Spectrum

A Collection of Engaging Essays

Megan Rizzoli

Breadan Publishing

Breadan Publishing

Spectrum: An Engaging Collection of Essays by Megan Rizzoli

Address for Domestic and International Orders:

Breadan Publishing
4706 N. Quail Lake Dr.,
Clovis, CA 93619

Website: http://breadanpublishing.com
Telephone: 559-291-2152
Fax: 559-291-1978

Printed in the United States of America

ISBN 978-0-615-92770-1

Publisher, English: Pat Nishimura
Editor, Writing: Susan Wiesick
Marketing: Lori Jones
Cover and text design: Russell Boldt

Table of Contents

VI: Hot-Button Issues

VII: Health and Well-Being

VIII: Jobs and the Economy

IX: Education

X: Art and Entertainment

XI: International Perspectives

XII. Technology

XIII: Politics and Governance

Alternate Table of Contents

I. Personal Narrative

II. Comparison/Contrast

III. Problem/Solution

IV. Argument/Persuasion

V. Cause/Effect

VI. Exposition

VII. Viewpoint (Thesis/Support)

Introduction

People read for a variety of reasons: for enjoyment, for knowledge, for inspiration, for self-improvement, to challenge their intellect, to challenge or reinforce their beliefs, to help them make decisions (whom to vote for, what computer to buy), to seek solutions to problems, or to help others. All of these reasons were taken into account in selecting the readings for *Spectrum*.

People's reading interests also vary greatly. With that in mind, the essays in *Spectrum* cover a wide range of topics divided into thirteen sections: technology, education, the economy, relationships, health and well-being, art and entertainment, science, international perspectives, politics and governance, cultural/ethnic perspectives, children's issues, values and ethics, and "hot-button" issues. Hopefully readers will find numerous topics of interest within these sections.

The authors of the readings in *Spectrum* also reflect the diversity of writers that exists today and merit the attention of readers: women and men of different ethnicities, professional writers, student writers, essayists, journalists, book authors, and bloggers. Never has there been such a plethora of written material at our fingertips, and numerous sources were mined in compiling the essays in this anthology.

The readings in *Spectrum* were also selected with a college reading audience in mind. Essays are included throughout the anthology that speak to the concerns and interests of many college students: the future job market, why students drop out of college, relationships and sexual mores, technological issues, educational trends, music, differing ethnic perspectives, physical and mental well-being, and issues involving children. At the same time, other essays were selected to broaden the knowledge and interests of readers beyond their current parameters and to make them think deeply about complex and significant issues.

Finally, at the end of each essay are questions for discussion. These "Discussion Starter" sections are just that: questions to help initiate discussion that will flow in the directions that reflect the readers' interests. Consider the questions as a starting point to launch discussions that you find most meaningful, enlightening, or interesting.

I. Perspectives in Science

Weather on Steroids

By Paul Barrett

Paul Barrett is a senior writer at Bloomberg Businessweek who writes on a range of issues from the energy industry to national politics to the environment. In this essay, Barrett contends that human-created climate change plays an undeniable role in the extreme weather events that are becoming more commonplace worldwide.

Yes, yes, it's unsophisticated to blame any given storm on climate change. Men and women in white lab coats tell us—and they're right—that many factors contribute to each severe weather episode. Climate deniers exploit scientific complexity to avoid any discussion at all. Clarity, however, isn't beyond reach. Hurricane Sandy demands it: At least 40 U.S. deaths. Economic losses expected to climb as high as $50 billion. Eight million homes without power. Hundreds of thousands of people evacuated. More than 15,000 flights grounded. Factories, stores, and hospitals shut. Lower Manhattan dark, silent, and underwater. Homes sit in ruin at the end of a bridge wrecked by flooding in Mantoloking, New Jersey.

An unscientific survey of the social networking literature on Sandy reveals an illuminating tweet (you read that correctly) from Jonathan Foley, director of the Institute on the Environment at the University of Minnesota. On Oct. 29, Foley thumbed thusly: "Would this kind of storm happen without climate change? Yes. Fueled by many factors. Is storm stronger because of climate change? Yes."

Eric Pooley, senior vice president of the Environmental Defense Fund, and former deputy editor of Bloomberg Businessweek, offers a baseball analogy: "We can't say that steroids caused any one home run by Barry Bonds, but steroids sure helped him hit more and hit them farther. Now we have weather on steroids."

In an Oct. 30 blog post, Mark Fischetti of Scientific American took a spin through Ph.D.-land and found more and more credentialed experts willing to shrug off the climate caveats. The broadening consensus: "Climate change amps up other basic factors that contribute to big storms. For example, the oceans have warmed, providing more energy for storms. And the Earth's atmosphere has warmed, so it retains more moisture, which is drawn into storms and is then dumped on us." Even those of us who are science- extended its geographical reach.

Pushing that cold air south was an atmospheric pattern, known as a blocking high, above the Arctic Ocean. Climate scientists Charles Greene and Bruce Monger of Cornell University, writing earlier this year in Oceanography, provided evidence that Arctic ice-melts linked to global warming contribute to the very atmospheric pattern that sent the frigid burst down across Canada and the eastern U.S.

If all that doesn't impress, forget the scientists ostensibly devoted to advancing knowledge and saving lives. Listen instead to corporate insurers committed to compiling statistics for profit.

On Oct. 17 the giant German reinsurance company Munich Re issued a prescient report titled "Severe Weather in North America." Globally, the rate of extreme weather events is rising, and "nowhere in the world is the rising number of natural catastrophes more evident than in North America."

From 1980 through 2011, weather disasters caused losses totaling $1.06 trillion. Munich Re found "a nearly quintupled number of weather-related loss events in North America for the past three decades."

By contrast, there was "an increase factor of 4 in Asia, 2.5 in Africa, 2 in Europe, and 1.5 in South America." Human-caused climate change "is believed to contribute to this trend," the report said, "though it influences various perils in different ways."

Global warming "particularly affects formation of heat waves, droughts, intense precipitation events, and in the long run most probably also tropical cyclone intensity," Munich Re said. This July was the hottest month recorded in the U.S. since record-keeping began in 1895, according to the National Oceanic and Atmospheric Administration. The U.S. Drought Monitor reported that two-thirds of the continental U.S. suffered drought conditions this summer. Granted, Munich Re wants to sell more reinsurance, backup policies purchased by other insurance companies, so maybe it has a selfish reason to stir anxiety. Yet it has no obvious motive for fingering global warming vs. other causes.

"If the first effects of climate change are already perceptible," said Peter Hoppe, the company's chief of geo-risks research, "all alerts and measures against it have become even more pressing."

Which raises the question of what alerts and measures to undertake. In his book *The Conundrum*, David Owen, a staff writer at the *New Yorker*, contends that as long as the West places high and unquestioning value on economic growth and consumer gratification—with China and the rest of the developing world right behind—we will continue to burn the fossil fuels whose emissions trap heat in the atmosphere. Fast trains, hybrid cars, compact fluorescent light bulbs, carbon offsets—they're just not enough, Owen writes. Yet even he would surely agree that the only responsible first step is to put climate change back on the table for discussion. The issue was missing-in-action during the presidential debates and is unlikely to appear on the near-term congressional calendar. After Sandy, that seems insane.

Former Republican nominee Mitt Romney went from being a supporter years ago of clean energy and emission caps to, more recently, a climate agnostic. He belittled Barack Obama's vow to arrest climate change, made during the 2008 presidential campaign. "President Obama promised to begin to slow the rise of the oceans and heal the planet," Romney told the Republican National Convention in storm-tossed Tampa. "My promise is to help you and your family." Two months later, in the wake of Sandy, submerged families in New Jersey and New York urgently needed some help dealing with that rising-ocean stuff.

Obama and his strategists clearly decided that in a tight race during fragile economic times, he should compete with Romney by promising to mine more coal and drill more oil. On the campaign trail, when Obama refers to the environment, he did so only in the context of spurring "green jobs."

During his time in office, Obama has made modest progress on climate issues. His administration's fuel-efficiency standards will reduce by half the amount of greenhouse-gas emissions from new cars and trucks by 2025. His regulations and proposed rules to curb mercury, carbon, and other emissions from coal-fired power plants are forcing utilities to retire some of the dirtiest old facilities. And the country has doubled the generation of energy from renewable sources such as solar and wind. Still, renewable energy accounts for less than 15 percent of the country's electricity. The U.S. can't shake its fossil fuel addiction by going cold turkey. Offices and factories can't function in the dark. Shippers and drivers and air travelers will not abandon petroleum overnight.

While scientists and entrepreneurs search for breakthrough technologies, the President should push an energy plan that exploits plentiful domestic natural gas supplies. Burned for power, gas emits about half as much carbon as coal. That's a trade-off already under way, and it's worth expanding. Environmentalists taking a hard no-gas line are making a mistake.

Conservatives champion market forces—as do smart liberals—and financial incentives should be part of the climate agenda. In 2009 the House of Representatives passed cap-and-trade legislation that would have rewarded more nimble industrial players that figure out how to use cleaner energy. The bill died in the Senate in 2010, a victim of Tea Party-inspired Republican obstructionism and Obama's decision to spend his political capital to push health-care reform. Republican fanaticism about all forms of government intervention in the economy aside, the idea of pricing carbon must remain a part of the national debate. One politically plausible way to tax carbon emissions is to transfer the revenue to individuals. Alaska, which pays dividends to its citizens from royalties imposed on oil companies, could provide inspiration, just as Romneycare in Massachusetts pointed the way to Obamacare.

Ultimately, the global warming crisis will require global solutions. Washington can become a credible advocate for moving the Chinese and Indian economies away from coal and toward alternatives only if the U.S. takes concerted political action. At the last United Nations conference on climate change in Durban, South Africa, the world's governments agreed to seek a new legal agreement that binds signatories to reduce their carbon emissions. Negotiators agreed to come up with a new treaty by 2015, to be put in place by 2020. To work, the treaty will need to include a way to penalize countries that don't meet emission-reduction targets —something the U.S. has until now refused to support.

If Hurricane Sandy does nothing else, it should suggest that we need to commit more to disaster preparation and response. The U.S. has allowed transportation and other infrastructure to grow obsolete and deteriorate, which poses a threat not just to public safety yet also to the nation's economic health. With once-in-a-century floods now occurring every few years, New York Governor Andrew Cuomo and New York City Mayor Michael Bloomberg said the country's biggest city will need to consider building surge protectors and somehow waterproofing its enormous subway system. "It's not prudent to sit here and say it's not going to happen again," Cuomo said. "I believe it is going to happen again."

David Rothkopf, the chief executive and editor-at-large of Foreign Policy, noted in an Oct. 29 blog post that Sandy also brought his hometown, Washington, to a standstill, impeding affairs of state. To lessen future impact, he suggested burying urban and suburban power lines, an expensive yet sensible improvement. Where to get the money? Rothkopf proposed shifting funds from post-Sept. 11 bureaucratic leviathans such as the Department of Homeland Security, which he alleges is shot through with waste.

In truth, what's lacking in America's approach to climate change isn't the resources to act but the political will to do so. A Pew Research Center poll conducted in October found that two-thirds of Americans say there is "solid evidence" the earth is getting warmer. That's down 10 points since 2006. Among Republicans, more than half say it's either not a serious problem or not a problem at all.

Such numbers reflect the success of climate deniers in framing action on global warming as inimical to economic growth. This is both shortsighted and dangerous. The U.S. can't afford regular Sandy-size disruptions in economic activity. To limit the costs of climate-related disasters, both politicians and the public need to accept how much they're helping to cause them.

Discussion Starters

1. What evidence does Barrett provide that extreme weather events are fueled by climate warming? How compelling do you find the evidence?
2. What "solutions" to the problem of global warming are presented? How realistic are they?
3. How big of a problem do you believe global warming is? What can individuals do to help solve the problem?

The Intelligence of Beasts

By Colin Woodard

Colin Woodard is an award-winning author and journalist who writes for The Washington Monthly, The Christian Science Monitor, and The Chronicle of Higher Education. In this essay, Woodard explores the intelligence of non-primates whose capabilities have often been both ignored and underestimated.

If you've ever doubted that elephants are contemplative, Joshua M. Plotnik has some video you should watch. Plotnik, a postdoctoral fellow in experimental psychology at the University of Cambridge, wanted to see if Asian elephants could pass a classic cooperation test designed for chimpanzees. The elephants already knew how to use a rope to pull a food-bearing table within reach. But what if the only way to move the table was two elephants pulling on separate ropes simultaneously?

On one video, one elephant ambles up to the rope and waits patiently, trunk and tail gently swinging, for its counterpart to arrive, half a minute later. Then, without hesitation, they grasp their respective ropes in synchronicity, pulling the food to themselves. In another segment, a young female simply stands on her rope, which—the way the mechanism is set up—forces her colleague to do all the work for the both of them. In 60 trials, all six pairs of elephants waited for their partners, with an average success rate of over 93 percent, suggesting that they easily understood cooperation.

"We were very excited by the results," Plotnik says into his cellphone as he walks home, after midnight, through the streets of Chiang Mai, Thailand, not far from his research sites. "Their behavior was comparable to that of the chimpanzees. We're getting further into understanding how intelligent they are."

For much of the last century, research on animal cognition focused almost exclusively on primates, on account of their relatively close evolutionary kinship with humans. But in recent years, many researchers wishing to understand how higher intelligence evolved have taken a different approach, looking to apparently intelligent species that are only distantly related to ourselves, like elephants, dolphins, or ravens. In the process, many cognitive traits once thought to be exclusive to humans—including some that are considered definitive of human uniqueness—have been found in far-flung provinces of the animal kingdom.

"In understanding evolution, human cognition is like the elephant's trunk: It's a very unusual thing, and it really stands out," says Evan L. MacLean, a doctoral student in evolutionary anthropology at Duke University, which is coordinating a collaborative project to compare 30 species, as varied as dogs and octopuses. "The best source of evidence we have are the closest relatives—chimps and bonobos—but we've been missing a ton of very interesting variation by just looking at primates."

Nine-week-old puppies have been shown to be very good at recognizing human gestures and interpreting them for their own benefit, while adult dogs provide and request information, predict social events, and perhaps even speculate on what their masters are thinking—for example, finding hidden food by picking up on subtle human cues. Dolphins recognize themselves in mirrors, while the New Caledonian crow fashions tools with which to capture grubs. The common raven has demonstrated the ability to test actions in its mind, solving complicated puzzles to obtain food on the first try.

"There used to be this chimpocentrism in the field, with research narrowly concentrated on primates," says Ádám Miklósi, a professor of ethology at Budapest's Eötvös Loránd University and an expert on canine cognition. "It's really great to see research in other species expand exponentially, because we really need the breadth and depth of species to be able to say anything meaningful about animal cognition."

While there are many reasons to study the thinking ability of animals—devising better conservation strategies, opening new pathways in artificial intelligence—the great evolutionary question driving many researchers is this: Under what evolutionary pressures do different types of cognitive abilities tend to develop? If several entirely unrelated species turn out to have a given intellectual ability—mirror recognition in humans, dolphins, and elephants, for instance—are there common denominators in the conditions they confront (membership in complex social groups, for example) that might explain the development? Can the study of such examples of convergent evolution help us understand how and why higher intelligence arises in nature? Researchers have taken only the first steps toward finding definitive answers to both of those questions.

Elephants are fascinating subjects in this regard. They have enormous brains, bigger than those of humans. Like many other animals thought to possess unusual intelligence, they live in complex societies in which individuals cooperate and interact to solve problems. They're also unrelated to humans. Whereas we and chimpanzees had a common ancestor about five million years ago, with elephants (and their relations, the aardvark and manatee), it was 100 million years ago, a relationship even more distant than the ones we have with dolphins and whales.

"If you find an elephant and a human sharing an ability that most other primates don't have, you can be pretty sure" it's an example of convergent evolution at work, says Richard W. Byrne, a professor of psychology at the University of St. Andrews, in Scotland, who has studied cognition in both primates and elephants. "If you can see shared circumstances in which these animals use this ability, that can help show what its biological function is."

Researchers like Byrne are finding that elephants have all sorts of intriguing cognitive abilities comparable to—and sometimes exceeding—our own. They recognize their reflections in mirrors. They act empathically toward fellow elephants in distress and offer them assistance. They mourn and even bury their dead. As Plotnik has shown, they're not flummoxed by cooperative problem solving. And both Asian and African elephants make tools for a variety of purposes, from flyswatters to backscratchers.

Byrne's fieldwork has taken place in Kenya's Amboseli National Park, site of a long-term, multidisciplinary study of elephants, in its 39th year. (That research is described in an edited collection, *The Amboseli Elephants: A Long-Term Perspective on a Long-Lived Mammal,* published this spring by the University of Chicago Press.) In recent years, Byrne and his colleagues have conducted field experiments that show two additional mental abilities not seen in any other animal.

In one experiment, elephants were presented garments worn by two different human ethnic groups: the Masai (who sometimes spear elephants) and the Kamba (an agrarian people who rarely interact with elephants). Whether given access to smells of previously worn clothing or to visual inspection of unworn clothing, the elephants responded with greater fear or aggression toward the Masai clothing. This led Byrne and his colleagues to conclude that elephants are able to categorize another species, humans, into subclasses. "We don't know any other animals that categorize dangers in this way, but that may be because they haven't been tested," he says.

In the second experiment, the researchers wanted to test if elephants understand "person permanence" and "invisible displacement"—that is, if they are aware that absent individuals exist and if they contemplate the movements and activities of those individuals in absentia, an ability that human beings develop in infancy. Knowing that the members of the extended elephant family they were working with sniffed one another's urine deposits, the researchers began moving the deposits around. "The nice thing was to see their surprised reaction when they encountered a sample from an individual who was actually a half-kilometer or more behind them, a much greater reaction than if the sample was from someone who was actually ahead of them," Byrne explains.

The results suggested that each elephant was keeping track of the location and expected movements of everyone else in its foraging group—17 individuals, in this case—a remarkable display of working-memory capacity.

"They don't use their eyes in the bright Amboseli sun, but they're still able to keep track of 17 individuals in an environment that they cannot scan," Byrne notes. "Think of a parent with 17 kids roaming around a department store; I think we would find it extremely challenging to keep track in our minds of where everyone is. This is an ability that appears to be rather more than humans can do."

Miklósi, who is using cognition work with dogs to program robots that will, doglike, anticipate, serve, and respond to human needs, suspects that scientists will discover many more instances in which animals are found to have mental powers that humans lack. "So far, no matter how much you read in the literature, there is this notion that humans are always the best at everything," he says. "If the tests were not so anthropocentric, we would probably lose a lot more often."

Some other researchers agree that animal-cognition research will inevitably challenge human presumptuousness. "From ancient times, it's always been us versus the rest of the animal world, and it wasn't really considered that animals were thinking creatures," says Diana Reiss, a professor of cognitive psychology at Hunter College of the City University of New York, who studies elephants and dolphins. "The big message is that we're not the pinnacle of the tree, the only creatures who are thinking complexly. We share the upper branches of the tree with many species, each so beautifully evolved for their own environmental niche and social structures."

But other scientists take a more skeptical view. They include David Premack, a professor emeritus of psychology at the University of Pennsylvania and the father of the influential "theory of mind," which refers to the ability to infer the mental states of others. "I have a prejudice that's not common among people who study animals, who tend to do so primarily to show similarities between the animal and the human," he explains. "That's a noble cause, but I feel it's easily abused, as when they leap from similarity to equivalence."

Humans and certain animals might similarly recognize that a large rock is more likely to break a branch than a small one, but Premack says there's no evidence that this understanding of a physical action is equivalent to causal reasoning. That is, if an animal comes across a large rock lying beside a crushed plant, it won't infer, as a human might, that the rock crushed the plant, he argues.

Microscopic study of the human brain, he notes, has revealed neural structures and forms of connectivity not found in any other animal. And cognitive research has not been able to keep pace with those developments. "Things that the naked eye can see—that the human is a very different entity than the nonhuman—is very much corroborated under the microscope," he says. "If you can't see we're special, you have to be permanently drunk."

Byrne agrees that it would be foolish to jump from similarity to equivalence, but he says comparative-cognition researchers are by no means trying to show that animals are "little humans in disguise." "None of the interpretations we make of our experiments require one to treat superficial resemblance as deep equivalence," he says.

As for his own research interests, Byrne would like to explore what creatures in other, unstudied corners of the animal kingdom might be thinking. Most species thought to be especially intelligent are social creatures, but what about large-brained nonsocial species? "I don't know anybody who's looking at bears. They have very large brains—I wonder why," he says. "If someone offered me a long-term study of grizzlies, I'd take it."

Discussion Starters

1. Why has the study of intelligence in animals other than primates been lacking historically? How do recent findings change our thinking about the intelligence of some non-primates?
2. How might the treatment of animals change given our understanding of their intelligence? What current practices regarding animal captivity should be examined?
3. What does the intelligence found in completely unrelated species – e.g. elephants, birds, dogs – infer about animal intelligence? What does it infer about evolution across the species?

The Amazing Teen Brain

By Nancy Shute

Nancy Shute is a senior writer at U.S. News and World Report. In this essay, Shute explores the effects of the still-developing brain on teen behavior and the potential risks and rewards that accompany it.

Behold the American teenager, a lump in a hoodie who's capable of little more than playing "Grand Theft Auto," raiding the liquor cabinet, and denting the minivan, thanks to a brain so unformed that it's more like a kindergartner's than a grown-up's. That's the message that seemed to emerge from the past decade's neuroscientific discoveries: that the brain, once thought to be virtually complete by age 6, is very much a work in progress during adolescence and *not* to be trusted. But experts now are realizing that the popular parental response—to coddle teens in an attempt to shield them from every harm—actually may be counterproductive.

Yes, teenagers make woefully errant decisions that factor big in the 13,000 adolescent deaths each year. And yes, their unfinished brains appear to be uniquely vulnerable to substance abuse and addiction. But they also are capable of feats of learning and daring marvelous enough to make a grown-up weep with jealousy. How they exercise these capabilities, it now appears, helps shape the brain wiring they'll have as adults. "You have this power you're given," says Wilkie Wilson, co-director of DukeLEARN, a new program at Duke University designed to teach teenagers how to best deploy their brains. Far from coddling the kids, he says, Mom and Dad need to figure out how to allow enough "good" risk-taking to promote growth and prevent wasted talent—while also avoiding disaster.

It can be a nerve-racking exercise. "These kids are such a crazy mix of impulsiveness and shrewdness," says Marcia Harrington, a survey researcher in Silver Spring, Md. She recalls the time she thought her then 16-year-old daughter, Alexandra Plante, had sleepover plans, but the girl instead ditched school and flew to Chicago to visit an acquaintance she'd met briefly during a family trip. The scheme was revealed only because bad weather delayed the flight home. Alex returned unharmed and has never conceded that the escapade was too risky. "She's going to be a great adult someday," says Harrington. "But, boy, there are moments that are terrifying." Further along the road to adulthood now, Alex has applied her daring spirit to becoming an emergency medical technician and volunteer for the local fire department, and to heading off to college 2,500 miles from home.

While society has known since forever that adolescents can be impulsive risk-takers, it wasn't until the 1990s, when MRI scans became a common research tool, that scientists could peek into the teenage cranium and begin to sort out why. What they found astonished them. The brain's gray matter, which forms the bulk of its structure and processing capacity, grows gradually throughout childhood, peaks around age 12, and then furiously "prunes" underused neurons.

By scanning hundreds of children as they've grown up, neuroscientists at the National Institute of Mental Health have been able to show that the pruning starts at the back of the brain and moves forward during adolescence. Regions that control sensory and motor skills mature first, becoming more specialized and efficient. The prefrontal cortex, responsible for judgment and impulse control, matures last. Indeed, the prefrontal cortex isn't "done" until the early 20s—and sometimes even later in men. Meantime, the brain's white matter, which acts as the cabling connecting brain parts, becomes thicker and better able to transmit signals quickly. Recent research shows that this myelination process of white matter continues well past adolescence, perhaps even into middle age.

Now, dozens of researchers are studying how all these changes might affect adolescent behavior, and also shape adult skills and behavior, for good and for ill. The maturation lag between emotional and cognitive brain centers may help explain why teenagers get so easily upset when parents see no reason, for example; teens seem to process input differently than do adults.

In one experiment, young teenagers trying to read the emotions on people's faces used parts of the brain designed to quickly recognize fear and alarm; adults used the more rational prefrontal cortex. Deborah Yurgelun-Todd, the researcher at McLean Hospital in Belmont, Mass., who led this work, believes young teens are prone to read emotion into their interactions and miss content. Therefore, parents may have better luck communicating with middle-schoolers if they avoid raising their voice (easier said than done) and instead explain how they're feeling.

Other experiments shed light on why even book-smart teenagers come up short on judgment: Their brain parts aren't talking to each other. When Monique Ernst, a child psychiatrist and neurophysiologist at NIMH, uses functional MRI to watch teenage and adult brains engaged in playing a gambling game, she finds that the "reward" center lights up more in teens than in adults when players are winning, and the "avoidance" region is less activated in teens when they're losing. There's also less activity in teens' prefrontal cortex, which adults use to mediate the "yes!" and "no" impulses from other brain regions. "The hypothesis is that there is this triumvirate of brain regions that needs to be in balance" in order to produce wise judgments, says Ernst, whether that's to wear a seat belt or use contraception.

Does an unfinished brain make for bad behavior? There is as yet no proven link between bright blobs on an MRI and real-life behavior, but researchers are hard at work trying to make that connection. In a 2005 study by Laurence Steinberg, a developmental psychologist at Temple University, teenagers in a simulated driving test were twice as likely to drive dangerously if they had two friends with them—and brain scans showed that the reward centers lit up more if teens were told that friends were watching. A savvy parent might conclude that what's needed in the teen years is more guidance, not less.

In fact, study after study has shown that one of the most powerful factors in preventing teenage pregnancy, crime, drug and alcohol abuse, and other seriously bad outcomes is remarkably simple: time with responsible adults. "It doesn't have to be parents, necessarily," says Valerie Reyna, a professor of psychology at Cornell University. But it does mean that teenagers should be directly monitored by responsible adults so they have less time to get in trouble. Reyna thinks adults also need to teach what she calls "gist" thinking, or the ability to quickly grasp the bottom line. Instead, she says, teenagers often overthink but miss the mark. When Reyna asks adults if they'd play Russian roulette for $1 million, they almost universally say no. Half of teenagers say yes. "They'll tell you with a straight face that there's a whole lot of money, and they're probably not going to die. It's very logical on one level, but on another level, it's completely insane."

If it's any comfort, the evidence suggests that teenagers' loopy behavior and combativeness is hard-wired to push them out of the nest. Adolescent primates, rodents, and birds also hang out with their peers and fight with their parents, notes B. J. Casey, a teen brain researcher who directs the Sackler Institute at Weill Medical College of Cornell University in New York City. "You need to take risks to leave your family and village and find a mate."

The revved-up adolescent brain is also built to learn, the new research shows—and those teen experiences are crucial. Neurons, like muscles, operate on a "use it or lose it" basis; a teenager who studies piano three hours a day will end up with different brain wiring than someone who spends that same time shooting hoops or playing video games. A 16-year-old who learns to treat his girlfriend with care and compassion may well develop different emotional brain triggers than one who's thinking just about the sex.

Only in early childhood, it turns out, are people as receptive to new information as they are in adolescence. The human brain is designed to pay attention to things that are new and different, a process called salience. Add in the fact that emotion and passion also heighten attention and tamp down fear, and teenagerhood turns out to be the perfect time to master new challenges. "You are the owners of a very special stage of your brain development," Frances Jensen, a neurologist at Children's Hospital Boston, tells teenagers in her "Teen Brain 101" lectures at local high schools. "You can do things now that will set you up later in life with an enhanced skill set. Don't waste this opportunity." (She was motivated to create the talks by her own befuddling experiences as a single mother of two teenage boys.)

Jordan Dickey is one teen who seized opportunity. As a 14-year-old high-school freshman, he asked his father for something unusual: a $26,000 loan to start a business. The Dickey family, of Ramer, Tenn., raised a few cattle, and Jordan had noticed that people paid a lot more for hay in square bales than for the same amount in less-convenient round bales. After doing a feasibility study as an agriculture class project, Jordan convinced his dad to give him a three-year loan to buy a rebaling machine. He worked nights and weekends, mowing, raking, and rebaling; paid friends $7 an hour to load the bales into a trailer; and hired drivers to deliver the hay to local feed marts, since he was too young to drive. "It taught me how to manage my own money," Jordan says.

That's an understatement. Not only did he pay off the loan in one year, he made an additional $40,000. Now 17 and a senior, he has saved enough money to pay for a big chunk of college, much to his parents' delight. "He likes for the job to get done and get done right," says Perry Dickey, who owns an electroplating shop. "It was a big responsibility for him, and I'm glad he took the lines and produced."

Teens can apply the new findings to learn more without more study, notes Wilson, whose DukeLEARN program will be tested in ninth-grade health classes next year. Key points:

- Brains need plenty of sleep because they consolidate memory during slumber.
- The brain's an energy hog and needs a consistent diet of healthful food to function well.
- Drugs and alcohol harm short- and long-term memory.

Teens' predisposition to learn plays a critical role in the vexing issue of teenage drinking, smoking, and drug use. Neuroscientists have learned that addiction uses the same molecular pathways that are used in learning, most notably those involving the neurotransmitter dopamine. Repeated substance use permanently reshapes those pathways, researchers say. In fact, they now look at addiction as a form of learning: Adolescent rats are far more likely to become hooked than adults.

And epidemiological studies in humans suggest that the earlier someone starts using, the more likely he or she is to end up with big problems. Last month, a study tracking more than 1,000 people in New Zealand from age 3 to age 32 found that those who started drinking or using drugs regularly before age 15 were far more likely to fail in school, be convicted of a crime, or have substance abuse problems as an adult. "You can really screw up your brain at this point," says Jensen. "You're more vulnerable than you think."

When can the brain handle a beer? The new brain science has been used as a weapon by both sides of the drinking-age debate, though there is no definitive evidence for a "safe" age. "To say that 21 is based on the science of brain development is simply untrue," says John McCardell, president of Choose Responsibility, which advocates lowering the drinking age to 18. But there's also no scientific basis for choosing 18. The bottom line for now, most experts agree: Later is better.

Jay Giedd, an NIMH neuroscientist who pioneered the early MRI research on teen brains, is fond of saying that "what's important is the journey." Researchers caution that they can't prove links between brain parts and behavior, or that tackling adult-size challenges will turn teenagers into better adults. But common sense suggests that Nature had a reason to give adolescents strong bodies, impulsive natures, and curious, flexible minds. "Our generation is ready for more," insists Alex Harris, 20, of Gresham, Ore., who, with his twin brother, Brett, writes a blog and has published a book urging teens to push themselves. Its title: "Do Hard Things."

Discussion Starters

1. How does the adolescent brain differ from the adult brain, and what, according to the essay, are the consequences?
2. What contradictory advice does the essay give parents on dealing with their teenagers? What kind of "balance" do you think makes the most sense between protecting adolescents from harm and allowing them to take risks?
3. What influence does teen behavior, according to the essay, have on adulthood? How do you view your own experiences and behavior, past or current, in the context of the essay?

Geoengineering for Atmospheric Restoration

By Robert B. Jackson and James Salzman

Robert B. Jackson is the Nicholas Professor of Global Environmental Change at Duke University. James Salzman is the Nicholas Institute Professor of Environmental Policy at Duke. In this essay, the authors present a variety of potential solutions for restoring earth's atmosphere to its pre-industrial condition.

A few decades ago, the notion of actively controlling Earth's climate resided primarily in the writings of science fiction authors such as Frank Herbert, Isaac Asimov, and Arthur C. Clarke. Today, planetary engineering is being discussed openly by scientists and policymakers in Congress, the UK House of Commons, and many other settings. Clarke's advice apparently struck a chord: "Politicians should read science fiction, not westerns and detective stories."

Geoengineering can be thought of as intentionally manipulating Earth's climate to offset the warming from greenhouse gas emissions. Its activities can be divided into two loose groups. One set of options cools Earth by removing carbon dioxide (CO_2) and other greenhouse gases from air, essentially reversing the process of fossil fuel emissions. The other cools the planet by blocking or reflecting sunlight, offsetting the consequences of increased greenhouse gases for temperature but leaving the buildup of greenhouse gas concentrations unchecked.

Several developments have fueled the rise of geoengineering from fiction to possible reality in a remarkably short period of time. The first is our inability to reduce greenhouse gas emissions in any substantive way. A wealth of scientific evidence shows that Earth's climate is already changing because of such gases, posing a threat to people and other animals and to plants. A second factor is the concern that some planetary engineering may already be needed to reduce the harmful effects of climate change, even if emissions fall in the future. A third is the hope that geoengineering could be cheaper than cutting emissions, even if it treats only a symptom of climate change, not the root cause.

The first category of geoengineering removes or "scrubs" CO_2 from the atmosphere. Carbon removal can be biological, including planting trees or fertilizing the oceans to stimulate phytoplankton growth. It can also be industrial. Industrial options include using chemicals to capture CO_2 from the air, with renewable energy regenerating the chemicals, or mining silicates or other geologic materials that react naturally with CO_2, reburying the deposits after they have absorbed carbon. Whether biological or industrial, the goal of the activities is to reduce greenhouse gas concentrations in the air.

The second type of geoengineering reflects or blocks sunlight to cool Earth without reducing CO_2 concentrations. Some commonly proposed "sunshades" include placing dust into the stratosphere with rockets and airplanes, placing space mirrors between Earth and the Sun, or increasing the extent and brightness of ocean clouds. Sunshade approaches are conceivable because reducing sunlight by a couple of percentage points is all that is needed to offset the warming from a doubling of atmospheric CO_2. There is a natural analog for this approach: volcanic eruptions, such as Mt. Pinatubo in 1991, which blasted sulfur dust into the stratosphere and cooled Earth by 1° Fahrenheit for more than a year. A concise description of both types of approaches can be found in the Royal Society report *Geoengineering the Climate*, published in 2009.

Sunshade and carbon removal approaches differ in how fast they can be applied and what they will cost. Sunshade technologies could be applied quickly and fairly cheaply to reduce Earth's temperature, at a price of perhaps several billion dollars per year and within months of a policy mandate for stratospheric dust seeding. This combination of speed and cost is the main reason why sunshade approaches are being discussed. No other technology allows us to alter the effects of global warming so quickly if Earth's climate begins to spin out of control.

In contrast, carbon removal technologies would take decades to scale up, at significantly higher cost. For instance, at a price or tax of $100 per metric ton of CO_2—roughly five times the European CO_2 price in May 2010 but cheaper than industry can scrub CO_2 from air today—removing a billion tons of CO_2 using industrial approaches would cost $100 billion. Removing the entire fossil fuel emissions from the United States would take about $600 billion annually, and $3 trillion would pay for removing the 30 billion tons of CO_2 emitted globally each year. These numbers dwarf the cost of sunshade approaches, even if cheaper biological options such as tree planting can help bring the price down.

How should we think about the geoengineering option? One promising model resides in the principle of restoration. In a well-cited primer from 2004, the Society for Ecological Restoration defined ecological restoration as "the process of assisting the recovery of an ecosystem that has been degraded, damaged, or destroyed. We propose to extend the concept of restoration to the atmosphere, suggesting the term "atmospheric restoration" as a guiding principle for prioritizing geoengineering efforts. The goal is to return the atmosphere to a less degraded or damaged state and ultimately to its preindustrial condition.

Given an umbrella of atmospheric restoration, we prioritize geoengineering efforts based on two principles. The first is to treat the cause of the disease itself, through CO_2 removal, instead of a symptom of the disease, through the use of sunshades. Because carbon-scrubbing technologies will take far longer to deploy than sunshades, policy incentives for research on them are needed now. Without such incentives, we will face unnaturally high greenhouse gas concentrations in our air (as compared to the past 100 million years of Earth history) or a world where sunshade approaches must be maintained for centuries once we start using them. For instance, large-scale stratospheric dust seeding, if stopped abruptly, would cause Earth's temperature to shoot up rapidly. (Consider the analogy of a dim cloud passing, exposing the Earth to full sunlight.) This rapid increase would likely be far more damaging environmentally than a gradual increase to the same temperature would have been. Is global governance likely to keep sunshades in place for 500 or 1,000 years?

A second principle is to prioritize activities with the greatest chance of public acceptance. We remain skeptical that the public will ever broadly accept sunshades, particularly stratospheric dust seeding, and some carbon removal strategies such as ocean fertilization. Recognizing this barrier provides another filter for prioritizing research. The likelihood of public acceptance suggests a few good geoengineering choices from among the broader set of less direct and potentially dangerous geoengineering activities.

Based on these principles and the Hippocratic spirit of first do no harm, we propose three forms of geoengineering that could provide the greatest climate benefits with the smallest chance of unintentional harm to the environment. All three are forms of atmospheric restoration, will probably have fewer unintended consequences than other forms of geoengineering, and are more likely to be accepted by the public than many other forms of geoengineering.

The first geoengineering activity, forest protection and restoration, is an opportunity available now. The other two, industrial carbon removal and bioenergy linked to carbon capture and storage, need extensive research to make them effective and to reduce their costs. Unlike forest protection, these will take decades to scale up to a level that lowers atmospheric CO_2 concentrations substantially, because they require a distributed network of facilities.

The most immediate opportunity is forest preservation and restoration. Plants and other photosynthetic organisms provide one of the oldest and most efficient ways to remove CO_2 from air. Efforts to regrow forests or keep forests from being cut both provide greenhouse gas benefits. If a policy incentive keeps a rainforest in Amazonia or Alaska from being harvested, carbon that would have moved to the atmosphere is "removed" from the atmosphere.

A second geoengineering opportunity that should be encouraged with research incentives is industrial carbon removal, specifically facilities that use renewable chemicals rather than continuously mined ones such as silicates. Imagine a series of power plants run in reverse. The facilities use renewable energy to drive a chemical reaction that removes CO_2 from the atmosphere and regenerates the chemical used in the reaction. It's as simple as that.

What isn't simple about the process is its cost. Current amine-based technologies or next-generation chilled-ammonia chemistry for capturing CO_2 from power plant smoke-stacks are too expensive to be used widely today. Moreover, CO_2 in air is far more dilute than in the exhaust of a coal- or gas-fired power plant, making the job even more difficult and costly. We need immediate research incentives to reduce the costs of industrial CO_2 capture.

Another aspect of cost with industrial carbon removal is where the carbon-free source of power comes from. For starters, are you really removing CO_2 from the atmosphere with this approach if you could instead plug the carbon-free energy consumed in it into the grid to offset emissions from a coal- or gas-fired plant somewhere else? One advantage here is that a carbon-removal facility could be set up anywhere on Earth where energy is plentiful. You don't have to be near a power grid in choosing locations. Renewable energy for the process could also be used at times and in places where it isn't needed for normal uses, such as off-peak hours.

Finally, for industrial carbon removal, you have to do something with the billions of tons of CO_2 removed from air. On the one hand, you could generate carbon-based fuels as one possibility. This use of the carbon does not really remove CO_2 from air unless the CO_2 is subsequently captured, perhaps analogous instead to generating corn ethanol and other biologically based renewable fuels. To be truly carbon-negative, however, you have to store the carbon permanently away from the atmosphere, most likely thousands of feet underground or under the oceans. This, too, is expensive and needs research to guarantee its safety and effectiveness.

The third technology that we believe needs immediate but perhaps more cautious research support combines bioenergy with carbon capture and storage. This technology fuses aspects of the previous two, including its focus on trees and other plants as a cheap way to capture CO_2 biologically instead of chemically, and its reliance on carbon capture and storage to move CO_2 from the atmosphere back underground. Unlike the previous option, it has the benefit of supplying its own energy generated from the biomass instead of requiring large energy inputs.

Bioenergy with carbon capture and storage also has some important differences, however. Although bioenergy provides energy from biomass rather than consuming it, harvesting the needed biomass will affect millions of acres of land if applied broadly. In that sense, bioenergy may in some places be at odds with the forest restoration and avoided deforestation efforts highlighted earlier. We acknowledge this contradiction, invoking a 19th-century adage for household management: "A place for everything, and everything in its place." There are places on Earth where habitat preservation and restoration are particularly important right now, including the tropics, whereas other places have lands that could be managed productively for fast-rotation biomass.

What bioenergy with carbon capture and storage provides is an extensive, cheaper complement to industrial carbon removal. Neither approach is perfect. Both will eventually be needed to draw down the concentration of CO_2 in the atmosphere, because energy efficiency and renewables alone can't get us to a carbon-negative economy.

In conclusion, to discuss even the possibility of engineering Earth's climate is to acknowledge that we have failed to slow greenhouse gas emissions and climate change. Emitting less CO_2 through increased energy efficiency and renewables should remain a top policy priority. These options will be cheaper than most forms of geoengineering and will provide many additional benefits, including improved air and water quality, national security, balance of trade, and human health.

Discussion Starters

1. Which of the geoengineering approaches to cooling the earth do you find most interesting or promising? Why do the authors introduce and then discount the possibility of blocking or reflecting sunlight? Do you agree with them?
2. Why do the authors support reducing the amount of carbon dioxide in the atmosphere over cooling the earth without reducing the CO2 level? Do you agree with them?
3. Based on the essay, are you encouraged that dramatically reducing the carbon dioxide level in the atmosphere and returning the earth the post-industrial condition is possible? Is it a worthwhile goal?

To Teach Evolution, Understand the Creationists

By Adam Laats

Adam Laats is a Professor in the School of Education at Binghamton University and author of Fundamentalism and Education: God, Darwin, and the Roots of America's Culture Wars. In this essay, Laats argues that scientists are not helping to promote the understanding and acceptance of evolution by belittling the beliefs of creationists.

If you follow the news about culture wars, evolution, and creationism, you've probably seen it by now. Earlier this fall, U.S. Rep. Paul C. Broun Jr., Republican of Georgia who ran unopposed for re-election, said in a widely distributed video that evolution, embryology, and the Big Bang theory were "lies straight from the pit of hell."

I don't agree. But the ferocious response to Broun's remarks tells us more about the widespread ignorance among evolution supporters than it does about ignorance among creationists. Broun, who serves on the House of Representatives' Science, Space, and Technology Committee, has long been one of the most staunchly conservative members of Congress. His comments have earned him widespread condemnation; Bill Nye, television's "The Science Guy," has called Broun "by any measure, unqualified to make decisions about science, space, and technology." In the blogosphere, comment has been even less restrained.

I disagree with Broun's views on evolution—and on a host of other topics, for that matter. But if we hope to understand creationism, we need to abandon the trope that only the ignorant can oppose mainstream evolutionary science. It is a comfortable delusion, a head-in-the-sand approach to improving evolution education in the United States. In the end, it stems from a shocking ignorance among evolutionists about the nature of creationist beliefs.

First of all, Broun is no ignoramus. He holds a bachelor's degree in chemistry and an M.D. He is the most recent in a long line of educated creationists. In the 1920s, William Jennings Bryan similarly defended his role as a man of science. In response to Clarence Darrow's accusation that only "bigots and ignoramuses" opposed evolution education, Bryan listed his many college degrees. As U.S. secretary of state, Bryan noted, he had met with "kings, emperors, and prominent public men." Throughout his career, Bryan complained he had never been called "an ignoramus...by anyone except an evolutionist."

Bryan's defense in 1925 could be revived by Broun today: "Christianity has nothing to fear from any *truth;* no *fact* disturbs the Christian religion or the Christian. It is the unsupported guess that is substituted for science to which opposition is made." Like Broun, Bryan insisted on his scientific credentials. Until his untimely death, in 1925, Bryan remained a member of the staunchly pro-evolution American Association for the Advancement of Science.

The notion that only the ignorant can oppose evolution does not hold water. As the political scientists Michael Berkman and Eric Plutzer demonstrate in *Evolution, Creationism, and the Battle to Control America's Classrooms* (Cambridge University Press, 2010), a slim majority of Americans are aware that mainstream scientific opinion supports evolution. Yet even among those 52 percent of Americans who know that scientists support evolution, large majorities still want schools to teach creationism. And, among those teachers who teach young-earth creationism, a majority—like Broun—hold a bachelor's degree or higher in science and almost half have completed 40 or more college credits in biology.

As it stands, scientists' blundering hostility toward creationism actually encourages creationist belief. By offering a stark division between religious faith and scientific belief, evolutionary scientists have pushed creationists away from embracing evolutionary ideas. And, by assuming that only ignorance could explain creationist beliefs, scientists have unwittingly fostered bitter resentment among the creationists, the very people with whom they should be hoping to connect. Nor can we take solace in the delusion that these teachers are somehow rogue agents of a vast right-wing creationist conspiracy. As Berkman and Plutzer demonstrate, the creationist beliefs of teachers embody the creationist beliefs of Americans in general. The teachers are not ignorant of evolution, yet they choose to reject it.

More-focused studies support those findings. David Long, an anthropologist and science educator now at George Mason University, conducted an in-depth ethnographic study of creationists in college, reported in his *Evolution and Religion in American Education* (Springer, 2011). Among his batch of creationist biology majors, only one abandoned her creationist beliefs. Most striking, this woman was not convinced by the scientific evidence in her biology classes; rather, her home life in high school, including an out-of-wedlock pregnancy, had turned her away from her conservative Protestant upbringing. Of the biology majors Long studied, none was convinced of the truth of evolutionary science by scientific coursework alone.

This commitment to creationism by those who know the facts of evolutionary science makes no sense to mainstream scientists, many of whom have always been utterly flummoxed by the durability of creationism. And a snarky insistence that Broun does not have the qualifications to serve on the House science committee blunders into an uncomfortable truth: Broun's views may fairly represent those of his constituents. Do we really want to demand that an elected official not fight for the ideas in which his constituents believe?

If we hope to spread the science of evolution, it does not help to charge forward in blissful ignorance about the nature and meanings of creationism. Broun may be wrong about evolution, embryology, and the Big Bang. But his scientific errors do not instantly disqualify him as a representative of the American people. Nor can they be explained away as a product of ignorance.

Rather, those of us who care about promoting evolution education must admit the hard truth. It is not simply that creationists such as Broun have not heard the facts about evolution. Broun—along with other informed, educated creationists—simply rejects those facts. Evolution educators do not simply need to spread the word about evolution. We need to convince and convert Americans who sincerely hold differing understandings about the nature and meaning of science.

Discussion Starters

1. Why does Laats believe that dismissing those who believe in creationism as "ignorant" does nothing to further widespread public acceptance of evolution? Do you agree with him?

2. Why do you think that the well-educated people Laats refers to embrace creationism over evolution? Why do you think that a majority of Americans want creationism taught in schools?

3. How does Laats feel that an understanding and acceptance of evolution can best be promulgated by the scientific community? Do you agree with him? What is your viewpoint on evolution and creationism?

Dr. Hans Holzer: Explaining the Unexplained

By Jeff Belanger

Jeff Belanger is one of the leading authors and experts on the paranormal. In this essay, Belanger interviews paranormal guru Dr. Hans Holzer, who makes the case that the study of the paranormal is a legitimate scientific endeavor.

This past January, Dr. Hans Holzer turned 85 years old. He laughs when you mention retirement. "I retire every day," he says with the hint of an Austrian accent. "Every night at midnight." After penning 138 books as well as several plays, musicals, films, and documentaries and hosting a television show, the only thing that slows him down today is a mishap from an operation on his leg three years ago. What does it slow him down from? "Swing dancing," he said. I laughed. Then I realized he wasn't kidding. "Not just swing dancing, *any* kind of dancing!"

Supernaturally speaking, Dr. Holzer has seen and heard it all. He's worked with psychic legends like Sybil Leek, he's investigated some of the most prominent haunted locations around the world, and he's come as close as a living person can to touching the "other side of life" – a term he's quick to point out that he invented. I spoke to Dr. Holzer about his life and work from his office in New York City. "I have no secrets," he said. "I mean, I have secrets, but I don't make them secret. If anybody wants to hear them, they can hear them." I wanted to hear them.

Born January 26, 1920 in Vienna, Austria, Holzer embraced the supernatural from a young age. He had an uncle Henry who used to tell him about fairies. Uncle Henry had many interests in the field of the paranormal, and he certainly left an impression on young Hans. "I was in kindergarten," Holzer said. "I was four years old – I see this as vividly today as when it happened – I see myself seated in a little yellow chair with all of the other kids around, and I was in the middle, pretending to read from an expired streetcar pass of my father's. I couldn't read at four, but I pretended. And I was 'reading' them ghost stories. Obviously fictional ghost stories, but the kids loved it. The only trouble was that they told their parents at home. The next thing that happened was the mothers came in and said, 'What kind of a kindergarten are we running here?' And so my mother was brought in, and the teacher said, 'Look, either he goes or I go.' At that point, I stopped telling ghost stories."

In 1938, 18-year-old Holzer saw a very big war coming to his region. He figured being that close to Nazi Germany while a World War was brewing wasn't healthy, so he and his brother came to New York. He's lived in New York City ever since.

"What was your first paranormal experience?" I asked.

"It's not a question of whether I had experiences," he said. "My interest has nothing to do with personal experiences. In other words, you don't have to be an investigator to experience things first-hand."

For Holzer, each case must withstand journalistic integrity, and journalism is just one of the many subjects he studied during his academic career. "I took ancient history and archaeology at the University of Vienna," he said. "Then I spent another three-and-a-half years at Columbia

University where I studied Japanese. In addition, I was a graduate of the Academy of Journalism in Vienna, which was a total waste of time. But I took it—it sounded nice. At the end, I studied at the London College of Applied Science which awarded me a master's in comparative religion, and then a year later a Ph.D. with a specialty in parapsychology." By the time his schooling was finished, his reputation was sealed as an investigator of the paranormal.

"I've read you don't like the term 'supernatural,'" I said.

"I use the term because it is the one that people use," Holzer said. "But nothing in my scientific view does not have an explanation. The question is, sooner we get it or later we get it, but there has to be an explanation. You can't say nobody knows. I don't accept that. And the paranormal is part of our experience – we just don't always understand it as such."

Eventually, we did get to speak about some of Holzer's personal experiences. And while some people in this field of study have had personal experiences and believe that in itself makes them expert on knowing if a location is haunted, Holzer wants witnesses – several of them preferably, and the not-crazy kind. "That's why I want to know my witness," he said. "I ask them, 'Who are you? What do you do for a living?' I interview the witnesses. If there is a crazy in front of me, I'll know it."

"My first visual experience was when I lived in New York City with my father in a penthouse apartment on Riverside Drive. I was asleep in bed, and I woke up and there was my mother dressed in a white nightgown, pushing my head back onto the pillow. My head had slipped off the pillow. At that time I was subject to migraines. Had I not had my head back on the pillow, I probably would've had one, and there would've been dizziness and I would've been out of business for a day. I said, 'Oh, hello, Mama.' And she disappeared."

We talked about the difference between a ghost or a spirit – how a ghost is a residual entity, like a psychic imprint left in an area that some people can pick up, whereas a spirit is intelligent and interactive. Holzer also mentioned a third category I hadn't heard about before: the "stay behinds."

"'Stay behinds are relatively common," he said. "Somebody dies, and then they're really surprised that all of a sudden they're not dead. They're alive like they were. They don't understand it because they weren't prepared for it. So they go back to what they knew most – their chair, their room, and they just sit there. Next, they want to let people know that they're still 'alive.' So they'll do little things like moving things, appear to relatives, pushing objects, poltergeist phenomena, and so on."

I asked him what we can expect to find waiting for us on the other side. His reply came without hesitation, and very matter-of-fact. "We all pass out of the physical body and we are now on the other side of life. It's a world just like this one – it has only two differences: there's no sense of time, and if you're ill when you die you're now no longer ill. But other than that, you'll find houses, trees, gardens, and your relatives, friends, and so on. It looks like a very real world. Maybe a little nicer, but still a normal, real world. And you are just the way you were before. Maybe a little bit younger-looking if you wish, but you're still in a very real world."

"You'll notice that the other side of life is a bureaucracy just like this one. You can't just call Uncle Frank [who's still living]. You have to get permission from a group of people who call themselves guides – spirit guides. They will say, 'Why do you want to make contact? What's your purpose?' And if they approve of it, they'll say, 'Okay, find yourself a medium somewhere, speak with them, and they will make contact for you.' Or if you're that strong, you can try to make contact yourself."

"And if you don't like where you are after a while—you may have a consciousness that you've been there a certain period and feel that you would rather be back on the other side with friends and loved ones. You'll say, 'I'd like to get reborn again.' These are the words I got from them, they're not my invention. They [the spirits] said you have to go to a line, and you have to register with the clerk. 'Clerk' is the word they used. So you get in line and register with the clerk that you want to go back. The clerk says, 'Okay, I'll let you know when I find an appropriate couple for you that will advance your development.' They have no real sense of time, so they just stand there, and eventually the clerk will say, 'I've got a couple for you.'"

"There is a well and they [the spirit about to go back] must walk through that well. They call it 'The Well of Forgetfulness.' They are sprayed with this water – not 100%, it never quite covers everything. That's why people have memories, dejá vu experiences, and recurrent dreams. And then they are a baby again."

"What I have learned in my investigations is that there are seven levels of consciousness on the other side of life that are concentric with our world. It's not up or down, it's just concentric. We can't see it because it moves at a different rate of speed than we move."

"The idea is reincarnation. This concept has been a part of many religions and belief systems for millennia." Holzer continued with his ideas on how our physical and spirit bodies connect. "There's three levels when you are born. You are born with a physical outer body, a duplicate inner body, and at the very moment of birth – that's very important – the moment the child is supposed to see the light [during childbirth], that is when the soul or the spirit is inserted from the pool of available spirits from the other side. Therefore all this nonsense about abortion killing a child is pure lies, pure nonsense. The fetus, until the spirit of the child is inserted, is a physical part of the mother. It does not have any life – it's not a separate entity."

Holzer said he worked with several mediums to compile this information on how things work in the afterlife. Holzer believes a good medium is the most critical element to a good supernatural investigation. He believes the medium is the person who can speak for those on the other side and deliver clear messages.

"That's putting a lot of faith in a person who is hopefully not a charlatan, but could be," I said.

"That's why you don't ask questions of a psychic," he said. "You just sit there and listen. I'll give you an example. Philip Solomon, a British trancemedium, once called me out of the blue because I had written a rather harsh piece in a magazine. It was about psychics who didn't deliver – not fakers – but incompetent psychics. So we talked on the phone and became friendly, and then he suddenly said, 'Your uncle Henry is here.' It became clear that he was talking about somebody who really is my uncle Henry. Weeks went on, and from time to time he would call me and give me messages from my parents and from Henry, which I found valid. Months went by, and he [Philip Solomon] said, 'Yes, Uncle Henry is here again.' So I said, 'If it's my uncle Henry, what does he want me to know?' And Philip said, 'Just a moment.' And then he came back and said, 'Your uncle Henry says the dog's name was Rigo.' Who the hell would know that? But it was Rigo."

"That's what I call evidence. There was no way that he could have known that my uncle's dog's name was Rigo. No way he could have known that—that was years and years ago. The only explanation of that particular case was that this was my uncle Henry. That was his way of proving himself. That's the kind of evidence I demand. It cannot be explained away."

Paranormal investigative groups are popping up everywhere. More people are studying this field today than ever before, and Holzer has met many of them. "We are living in a technological age," he said, "and they [paranormal investigators] think, or at least some of them that I've met, in all sincerity, that running around with Geiger counters and cameras and instruments that can measure cold spots will be the way to investigate a haunting or a ghost. That's bullshit. Because if you really are an investigator of the paranormal, and you're dealing with ghosts or hauntings, you're dealing with a human being – nothing more, nothing less. Therefore you should have with you a good trancemedium who can lend her body or his body temporarily for that entity to speak through so you can find out what the trouble is. That's the way it works – not a Geiger counter."

"But certainly a Geiger counter is more accessible than a trancemedium for most people," I said.

"And it looks more professional to them," Holzer said. "But it really is bullshit."

The one piece of equipment Holzer doesn't completely dismiss is the camera. "I have worked with psychic photographers," he said. "That's a special form of mediumship. Psychic photography is a gift. Some have it. I've used these people in haunted places. When there was something there, they would photograph it."

"Have you ever been afraid during an investigation?" I asked.

"Fear is the absence of information," he said. "Fear is created by not understanding something. You bring on the fear. There is no object to fear. I've never been afraid during an investigation. I shouldn't be in this business if I was. There's nothing out there that isn't one way or the other human. Hollywood notwithstanding, there are no monsters out there. There is no other supernatural race, no devils, no fellows in red underwear. It doesn't exist."

"What have you learned about yourself during all of these years of investigations?" I asked.

"My purpose is that I have a job. First of all, the other side, being a bureaucracy and being a well-ordered world, invests in people's abilities. When the other side decides some individuals have very good minds and good hearts, then they are given talents with the proviso that they will use those talents for the betterment of the world and mankind. If you don't, they won't like it. So they make it very plain: you have a gift. Use it. I found out early enough that they had something in mind for me. I accepted that it's an assignment. I noticed that what happened to me was kind of programmed – I met some people who were important for my career, or for my enlightenment – it was all arranged. So I finally said, 'Friends, I noticed you're running my life. It's okay with me. I will do it.' And I hear this in my right ear: 'We will guide you, help you. Use your gifts. You have two separate paths, one has to do with science, parapsychology research, and the other has to be the entertainment business. But you combine them to let the world know what you find.' And that's what I do."

Holzer is fortunate to be doing what he loves to do. So there is certainly no need to retire. "People can be unhappy for two reasons," he said. "Because they have the wrong mate or because they have the wrong job. They can change both."

"How do you want to be remembered?" I asked.

"As a man who told the truth. I won't have a tombstone. Cemeteries are real estate wastes, and I don't believe in funerals of any kind. The sooner you burn the body the better. It's just a shell.

"What will you be doing on your 100th birthday?"

"Looking forward to my 101st," he said. "I do what I'm meant to do. A man who takes himself too seriously, others won't take seriously, so I'm very careful about that. I want to be factual and to be useful – and I try to help anybody who wants help."

"And you want to keep swing dancing." I said.

"Yes," he said. "Not just swing, any form of dancing. When my daughter saw me at the wedding of my younger daughter, my older daughter saw all of us on the dance floor and said, 'I didn't know you had in you, Daddy.' I said, 'What do you think I do, the Govotte?'"

Thanks for dancing with me, Dr. Holzer.

Discussion Starters

1. Do you believe, like Dr. Holzer, that study of the paranormal is a science? Why?
2. Dr. Holzer claimed that a medium conversed with Holzer's dead uncle and provided information that he could only have gotten from the uncle. Do you believe his claim? Why?
3. Dr. Holzer has very specific information about what the "afterlife" is like, information he gleaned from his investigations and various mediums. What do you think of his depiction of an afterlife? Do you agree that an afterlife exists?

II. Cultural/Ethnic Perspectives

Why Chinese Mothers Are Superior

By Amy Chua

Amy Chua is a professor at Yale Law School and author of The Battle Hymn of the Tiger Mother. In this essay, Chua satirizes the manner in which Chinese mothers raise their daughters, implying that there is a better way.

A lot of people wonder how Chinese parents raise such stereotypically successful kids. They wonder what these parents do to produce so many math whizzes and music prodigies, what it's like inside the family, and whether they could do it too. Well, I can tell them, because I've done it. Here are some things my daughters, Sophia and Louisa, were never allowed to do:

- attend a sleepover
- have a playdate
- be in a school play
- complain about not being in a school play
- watch TV or play computer games
- choose their own extracurricular activities
- get any grade less than an A
- not be the No. 1 student in every subject except gym and drama
- play any instrument other than the piano or violin
- not play the piano or violin.

I'm using the term "Chinese mother" loosely. I know some Korean, Indian, Jamaican, Irish and Ghanaian parents who qualify too. Conversely, I know some mothers of Chinese heritage, almost always born in the West, who are not Chinese mothers, by choice or otherwise. I'm also using the term "Western parents" loosely. Western parents come in all varieties.

All the same, even when Western parents think they're being strict, they usually don't come close to being Chinese mothers. For example, my Western friends who consider themselves strict make their children practice their instruments 30 minutes every day. An hour at most. For a Chinese mother, the first hour is the easy part. It's hours two and three that get tough.

When it comes to parenting, the Chinese seem to produce children who display academic excellence, musical mastery and professional success - or so the stereotype goes. Despite our squeamishness about cultural stereotypes, there are tons of studies out there showing marked and quantifiable differences between Chinese and Westerners when it comes to parenting. In one study of 50 Western American mothers and 48 Chinese immigrant mothers, almost 70% of the Western mothers said either that "stressing academic success is not good for children" or that "parents need to foster the idea that learning is fun." By contrast, roughly 0% of the Chinese mothers felt the same way. Instead, the vast majority of the Chinese mothers said that they believe their children can be "the best" students, that "academic achievement reflects successful parenting," and that if children did not excel at school then there was "a problem" and parents "were not doing their job." Other studies indicate that compared to Western parents, Chinese parents spend approximately 10 times as long every day drilling academic activities with their children. By contrast, Western kids are more likely to participate in sports teams.

What Chinese parents understand is that nothing is fun until you're good at it. To get good at anything you have to work, and children on their own never want to work, which is why it is crucial to override their preferences. This often requires fortitude on the part of the parents because the child will resist; things are always hardest at the beginning, which is where Western parents tend to give up. But if done properly, the Chinese strategy produces a virtuous circle. Tenacious practice, practice, practice is crucial for excellence; rote repetition is underrated in America. Once a child starts to excel at something—whether it's math, piano, pitching or ballet—he or she gets praise, admiration and satisfaction. This builds confidence and makes the once not-fun activity fun. This in turn makes it easier for the parent to get the child to work even more.

Chinese parents can get away with things that Western parents can't. Once when I was young—maybe more than once—when I was extremely disrespectful to my mother, my father angrily called me "garbage" in our native Hokkien dialect. It worked really well. I felt terrible and deeply ashamed of what I had done. But it didn't damage my self-esteem or anything like that. I knew exactly how highly he thought of me. I didn't actually think I was worthless or feel like a piece of garbage.

As an adult, I once did the same thing to Sophia, calling her garbage in English when she acted extremely disrespectfully toward me. When I mentioned that I had done this at a dinner party, I was immediately ostracized. One guest named Marcy got so upset she broke down in tears and had to leave early. My friend Susan, the host, tried to rehabilitate me with the remaining guests.

The fact is that Chinese parents can do things that would seem unimaginable—even legally actionable—to Westerners. Chinese mothers can say to their daughters, "Hey fatty—lose some weight." By contrast, Western parents have to tiptoe around the issue, talking in terms of "health" and never ever mentioning the f-word, and their kids still end up in therapy for eating disorders and negative self-image. (I also once heard a Western father toast his adult daughter by calling her "beautiful and incredibly competent." She later told me that made her feel like garbage.)

Chinese parents can order their kids to get straight As. Western parents can only ask their kids to try their best. Chinese parents can say, "You're lazy. All your classmates are getting ahead of you." By contrast, Western parents have to struggle with their own conflicted feelings about achievement, and try to persuade themselves that they're not disappointed about how their kids turned out.

I've thought long and hard about how Chinese parents can get away with what they do. I think there are three big differences between the Chinese and Western parental mind-sets.

First, I've noticed that Western parents are extremely anxious about their children's self-esteem. They worry about how their children will feel if they fail at something, and they constantly try to reassure their children about how good they are notwithstanding a mediocre performance on a test or at a recital. In other words, Western parents are concerned about their children's psyches. Chinese parents aren't. They assume strength, not fragility, and as a result they behave very differently.

For example, if a child comes home with an A-minus on a test, a Western parent will most likely praise the child. The Chinese mother will gasp in horror and ask what went wrong. If the child comes home with a B on the test, some Western parents will still praise the child. Other Western parents will sit their child down and express disapproval, but they will be careful not to make their child feel inadequate or insecure, and they will not call their child "stupid," "worthless" or "a disgrace." Privately, the Western parents may worry that their child does not test well or have aptitude in the subject or that there is something wrong with the curriculum and possibly the whole school. If the child's grades do not improve, they may eventually schedule a meeting with the school principal to challenge the way the subject is being taught or to call into question the teacher's credentials.

If a Chinese child gets a B—which would never happen—there would first be a screaming, hair-tearing explosion. The devastated Chinese mother would then get dozens, maybe hundreds of practice tests and work through them with her child for as long as it takes to get the grade up to an A.

Chinese parents demand perfect grades because they believe that their child can get them. If their child doesn't get them, the Chinese parent assumes it's because the child didn't work hard enough. That's why the solution to substandard performance is always to excoriate, punish and shame the child. The Chinese parent believes that their child will be strong enough to take the shaming and to improve from it. (And when Chinese kids do excel, there is plenty of ego-inflating parental praise lavished in the privacy of the home.)

Second, Chinese parents believe that their kids owe them everything. The reason for this is a little unclear, but it's probably a combination of Confucian filial piety and the fact that the parents have sacrificed and done so much for their children. (And it's true that Chinese mothers get in the trenches, putting in long grueling hours personally tutoring, training, interrogating and spying on their kids.) Anyway, the understanding is that Chinese children must spend their lives repaying their parents by obeying them and making them proud.

By contrast, I don't think most Westerners have the same view of children being permanently indebted to their parents. My husband, Jed, actually has the opposite view. "Children don't choose their parents," he once said to me. "They don't even choose to be born. It's parents who foist life on their kids, so it's the parents' responsibility to provide for them. Kids don't owe their parents anything. Their duty will be to their own kids." This strikes me as a terrible deal for the Western parent.

Third, Chinese parents believe that they know what is best for their children and therefore override all of their children's own desires and preferences. That's why Chinese daughters can't have boyfriends in high school and why Chinese kids can't go to sleepaway camp. It's also why no Chinese kid would ever dare say to their mother, "I got a part in the school play! I'm Villager Number Six. I'll have to stay after school for rehearsal every day from 3:00 to 7:00, and I'll also need a ride on weekends." God help any Chinese kid who tried that one.

Don't get me wrong: It's not that Chinese parents don't care about their children. Just the opposite. They would give up anything for their children. It's just an entirely different parenting model.

Here's a story in favor of coercion, Chinese-style. Lulu was about 7, still playing two instruments, and working on a piano piece called "The Little White Donkey" by the French composer Jacques Ibert. The piece is really cute—you can just imagine a little donkey ambling along a country road with its master—but it's also incredibly difficult for young players because the two hands have to keep schizophrenically different rhythms.

Lulu couldn't do it. We worked on it nonstop for a week, drilling each of her hands separately, over and over. But whenever we tried putting the hands together, one always morphed into the other, and everything fell apart. Finally, the day before her lesson, Lulu announced in exasperation that she was giving up and stomped off.

"Get back to the piano now," I ordered.

"You can't make me."

"Oh yes, I can."

Back at the piano, Lulu made me pay. She punched, thrashed and kicked. She grabbed the music score and tore it to shreds. I taped the score back together and encased it in a plastic shield so that it could never be destroyed again. Then I hauled Lulu's dollhouse to the car and told her I'd donate it to the Salvation Army piece by piece if she didn't have "The Little White Donkey" perfect by the next day. When Lulu said, "I thought you were going to the Salvation Army, why are you still here?" I threatened her with no lunch, no dinner, no Christmas or Hanukkah presents, no birthday parties for two, three, four years. When she still kept playing it wrong, I told her she was purposely working herself into a frenzy because she was secretly afraid she couldn't do it. I told her to stop being lazy, cowardly, self-indulgent and pathetic.

Jed took me aside. He told me to stop insulting Lulu—which I wasn't even doing, I was just motivating her—and that he didn't think threatening Lulu was helpful. Also, he said, maybe Lulu really just couldn't do the technique—perhaps she didn't have the coordination yet—had I considered that possibility?

"You just don't believe in her," I accused.

"That's ridiculous," Jed said scornfully. "Of course I do."

"Sophia could play the piece when she was this age."

"But Lulu and Sophia are different people," Jed pointed out.

"Oh no, not this," I said, rolling my eyes. "Everyone is special in their special own way," I mimicked sarcastically. "Even losers are special in their own special way. Well don't worry, you don't have to lift a finger. I'm willing to put in as long as it takes, and I'm happy to be the one hated. And you can be the one they adore because you make them pancakes and take them to Yankees games."

I rolled up my sleeves and went back to Lulu. I used every weapon and tactic I could think of. We worked right through dinner into the night, and I wouldn't let Lulu get up, not for water, not even to go to the bathroom. The house became a war zone, and I lost my voice yelling, but still there seemed to be only negative progress, and even I began to have doubts.

Then, out of the blue, Lulu did it. Her hands suddenly came together—her right and left hands each doing their own imperturbable thing—just like that. Lulu realized it the same time I did. I held my breath. She tried it tentatively again. Then she played it more confidently and faster, and still the rhythm held. A moment later, she was beaming.

"Mommy, look—it's easy!" After that, she wanted to play the piece over and over and wouldn't leave the piano. That night, she came to sleep in my bed, and we snuggled and hugged, cracking each other up. When she performed "The Little White Donkey" at a recital a few weeks later, parents came up to me and said, "What a perfect piece for Lulu—it's so spunky and so her."

Even Jed gave me credit for that one. Western parents worry a lot about their children's self-esteem. But as a parent, one of the worst things you can do for your child's self-esteem is to let them give up. On the flip side, there's nothing better for building confidence than learning you can do something you thought you couldn't.

There are all these new books out there portraying Asian mothers as scheming, callous, overdriven people indifferent to their kids' true interests. For their part, many Chinese secretly believe that they care more about their children and are willing to sacrifice much more for them than Westerners, who seem perfectly content to let their children turn out badly. I think it's a misunderstanding on both sides. All decent parents want to do what's best for their children. The Chinese just have a totally different idea of how to do that.

Western parents try to respect their children's individuality, encouraging them to pursue their true passions, supporting their choices, and providing positive reinforcement and a nurturing environment. By contrast, the Chinese believe that the best way to protect their children is by preparing them for the future, letting them see what they're capable of, and arming them with skills, work habits and inner confidence that no one can ever take away.

Discussion Starters

1. Discuss the differences between the Chinese and Western "mothering" in the essay. Do you find one method superior to the other? Why? What kind of a balance between the two methods might be best?
2. Chua has said that the essay is intended to be satirical. Reading the essay as satire, what is being satirized and what is being praised?
3. Discuss your own parental upbringing regarding school and achievement. How do you feel it affected (affects) your life? How would you raise (or do you raise) your own children?

I'm an Illegal Immigrant at Harvard

The author withholds her name due to her current status as an undocumented resident. In this essay, the author reveals the negative impact that being an "illegal immigrant" and living in legal limbo has on her and others in the same situation.

I'm a senior at Harvard and I'm undocumented. I've spent most of my life keeping my immigration status a secret, but in retrospect it seems that I could have been more discreet at times.

I watched the live vote of the DREAM Act—the controversial legislation that would pave the way toward amnesty for illegal immigrants who have grown up and gone to college here—as I pretended to take notes in one of my political science seminars. Classmates on either side of me, who may have suspected my secret, shot me glances that alternated between the confused and the sorry as I fumbled with my laptop and watched the C-Span live stream on mute. It didn't look to be going well. Harry Reid looked flustered. And then I saw the news ticker flash announce what I already knew—the DREAM Act was not going in for a vote.

As this lame-duck session drew to a close, and even as Reid and Nancy Pelosi make promises to bring the legislation up for a vote again, I am still fumbling with my laptop, signing petitions I fear are useless, and watching the news alerts pour into my inbox. This time, I am protecting my heart. I know the DREAM Act will probably once again wither away. I know supporting it is political suicide and I don't expect anyone to put their political careers on the line for me or my family. It's always been just the four of us and I know it probably always will be. I'm a senior at Harvard and I'm undocumented.

An immigration lawyer recently told me I had no way of regulating my status, save for marriage or legislation, and did I feel OK about that? How can I answer that question? I was born in South America and lived there until I was 4, but I've lived here since I started kindergarten. That's how I've always measured my life, in increments of semesters and trimesters and marking periods. School has always been my sanctuary, a place where I could be alone with my books and words, a respite from reality, a place where I could be loved and appreciated for my mind and my heart. Opponents of the DREAM Act say citizenship is not a right, it's a privilege, and no amount of patriotism can entitle you to it, no matter how hard-earned or heartfelt—you cannot deserve your way into becoming American. But despite that rhetoric, the discourse of immigration reform always falls into a discussion of individual merits and goodness.

My parents were only a little older than I am now when they overstayed their visas. I hadn't even learned the alphabet when I overstayed mine. It is important that I make clear I was the valedictorian of my high school class and got full scholarships to the country's best schools. It is important that I point out I have been published in some of the top magazines and am currently working on a book, an excerpt of which has already been published. And it might be worth emphasizing that we'd make excellent permanent neighbors. My parents have been paying taxes for years, even procuring a special taxpayer ID number from the IRS in order to be able to do so. We go to church every Sunday. We've adopted from the animal shelter. We go running together in the summers. We recycle. But you and I both know this changes nothing.

Immigration law has never been straightforward, and 9/11 made it impossible to do anything about it. I am 21 years old and this is a burden I've had to carry for most of my life. I'm emotionally exhausted from living my life in a perpetual state of purgatory and I now know I am expected to also live in a perpetual state of penance. We broke the law and deserve to be punished, the argument goes. So why haven't we been punished?

I don't have an answer to that question, but in lieu of an answer, I could tell you that perhaps we have been—daily, privately, painfully. Punishment isn't made legitimate by the presence of an audience.

There was the time, years and years ago, when I got on the bus and an elderly woman walked past me and said loudly but to no one in particular, "Why can't these Mexicans just learn English?" Or the time my father's boss looked me up and down, letting his eyes linger where they may, and offered me a job at his restaurant, the first and only post-Harvard job offer extended not despite but because of my legal status.

I can tell you that I spent my first two years at Harvard paralyzed by fear and self-loathing. I can tell you about the day my father's driver's license was suspended. He had worked as a cab and ambulette driver since setting foot in the country and was suddenly out of work. Our family's only government-issued identification card was suddenly gone. My father collapsed into my arms the minute he walked into our apartment. He buried his face in my hair and sobbed violently—it remains the only time I've seen him cry. He was unemployed for a couple weeks and then began doing deliveries by foot at a restaurant in our city's financial district. Our family lives off his tips. Sometimes he needs me to help him stand up after he's been sitting for a while. I hold onto his arm and lift him while he closes his eyes and tries not to grimace. The doctor says his back and knees are so bad he will have to retire early. He is 45.

I can tell you the sight of a police officer makes my heart beat fast. I can tell you I've had to sit through my friends' thousand-picture slide shows of their backpacking trips through Europe and that I feel more and more deflated after each click because I can't leave this country and I can't study abroad and I'm even afraid to take the Greyhound. I can tell you I am only now beginning to trust people enough to talk about what we refer to as "my situation." I can try to tell you I'm scared and you might be able to figure out who I am and I will be deported. I can tell you so many things.

Joan Didion once explained that someone with a plane schedule in their drawer lives according to a slightly different calendar than everyone else. Will these next seven months be the last I spend in the United States? It is November and I have already lost the ability to think in the future tense, as if my heart had anesthetized my mind in preparation for the possible disappointments of the next several months. I sleep without setting any alarm clocks. I speak faster in hopes that I might get more English words in. I kiss slower to feel more, here, longer. I'm at a road that bifurcates into continents and I am terrified because I know I might once again have to live with a decision that is not mine to make. It would hurt to be forced to leave, but it hurts to stay the way I'm staying now. I belong to this place but I also want it to belong to me.

Discussion Starters

1. What did you learn from the essay about what life is like for undocumented people living in the U.S.? How are their lives markedly different from U.S. citizens?

2. The DREAM act would grant legal residence to undocumented persons who graduated from high school in the U.S. and came to the country as minors. Do you support such legislation?

3. Discuss your personal experience or those of people you know who are undocumented. What do you think is the best legislative solution for all undocumented persons in the U.S.?

"I Stayed to Fight"—Being a Muslim Immigrant in Post 9/11 America

By Mona Eltahawy

Mona Eltahawy is an award-winning columnist and public speaker on Arab and Muslim issues. In this essay, Eltahawy provides an American Muslim's perspective on the 9/11 attacks, the post-9/11 consequences for American Muslims, and what she would like readers whose only frame of reference for Muslims is 9/11 to know.

For most of my life, the US was never anything more than vacation memories. My family visited almost 30 years ago for a vacation that marked the end of our years of living in the UK and which came just before we moved to Saudi Arabia. New York City dazzled, of course, and a road trip with an uncle and his family from Wyoming through the Rockies to California where Mickey Mouse greeted us in Disneyland, was a lesson in the sheer vastness that is the United States.

But then I fell in love with an American and I flew to NYC to meet him for the millennium celebrations and even though we fought and I gave him back his engagement ring, I agreed to marry him and I did what I vowed I'd never do: I left my job and my home for a man.

The year after I moved to be with him in Seattle, early one Tuesday, his mother called us from her home at the other end of the country – three time zones away in Florida – urging us to turn on the television because something terrible was happening in New York. I rushed to awaken my brother and his wife who were visiting us.

That morning of 11 September 2001 as we watched the twin towers crumble on live television, America and I would develop a bond that has proven deeper and more enduring – for better or worse, through sickness and health – than the one I had with my now ex-husband.

"If this is Muslims, they're going to round us up," I told him. He took the day off work and we didn't leave the apartment for two days, worried that my sister-in-law would be attacked for her headscarf. A drunk unsuccessfully tried to set our local mosque on fire; the neighborhood stood guard outside the mosque for weeks afterwards holding signs that read "Muslims are Americans". "What's it like to f**k a terrorist?" a group of young men asked the white American husband of a Pakistani-American woman I knew.

I left my husband a year after 9/11. Not because he was an American and I an Egyptian, nothing to do with culture or religion; nothing to do with 9/11. We brought out the worst in each other. But before we separated we visited NYC one more time together for a friend's engagement and we went to pay our respects at the site of the attacks. I had no words. Just tears and prayers as we took in the gaping hole, the makeshift shrines of teddy bears and notes desperately seeking the whereabouts of loved ones.

Ironically, he now lives in Asia and I've stayed in the US. I stayed to fight. To say that's not my Islam. To yell Muslims weren't invented on 9/11. Those planes crashing again and again into the towers were the first introduction to Islam and Muslims for too many Americans but we – American Muslims – are sick and tired of explaining. None of those men was an American Muslim and we're done explaining and apologizing. Enough.

I stayed to give my middle finger to Tea Partiers who tried to intimidate a group of us in 2010 because we supported the right of an Islamic community center to build near the site of the attacks. They came to bully us and I bullied them right back. I wanted them to know Muslims will not be intimidated so think twice before you try to bully another one.

I became an American in April of this year, almost 11 years after I moved here. I could've become naturalised earlier but I realized soon after I took the oath and we watched a video of President Obama congratulating us that if it had been President Bush I would've probably run out, screaming. Despite an appearance by Bush at a mosque after 9/11 to show he didn't hold all Muslims responsible, his administration proceeded to do exactly that: military trials for civilians, secret prisons, the detention of hundreds of Muslim men without charge, the torture and harsh interrogation of detainees and the invasions of two Muslim-majority countries.

And the latest stain on the US civil liberties record: an Associated Press expose in August on ways the CIA and the NYPD are combining forces to spy on Muslims in New York City. The thought that someone could be following me to my favorite book shops or night clubs is as pathetic and sinister as when the Mubarak regime tapped my phone and had me followed when I lived in Egypt.

And I will continue to stay in the US for my nieces and nephews. I have chosen not to have children. I am a happy aunt to two girls and two boys between the ages of three and eight. They were the first Americans in our family and the thought that anyone could question either their nationality or faith – or demand they choose between the two – enrages me.

Over the past 10 years, American Muslims have fought not just the hate and stereotypes and the profiling from those outside the community, we've also had major fights within the Muslim community. As a friend described it, 9/11 pushed many Muslims to "come out" as liberals or progressives. For too long, huge, conservative national organizations claimed to speak for all of us but there is a much greater diversity of American Muslim voices now and that benefits everyone. Conservative does not equal authentic.

People think I'm Brazilian, Dominican, Puerto Rican, anything but Muslim because many people equate a Muslim woman with the wearing of a headscarf. So like someone who's gay who might make sure to tell you soon after you meet, I try to include within the first three sentences of a new meeting that I'm a Muslim.

Before 9/11, some Muslims lived quiet, uneventful suburban lives; the dentists and the accountants and the attorneys. 9/11 robbed them of that boring existence. But in struggling to become boring again, American Muslims have over the past 10 years made our community here the most vibrant of any Muslim community in the world.

We're your friends, lovers and spouses, America. We're your comedians, taxi drivers, chefs, politicians and singers. And we're your doctors, like my brother and his wife who were visiting me from the Midwest in Seattle 10 years ago.

My brother, a cardiologist, was visited by special agents from the FBI in November 2001 who asked him if he knew anyone who celebrated the attacks. His wife is an obstetrician/gynecologist. One day she and I were watching one of those medical dramas when she told me an anecdote that neatly sums it all up: "I was delivering a baby the other day and the father was watching via Skype cam. He was a soldier in Afghanistan. And I thought, here I am: a Muslim doctor in a headscarf delivering a baby whose father is an American soldier in Afghanistan, a Muslim country."

Let's draw the curtain on 9/11 anniversaries after this 10th one. Every year on 11 September you can taste the grief in NYC. The wound will never heal if every year we scratch the scar off and open the way to hate and prejudice.

Some of the earliest Muslims came to the US across the Atlantic on slave ships from West Africa. Not far from where I live in Harlem, there's a West African community complete with a mosque, restaurants and French-speaking people. 9/11 changed everything and 9/11 changed nothing at all. America – I'm not going anywhere.

Discussion Starters

1. What did you learn about Muslim Americans from the essay that you may not have known? Are they any different, in your opinion, from Americans of other religious affiliations? Why?

2. What treatments of Muslim Americans does Eltahawy find unfair and indefensible since 9/11? Do you agree with her? Why?

3. What is your own attitude towards Muslim Americans? How can Americans best separate the radical Islamic terrorists from the millions of Muslim Americans who love their country?

What a Wall Can't Stop

By Richard Rodriguez

Richard Rodriguez is an award-winning American writer and author of the acclaimed The Hunger Of Memory: The Education of Richard Rodriguez. In this essay, Rodriguez contends that the "Mexicanization" of America is so well established that any measures to fortify the border against illegal entry are irrelevant.

To placate the nativist flank of his Republican Party, former President Bush promised to brick up the sky. But that will not prevent the coming marriage of Mexico and the United States. South and north of the line, we are becoming a hemispheric people—truly American—in no small part because of illegal immigrants.

As the son of Mexican immigrants legally in the United States, I have long wondered about the future of Mexico, a nation that every night for nearly a century has lost hundreds of its most hopeful youths to its neighbor and rival, the North.

I think historians will come to recognize the illegal immigrant as the great prophetic figure within the Americas. The illegal immigrant Americanized us all by a simple and frugal migration; by sojourning in the North; and by sending the dream of the North (a money-gram) back into Mexico.

From the early 20th century, the migrant worker commuted between here and there, hot and cold, high and low, past and future, rich and poor, Spanish and English, life and death. The legend of the North spread throughout the Americas. Today Peruvians and Bolivians know when there are apple-picking jobs in the Yakima Valley; when the god-awful fisheries in Alaska will begin to hire; when a dishwashing job in a Bronx restaurant is coming open.

By the late 20th century, the rumor of the North had ascended to the middle and the upper class in Mexico. They, too, followed the peasant's lead. In Mexico City, a capital of abundant but vulnerable wealth, the rich have learned the prudence of a second home in La Jolla.

The Americanization of Mexico is as inevitable as the Mexicanization of the United States, though the cross-pollination will never be equal because the United States is the more potent transgressor.

Americans take our imperial influence for granted. We assume, do we not, the desirability of Wal-Mart? Shouldn't we build Wal-Mart in Mexico? Of course we should. Where shall we build Wal-Mart in Mexico? How about right there—where it will appear in the photograph of the Pyramid of the Sun.

Commentators did not seem to know what they were watching when millions of brown people recently marched along U.S. streets. This was obviously a "demonstration," but a demonstration of what? I believe it was a reunion—of family, of hemisphere. Children and parents walked as one family. Brothers born there, sisters born here, walked as one hemisphere.

A great many Americans are alarmed by how much of Mexico is within the United States—the tongue, the tacos, the soccer balls, the street gangs, the Spanish Catholic Masses, the workforce swarming into New Orleans in the wake of Hurricane Katrina. The extent of the Mexicanization of U.S. culture renders any notion of a fortified border irrelevant.

Twenty-five years ago, Joel Garreau wrote "The Nine Nations of North America," in which he described a nation he called "MexAmerica"—a puzzle to both Washington and Mexico City—encompassing much of the U.S. Southwest and Northern Mexico as well as Baja California. A quarter-century later, one is struck by how prescient Garreau was but also how modest his forecast was. MexAmerica now includes vast sections of Chicago and blocks along Main Street in Kansas, as well as the Baptist Church in North Carolina.

In the other direction, MexAmerica includes not just the Mexican border towns that have become drug supply centers for U.S. addiction but also Jalisco, Colima, Michoacan and points south.

Mexico, the poorer country, does not have the luxury of an appalled demeanor when the Atlanta couple transforms a beachfront property into a saltwater Tara or when senior citizens from Ohio park their retirement village in Baja.

And watch closely—I implore you—watch the eyes of Mexican busboys and waiters as they observe U.S. college students conducting wet T-shirt competitions on the beaches of Cancun. Do not believe, America, that you are alone in your reservations concerning this marriage.

Discussion Starters

1. What does Rodriguez mean by the "Mexicanization" of America? What examples does he provide? Do you agree with him that any notion of a fortified border is "irrelevant?"
2. Likewise, Rodriguez sees the "Americanization" of Mexico. What examples does he provide? How does the "Mexicanization" of America differ sharply from the "Americanization" of Mexico?
3. The Latino population is by far the fastest growing in the U.S., with California nearly 40% Latino. What impact will this growth have on the culture, the economy, and U.S. politics?

How Black is Black Enough?

By Leonard Pitts Jr.

Leonard Pitts Jr. is a Pulitzer Prize-winning editorialist for the Miami Herald. In this essay, Pitts takes exception to the viewpoint of former ESPN commentator Rob Parker that to be black carries with it a particular criteria which many blacks, including Pitts, don't fit.

I suddenly find myself concerned about my blackness. It had never occurred to me to worry about it before. Then came the incident on ESPN's "First Take" program that initially got commentator Rob Parker suspended and then, last week, fired outright. It seems Parker, who is black, analyzed what he saw as the insufficient blackness of Robert Griffin III, rookie quarterback for the Washington, D.C., football team that is named for a racial slur.

Having returned their team to relevance for the first time since the Clinton era, RG3, as he is known, can do no wrong in the eyes of Slurs fans. But Parker, saying that the young man's fiancee is (gasp!) white and that he himself is rumored to be—cover the children's ears—a Republican, found him lacking in the area of authentic blackness. "My question," he said, "which is just a straight, honest question: is he a brother, or is he a cornball brother? He's not really...OK, he's black, he kind of does the thing, but he's not really down with the cause. He's not one of us. He's kind of black, but he's not really like the guy you really want to hang out with..."

That explosion you hear is the sound of my mind, blown. I'm left second-guessing my own blackness. I mean, I listen to Bruce Springsteen, for crying out loud! There's even a Dixie Chicks album on my iPod. And I read books sometimes, man—even when no one's making me do it. Some of them are thick as bricks. Some aren't even about African-American themes.

It gets worse. I have no natural rhythm, no criminal record and can correctly pronounce the word "ask." I don't curse nearly as much as I ought to. Oh, and I went and married my baby mama. Obviously, my blackness is on life support.

Many of us have been taught that it is demeaning and delimiting when someone presumes to say who you are, how you will behave, what you think, what you like, and how intelligent you are, from the color of your skin. We have been taught that such behavior abridges the other person's individuality. But apparently, that's only when white people do it to black people. When black people do it to black people, it's called assessing your blackness, making sure you aren't some "cornball brother."

How enlightening to learn that. It is even more enlightening to discover that we have such easy-peasy rubrics to go by. You can't be black if you are a Republican? That means Colin Powell isn't black. Neither, if published reports are to be believed, are rappers LL Cool J and 50 Cent. Who'd have thought?

Poor Frederick Douglass has a double whammy. He was a Republican and had a white wife. Who'd have thought this former slave, one of the towering heroes of African-American history, wasn't black enough?

It is this kind of bold insight and trenchant analysis ESPN loses in sacking Rob Parker. What is the network thinking? Parker, who also contributes commentary to WDIV television in Detroit, defended himself in an interview with the station that aired just before ESPN dropped the ax. He pronounced himself shocked by the fallout and suggested his comments were taken out of context.

"You can't be afraid to talk about race," he said. He's exactly right. In discussing race, we must be fearless. We must also be thoughtful. And informed. And exact. And alive to the ramifications of what we say. Surely, Parker knows this. Or if he didn't before, he does now.

As for being black enough, he is probably a greater expert than he was before. He is, after all, a man out of work. It doesn't get much blacker than that.

Discussion Starters

1. How does Pitts attack Parker's contention that you aren't *really* black unless you fit a particular criteria? Do you find his response effective? Why?
2. Pitts enlists his own black stereotypes to show he doesn't fit the mold: blacks don't read, swear too much, have wedlock children, and don't have jobs. Is such stereotyping of blacks by a black man defensible in any way?
3. Discuss racial stereotypes of blacks, whites, Asians, and Latinos. What are such stereotypes based on and how are they harmful?

Paper Tigers

By Wesley Yang

Wesley Yang is an American writer and critic whose essays have appeared in several publications. In this essay, Yang contends that the stereotypical perception of Asians as hardworking, monochromatic achievers accurately characterizes the majority, and he challenges young Asians to break the mold as he himself has tried to do.

Sometimes I'll glimpse my reflection in a window and feel astonished by what I see. Jet-black hair. Slanted eyes. A pancake-flat surface of yellow-and-green-toned skin. An expression that is nearly reptilian in its impassivity. I've contrived to think of this face as the equal in beauty to any other. But what I feel in these moments is its strangeness to me. It's my face. I can't disclaim it. But what does it have to do with me?

Millions of Americans must feel estranged from their own faces. But every self-estranged individual is estranged in his own way. I, for instance, am the child of Korean immigrants, but I do not speak my parents' native tongue. I have never called my elders by the proper honorific, "big brother" or "big sister." I have never dated a Korean woman. I don't have a Korean friend. Though I am an immigrant, I have never wanted to strive like one.

You could say that I am, in the gently derisive parlance of Asian-Americans, a banana or a Twinkie (yellow on the outside, white on the inside). But while I don't believe our roots necessarily define us, I do believe there are racially inflected assumptions wired into our neural circuitry that we use to sort through the sea of faces we confront. And although I am in most respects devoid of Asian characteristics, I do have an Asian face.

Here is what I sometimes suspect my face signifies to other Americans: an invisible person, barely distinguishable from a mass of faces that resemble it. A conspicuous person standing apart from the crowd and yet devoid of any individuality. An icon of so much that the culture pretends to honor but that it in fact patronizes and exploits. Not just people "who are good at math" and play the violin, but a mass of stifled, repressed, abused, conformist quasi-robots who simply do not matter, socially or culturally.

I've always been of two minds about this sequence of stereotypes. On the one hand, it offends me greatly that anyone would think to apply them to me, or to anyone else, simply on the basis of facial characteristics. On the other hand, it also seems to me that there are a lot of Asian people to whom they apply.

Let me summarize my feelings toward Asian values: F**k filial piety. F**k grade-grubbing. F**k Ivy League mania. F**k deference to authority. F**k humility and hard work. F**k harmonious relations. F**k sacrificing for the future. F** earnest, striving middle-class servility.

I understand the reasons Asian parents have raised a generation of children this way. Doctor, lawyer, accountant, engineer: These are good jobs open to whoever works hard enough. What could be wrong with that pursuit? Asians graduate from college at a rate higher than any other ethnic group in America, including whites. They earn a higher median family income than any other ethnic group in America, including whites. This is a stage in a triumphal narrative, and it is a narrative that is much shorter than many remember. Two thirds of the roughly 14 million Asian-Americans are foreign-born. There were less than 39,000 people of Korean descent living in America in 1970, when my elder brother was born. There are around 1 million today.

Asian-American success is typically taken to ratify the American Dream and to prove that minorities can make it in this country without handouts. Still, an undercurrent of racial panic always accompanies the consideration of Asians, and all the more so as China becomes the destination for our industrial base and the banker controlling our burgeoning debt. But if the armies of Chinese factory workers who make our fast fashion and iPads terrify us, and if the collective mass of high-achieving Asian-American students arouse an anxiety about the laxity of American parenting, what of the Asian-American who obeyed everything his parents told him? Does this person really scare anyone?

Earlier this year, the publication of Amy Chua's *Battle Hymn of the Tiger Mother* incited a collective airing out of many varieties of race-based hysteria. But absent from the millions of words written in response to the book was any serious consideration of whether Asian-Americans were in fact taking over this country. If it is true that they are collectively dominating in elite high schools and universities, is it also true that Asian-Americans are dominating in the real world? My strong suspicion was that this was not so. If we are a collective juggernaut that inspires such awe and fear, why does it seem that so many Asians are so readily perceived to be, as I myself have felt most of my life, the products of a timid culture, easily pushed around by more assertive people, and thus basically invisible?

I finished school alienated both from Asian culture (which, in my hometown, was barely visible) and the manners and mores of my white peers. I wanted to be an individual. I had refused both cultures as an act of self-assertion. An education spent dutifully acquiring credentials through relentless drilling seemed to me an obscenity. So did adopting the manipulative cheeriness that seemed to secure the popularity of white Americans.

Instead, I set about contriving to live beyond both poles. I wanted what James Baldwin sought as a writer—"a power which outlasts kingdoms." Anything short of that seemed a humiliating compromise. I would become an aristocrat of the spirit, who prides himself on his incompetence in the middling tasks that are the world's business. Who does not seek after material gain. Who is his own law.

This, of course, was madness. A child of Asian immigrants born into the suburbs of New Jersey and educated at Rutgers cannot be a law unto himself. The only way to approximate this is to refuse employment, because you will not be bossed around by people beneath you, and shave your expenses to the bone, because you cannot afford more, and move into a decaying Victorian mansion in Jersey City, so that your sense of eccentric distinction can be preserved in the midst of poverty, and cut yourself free of every form of bourgeois discipline, because these are precisely the habits that will keep you chained to the mediocre fate you consider worse than death.

Throughout my twenties, I proudly turned away from one institution of American life after another (for instance, a steady job), though they had already long since turned away from me. Academe seemed another kind of death—but then again, I had a transcript marred by as many F's as A's. I had come from a culture that was the middle path incarnate. And yet for some people, there can be no middle path, only transcendence or descent into the abyss. I was descending into the abyss.

All this was well deserved. No one had any reason to think I was anything or anyone. And yet I felt entitled to demand this recognition. I knew this was wrong and impermissible; therefore I had to double down on it. The world brings low such people. It brought me low. I haven't had health insurance in ten years. I didn't earn more than $12,000 for eight consecutive years. I went three years in the prime of my adulthood without touching a woman. I did not produce a masterpiece.

I recall one of the strangest conversations I had in the city. A woman came up to me at a party and said she had been moved by a piece of writing I had published. She confessed that prior to reading it, she had never wanted to talk to me, and had always been sure, on the basis of what she could see from across the room, that I was nobody worth talking to, that I was in fact someone to avoid. But she had been wrong about this, she told me: It was now plain to her that I was a person with great reserves of feeling and insight. She did not ask my forgiveness for this brutal misjudgment. Instead, what she wanted to know was—why had I kept that person she had glimpsed in my essay so well hidden? She confessed something of her own hidden sorrow: She had never been beautiful and had decided, early on, that it therefore fell to her to "love the world twice as hard." Why hadn't I done that?

Here was a drunk white lady speaking what so many others over the years must have been insufficiently drunk to tell me. It was the key to many things that had, and had not, happened. If you are a woman who isn't beautiful, it is a social reality that you will have to work twice as hard to hold anyone's attention. You can either linger on the unfairness of this or you can get with the program. If you are an Asian person who holds himself proudly aloof, nobody will respect that, or find it intriguing, or wonder if that challenging façade hides someone worth getting to know. They will simply write you off as someone not worth the trouble of talking to.

Having glimpsed just how unacceptable the world judges my demeanor, could I too strive to make up for my shortcomings? Practice a shit-eating grin until it becomes natural? Love the world twice as hard? I see the appeal of getting with the program. But this is not my choice. Striving to meet others' expectations may be a necessary cost of assimilation, but I am not going to do it.

Often I think my defiance is just delusional, self-glorifying bullshit that artists have always told themselves to compensate for their poverty and powerlessness. But sometimes I think it's the only thing that has preserved me intact, and that what has been preserved is not just haughty caprice but in fact the meaning of my life. I care, in the end, about expressing my obdurate singularity at any cost. I love this hard and unyielding part of myself more than any other reward the world has to offer a newly brightened and ingratiating demeanor, and I will bear any costs associated with it.

The first step toward self-reform is to admit your deficiencies. Though my early adulthood has been a protracted education in them, I do not admit mine. I'm fine. It's the rest of you who have a problem.

Amy Chua returned to Yale from a long, exhausting book tour in which one television interviewer had led off by noting that Internet commenters were calling her a monster. By that point, she had become practiced at the special kind of self-presentation required of a person under public siege. "I do not think that Chinese parents are superior," she declared at the annual gathering of the Asian-American Students Alliance. "I think there are many ways to be a good parent."

Much of her talk to the students, and indeed much of the conversation surrounding the book, was focused on her own parenting decisions. But just as interesting is how her parents parented her. Chua was plainly the product of a brute-force Chinese education. *Battle Hymn of the Tiger Mother* includes many lessons she was taught by her parents. "Be modest, be humble, be simple," her mother told her. "Never complain or make excuses," her father instructed. "If something seems unfair at school, just prove yourself by working twice as hard and being twice as good."

"The loudest duck gets shot" is a Chinese proverb. "The nail that sticks out gets hammered down" is a Japanese one. Its Western correlative: "The squeaky wheel gets the grease." Chua had told her story and been hammered down. Yet here she was, fresh from her hammering, completely unbowed.

There is something salutary in that proud defiance. And though the debate she sparked about Asian-American life has been of questionable value, we will need more people with the same kind of defiance, willing to push themselves into the spotlight and to make some noise, to beat people up, to seduce women, to make mistakes, to become entrepreneurs, to stop doggedly pursuing official paper emblems attesting to their worthiness, to stop thinking those scraps of paper will secure anyone's happiness, and to dare to be interesting.

Discussion Starters

1. Wang rails against everything that has underscored the Asian success story in America: hard work, good grades, college degrees, professional jobs. What does he find lacking in this formula for success? Do you agree with him?

2. Wang believes more Asians should "push themselves into the spotlight and to make some noise, to beat people up, to seduce women, to make mistakes, to become entrepreneurs, to stop doggedly pursuing official paper emblems attesting to their worthiness, to stop thinking those scraps of paper will secure anyone's happiness, and to dare to be interesting." Why does he offer such advice? Do you agree with him?

3. Wang sees himself as "an invisible person, barely distinguishable from a mass of faces that resemble it." Is this an accurate assessment of how Asian people are viewed in America?

Black Teenagers Defy Pop Culture Portrayals

By Laura Stepp

Laura Stepp is a Pulitzer Prize-winning journalist for The Washington Post. In this essay, Stepp juxtaposes the negative stereotypical perception of young black people with a more positive reality based on an extensive research survey.

If you got your ideas about young black people just from the entertainment industry, you'd think they were all players and baby mamas—and you'd be sorely mistaken.

In fact, the pregnancy rate of black teenage girls has dropped 44% over the last two decades, the teen birth rate 47%. Over that same period, both pregnancy and birth rates declined among all youth, but black youth had the largest declines. And those black Casanovas? Also a stereotype. Young black men, as well as young black women, value relationships over sex.

These are some of the findings reported in *Essence* magazine. *Essence*, in partnership with The National Campaign to Prevent Teen and Unplanned Pregnancy, hired an independent research firm to survey 1,500 African-Americans ages 13 to 21 about their attitudes toward sex, relationships and media.

Not all results were positive. Among young African-American males in the *Essence* survey who had had sex, 65% had done so at least once without using protection. And national data show that almost 50% of African-American females ages 13-21 will get pregnant before they turn 20.

But sexual behavior is improving, and unlike the impression we get from popular culture, young people have got other things on their minds in addition to "doing it." The survey reported, for example, that four out of five girls and guys said they'd rather get straight A's in school than be thought of as "hot." Also, three of four males said they'd rather be in a relationship with no sex than have sex with no relationship, and three of five said guys have more respect for girls who want to wait to have sex.

Both young men and young women said they felt more sexual pressure from society and the media than from their partners. The media—including television, movies and videos—took a particular beating from young women: 72% said that media send a message that sex appeal is a black woman's most important quality.

As Kendralyn, a college freshman, told me, VH1's "Basketball Wives" or Oxygen's "Bad Girls' Club" are "not what being a black woman is all about." Naomi, a high school senior, singled out the BET network. "It's just too much. There's so much sass, playing on the stereotype."

Turning off the television—even if a parent could—is not going to help. As the *Essence* article pointed out, young people carry the media around in their smart phones, leaving grayheads clueless about what the teens are watching, listening to and talking about. And TV and video characters are not the only ones pushing sexual stereotypes. Older adults, especially white adults, can be quick to make generalizations based on how black youth dress or talk, Naomi said. She and her friends pick up on suggestive stares and snide comments.

Kendralyn noted, correctly, that older adults have always made negative generalizations about youth. (Indeed. "Bye-Bye Birdie" anyone?) "Every young generation is underestimated and sometimes misjudged," Kendralyn said. What she would like to see, especially for black girls, are more ways for them to showcase their talents beyond what their bodies offer.

She offered one more piece of advice to adults: Listen before you talk. That means starting with the right questions, according to *Essence* writer Jeannine Amber. Steer away from "Don't, don't, don't," she wrote. Ask young people what they're doing, how they're feeling, what they're thinking about—not just when it comes to sex, but also about their relationships. Parents who are uncomfortable with such conversations can steer their kids to an aunt, uncle or other substitute, Amber said.

Almost all kids in school today learn the mechanics of sexual intercourse, the dangers of unprotected sex and the precautions they should take if they're going to have sex. It's a good bet that sex education - as spotty as it is in this country - has had something to do with the decline of teen pregnancies and teen births.

But let's also give credit to black teens themselves. After all, in the moment when it counts, they're the ones making the decision to wait to have sex or to use protection. Adults' role is not to judge, but to help them do what many, if not most, already want to do.

Discussion Starters

1. What, if anything, surprised you in the survey of black teens presented in the essay? How do those findings contradict prevalent stereotypes about black teen behavior and attitudes?

2. Teens girls interviewed in the essay decried the image of black women on reality shows and the Black Television Network. Why do you think there is such a disparity between how blacks are portrayed on television compared to reality?

3. To evaluate the validity of the *Essence* survey results, what would you want to know about the respondents to assess their "representativeness" of black teens in general? Do you think the survey results would be similar for other ethnic/racial groups?

III. Family and Relationships

The Changing American Family

By Herbert S. Klein

Herbert S. Klein is a research fellow at the Hoover Institution located at Stanford University. In this essay, Klein examines the dramatic changes in the American family in the past thirty years and the effects of those changes.

For all the changes in fertility and mortality that Americans have experienced from the colonial period until today, there has been surprisingly little change in the structure of the family until the past quarter century. Until that point, the age of marriage changed from time to time, but only a minority of women never married and births outside marriage were traditionally less than 10 percent of all births.

But this fundamental social institution has changed profoundly since 1980. In fact, if one were to define the most original demographic feature in the post-1980 period in the United States, it would be the changes that were occurring in both families and households for all sections of the national population. The traditional American family has been undergoing profound transformations for all ages, all races, and all ethnic groups. Every aspect of the American family is experiencing change. These include the number of adults who marry, the number of households that are formed by married people, the number of children that are conceived, the economic role of mothers, the number of non-family households, and even the importance of marriage in accounting for total births.

The proportion of persons over 20 years of age who had never married reached historic levels in 2000 when a third of the men and a quarter of the women were listed as never having married. The decline in marriage among whites is occurring at a slower pace than among blacks, but both are experiencing rising trends in unmarried adults. By 2000, 22 percent of adult white women and 42 percent of adult black women had never married. This rise in the ratio of persons never married is also reflected in historical changes in the relation between families and households. Non-family households had always existed as a small share of the total households in the United States, usually made up of elderly persons with no families left. But now they are formed by young adults, many of whom never married, or by older persons who no longer reside with children.

Also, the proportion of two-parent households, even in family households with children, is on the decline, as single-parent-plus-children households are on the rise. As late as 1960, at the height of the Baby Boom, married families made up almost three-quarters of all households but by the census of 2000 they accounted for just 53 percent of them, a decline that seems to have continued in the past few years. Non-family households now account for 31 percent of households, and families headed by a single parent with children account for the rest, making up to 27 percent of all such families with children. Black families experienced the fastest decline of dual-parent households; by the end of the century married couples with children accounted for only 4 out of 10 of all black family households with children. But no group was immune to this rising trend of single-parent households.

Not only have family households been on the decline, as a consequence of the rise of single-person and childless-couple households, but even women giving birth are now having far fewer children, are spacing them further apart, and are ending their fertility at earlier ages than ever before, which has brought fertility levels in the United States to their lowest level in history. In the colonial period the average woman produced more than seven children during the course of her lifetime. Since the 1970s the rate has been under two children for the majority non-Hispanic white population. The national fertility total currently barely reaches its replacement level; fluctuating between 2.0 and 2.1 children per woman over the past quarter century; by 2000 non-Hispanic white women were averaging just 1.8 children. Among all groups it was only the Hispanic women—who are at a total fertility rate of 2.5 children—who are above the replacement level. Even among Hispanic women, it is primarily Mexican-American women, the largest single group, which maintained very high fertility rates. Cuban-American women were close to the non-Hispanic whites, and the Puerto Rican women were closer to the fertility patterns of non-Hispanic black women.

Although the U.S. fertility rate declined to the lowest level in history, single women now make up an increased percentage of those having children. The rapid and very recent rise in births outside marriage means that married women no longer are the exclusive arbiters of fertility. Whereas at mid-century such extramarital births were an insignificant phenomenon, accounting for only 4 percent of all births, by 2000 they accounted for a third of births, and that proportion is rising. Although all groups experienced this change, non-Hispanic whites experienced a slower rise than all other groups. Although some have thought this to be a temporary aberration in historic patterns, the increasing unmarried pregnancy rates in Europe suggest that North America is following modern advanced Western European trends.

In the 1970s, when the issue began to be perceived by the public as one of major concern, it was the teenagers who had the highest rates of births outside marriage, and those births seemed to be rising at the time. But by the end of the century older women's rates of unmarried pregnancies were highest and rising; those for teenage girls were falling in both relative and absolute numbers.

That this increase of births outside marriage was not due to poverty per se can be seen in the fact that the United States was not unique in this new pattern of births and the declining importance of traditional marriage. Other wealthy countries, such as Sweden, have also experienced this trend. Although Sweden in 1950 had fertility patterns comparable to those of the United States, by the end of the century its rate of non-marital births was more than half of all births. Even such Catholic countries as Spain and Portugal had arrived at 16 percent and 22 percent rates of non-marital births, respectively, and France was up to 38 percent by 1996. Thus the belief that this was a temporary or uniquely North American development does not appear to be the case. The factors influencing these trends everywhere in the modern industrial world seem to be the same— late marriages, women increasing their participation in the workforce and thus having higher incomes, and changing beliefs in the importance and necessity of marriage. These changes seem to be affecting all Europe and North America at approximately the same time.

This trend is also reflected in the changing economic role of women even in dual-parent households with children. The traditional family with a single male breadwinner working alone to sustain the family is no longer the norm. By the end of the century, only one in five married couples had just a single male breadwinner working outside the home. Among married couples with children under six years of age, only 36 percent had the mother staying at home with the children and not working, and in families where women had given birth to a child during the previous year, the majority of these mothers at the end of the year were working outside the home—more than half of them in 2000 compared to just under one third in 1967. Not only were more women in the workforce—a ratio that was constantly on the rise through the second half of the century—but the vast majority of married mothers with young children were working outside the home by 2000.

All of these changes are having an impact on U.S. fertility rates. Not only is formal marriage no longer the exclusive arbiter of fertility, but more and more women are reducing the number of children they have. This is not due to women forgoing children. In fact, there has been little change in the number of women going childless, which has remained quite steady for the past 40 years. This decline in fertility is due to the fact that women are deliberately deciding to have fewer children. They are marrying later, thus reducing their marital fertility, they are beginning childbearing at ever later ages, they are spacing their children farther apart, and they are terminating their fertility at earlier ages. Not only did the average age of mothers having their first children rise by 2.7 years from 1960 to 1999, but it rose significantly for every subsequent child being born as well, while the spacing between children also increased. Although the average age of mothers at first birth for the entire population was now 24.9 years, for non-Hispanic white women it was 25.9 years.

Clearly the American family, like all families in the Western industrial countries, is now profoundly different from what it had been in the recorded past. It typically is a household with few children, with both parents working, and with mothers producing their children at ever older ages. At the same time, more adults than ever before are living alone or with unmarried companions and more women than ever before are giving birth out of wedlock. These trends have profoundly changed the American family and are unlikely to be reversed any time soon.

Discussion Starters

1. What are the major changes in the American family that the essay presents? What do you think the impact of these changes are on children, women, and men?
2. Discuss your own family situations in which you were raised. How do they reflect the trends noted in the essay?
3. What is your viewpoint on marriage and family? What future do you see for yourself regarding marriage, singleness, and children?

Gay Men: Fusing the Erotic and Aesthetic

By David Halperin

David Halperin is a professor at the University of Michigan, the author of How to be Gay, and a prominent gay rights activist. In this essay, Halperin presents a very different reality of growing up gay compared to heterosexual and how the formative adolescent years of gay men have a profound and lasting effect on their lives.

In his inexhaustible study of gay male culture, Neil Bartlett devotes an entire chapter called "Possessions" to gay men's relationship to their *things*. Like "the excessive sentimentality that was the necessary condition of sentiments allowed no real object," gay men's insistent desire for precious possessions springs, according to Bartlett, from a permanent sense of fundamental frustration at the particular unavailability to us of the objects we most want. "Material wealth and sensual pleasure have a very special function for us," Bartlett explains; "they compensate for other forms of poverty." Bartlett carefully left those other forms of poverty unspecified – he clearly had in mind a broad spectrum of social and political deprivations – but he allowed for the possibility that there might be a very specific "hunger that gapes beneath" our quest for possessions.

The true sense of that hunger, Bartlett implied, is a lack of erotic satisfaction of a very general and basic kind. Sexual deprivation is fundamental, and crucial, to the subjective experiences of gay men, not because we are all pathetic, sex-starved rejects who never succeed in finding acceptable partners, but because adult satisfaction cannot quite make up for a previous history of unfulfillment. As George Haggerty says, speaking of the gayness of the pastoral elegy, "A love that is constituted in loss is a love that yields a longing that can never be fulfilled."

Early on in our lives, whenever we become urgently aware of our desires, gay men discover that most of the human beings that attract us are not the least bit interested in having a sexual relationship with us, that they are not and cannot be attracted to us in return, and that some of them regard the mere fact of our desire for them as abhorrent. To be sure, it is possible to generalize this phenomena to people other than gay men, but at least heterosexuals do not experience their love objects as being *categorically* off limits to them, on account of them belonging to the wrong sex, which is what gay men experience. Even as adults, we do not escape the awareness that, in the eyes of most men, we fail to qualify as candidates for either sex or love. So our desire for men, in many cases, is impossible from the start, *impossible as such*. It is therefore infinite, and necessarily confined in the first instance to *fantasizing* about them. We develop, early on, a habit of communing with imaginary lovers, and it is a habit we never quite abandon.

What may be in and of itself an easy desire to satisfy becomes, when it is denied and frustrated, an impossible dream. The protracted experience of erotic lack which all gay men who grow up in straight society necessarily and painfully undergo turns the ordinary fulfillment of ordinary homosexual desire into an unattainable fantasy, which it often remains even when, later in life, a small-town boy moves to a gay metropolis where the sexual fulfillment of his former erotic daydreams turns out at last to be child's play. For belated access to sexual objects, no matter how numerous or glamorous they may be, can do little to close the long-established gap between fantasy and reality in the demand for erotic gratification. (Which is why the myriad opportunities for sexual satisfaction and love that gay liberation offers us have led not to a withering away of the gay porn industry but to its hypertrophic expansion.) Once the very prospect of "getting what you want" has been consigned to the realm of fantasy, erotic gratification ineluctably takes on hyperbolic proportions, exits the realm of the attainable, and becomes indissolubly associated with impossible rapture.

No wonder homosexual desire routinely verges on an obsession with absolute, unearthly perfection, with flawless archetypes or Platonic essences (the perfectly beautiful man: Dorian Gray; the technically flawless image of a beautiful man: Robert Mapplethorpe's "The Perfect Moment;" the perfect operatic diva: the Lisbon Traviata).

Since they devote so much solitary time and effort early on in their lives to studying the perfect attributes of their ideal love objects, determining what combination of features – or what social form – corresponds most exactly to the requirements of their desire, gay men tend, while still quite young, to arrive at a detailed and rigorous mental picture of what it is that they want. And they are not likely to settle for anything less. Also, if most of the men you grew up wanting were bound to reject you anyway through no fault of your own, and if your prohibited desire for them was therefore destined to express itself only in dreams, in hopeless fantasies of sexual fulfillment and romantic bliss, then you had no reason to let the world constrain your daydreams or limit the scope of your fantasies to the narrow field of the possible. And so, when the time eventually comes to leave that dreamscape, you may find it difficult to make compromises with humdrum reality.

The commitment to perfection, and the refusal to settle for anything (or anyone) less, generate the peculiar merging of eroticism and aestheticism that is distinctive to gay culture. For an impossible but perfect object excites a very particular kind of desire. The ecstatic practice of erotic worship, combined with a despair of sexual satisfaction, produces a specific attitude toward objects of longing that is characteristic of gay male culture: an attitude of passionate but detached contemplation, at once critical and idealistic. By mingling the rapt transports of sexual idolatry with a distant, almost clinical appreciation of beauty, gay men achieve a kind of disinterestedness in their relation to erotic objects that brings their experience of sexual desire very close to that of pure aesthetic contemplation.

At least since Kant, it has been conventionally assumed that physical beauty and artistic beauty awaken very different kinds of response in normal (heterosexual) human subjects. The alleged difference between our responses to beautiful bodies and beautiful works of art is supposed to ground a fundamental distinction between interested and disinterested attraction, between instrumental, selfish, egoistic excited interestedness and non-instrumental, selfless, altruistic, contemplative disinterestedness. Aestheticism, moreover, is usually thought to express a quest for perfection, or a commitment to perfect beauty, that is largely irrelevant to the cruder, baser workings of sexual excitation. Gay male culture, by contrast, is notorious for its habit of fusing erotics and aesthetics.

Discussion Starters

1. What permanent effects, according to Halperin, does the fact that most men (i.e. heterosexual) a gay man is attracted to in his early years are "*categorically* off limits" have on him? How does this create a very different mindset among gay men compared to heterosexuals?
2. Why, according to Halperin, do gay men fuse the erotic and the aesthetic while heterosexuals, in general, do not? Is this an important distinction?
3. What, if anything, did you learn from the essay about the gay perspective? Do you feel that as a gay man, Halperin is relating the universal gay experience?

More College 'Hookups,' but More Virgins, Too

By Sharon Jayson

Sharon Jayson writes articles about relationships and behavior for USA TODAY. In this essay, Jayson analyzes the seeming paradox of more college students "hooking up" for sex and more students simultaneously remaining virgins, and some probable causes.

It wasn't until the second semester of her senior year at Fordham University in New York that Kathleen Adams had a college boyfriend. "You just don't date at colleges," says Adams, 23, now a Fordham graduate student in urban studies.

But there's no shortage of casual sex on campus, she says—in part because Fordham, like many colleges, has significantly more women than men. Adams says that means guys have the upper hand when it comes to intimacy. "It's kind of like a competition," she says. "The guys have their choice of whoever they want. So they think, 'Why would I date?' "

The relationship game among college-age adults today is a muddle of seemingly contradictory trends. Recent studies indicate that traditional dating on campuses has taken a back seat to no-strings relationships in which bonds between young men and women are increasingly brief and sexual. A new website to arrange these encounters that began at the University of Chicago last month now is expanding to other campuses.

But even as casual sex—often called "hookups" or "friends with benefits"—is a dominant part of campus life, a new report by the National Center for Health Statistics indicates the percentages of men and women 18-24 who say they are virgins also are increasing. It all reflects an emerging paradigm that is altering the nature of sex and relationships among young adults: fewer men than women on campuses; a more openly sexual society that often takes cues from media, and a declining desire to make relationship commitments early in life.

Adams' experience is the reality for many of today's college students, says Mark Regnerus, an associate professor of sociology at the University of Texas-Austin. His research suggests that the higher proportion of women on campuses has contributed to the ascent of the hookup culture. Overall, women made up more than 56% of the college population in 2009, according to the recent Census data on enrollments; more women are found on many campuses that serve both sexes.

"The women wind up competing with each other for access to the men, and often, that means relationships become sexual quicker," says Regnerus, co-author of *Premarital Sex in America: How Young Americans Meet, Mate, and Think About Marrying*. It is based on an analysis of four national studies representing a total of 25,000 young people ages 18-23 and more than 200 additional interviews. "Men don't have to work as hard as they used to, to woo a woman," he says. "I've talked to various interviewees who had never been on a date, which doesn't really make sense, given they're pretty attractive. It's just that less seems to be required to be in the company of a woman."

Justin Garcia, a State University of New York doctoral fellow at Binghamton (N.Y.) University who conducts research on hookups, says this general lack of dating means many young adults don't even know how to get a relationship started. "For the majority of students, they're not going to dinner and a movie unless they've hooked up with someone. Some physical interaction comes before the dating," he says. Often, "dates happen after a relationship, rather than before."

Many young people are eschewing relationships as too much hassle, especially when they plan to study abroad, leave town for internships or go to graduate school, says sociologist Teresa Downing-Matibag of Iowa State University. "They want to have their freedom and are not always interested in these committed relationships. At the same time, they'll tell you they will not be in a relationship without sex being an important part of it," she says.

The down economy has forced many students to work because their parents aren't as capable of funding their education; that means they're juggling school and work and are less likely to have time to devote to a relationship, she adds. "With the people that I know, there is a fair share of hooking up just to have sex, and the intention is to only do it once and possibly never see that person again," says Rachel Curtis, 22, an Iowa State grad student. "I know a few girls who would like to hook up every weekend, but sometimes the opportunity doesn't present itself. They call that an 'unlucky night.' "

The cryptic nature of what a hookup involves appeals to many young people: They deliberately want to be vague so they can exaggerate or hide their actions from their friends, analysts say. 'Hookup' leaves it to the imagination. The ambiguity is intentional," says Michael Bruce of San Francisco, co-editor of College Sex: Philosophy for Everyone: Philosophers with Benefits. "Hooking up is very vague. It can be anything from kissing on the dance floor to you go back and have sex in the room and sleep over," says Leah Reis-Dennis, 19, a Harvard University sophomore from Eugene, Ore.

"It's called hanging out, but it's really hooking up," adds Kirsten Ellermann, 20, a junior at Iowa State University who has been in a relationship for more than a year. "You know what it means when a guy says he wants to come over and hang out. He's not taking you to dinner." "In a big way, hookups have kind of taken the place of—not exactly eclipsed—relationships, but hooking up is kind of an easier way for college students to act on their sexual desire without making a big commitment," says Reis-Dennis, a history and literature major.

Even so, "it's not like everyone is having casual sex all the time," says sociologist Paula England of Stanford University, whose ongoing research since 2005 has surveyed more than 17,000 students from 20 colleges and universities. "Some people are hooking up a bunch of times with the same person but are not calling it a relationship. Others are never doing anything you would call a hookup." Her latest data finds that by senior year, 72% of both sexes reported having at least one hookup, with the average of 9.7 for men and 7.1 for women. Just under one-quarter (24%) of seniors say they are virgins, she says.

The percentage of those who claim virginity appears to be increasing, according to a National Center for Health Statistics study released this month of 2006-08 data. Among 18- and 19-year-olds, about one-quarter of men and women said they hadn't had sexual contact with another person, up from 17% of women and 22% of men in 2002. Among those ages 20-24, 12% of women and 13% of men said they were virgins, up from 8% for both sexes in 2002. "Friends my age have not said they have chosen to be virgins," says Ashley Thompson, 23, who will receive her master's degree in public health from Ohio State University-Columbus in June.

Thompson, of Perrysburg, Ohio, is engaged, but "a lot of my peers, as women, have got a lot of other things going on. I think the fact that young women are able to focus on other life goals such as school or career could change the way they form relationships, which inherently would impact their sexual activity."

Some studies find virgins in even higher numbers. Responses collected from 1,500 Duke University freshmen and seniors at the Durham, N.C., campus in 2007 found that about 53% of women and 40% of the men said they were virgins, says Wendy Brynildsen, a Duke doctoral student who will share that data in a paper at the annual meeting of the American Sociological Association in August. "Many people think I'm crazy" for not having sex, says Jon Haron, 21, of Highlands Ranch, Colo., a part-time college student studying aviation technology and air-traffic control. He also works part-time as a flight instructor. "My core group of guy friends—my close friends—we've all made the decision to not have (sexual intercourse) until we're married," Haron says. But several friends, he adds, think it's OK to engage in other sexual activity.

Although the government data offers no explanations for the growing percentage of virgins, there has been plenty of speculation, ranging from more open discussion about the health risks associated with casual sex to the busy lives of young people. Some cite the rise of the abstinence movement, while others point to easy access to Internet porn and an overtly sexualized culture that has made young people somewhat blase about sex.

"We're seeing that the choice to remain abstinent is increasingly resonant," says Valerie Huber, executive director of the non-profit National Abstinence Education Association, which will launch a campaign next year to "rebrand the cultural message" and tell young people that "sexual activity as a rite of passage" is no longer an expectation for teens and young adults.

While sexual experimentation is a part of life for many young people, Reis-Dennis, a history and literature major, says there also are many who don't want to have a "throwaway sexual experience." "Personally, a lot of my friends at school have had sex," she says. "As many, if not more, haven't."

Haron says his circle of friends, which includes about 15 guys, some with girlfriends, all have looked at porn and are trying to stay away from it. "Porn is easy," he says. "I think that's why a lot of guys are drawn to that. It's so easy to get and they're not going to be rejected, so why try with a girl?"

Researchers are well aware how the Internet has made porn and sex websites so accessible and appealing; Downing-Matibag says her students have shown her websites for virtual sex. "They can go to those websites and have sexual relationships watching a webcam. They can still be a virgin and have 100 different partners online through chat rooms or webcams," she says. "Young people have avatars (on-screen characters representing themselves online) and enter these virtual worlds that involve sexual encounters."

But some of those who work to educate young people about sex say the new data about more virgins could signal change. "The hookup culture seems to be predominating, but there might be the beginning of a pushback and relationships playing a much stronger role," says James Wagoner, president of Advocates for Youth, a Washington-based non-profit.

Still, most young people are having some kind of sexual contact. "Humans are biological beings," Garcia says. "We have a sex drive. To not recognize that in talking to young adults is foolish."

Discussion Starters

1. What might be the reasons for the contradictory sexual behavior presented in the essay: more sexual "hook-ups" but more college-age virgins?
2. What effects do you think that the casual/no strings approach to sex has on those who experience it? What is your personable viewpoint on "hooking up?"
3. The essay presents a rather discouraging picture for women on campus: not enough guys, more competition, more need to gratify men sexually. Does this picture conform to your college experience? Does the essay reflect the sexual/relationship situation for most college students?

Fathering in America: What's a Dad Supposed to Do?

By Marie Hartwell-Walker

Marie Hartwell-Walker is a psychologist, professor at the University of Massachusetts, and writer for the Huffington Post. In this essay, Hartwell-Walker contends that no matter the kind of family situation children are in, fathers are a critical part of the equation, and reveals how all fathers can contribute to the happiness and well-being of their children.

Americans seem more confused than ever about the role of fathers in children's lives. On the one hand, more and more fathers are absent for all or significant periods of time. According to the 2006 Census, 23 percent of children under the age of 18 don't live with their biological father and the number is climbing. On the other hand, search "fatherhood" on the web and you'll find dozens of websites dedicated to teaching, encouraging, and supporting men in becoming more nurturing and involved fathers.

Meanwhile, many TV sitcoms and animated shows continue to portray dads as dolts or, at best, well-meaning but misguided large children whose wives have to mother them as well as their offspring. If an alien in another universe happens to tune in to *The Simpsons, Everyone Loves Raymond, Family Guy*, etc., he (it?) will come away with a rather skewed idea of how men function in American families.

I'll leave it to the sociologists to explain the many and complicated variables of race, class, gender issues, social policy, employment issues, and governmental interventions that are at the root of the diverging trends and the pejorative TV scripts. It's enough to note that there is a major rethinking of fathers' roles and responsibilities going on within the context of lots of rethinking in America.

We may be reconsidering how family should be defined. We may be confused about gender roles. We may be struggling with knowing how to parent well in a complicated time. But in the midst of all this confusion, there is a growing consensus that what kids need, at least, is clear. Kids need their fathers as well as their mothers.

Regardless of whether the father lives with his children, active participation in raising those children is good for everyone. The kids become healthier adults. The fathers come to a fuller and more complex maturity. The mothers have a reliable co-parent to share the responsibilities and challenges as well as the accomplishments of parenting. How does this idea of "involved father" translate to daily life? Current research points to the following practical guidelines for responsible fatherhood.

What's a Father to Do?

Embrace your responsibility. Once you are a father, you are a father for life. The knowledge of fatherhood changes a man. It can be a source of pride and maturity or a source of shame and regret. Even if you have good reasons for not being actively involved, acknowledging your paternity is a minimal gift you can provide to your child. With it come many legal, psychological, and financial benefits. If you want to be in your child's life, it also protects your rights to have time with your child should you and the child's mother have a falling out.

Be there. In study after study, kids consistently say they would like to have more time with their dads. Regardless of whether a dad shares a home with the children and their mother, the kids need dad time. Working together on a chore or simply hanging out can be as meaningful as attending events or having adventures. Kids want to know their fathers. Just as important, they want their fathers to know them.

Be there throughout their childhoods. There is no time in a child's life that doesn't count. Research has shown that even infants know and respond to their fathers differently than they do to their mothers. The bond you make with a baby sets the foundation for a lifetime. As the kids get older, they'll need you in different ways but they will always need you. Insistent toddler, curious preschooler, growing child, prickly adolescent: Each age and stage will have its challenges and rewards. Kids whose parents let them know that they are worth their parents' time and attention are kids who grow up healthy and strong. Boys and girls who grow up with attention and approval from their dads as well as their moms tend to be more successful in life.

Respond to the needs of the kids, not your relationship with their mother. Regardless of whether you are getting along with your girlfriend or wife (present or ex), your relationship with the kids is exactly that: your relationship with the kids. The kids need predictability. They need care. They need a loving relationship with you. They need whatever financial support you can provide. None of these things should depend on whether you've had a disagreement or fight with their mom. None of these things should ever be withheld as a way to get even with her.

Be in a respectful and appreciative relationship with their mother. Being a good dad is certainly possible both inside and outside of marriage. Regardless of whether you and their mom can work out how to be a committed couple, you can support each other as parents. Kids grow best when their parents treat each other with respect and appreciation. The kids then don't feel torn between the two people they love.

Do your financial share. Kids need to be fed, clothed, housed, and cared for. Children whose parents provide for them live better lives, feel valued, and have better relationships with both their parents. They need the role model of a responsible male acting responsibly. Just as they need you to be present in their lives, regardless of whether you live with their mom, they also need you to live up to financial obligations to the very best of your ability.

Balance discipline with fun. Some dads make the mistake of being only the disciplinarian. The kids grow up afraid of their dads and unable to see the man behind the rules. An equal and opposite mistake is being so focused on fun that you become one of the kids, leaving their mother always to be the heavy. Kids need to have fathers who know both how to set reasonable, firm limits and how to relax and have a good time. Give yourself and the kids the stability that comes with clear limits and the good memories that come with play.

Be a role model of adult manhood. Both boys and girls need you as a role model for what it means to be adult and male. Make no mistake: The kids are observing you every minute. They are taking in how you treat others, how you manage stress and frustrations, how you fulfill your obligations, and whether you carry yourself with dignity. Consciously or not, the boys will become like you. The girls will look for a man very much like you. Give them an idea of manhood (and relationships) you can be proud of.

Beyond these considerations, there is little agreement about how an "ideal father" should behave. It doesn't seem to matter (in terms of the mental health of children) whether fathers work out of the home or stay home with the kids. It doesn't seem to matter what job a dad has or how much money a dad makes, as long as he is doing his best. It doesn't seem to matter what his interests and skills are, as long as he shares them with his children. It doesn't seem to matter whether a father is very physically affectionate or loves more quietly as long as the kids know that he most certainly cares about them. What matters is for fathers to be committed to their children and involved with them over time. When fathers take that responsibility seriously, their children are more likely to do well and the fathers have few regrets.

Discussion Starters

1. The essay is based on the assumption that fathers are very important in a child's life. Do you agree with the assumption? Why?
2. Discuss the eight recommendations that Hartwell-Walker makes for successful fathering. Do you agree with each recommendation? Are some more important than others?
3. Discuss the role that a father (or lack of a father) has played in your life. How do you view fatherhood in your own future (or how do women view the importance of raising children with a father in their future)?

Looking for Someone: Sex, Love, and Loneliness on the Internet

By Nick Paumgarten

Nick Paumgarten is a staff writer for The New Yorker. In this essay, Paumgarten explores the world of online dating, its place in the "love-connection" landscape, and the range of experiences of those who seek love on the Internet.

The process of selecting and securing a partner, whether for conceiving and rearing children, or for enhancing one's socioeconomic standing, or for attempting motel-room acrobatics, or merely for finding companionship in a cold and lonely universe, is as consequential as it can be inefficient or irresolute. Lives hang in the balance, and yet we have typically relied for our choices on happenstance—offhand referrals, late nights at the office, or the dream of meeting cute.

Online dating sites, whatever their more mercenary motives, draw on the premise that there has got to be a better way. They approach the primeval mystery of human attraction with a systematic and almost Promethean hand. They rely on algorithms, those often proprietary mathematical equations and processes which make it possible to perform computational feats beyond the reach of the naked brain. Some add an extra layer of projection and interpretation; they adhere to a certain theory of compatibility, rooted in psychology or brain chemistry or genetic coding, or they define themselves by other, more readily obvious indicators of similitude, such as race, religion, sexual predilection, sense of humor, or musical taste. There are those which basically allow you to browse through profiles as you would boxes of cereal on a shelf in the store. Others choose for you; they bring five boxes of cereal to your door, ask you to select one, and then return to the warehouse with the four others. Or else they leave you with all five.

The obvious advantage of online dating is that it provides a wider pool of possibility and choice. In some respects, for the masses of grownups seeking mates, either for a night or for life, dating is an attempt to approximate the collegiate condition—that surfeit both of supply and demand, of information and authentication. A college campus is a habitat of abundance and access, with a fluid and fairly ruthless vetting apparatus. A city also has abundance and access, especially for the young, but as people pair off, and as they corral themselves, through profession, geography, and taste, into cliques and castes, the range of available mates shrinks. We run out of friends of friends and friends of friends of friends. You can get to thinking that the single ones are single for a reason.

If your herd is larger, your top choice is likely to be better, in theory, anyway. This can cause problems. When there is something better out there, you can't help trying to find it. You fall prey to the tyranny of choice—the idea that people, when faced with too many options, find it harder to make a selection. If you are trying to choose a boyfriend out of a herd of thousands, you may choose none of them. Or you see someone until someone better comes along. The term for this is "trading up." It can lead you to think that your opportunities are virtually infinite, and therefore to question what you have. It can turn people into products.

For some, of course, there is no end game; Internet dating can be sport, an end in itself. One guy told me he regarded it as "target practice"—a way to sharpen his skills. If you're looking only to get laid, the industry's algorithmic-matching pretense is of little account; you merely want to be cut loose in the corral. The Internet can arrange this for you.

But if you really are eager, to say nothing of desperate, for a long-term partner you may have to contend with something else—the tyranny of unwitting compromise. Often the people who go on the sites that promise you a match are so primed to find one that they jump at the first or the second or the third who comes along. The people who are looking may not be the people you are looking for. "It's a selection problem when you round up a bunch of people who want to settle down," Chris Coyne, one of the founders of a site called OK Cupid, told me. Some people are too picky, and others aren't picky enough. Some hitters swing at every first pitch, and others always strike out looking. Many sites, either because of their methods or because of their reputations, tend to attract one or the other.

"Internet dating" is a bit of a misnomer. You don't date online, you meet people online. It's a search mechanism. The question is, is it a better one than, say, taking up hot yoga, attending a lot of book parties, or hitting happy hour at Tony Roma's?

Match.com, one of the first Internet dating sites, went live in 1995. It is now the biggest dating site in the world and is itself the biggest aggregator of other dating sites; under the name Match, it owns thirty in all, and accounts for about a quarter of the revenues of its parent company, I.A.C., Barry Diller's collection of media properties. In 2010, fee-based dating Web sites grossed over a billion dollars.

According to a recent study commissioned by Match.com, online is now the third most common way for people to meet. (The most common are "through work/school" and "through friends/family.") One in six new marriages is the result of meetings on Internet dating sites. (Nobody's counting one-night stands.) For many people in their twenties, accustomed to conducting much of their social life online, it is no less natural a way to hook up than the church social or the night-club-bathroom line.

There are thousands of dating sites; the big ones, such as Match.com and eHarmony (among the fee-based services) and PlentyOfFish and OK Cupid (among the free ones), hog most of the traffic. Pay sites make money through monthly subscriptions; you can't send or receive a message without one. Free sites rely on advertising. Mark Brooks, the editor of the trade magazine *Online Personals Watch*, said, "Starting a site is like starting a restaurant. It's a sexy business, looks like fun, yet it's hard to make money." There is, as yet, a disconnect between success and profit. "The way these companies make money is not directly correlated to the utility that users get from the product," Harj Taggar, a partner at the Silicon Valley seed fund Y Combinator, told me. "What they really should be doing is making money if they match you with people you like."

Some sites proceed from a simple gimmick. ScientificMatch attempts to pair people according to their DNA, and claims that this approach leads to a higher rate of female orgasms. A site called Ashley Madison notoriously connects cheating spouses. Howaboutwe.com asks only that you complete a sentence that begins "How about we . . ." with a suggestion for a first date, be it a Martini at the Carlyle or a canoe trip on the Gowanus Canal. The cutting edge is in mobile and location-based technology, such as Grindr, a smartphone app for gay men that tells subscribers when there are other willing subscribers in their vicinity. Many Internet dating companies, including Grindr, are trying to devise ways to make this kind of thing work for straight people, which means making it work for straight women, who may not need an app to know that they are surrounded by willing straight men.

For the purposes of this essay, I didn't do any online dating of my own. Instead, I went out for coffee or drinks with various women who, according to their friends, had had extraordinary or, at least, numerous adventures dating online. To the extent that a date can sometimes feel like an interview, these interviews often felt a little like dates. We sized each other up. We doled out tidbits of immoderate disclosure.

I talked to men, too, of course, but there is something simultaneously reductive and disingenuous in most men's assessments of their requirements and conquests. Some research has suggested that it is men, more than women, who yearn for marriage, but this may be merely a case of stated preference. Men want someone who will take care of them, make them look good, and have sex with them—not necessarily in that order. It may be that this is all that women really want, too, but they are better at disguising or obscuring it. They deal in calculus, while men, for the most part, traffic in simple sums.

A common observation, about both the Internet dating world and the world at large, is that there is an apparent surplus of available women, especially in their thirties, and a shortage of recommendable men. The explanation for this asymmetry, which isn't exactly news, is that men can and usually do pursue younger women, and that often the men who are single are exactly the ones who prefer them. For women surveying a landscape of banished husbands or perpetual boys, the biological rationale offers little solace. Neither does the Internet.

Everyone these days seems to have an online-dating story or a friend with online-dating stories. Pervasiveness has helped to chip away at the stigma; people no longer think of online dating as a last resort for desperadoes and creeps. The success story is a standard of the genre. But anyone who has spent a lot of time dating online, and not just dabbling, has his or her share of horror stories, too.

Earlier this year, a Los Angeles filmmaker named Carole Markin sued Match.com in California state court after she was allegedly raped by a man she met on the site; he turned out to be a convicted sex offender. Markin's suit asked not for money but for an injunction against Match.com to prevent it from signing up any new members until it institutes a system for background checks. (A few days later, the company announced that it would start checking subscribers against the national registry of sex offenders.) To some extent, such incidents, as terrible as they are, merely reflect the frequency of such transactional hazards in the wider world. Bars don't do background checks, either.

Most bad dates aren't that kind of bad. They are just awkward, or excruciating. One woman, a forty-six-year-old divorced mother of two, likened them to airplane crashes: the trouble usually occurs during takeoff and landing—the minute you meet and the minute you leave. You can often tell right away if this person who's been so charming in his e-mails is a creep or a bore. If not, it becomes clear at the end of the evening, when he sticks his tongue down your throat. Or doesn't. One woman who has dated fifty-eight men since her divorce, a few years ago, told me that she maintains a chart, both to keep the men straight and to try to discern patterns—as though there might be a unified-field theory of why men are dogs.

I had a talk-about-dating date with a freelance researcher named Julia Kamin, who, over twelve years as a dater on various sites, has boiled down all the competing compatibility criteria to the question of, as she put it, "Are we laughing at the same shit?" This epiphany inspired her to build a site—makeeachotherlaugh.com—on which you rate cartoons and videos, and the algorithms match you up. As she has gone around telling people about her idea, she says, "women get instantly excited. Men are, like, 'Um, O.K., maybe.' " It might be that women want to be amused while men want to be considered amusing. "I really should have two sites," Kamin said. "Hemakesmelaugh. com and shelaughsatmyjokes.com." (She bought both URLs.)

It's senseless, at least in the absence of divine agency, to declare that any two people were made for each other, yet we say it all the time, to sustain our belief that it's sensible for them to pair up. The conceit can turn the search for someone into a search for *that* someone, which is fated to end in futility or compromise, whether conducted on the Internet or in a ballroom. And yet people find each other, every which way, and often achieve something that they call happiness.

Look around a Starbucks and imagine that all the couples you see are Internet daters complying with the meet-first-for-coffee rule of thumb: here's another bland, neutral establishment webbed with unspoken expectation and disillusionment. One evening, I found myself in such a place with a thirty-eight-year-old elementary-school teacher who had spent more than ten years plying Match. com and Nerve.com, as well as the analogue markets, in search of someone with whom to spend the rest of her life. She'd met dozens of men. Her mother felt that she was being too picky.

In December, she started corresponding online with a man a couple of years older than she. After a week and a half, they met for drinks, which turned into dinner and more. He was clever, handsome, and capable. In their e-mails, they'd agreed that they'd reached a time and place in their lives to be less cautious and cool, in matters of the heart, so when, two days later, he sent a photograph of a caipirinha, the national cocktail of Brazil, where he'd gone for a few weeks on business, she found herself suggesting that she join him there. He made the arrangements. Her mother approved. She flew down to Rio the next week, and he came to the airport with a driver to meet her.

Months later, she savored the memory of that moment when he greeted her with a passionate hug, and the week and who knows what else lay before them. A swirl of anticipation, uncertainty, and desire converged into an instant of bliss. For that feeling alone—to say nothing of the chance to go to Brazil—she would do it all over again, even though, during the next ten days, with nothing but sex to stave off their corrosive exchanges over past and future frustrations, they came to despise each other. When they returned to New York, they split up, and went back online.

Discussion Starters

1. What, if anything, did you learn about online dating sites that you didn't know? Do you view online dating any differently as a result?
2. What are the positives and negatives of online dating? Does it appear to be a viable way of meeting a future partner?
3. What is your personal experience, or the experience of people you know, with online dating? Might you try it someday if you haven't?

Domestic Violence and Abuse

By Jeanne Segal

Jeanne Segal is a sociologist, psychologist, author, and co-creator of Helpguide.org. In this essay, Segal explains what constitutes domestic violence, presents signs that indicate a person may be in an abusive relationship, reveals ways in which abusers attempt to control their victims, and provides advice on how to help a person who may be abused.

Domestic violence and abuse can happen to anyone, yet the problem is often overlooked, excused, or denied. This is especially true when the abuse is psychological rather than physical. Noticing and acknowledging the signs of an abusive relationship is the first step to ending it. No one should live in fear of the person they love. If you recognize yourself or someone you know in the following warning signs and descriptions of abuse, reach out. There is help available.

Domestic abuse, also known as spousal abuse, occurs when one person in an intimate relationship or marriage tries to dominate and control the other person. Domestic abuse that includes physical violence is called domestic violence.

Domestic violence and abuse are used for one purpose and one purpose only: to gain and maintain total control over you. An abuser doesn't "play fair." Abusers use fear, guilt, shame, and intimidation to wear you down and keep you under his or her thumb. Your abuser may also threaten you, hurt you, or hurt those around you.

Domestic violence and abuse does not discriminate. It happens among heterosexual couples and in same-sex partnerships. It occurs within all age ranges, ethnic backgrounds, and economic levels. And while women are more commonly victimized, men are also abused—especially verbally and emotionally, although sometimes even physically as well. The bottom line is that abusive behavior is never acceptable, whether it's coming from a man, a woman, a teenager, or an older adult. You deserve to feel valued, respected, and safe.

Domestic abuse often escalates from threats and verbal abuse to violence. And while physical injury may be the most obvious danger, the emotional and psychological consequences of domestic abuse are also severe. Emotionally abusive relationships can destroy your self-worth, lead to anxiety and depression, and make you feel helpless and alone. No one should have to endure this kind of pain—and your first step to breaking free is recognizing that your situation is abusive. Once you acknowledge the reality of the abusive situation, then you can get the help you need.

There are many signs of an abusive relationship. The most telling sign is fear of your partner. If you feel like you have to walk on eggshells around your partner—constantly watching what you say and do in order to avoid a blow-up—chances are your relationship is unhealthy and abusive. Other signs that you may be in an abusive relationship include a partner who belittles you or tries to control you, and your personal feelings of self-loathing, helplessness, and desperation.

Do you feel afraid of your partner much of the time, avoid certain topics out of fear of angering him, feel that you can't do anything right for him, believe that you deserve to be hurt or mistreated, or feel emotional numb or helpless? Does your partner humiliate or yell at you, criticize and put you down regularly, treat you so badly that you're embarrassed for your friends or family to see, ignore or put down your opinions or accomplishments, blame you for his abusive behavior, or see you as property or a sex object? Does he have a bad or unpredictable temper, has hurt you or threatened to hurt or kill you, threatened to take your children away or harm them, threatened to commit suicide if you leave, forced you to have sex, or destroyed your belongings? Is he excessively jealous and possessive, does he control where you go and what you do, keep you from seeing your family or friends, limit your access to money, a car, or a phone, or constantly check up on you? Any of these signs can indicate an abusive and unhealthy relationship.

When people talk about domestic violence, they are often referring to the physical abuse of a spouse or intimate partner. Physical abuse is the use of physical force against someone in a way that injures or endangers that person. Physical assault or battering is a crime, whether it occurs inside or outside of the family. The police have the power and authority to protect you from physical attack.

Any situation in which you are forced to participate in unwanted, unsafe, or degrading sexual activity is sexual abuse. Forced sex, even by a spouse or intimate partner with whom you also have consensual sex, is an act of aggression and violence. Furthermore, people whose partners abuse them physically *and* sexually are at a higher risk of being seriously injured or killed.

It is still abuse if the incidents of physical abuse seem minor when compared to those you have read about, seen on television or heard other women talk about. There isn't a "better" or "worse" form of physical abuse; you can be severely injured as a result of being pushed, for example. It is still abuse if the incidents of physical abuse have only occurred one or two times in the relationship. Studies indicate that if your spouse/partner has injured you once, it is likely he will continue to physically assault you. It is still abuse if the physical assaults stopped when you became passive and gave up your right to express yourself as you desire, to move about freely and see others, and to make decisions. It is not a victory if you have to give up your rights as a person and a partner in exchange for not being assaulted!

When people think of domestic abuse, they often picture battered women who have been physically assaulted. But not all abusive relationships involve violence. Just because you're not battered and bruised doesn't mean you're not being abused. Many men and women suffer from emotional abuse, which is no less destructive. Unfortunately, emotional abuse is often minimized or overlooked—even by the person being abused.

The aim of emotional abuse is to chip away at your feelings of self-worth and independence. If you're the victim of emotional abuse, you may feel that there is no way out of the relationship or that without your abusive partner you have nothing. Emotional abuse includes *verbal abuse* such as yelling, name-calling, blaming, and shaming. Isolation, intimidation, and controlling behavior also fall under emotional abuse. Additionally, abusers who use emotional or psychological abuse often throw in threats of physical violence or other repercussions if you don't do what they want. You may think that physical abuse is far worse than emotional abuse, since physical violence can send you to the hospital and leave you with scars. But the scars of emotional abuse are very real, and they run deep. In fact, emotional abuse can be just as damaging as physical abuse—sometimes even more so.

An abuser's goal is to control you, and he or she will frequently use money to do so. Economic or financial abuse includes rigidly controlling your finances, withholding money or credit cards, making you account for every penny you spend, withholding basic necessities (food, clothes, medication, shelter), restricting you to an allowance, preventing you from working or choosing your own career, sabotaging your job (making you miss work, calling constantly), or stealing from you or taking your money.

Despite what many people believe, domestic violence and abuse is not due to the abuser's loss of control over his or her behavior. In fact, abusive behavior and violence is a deliberate choice made by the abuser in order to control you. Abusers use a variety of tactics to manipulate you and exert their power:

- Dominance – Abusive individuals need to feel in charge of the relationship. They will make decisions for you and the family, tell you what to do, and expect you to obey without question. Your abuser may treat you like a servant, child, or even as his or her possession.
- Humiliation – An abuser will do everything he or she can to make you feel bad about yourself or defective in some way. After all, if you believe you're worthless and that no one else will want you, you're less likely to leave. Insults, name-calling, shaming, and public put-downs are all weapons of abuse designed to erode your self-esteem and make you feel powerless.
- Isolation – In order to increase your dependence on him or her, an abusive partner will cut you off from the outside world. He or she may keep you from seeing family or friends, or even prevent you from going to work or school. You may have to ask permission to do anything, go anywhere, or see anyone.
- Threats – Abusers commonly use threats to keep their partners from leaving or to scare them into dropping charges. Your abuser may threaten to hurt or kill you, your children, other family members, or even pets. He or she may also threaten to commit suicide, file false charges against you, or report you to child services.
- Intimidation – Your abuser may use a variety of intimidation tactics designed to scare you into submission. Such tactics include making threatening looks or gestures, smashing things in front of you, destroying property, hurting your pets, or putting weapons on display. The clear message is that if you don't obey, there will be violent consequences.
- Denial and blame – Abusers are very good at making excuses for the inexcusable. They will blame their abusive and violent behavior on a bad childhood, a bad day, and even on the victims of their abuse. Your abusive partner may minimize the abuse or deny that it occurred. He or she will commonly shift the responsibility on to you: Somehow, his or her violent and abusive behavior is your fault.

Abusers *are* able to control their behavior—they do it all the time:

- Abusers pick and choose whom to abuse. They don't insult, threaten, or assault everyone in their life who gives them grief. Usually, they save their abuse for the people closest to them, the ones they claim to love.
- Abusers carefully choose when and where to abuse. They control themselves until no one else is around to see their abusive behavior. They may act like everything is fine in public, but lash out instantly as soon as you're alone.

- Abusers are able to stop their abusive behavior when it benefits them. Most abusers are not out of control. In fact, they're able to immediately stop their abusive behavior when it's to their advantage to do so (for example, when the police show up or their boss calls).
- Violent abusers usually direct their blows where they won't show. Rather than acting out in a mindless rage, many physically violent abusers carefully aim their kicks and punches where the bruises and marks won't show.

Domestic abuse falls into a common pattern, or cycle of violence. Your abusive partner lashes out with aggressive, belittling, or violent behavior. The abuse is a power play designed to show you "who is boss." After abusing you, your partner feels guilt, but not over what he's done. He's more worried about the possibility of being caught and facing consequences for his abusive behavior. Next, your abuser rationalizes what he or she has done. The person may come up with a string of excuses or blame you for the abusive behavior—anything to avoid taking responsibility. Then the abuser does everything he can to regain control and keep the victim in the relationship. He may act as if nothing has happened, or he may turn on the charm. This peaceful honeymoon phase may give the victim hope that the abuser has really changed this time. Finally, your abuser begins to fantasize about abusing you again. He spends a lot of time thinking about what you've done wrong and how he'll make you pay. Then he makes a plan for turning the fantasy of abuse into reality. Your abuser sets you up and puts his plan in motion, creating a situation where he can justify abusing you.

Your abuser's apologies and loving gestures in between the episodes of abuse can make it difficult to leave. He may make you believe that you are the only person who can help him, that things will be different this time, and that he truly loves you. However, the dangers of staying are very real.

It's impossible to know with certainty what goes on behind closed doors, but there are some telltale signs and symptoms of emotional abuse and domestic violence. If you witness any warning signs of abuse in a friend, family member, or co-worker, take them very seriously.

People who are being abused may seem afraid or anxious to please their partner, go along with everything their partner says and does, check in often with their partner to report where they are and what they're doing, receive frequent, harassing phone calls from their partner, or talk about their partner's temper, jealousy, or possessiveness. People who are being physically abused may have frequent injuries, with the excuse of "accidents," frequently miss work, school, or social occasions without explanation, or dress in clothing designed to hide bruises or scars (e.g. wearing long sleeves in the summer or sunglasses indoors)

People who are being isolated by their abuser may be restricted from seeing family and friends, rarely go out in public without their partner, or have limited access to money, credit cards, or the car. People who are being abused may have very low self-esteem, even if they used to be confident, display major personality changes (e.g. an outgoing person becomes withdrawn), or be depressed, anxious, or suicidal.

If you suspect that someone you know is being abused, speak up! If you're hesitating—telling yourself that it's none of your business, you might be wrong, or the person might not want to talk about it—keep in mind that expressing your concern will let the person know that you care and may even save his or her life.

You can ask your friend or family member if something is wrong, express concern, listen and validate, offer help, and support her decision. Don't wait for her to come to you, judge or blame, pressure her in any way, give advice, or place conditions on your support ("If you don't leave him, I can't help you."). Talk to the person in private and let her know that you're concerned. Point out the things you've noticed that make you worried. Tell the person that you're there whenever she feels ready to talk. Reassure the person that you'll keep whatever is said between the two of you to yourself, and let her know that you'll help in any way you can.

Remember, abusers are very good at controlling and manipulating their victims. People who have been emotionally abused or battered are depressed, drained, scared, ashamed, and confused. They need help to get out, yet they've often been isolated from their family and friends. By picking up on the warning signs and offering support, you can help them escape an abusive situation and begin healing.

Discussion Starters

1. What, if anything, did you learn about physical or mental abuse from the essay? What did you learn about abusers?
2. How can a person distinguish between a mentally abusive relationship and a relatively "normal" relationship, which may have its share of arguments and harsh words?
3. Based on the signs of abuse in the essay, have you ever been (or are) in an abusive relationship? Do you know of others who might be in one? How does a person extricate herself from an abusive relationship? (The essay doesn't cover how to leave such a relationship.)

IV. Children's Issues

Who Would Peter be Today?

By Ismael Estrada

Ismael Estrada is a producer and contributor for Anderson Cooper 360 Degrees on CNN. In this essay, Estrada details the early life of a bullied child who ultimately committed suicide and Estrada's remorse for standing by, like so many other children, and doing nothing to stop the bullying.

It's a question I ask myself all the time. Where would Peter be living? What would his life be like? What would he have chosen as a career?

I knew Peter for many years when we were kids. We grew up in the same town, but we weren't friends. In fact, I can't remember a meaningful conversation Peter and I ever shared. We had many classes together and we were both in the school band. He was definitely a more talented musician. I struggled in my attempts to play the saxophone. Peter mastered playing the tuba. I was more interested in sports, since I also played baseball and football. Peter focused on his classroom studies and his music.

Peter didn't have many friends. He wasn't like us. Everything about him was different. He didn't dress like the rest of us; he didn't have the same interests as most of us; Peter just didn't fit in.

For as long as I can remember, Peter was bullied. Bullied probably isn't the right word to describe the way Peter was treated. I'm disgusted thinking of the days of our youth and remembering how he had to go through his life at school. The abuse was relentless. Students would heckle loudly as he walked by; he was laughed at and teased at almost every corner. People would shout out, "Peter the nerd!" or "Geek!" every chance they could.

Almost everyone I knew would join in. I'm ashamed to admit that I'm not innocent either. I honestly don't remember any specific taunt or harsh words I may have said toward Peter or his close circle of friends, but I know I laughed along with the others in my crowd. I watched as he was kicked and I did nothing. I didn't say anything to a teacher, nor did anyone else. I watched as people would trip him or knock his books from his hands. I did and said nothing.

I once saw him lose his temper as he was getting smacked in the back of the head. As he ran toward those taunting him, I stopped him and told him he didn't want to get in trouble. I advised him to turn around and go back to class. I saw the anger and hurt in his eyes, yet I did and said nothing. I think I was convinced that if I let him continue his chase, it wouldn't have ended in Peter's favor.

This was the life Peter had to lead in school for years. It never seemed to get better for him; it only got worse as we grew older. One night in 1986, as we entered our freshman year in high school, Peter had enough. He ended his life of abuse and ridicule with a single gunshot to his head. He was only 15-years-old.

Friends told me the news as we were waiting for the school bus in the morning. I remember feeling sick to my stomach thinking that this didn't have to happen. We all knew why he took his life. It was never a question. I don't know that I would have been strong enough to endure the abuse he took for so many years. I don't know anyone who would be able to handle that kind of pain.

I didn't attend Peter's funeral. I didn't feel I earned the right to say good-bye. I was upset with my fellow classmates who didn't seem to feel badly or somewhat responsible for his death. I was mostly upset with myself for laughing at some of those taunts and not telling any of my friends to stop.

I was sitting in class when Peter's father returned some of the school issued equipment. All he said was, "I'm sorry, but Peter won't need these anymore." I'll never forget that moment for as long as I live. His father turned and walked out of the classroom without looking at any of us.

Last week, I called some old friends to talk about Peter. We hadn't talked about Peter in over 25 years, yet we all remembered the same thing: no one at the school ever talked to the student body about Peter's death. There were no lectures, no demands for this type of abuse to end. No speeches, nothing. The teachers knew why he took his life, the students knew, yet our life continued like nothing happened. I even searched newspaper archives from that time. Nothing was ever written about him.

I think about Peter all the time. I try to teach my own kids not to bully and to stand up for those who are mistreated. I also remind them to talk to us about things that happen at school. Most importantly, a day doesn't pass when I don't tell my kids I love them.

I wish I could go back and talk to Peter. I'd invite him to sit at our table for lunch. I'd ask him what his interests were, or just share a laugh together. I also wish I could go back and talk to me. I would like to talk to the kid I once was and tell him how much even a laugh or a taunt hurts. I would tell him there was no place for bullying.

I'm not sure where Peter would be today or what his life would be like. Sadly, he wasn't given that chance. I only hope that I can take the most serious lesson I have ever learned in life and teach others about the consequences of bullying.

Discussion Starters

1. As a youngster, Estrada's response to Peter's bullying – going along with it – is typical of many children. Based on your experiences as a child, why do you think many children accept other children being bullied, or even participate, and seldom try to intervene?
2. The educational emphasis on bullying today is far different from Estrada's school days. Do you think the anti-bullying message is changing the way children treat one another?
3. What is your experience, or the experience of others you know, with being the bullied child or the bully? How did it affect your life (or other people's lives)?

For Kids, It's Better to Give Than Receive

By Amanda Enayati

Amanda Enayati is a columnist and contributor to CNN.com, NPR, and The Washington Post. In this essay, Enayati presents research supporting the contention that children derive greater pleasure, and benefit, from giving rather than receiving.

There's a good chance you've seen the 7-year-old tragicomic superstar of TLC's "Here Comes Honey Boo Boo" declare in a jaw-dropping video clip: "A dollar makes me holler." Whether you almost fell off your chair laughing or recoiled in horror at the child's statement, you might be one of the multitudes of parents who, consciously or not, subscribes to the broader principle that spending your dollars does, in fact, make your child holler with joy.

But a growing body of research paints a compelling picture that may help us rethink some of our over-the-top spending on children. These studies confirm some age-old wisdom about happiness: If the goal really is to make our children happy, perhaps what we ought to be doing is not over-indulging them, but giving them the opportunity to give.

According to the annual Tooth Fairy survey, the Fairy is delivering an average of $3 per tooth, up 15% from last year, with some children hitting the jackpot with as much as $20 per tooth.

Last June Bundle, a site that analyzes spending patterns, rated the American cities that spoil their children the most, as measured by household spending on purchases from children's toy and clothing stores, and other "kids' services" (you know, like toddler mani-pedis and 150-person catered birthday parties in hotel ballrooms). New York City and Brooklyn (which, alas, introduced the world to "babyccinos"; maybe baby Spanx are next?) topped the list of child spoilers. Other cities at the top of the list included Miami, Minneapolis, Tulsa, Dallas, Atlanta and Los Angeles.

But are the cash, toys, clothes and foamy pretend-coffees making our children happy? Probably not. Extreme birthday parties: How much is too much? According to a recent study by psychologists at the University of British Columbia, young children are happier to give than to receive. In the study, toddlers who were asked to give away their own treats, as well as extra treats, showed greater happiness about sharing their own possessions, suggesting that the act of personal sacrifice was emotionally rewarding.

While the children in the study were giving away a personal belonging—their goldfish crackers—the study's principle rests more generally on pro-social spending, says lead author Lara Aknin, assistant professor of psychology at Simon Fraser University in Vancouver, British Columbia.

"You can construe that pro-social behavior broadly to include giving time volunteering, giving money to causes or giving other resources. All of these correlate to happiness." The joy of helping others, says Aknin, is an inherent part of human nature.

The research was about seeing if the same joy of giving we see in adults is also present in our earliest acts of giving, notes J. Kiley Hamlin, assistant professor of developmental psychology at the University of British Columbia, who was also involved in the study. "Many people think that children are inherently selfish and we need to teach them how to be nice and feel good about giving to others."

But maybe we don't need to train children to feel good about giving, says Hamlin. As it turns out, children are naturally altruistic. The benefits of giving and cooperating with others may be part of the system from the get-go, she observes.

Moreover, pro-social spending can be a virtuous cycle. When people recall a time they spent generously, it makes them happy. That sets up and triggers a positive feedback loop between generous spending and happiness, according to Aknin. "We found that spending money on others leads to higher levels of happiness than spending money on yourself." But the giving does not have to be extravagant, she says. In a 2008 study involving students, Aknin and her colleagues found that spending as little as $5 on others has emotional benefits.

Another fascinating nuance to our inclination to spoil children is the potential for the overindulgence to dampen their ability to savor everyday joys. In a 2010 study, titled "Money Giveth, Money Taketh Away," Dr. Jordi Quoidbach and his colleagues found evidence that "having access to the best things in life may actually undermine one's ability to reap enjoyment from life's small pleasures."

How many times have you heard parents grouse that their children are ungrateful? Is it possible that we have an unwitting hand in this perceived lack of gratitude? We may well be anesthetizing our children by constantly plying them with stuff. That is a reasonable hypothesis, says Hamlin, adding that providing external rewards for things like jobs well done can inhibit the emotional benefits children get from them. "We should be striving for internal rewards as much as possible."

"Research shows that underindulgence—indulging a little less than you usually do—holds one key to getting more happiness for your money," writes Dr. Elizabeth Dunn, associate professor of psychology at the University of British Columbia researcher, who has also worked on several of the studies mentioned above, in a recent New York Times opinion piece.

In the end, the work of Aknin and her colleagues may help shift how we seek to make our children happy. "Consider that maybe children would be happier giving things away than receiving them," says Aknin. "Give them the opportunity to give."

Discussion Starters

1. Based on your experience, do you agree with the essay's thesis that children are happier when they give than when they receive? Why?
2. In the essay, Dr. Elizabeth Dunn is quoted, "Research shows that underindulgence - indulging a little less than you usually do—holds one key to getting more happiness for your money." Do you agree? Why?
3. Discuss your experiences as a child. Do you think you were "overindulged?" Do you recall giving to others and feeling good about it? Do you agree with the essay that children are "naturally altruistic?"

Overcoming Abuse - My Story

By Shawna Platt

Shawna Platt is an essayist, poet, and short story and screenplay writer. In this essay, Platt relates her life as a child growing up with abusive parents and how she survived and ultimately overcame the cycle of abuse.

Where do I begin? I grew up in an environment of alcoholism. This environment was filled with physical abuse, emotional abuse, neglect, anxiety and most importantly...denial. We weren't allowed to discuss what went on in our home. It was to be swept under the rug, like the dirty little secret it was.

I can't count how many times we had to silently put the house back together while my dad slept it off on the couch. I guess it was simply easier to pretend it didn't happen. I guess not acknowledging it meant we didn't have to deal with it. But we did have to deal with it and not discussing it didn't make it go away...it allowed it to continue.

I could start with the emotional issues domestic violence causes. Or the anxiety and panic attacks. The issues of trust and constantly being guarded. Always looking over your shoulder, waiting for the next bomb to drop. The effort to accept and forgive...at least enough to move on and live a normal daily life. I could start with the importance of breaking the cycle so this doesn't move on to the next generation. Or the importance of releasing the anger and becoming a productive human being. These are all important topics that need to be addressed and I will try to include them all.

I could start with some of my own personal experiences. The constant physical fights. The yelling and screaming. The broken "things." Being picked up by the throat while my mom stood by and did nothing. Watching my mom get shoved through a kitchen window by the hair, pulled back through, and pushed out the door onto the porch. Then being told by my dad that if we tried to let her in, he'd shoot us.

I could talk about the small travel trailer that was pulled from place to place, sometimes with no running water and illegally wired electricity. Relocating was a constant. There was no need to feel secure, because in no time at all, we'd be on the move again.

I could discuss the countless times my parents left us with people we didn't even know, sneaking out when they thought we weren't aware. And there were times those people made it very clear that we were not wanted there. I could never understand how I could be placed somewhere I wasn't truly wanted. But it happened time and time again. I remember my brother and I spending some time on the porch because we weren't allowed to enter the house while the other kids got to have their bowl of ice cream.

I remember wearing the same clothes every day and let me tell you...other kids aren't afraid to remind you of it. I could also talk about the sexual abuse I endured from one of my dad's drunk friends when I was five years old. I could dwell on my mom's attitude of, "If I can't beat him, I'll join him" and how she spent her share of time on the bar stool beside him while we were left at home alone, probably because no one would take us for the night. And of course, there's my mom's denial and how, "My kids always came first."

I started taking care of my sister when she was a baby. I was ten years old and had no idea how to care for an infant. I recall the first time I was left alone with her. I stood out at the end of the driveway, looking up the street, begging them to come back. That was the day something shifted in me.

I became hard as survival issues kicked in. When my parents would conveniently find a different sitter for the night, I always seemed to run them off. I literally had babysitters walk out on me because I made their experience with us a living hell. Who did they think they were, coming into my home and telling me what to do, thinking they could take care of my baby sister better than I could? I've been handling things just fine, thank you very much. I certainly didn't need them. Over time, my mom told me since I kept running them off, I would just do it on my own. Like I hadn't been doing that already. My sister wouldn't respond to anyone but me anyway.

I was never shown how to change a diaper or make a bottle. I guess it was assumed I would figure it out. After all, they would only be gone "a couple of hours." What could possibly go wrong? But those couple hours always turned into a day-long event, usually extending into the early morning hours, which would end with them coming home in a fight. Do you realize how scary it is to a ten year old child to be left at home alone, with an infant, especially when it gets dark? We rarely had a phone, so I never had any way of checking in to see when they'd be home. I was forced to learn to deal with it.

These few examples I've shared are only the tip of the iceberg. The emotional issues from domestic abuse could fill a book. The programming that comes from living in an abusive household is devastating to the human mind. In order to survive, the mind has to adapt and it becomes programmed to work in a certain way. It remembers everything and protects against danger in ways we still don't understand. The human mind literally has the ability to protect itself and it does this by altering what we think, which affects the way we see things. When our programming changes the way we think, it also affects the way we feel because the mind and body are tightly connected. What affects one affects the other.

Emotional abuse is one of the hardest to overcome because of the programming done to the mind. You can reprogram the mind to think and operate in a different manner, but it takes time and a lot of hard, heavy and deep soul searching, which is hardly a walk in the park.

Anxiety and panic attacks are also experiences that come from abuse. In most cases, the attacks are chronic because the mind/body are used to working in a fight or flight mode. When the mind is trained to live this way, it will continue to do so, even when there is no reason for it. It simply doesn't know any different. I've been experiencing anxiety since I was five years old and it wasn't until a few years ago that I finally figured it out. I still get anxious from time to time, but I've learned to deal with attacks.

Growing up in an abusive environment made me hard, guarded and non-trusting. You'll never see me cry. It doesn't mean I don't...it just means you won't see it. I view life differently and I respond to it differently. I don't drink. How could I? Drinking is what caused my childhood to be the way it was. The thought of putting alcohol in my system makes me physically ill and brings on anxiety instantly.

I've had to overcome serious trust issues. How could I possibly believe what you tell me? You're not really going to be there for me, so I simply won't count on it. I've learned to survive and I can take care of myself. I've learned to accept certain things and I've learned to forgive. I've done this for ME. Not for my parents, not for the bullies I encountered, not for the other adults who treated me as less than the trash in their garbage…but for ME. For my own sanity and well-being. For my own piece of mind. I'm happy with the person I've become and I've become that person on my own.

I decided a long time ago that I would not remain a victim and I would not become a product of my environment. I decided I would forgive as much as I could. Does that mean the circumstances I encountered were justified? Not for a second! But where do I place blame? With my father, who didn't know how to stop? With my mother, who allowed it to happen? I feel they both should be held responsible. But I'm no longer a victim of their circumstance. Their life is theirs to live as they choose. I simply choose to move in a difference direction.

I decided the cycle stops with me. It will not be passed on to the next generation that I brought into this world. Which means my kids won't pass it on to theirs and nothing makes me happier! At least I can sleep at night knowing that.

Discussion Starters

1. The author detailed her years of abuse as a child. What incidents stand out in your mind as the most destructive? How was the author able to survive the abuse?
2. Many abused children end up as abusers themselves as adults. How do you think the author was able to stop the "cycle" and raise her own children differently?
3. Discuss any childhood abuse that you or others you know have gone through. How has it affected your (or their) life, and how have you dealt with it?

Weighing In - Healthy at Any Size?

By Camille Jackson

Camille Jackson is a free-lance writer and regular contributor to Teaching Tolerance periodical. In this essay, Jackson reveals the discrimination faced by overweight children and questions whether today's emphasis on childhood obesity and weight loss is doing more to hurt children than help them.

Celebrities like singer Jennifer Hudson and actress Kirstie Alley parade their drastic weight loss in commercials and magazine articles. Popular TV shows like "The Biggest Loser" promote fast, extreme weight loss. And fat jokes cut across race, ethnicity and gender lines to provide easy laughs for comedians at the expense of the heavyset.

Society is more fatphobic than ever before, with subtle and overt messages all around us that not only is fat bad, but so are fat people. It's easy for overweight children to feel singled out and shamed about their body size, at home and at school. Experts say children can easily interpret even the well-intentioned "war on childhood obesity," meant to promote health, to mean a war on their bodies and on them.

"The number of obese kids has increased, so negativity has increased," says Reginald Washington, the chief medical officer at Rocky Mountain Hospital for Children and a leader in the fight against childhood obesity. "It is true that if you are obese you are discriminated against in schools and the workplace, and even in your home. Physical education teachers see them as lazy and are harder on them in class. Studies have shown this."

Size-based stigma stems in large part from the myth that being fat is a result of a lack of self-control and willpower, says Rebecca Puhl, a psychologist and coordinator at Yale's Rudd Center for Food Policy and Obesity. "There are prevailing public perceptions about the causes of obesity, like the widespread belief that obesity is simply an issue of laziness," Puhl says. "This perception drastically oversimplifies the complex causes—societal and biological—of obesity."

Lamar Richardson (not his real name), 25, of Greenville, N.C., remembers being humiliated in his sixth-grade physical education class when the coach jokingly suggested he wear a training bra. Richardson can still hear the laughter of his classmates. "It affected me for a very long time," says Richardson. "I was not comfortable with my body image. Even when I got to high school, after football practice I would go straight home and shower, rather than go to the locker room." He is now in a fitness program at a local gym but says he "still has the same issues."

Megan Hansen, the founder of a healthy-lifestyle support group in North Carolina, also isolated herself in high school because of her weight: "When you're fat you walk with your head down," she says. "You go from class to class not wanting anybody to see you." Megan says she was careful not to stand next to cheerleaders, for fear of being compared with them.

Lavinia Rodriguez, a clinical psychologist in Land O' Lakes, Fla. who treats eating disorders and weight issues, says most of the size-discrimination stories she's heard have come from adult patients. "Younger kids don't want to talk about that," she says. "They don't bring it up. The things they talk about suggest [size bullying], but they don't state it overtly." Richardson agrees: "I didn't talk to anybody about it," he says. "As a guy you're taught not to really share your feelings like that. You just suck it up."

Rodriguez points out that girls are more likely to talk about their body-image issues and self-esteem than boys. "Girls tend to remember name-calling and boys remember getting beat up," she says.

Unfortunately, educators often promote the negative stereotypes overweight students face. Studies show teachers tend to call on lean children over obese students. Some are less likely to give a favorable grade to overweight kids, and they generally perceive these children to be less successful. According to the Obesity Action Coalition, teachers often view overweight students as untidy and more emotional, among other problems. Obese students are also less likely to be accepted to college, despite having equivalent application rates and academic achievement.

State efforts regarding size bias in schools have thus far focused on reducing weight, not reducing prejudice. For instance, in 2003 Arkansas became the first state to record students' body mass index (BMI) and send the results home in a report card. However, federal agencies, including the Centers for Disease Control and Prevention, have not found enough evidence to recommend such programs as an effective strategy against childhood obesity.

The Arkansas program had no effect on obesity levels, according to a 2010 report by the state's Center for Health Improvement. And experts disparaged Arkansas's program coverage: "They didn't go the next step to give parents tools on how to design better meals and find afterschool activities," says Washington of the Rocky Mountain Hospital.

Yet Pennsylvania, New York, Massachusetts and other states soon followed with similar BMI-measuring programs. Georgia started a statewide school fitness program, the Georgia Student Health and Physical Education initiative, which seems to approach the issue in a more constructive way. In Georgia, kids are not labeled by their weight, says Therese McGuire of Georgia's Department of Education. Rather, "some kids will learn they are not in the healthy zone. It just means they need to make positive changes." Teachers will receive the students' data in aggregate form, she says, so that schools can customize their curriculum, for example by starting a running club.

Children should be legally protected from size-based teasing and harassment in school, says the National Association to Advance Fat Acceptance (NAAFA). The organization has called for changes in the proposed Safe Schools Improvement Act to add weight, height and physical appearance as protected categories, alongside race, religion and sexual orientation.

At a news conference last August in Washington, D.C., Peggy Howell, the organization's public relations director, unveiled NAAFA's online child advocacy toolkit, a 50-page booklet for parents and educators about size diversity. "Discrimination continues to increase against people of all ages," Howell told a room full of reporters. One in six children are bullied, she said, and of those, 85 percent are bullied for their size or physical appearance. And Howell argues that programs such as first lady Michelle Obama's "Let's Move!" campaign, which began in February 2010, do not help matters. NAAFA contends that the campaign, intended to "solve the problem of obesity within a generation," should focus on the overall health of children rather than on body size alone. "Low body weight does not equal health, high body weight does not equal disease," Howell said.

Rocky Mountain Hospital's Washington disagrees. He points out that obese and overweight children are more likely to have high blood pressure, diabetes, bone issues and other substantial problems. And obesity-related health problems cost states billions of dollars each year. However, Washington does agree with NAAFA that size discrimination is increasing, and says that it is up to adults to be self-reflective about their personal prejudice against overweight people. "Teachers have to look within themselves to ask, 'Am I a part of this problem?,'" he says.

Schools can avoid perpetuating size-based stigma by de-emphasizing weight and BMI numbers and focusing on overall health for all children. Psychologist Rodriguez says attention needs to be paid to behaviors, not to numbers. "Don't focus on one child as the one who has to do something different," she said. "It should be a family or school project. Parents are so focused on size, the weight, the number, they look at the symptom and just want to make the child lose weight."

Rebecca Puhl at Yale's Rudd Center says that teachers must be more aware of their own attitudes toward overweight and obese children. Those attitudes affect the overweight children directly and can indirectly promote bullying by other students. "Essentially, weight bias is rarely challenged, and often ignored," she says. "As a result many youth who are struggling with their weight are vulnerable."

Discussion Starters

1. In the essay, obesity expert Rebecca Puhl says that there is "widespread belief that obesity is simply an issue of laziness" while in fact there are "complex causes – societal and biological – of obesity." What do you think those causes are?

2. The essay contends that discrimination against overweight children is pervasive, involving other children, parents, teachers, schools, and government programs. How do you think such widespread discrimination can be eliminated or reduced?

3. What is your personal experience (or that of others you know) with size discrimination, and what are the effects?

Who Are America's Poor Children?

By Vanessa R. Wight, Michelle Chau, and Yumiko Aratani

Wright, Chau, and Aratani are researchers and writers at the National Center for Children in Poverty. In this essay, the authors explore the serious problem of poverty among America's children, identify which children are most prone to live in poverty, the effects of poverty on their lives, and what needs to be done to eradicate the problem.

Over 15 million American children live in families with incomes below the federal poverty level, which is $22,050 a year for a family of four. The number of children living in poverty increased by 33 percent between 2000 and 2009. There are 3.8 million more children living in poverty today than in 2000.

Not only are these numbers troubling, the official poverty measure tells only part of the story. Research consistently shows that, on average, families need an income of about twice the federal poverty level to make ends meet. Children living in families with incomes below this level – for 2010, $44,100 for a family of four – are referred to as low income. Forty-two percent of the nation's children – more than 31 million in 2009 – live in low-income families. Nonetheless, eligibility for many public benefits is based on the official poverty measure. This fact sheet describes some of the characteristics of American children who are considered poor by the official standard.

The percentage of children living in poverty and extreme poverty (less than 50 percent of the federal poverty level) has increased since 2000. Twenty-one percent of children live in families that are considered officially poor (15.3 million children). Nine percent of children live in extreme poor families (6.8 million).

What are some of the characteristics of children who are officially poor in America?

- Twelve percent of white children live in poor families. Across the 10 most populated states, rates of child poverty among white children do not vary dramatically; the range is nine percent in California and Texas to 16 percent in Ohio.
- Thirty-six percent of black children live in poor families. In the 10 most populated states, rates of child poverty among black children range from 30 percent in California and New York to 46 percent in Ohio and Michigan.
- Fifteen percent of Asian children, 34 percent of American Indian children, and 24 percent of children of some other race live in poor families (comparable state comparisons are not possible due to small sample sizes).
- Thirty-three percent of Hispanic children live in poor families. In the 10 most populated states, rates of child poverty among Hispanic children range from 25 percent in Florida and Illinois to 41 percent in North Carolina and Georgia.

- Twenty-seven percent of children in immigrant families are poor; 19 percent of children with native-born parents are poor.
- In the six states with the largest populations of immigrants – California, Florida, Illinois, New Jersey, New York, and Texas – the poverty rate among children in immigrant families ranges from 16 per cent to 34 per cent.
- Twenty-four percent of children younger than age 6 live in poor families; 19 percent of children age 6 or older live in poor families.
- In about two-thirds of the states (35 states), 20 percent or more of children younger than age 6 are poor, whereas only about a half (24 states) have a poverty rate for all children (younger than age 18) that is as high.

What are some of the hardships faced by children in America?

- Twenty-one percent of households with children experience food insecurity. The share of households with children experiencing food insecurity was split with about half (10 percent) reporting food insecurity among adults, only, and the other half (about 11 percent) reporting low and very low food security among children.
- Nearly 50 percent of tenants living in renter-occupied units spend more than 30 percent of their income on rent.
- Although crowded housing is relatively uncommon, five percent of poor households and nearly two percent of all households are moderately crowded with 1.01–1.50 persons per room. Severe crowding with 1.51 or more persons per room characterizes about 1.1 percent of poor households and 0.3 percent of all households.
- Compared to white families with children, black and Latino families with children are more than twice as likely to experience economic hardships, such as food insecurity.
- Sixteen percent of poor children lack health insurance, whereas 11 percent of all children (poor and non-poor) lack health insurance.
- In the 10 most populated states, the percentage of poor children who lack health insurance ranges from 12 percent in New York to 38 percent in Texas.

Research suggests that being poor during childhood is associated with being poor as an adult. Yet, child poverty is not intractable. Policies and practices that increase family income and help families maintain their financial footing during hard economic times not only result in short-term economic security, but also have lasting effects by reducing the long-term consequences of poverty on children's lives. NCCP (National Center for Children in Poverty) recommends a number of major policy strategies to improve the well-being of children and families living in poverty:

Make work pay
Since research is clear that poverty is the greatest threat to children's well being, strategies that help parents succeed in the labor force help children. Increasing the minimum wage is important for working families with children because it helps them cover the high cost of basic necessities, such as child care and housing. Further, policies aimed at expanding the Earned Income Tax Credit and

other tax credits such as the Additional Child Tax Credit and the Making Work Pay Tax Credit are particularly instrumental in putting well-needed dollars back into the hands of low-earning workers.

Finally, many low-wage workers need better access to benefits such as health insurance and paid sick days. Reducing the costs of basic needs for low-income families. Medicaid/ SCHIP not only increase access to health care, but also helps families defray often crippling health care costs by providing free or low-cost health insurance. The Patient Protection and Affordable Care Act signed into law by President Obama promises to provide more affordable coverage and to prevent families from bankruptcy or debt because of health care costs. Further, housing is known to be a major expense for families. However, current housing subsidy programs are available for a small percentage of eligible families due to inadequate funding. Housing subsidies have been shown to be positively related to children's educational outcomes. Thus, it is important to increase funding for housing subsidies for families with children.

Support parents and their young children in early care and learning
To thrive, children need nurturing families and high quality early care and learning experiences. Securing child care is particularly important for working parents with young children. Research has found that child care subsidies are positively associated with the long-term employment and financial well-being of parents. Along with providing child care subsidies, policies and practices that ensure high-quality child care are also important. For example, programs that target families with infants and toddlers, such as Early Head Start, have been shown to improve children's social and cognitive development, as well as improve parenting skills. Investments in preschool for 3- and 4-year-olds are just as critical. In short, high-quality early childhood experiences can go a long way toward closing the achievement gap between poor children and their more well-off peers.

Support asset accumulation among low-income families
Many American families with children are asset poor, which means they lack sufficient savings to live above the poverty line for three months or more in the event of parental unemployment or illness when no earnings are available. This type of economic vulnerability is typically masked by conventional poverty measures based on income. Unlike wages, income generated from assets provides a cushion for families. Further, parental saving promotes both positive cognitive development and subsequent college attendance among children.

There are two ways to support asset accumulation among low income families. First, eliminating asset tests from major means-tested programs reduces the risk of running up large amounts of debt and increases the amount of financial resources parents have to invest in children. Second, there are programs that actively promote and encourage the development of saving habits among asset-poor families through matching funds incentives, such as the Individual Development Accounts (IDA) program and the Saving for Education, Entrepreneurship, and Down-payment (SEED) National Initiative programs.

Discussion Starters

1. What statistics in the essay regarding the percentages of poor children and the hardships they face stand out to you? How can the richest nation in the world have among the highest child poverty rates of all industrialized nations?
2. Why do you think that the solutions presented to eradicate poverty – raising the minimum wage, providing affordable day care, providing health care for all children – have not been universally instituted in the U.S.?
3. Discuss your own experience or that of others you know growing up "poor" by essay definition. What effects did it have on you as a child and as an adult?

The Favorite Child

By Ellen Weber Libby

Ellen Weber Libby is a practicing psychologist and author of the book The Favorite Child. In this essay, Libby contends that it is common for parents to favor one child over another or others, and presents the negative effects that such favoritism can have on both the favored and the unfavored child.

"Admitting to a favorite kid is one of the biggest taboos in parenting, although the vast majority of moms—and pretty much all kids - perceive that there is a golden child in just about every family," blogs Amy Kuras in *Toddler Newsletter*. Wrong. Admitting to having a favorite kid isn't one of the biggest taboos in parenting. NOT admitting to having a favorite is! Denying what is true can be disturbing to everyone in the family, making everyone feel a little crazy and eroding healthy family relationships.

The vast majorities of moms describe having a child whom they prefer and who receives special treatment, and still, parents have a hard time admitting that they favor one child over others. The terms differ but the message is the same—there is a favorite child. Children seem freer to acknowledge the existence of favoritism in the family. Each child is an individual and so is each parent. It is perfectly natural that a given child and a given parent have a special resonance; sometimes it is brief and sometimes it is more permanent.

Two recently published studies, independent from one another, agree that favoritism is common to families and can contribute to depression in both the favored and unfavored child and impacts all family members for life. One study, directed by Cornell University gerontologist Karl Pillemer and published in the April issue of *Journal of Marriage and the Family,* found that "Perceived favoritism from one's mother still matters to a child's psychological well-being even if they have been living for years outside the parental home and have started families of their own." The second study, recently published by this author in the book *The Favorite Child*, explains that favored and unfavored children are vulnerable to depression because there is tension associated with being chosen as well as not being chosen by the parent.

Children growing up as the golden child or the unfavored child are equally vulnerable to suffering from symptoms of depression. Longing to be the favorite child or working to maintain that status creates complicated issues for both the unfavored and favorite child. The personalities of each are likely to be marred by symptoms of depression: Each child may struggle with loneliness or emotional isolation; achieving psychological independence; having addictions that undermine the quality of their lives.

There are advantages to being chosen. In species of birds and animals, life can depend on being selected as mothers offer their milk to some infants, who survive, and not to others, who die. In humans, while being selected and its consequences are usually not so dramatic, the emotional health of the child largely depends on that child's feeling secure in his mother's love. Commonly, children not only crave their parents' love but also want to believe that this love is greater than the love parents feel for anyone else. Adults smile as toddlers ask their mothers and fathers, "Do you love me more than anyone else in the whole wide world?" As children grow-up, a major task to be accomplished, necessary for their healthy functioning, is to learn to feel secure in the world without requiring ongoing parental affirmation. To the degree that children do not accomplish this important milestone, they are vulnerable to depression.

Children who have never felt this affirmation, the unfavored child, often live their lives looking for this validation. They look to others to choose them as they had hoped their parents would. Since no one can fill the void created by parental neglect or oversight, these unfavored children often grow up insecure and not believing themselves lovable. One father, who grew up feeling unfavored, lamented the pain he feels each Father's Day as he doesn't trust his children's celebration of him. He knows the problem resides within himself as his heart is not fully open to their embrace. A lifetime of disappointment has taught him that there is emotional safety in being walled off to the expectation that he will be chosen for special kudos.

These children are especially vulnerable to struggling with establishing intimacy, or being easily frustration or angered. First, to be intimate, one's heart has to be open to others, and like the father described above, unfavored children often have developed defenses to protect themselves against being disappointed that they are not chosen by people important to them. This tendency to close one's heart makes establishing and maintaining intimacy difficult.

Second, children who grew up unfavored often have adopted the attitude that no matter how hard they try, they will not achieve the desired outcome. Throughout their childhood, they may have worked hard to achieve the more preferred status; but as hard as they worked, they failed to achieve this position. They never grasped that most likely their unfavored status was rooted primarily in their parent's inadequacy, not in theirs. These children easily feel defeated, and overtime, develop the opinion that hard work does not bring the desired reward. They are easily frustrated and walk away from challenges.

Third, unfavored children are vulnerable to developing personalities impacted by underlying anger. They are angry at the parent who treats them as the unfavored child. They are angry with the other parent for not altering the course of events. They may be angry at the sibling who is favored, especially if that sibling exploits the advantages of being favored. Unfortunately, as the child grow up, their anger is likely to be easily ignited and inappropriately expressed.

Golden children are also vulnerable to depression. They are likely to develop unhealthy personality traits, and be robbed of knowing themselves well. First, favorite children, having grown up mastering the art of knowing how to get what they want from the adoring parent, have mastered the art of manipulation. They expect the quid pro quo to be enacted: The child believes that in exchange for making important people in their adult worlds feel valued, these adults will give them what they want and not hold them accountable for questionable behaviors. These golden children grow up knowing how to get what they want, when they want it, and to feeling entitled.

Second, favorite children are likely to mature without having forged their own identities. These children, wanting to insure their favorite status, can be preoccupied with pleasing the important parent. A gay man called in during one of my NPR interviews to report that he was frightened to come out to his parents. If he did he knew that he would loose his favorite child status, and he did not trust that he could function successfully in the world without it. Yet, he acknowledged that his heavy drinking permitted him to escape the discomfort he felt in living with the secret.

Third, ultimately favorite children are prone to harbor underlying anger at the parents who favor them. The children tend to feel trapped by the relationship. As one woman expressed, "Do I have wait for my mother to die to have my own life?"

Open communication among all family members is the best technique to prevent hurt feelings within a family to fester and to begin to remedy the injury that has corroded family relationships. Such dialogue is difficult to obtain. All family members must value it, and everyone has to be willing to work for it. Everyone must:

> LISTEN to each other.
> RESPECT different viewpoints.
> STRIVE to accept the truth of different perceptions.
> WORK deliberately at not being defensive.
> FEEL safe to express words of personal truth.

Discussion Starters

1. Do you agree with Libby that parents often favor a particular child? Does your own childhood experience influence your belief?
2. Discuss the negative effects presented in the essay of being the favored or unfavored child. Based on these effects, how as a parent would you (or do you) handle the "natural" inclination to favor a particular child?
3. Discuss your own "status" within your family as a child. What effects has that status had on your life?

V. Values and Ethics

A Positive Solution for Plagiarism

By Jeff Karon

Jeff Karon is a visiting instructor in the English department at the University of South Florida and contributor to The Chronicle of Higher Education. In this essay, Karon evaluates the different approaches that college instructors take to addressing the problem of plagiarism and presents his own positive approach and explains why he takes it.

We know that students plagiarize. We suppose that plagiarism, as well as academic dishonesty in general, has increased over the past few years, decades, or century—depending on which academic ax we choose to grind.

The caveats are familiar: Perhaps cheating just is easier than it used to be (most honors students who are caught plagiarizing say they did so because it was "easy"). Perhaps we are better at detecting plagiarism because of software such as Google and Turnitin. Or perhaps we forget that every generation, at least since the ancient Romans and Greeks, complains that the next one is composed of lazy, possibly illiterate, youngsters willing to cut ethical corners.

But a good dose of skepticism toward the doomsayers doesn't make the worry go away. For example, a July 21 article in *The Chronicle* on a New York University professor who vowed to stop pursuing plagiarists has drawn 249 comments, several of which were impassioned denunciations of institutional responses to the problem. Dealing with student plagiarism is a nagging, seemingly endless problem for academics, judging from the number of articles, blog posts, and forum discussions on the topic. Indeed, I've contributed to some of those discussions but have yet to find any consensus emerge.

I've organized and participated in conference panels on plagiarism, held workshops for college instructors and schoolteachers on the subject, and for several years have used the methods I'm about to describe. I also began my teaching career with a zero-tolerance policy, which meant that I have been involved in campus judicial proceedings, a step that drains just about everyone touched by the accusation.

But as the Internet has matured, I decided that I did not want to spend time as a cyber-cop. More important, my goal should be to help inculcate honor and integrity rather than build a culture of fear and accusation.

It's easy to find excellent articles and Web sites on dealing with plagiarism. From those sources, we can develop four general guidelines for an effective response:

- The solution should be positive; that is, show students how to act as responsible scholars and writers. The same tone should be reflected in the syllabus. I have seen many syllabi in which the penalties for plagiarism are laid out in excruciating detail, with no positive models or behavior mentioned. Surely by now we know that positive motivation trumps the negative variety.

- It should help students avoid plagiarism rather than focus on our catching it.
- The solution should objectively strengthen both students and teachers.
- It should also make students and teachers feel as though they are stronger.
- Those seem to me to be minimal requirements, yet they often are not met in practice. Before laying out a workable solution, let's review some approaches whose weaknesses contribute to the seemingly endless discussions of plagiarism:

Draconian consequences. The instructor who threatens maximum damage if plagiarism is detected usually stakes out the moral high ground. Syllabi and accompanying class discussions list everything that will befall the student, including possible expulsion.

Strength: If applied consistently, without regard for extenuating circumstances, this approach seems to work particularly well for teachers who are both imperious and admired by their students. I knew one colleague, a tenured professor of literature and writing, who threatened to ruin, as nearly as possible, the reputations of offending students. Somehow he still inspired them.

Weakness: Instructors who use this tactic set an adversarial tone at the beginning of a course. Although some can inhabit the Professor Kingsfield character from The Paper Chase, many simply come off as nasty or suspicious. And approaching plagiarism this way is dispiriting—it never energizes students or teachers. In the end, it often doesn't prevent enough plagiarism to counter its weaknesses.

Preventive construction. A teacher who is concerned about plagiarism and has read about strategies may attempt to construct every assignment in a way that precludes plagiarism.

Strength: Rethinking assignments—freshening them up—often produces new energy in a course. Those who reflect often on pedagogy will be attracted to this approach.

Weakness: The approach often means devising assignments with a narrow scope. But it's important to train students to explore widely. They need to be able to sift through all sorts of sources, and closely tailored assignments may be too restrictive. Such assignments certainly don't simulate the strengths needed in graduate or professional school. And sooner or later, we either will run out of ideas for assignments or will be lulled into a false sense of security.

Dedicated discussion. Some teachers discuss extensively in class the nature and consequences of plagiarism, believing that such time is well spent.

Strength: Some students may not understand what constitutes plagiarism or its consequences. By discussing it carefully in class, instructors demonstrate an awareness of that problem.

Weakness: Merely talking with students, especially about a critical topic, is a poor way to ensure that they will act correctly. Giving quizzes on the topic is a move in the right direction. But a quiz still encourages passivity. Plagiarism and academic dishonesty are actions taken by people; powerful lessons about it require actions as well.

A workable solution. The first writing assignment I give students in my writing courses involves plagiarism as a topic. I ask them to investigate and read resources on the Web assembled by experts on the subject such as Nick Carbone, a new-media consultant for Bedford/St. Martin's, and Bruce Leland, a professor emeritus at Western Illinois University. I ask students to take notes on the readings, especially on how both authors are unhappy with standard approaches to preventing plagiarism and academic dishonesty. I tell them to pay special attention to Carbone's discussion of Dos and don'ts, a list he developed after deciding that his previous approaches to fighting plagiarism adopted an inappropriate tone, and to Leland's extensive list of resources that instructors can use to deal with plagiarism.

Then I ask students to find a Web site that offers free essays for download. I provide a central source, such as "Cheating 101: Internet Papers" though there are many others. Each student has to download one paper (or as much of one as is permitted by the site) and analyze its strengths and weaknesses. They must bring to class a copy of the paper as well as their notes on their reading, and deliver oral reports.

The idea is for students to read materials written by teachers for teachers, rather than something written just for students. The explicit lesson is for them to learn about plagiarism and academic dishonesty. An implicit lesson is that instructors already are aware of free papers and other Internet dodges. Even if a faculty member is not particularly computer-savvy, students will assume from this assignment that he or she understands how to track down plagiarism.

By analyzing these "free essays" before the class, students learn firsthand that the papers available over the Internet often are far inferior to what they could produce on their own. When they occasionally happen on a strong paper, they will remark that it is too good: No professor would believe that such a professionally written piece had come from a student for a course assignment.

You need not guide the students' choices of papers: Their own interests and majors will do that. Through this assignment, they are engaging in research from the first day of the course, and are practicing critical reading. They understand that you will treat them like adults, since you have assigned them to read authoritative, friendly articles from Web sites that speak to adult professionals. And other than require that they concentrate on a paper's strengths and weaknesses, you need not guide the analyses: Students of all writing levels will demonstrate that they can pick apart someone else's work.

Faculty can substitute other Web sites or articles, of course. But they should give students separate credit for their Web-site notes and for their critique of the downloaded paper—both of which should be physical copies. Students who took notes can be distinguished easily from those who did not, which allows instructors to teach the lesson that strong scholars or professionals take notes. The physical copies also allow instructors to collect the assignments if they run short on time for the oral reports, though I encourage faculty to allow everyone to present.

This assignment builds: (1) a direct awareness of plagiarism and its responses; (2) research skills, since students immediately follow and analyze reliable Web sources; and (3) presentation skills, all without creating a hostile or adversarial atmosphere. The assignment can be adapted for large (or online) courses by creating a blog or online discussion area, although nothing beats the in-person connection. (I also ask students to introduce themselves by name every time they present. My philosophy is to maximize what any assignment can achieve.)

I have employed this approach with undergraduate and graduate, traditional and nontraditional students. During the past two semesters, I used it in online classes to great effect. Any method that makes both students and professors feel strong is worth trying.

Discussion Starters

1. Discuss the various approaches to plagiarism Karon presents that instructors tend to use. What is your opinion on each approach and how effective it would be?
2. Evaluate Karon's approach to plagiarism: the assignment he gives to counter plagiarism and the positive approach he uses. Do you feel that his approach is better than the other ones presented in combating plagiarism? Why?
3. What is your opinion on academic cheating (plagiarism and cheating on tests)? Is such cheating commonplace at your school? Why do many students cheat, and how do they justify it?

Why Money Doesn't Buy Happiness

By Sharon Begley

Sharon Begley is the senior health & science correspondent at Reuters and former science editor and science columnist at Newsweek. In this essay, Begley presents findings that support the contention that greater wealth doesn't buy greater happiness and that Americans' obsession with material gain is misguided.

All in all, it was probably a mistake to look for the answer to the eternal question—"Does money buy happiness?"—from people who practice what's called the dismal science. For when economists tackled the question, they started from the observation that when people put something up for sale they try to get as much for it as they can, and when people buy something they try to pay as little for it as they can. Both sides in the transaction, the economists noticed, are therefore behaving as if they would be more satisfied (happier, dare we say) if they wound up receiving more money (the seller) or holding on to more money (the buyer). Hence, more money must be better than less, and the only way more of something can be better than less of it is if it brings you greater contentment. The economists' conclusion: the more money you have, the happier you must be.

Depressed debutantes, suicidal CEOs, miserable magnates and other unhappy rich folks aren't the only ones giving the lie to this. "Psychologists have spent decades studying the relation between wealth and happiness," writes Harvard University psychologist Daniel Gilbert in his best-selling "Stumbling on Happiness," "and they have generally concluded that wealth increases human happiness when it lifts people out of abject poverty and into the middle class but that it does little to increase happiness thereafter."

That flies in the face of intuition, not to mention economic theory. According to standard economics, the most important commodity you can buy with additional wealth is choice. If you have $20 in your pocket, you can decide between steak and peanut butter for dinner, but if you have only $1 you'd better hope you already have a jar of jelly at home. Additional wealth also lets you satisfy additional needs and wants, and the more of those you satisfy the happier you are supposed to be.

The trouble is, choice is not all it's cracked up to be. Studies show that people like selecting from among maybe half a dozen kinds of pasta at the grocery store but find 27 choices overwhelming, leaving them chronically on edge that they could have chosen a better one than they did. And wants, which are nice to be able to afford, have a bad habit of becoming needs (iPod, anyone?), of which an advertising- and media-saturated culture create endless numbers. Satisfying needs brings less emotional well-being than satisfying wants.

The nonlinear nature of how much happiness money can buy—lots more happiness when it moves you out of penury and into middle-class comfort, hardly any more when it lifts you from millionaire to decamillionaire—comes through clearly in global surveys that ask people how content they feel with their lives. In a typical survey people are asked to rank their sense of well-being or happiness on a scale of 1 to 7, where 1 means "not at all satisfied with my life" and 7 means "completely satisfied." Of the American multimillionaires who responded, the average happiness score was 5.8. Homeless people in Calcutta came in at 2.9. But before you assume that money does buy happiness after all, consider who else rated themselves around 5.8: the Inuit of northern Greenland, who do not exactly lead a life of luxury, and the cattle-herding Masai of Kenya, whose dung huts have no electricity or running water. And proving Gilbert's point about money buying happiness only when it lifts you out of abject poverty, slum dwellers in Calcutta—one economic rung above the homeless—rate themselves at 4.6.

Studies tracking changes in a population's reported level of happiness over time have also dealt a death blow to the money-buys-happiness claim. Since World War II the gross domestic product per capita has tripled in the United States. But people's sense of well-being, as measured by surveys asking some variation of "Overall, how satisfied are you with your life?," has barely budged. Japan has had an even more meteoric rise in GDP per capita since its postwar misery, but measures of national happiness have been flat, as they have also been in Western Europe during its long postwar boom, according to social psychologist Ruut Veenhoven of Erasmus University in Rotterdam.

A 2004 analysis of more than 150 studies on wealth and happiness concluded that "economic indicators have glaring shortcomings" as approximations of well-being across nations, wrote Ed Diener of the University of Illinois, Urbana-Champaign, and Martin E. P. Seligman of the University of Pennsylvania. "Although economic output has risen steeply over the past decades, there has been no rise in life satisfaction...and there has been a substantial increase in depression and distrust."

That's partly because in an expanding economy, in which former luxuries such as washing machines become necessities, the newly affluent don't feel the same joy in having a machine do the laundry that their grandparents, suddenly freed from washboards, did. They just take the Maytag for granted. "Americans who earn $50,000 per year are much happier than those who earn $10,000 per year," writes Gilbert, "but Americans who earn $5 million per year are not much happier than those who earn $100,000 per year." Another reason is that an expanding paycheck, especially in an expanding economy, produces expanding aspirations and a sense that there is always one more cool thing out there that you absolutely have to have. "Economic success falls short as a measure of well-being, in part because materialism can negatively influence well-being," Diener and Seligman conclude.

If money doesn't buy happiness, what does? Grandma was right when she told you to value health and friends, not money and stuff. Or as Diener and Seligman put it, once your basic needs are met "differences in well-being are less frequently due to income, and are more frequently due to factors such as social relationships and enjoyment at work." Other researchers add fulfillment, a sense that life has meaning, belonging to civic and other groups, and living in a democracy that respects individual rights and the rule of law. If a nation wants to increase its population's sense of well-being, says Veenhoven, it should make "less investment in economic growth and more in policies that promote good governance, liberties, democracy, trust and public safety."

Curiously, although money doesn't buy happiness, happiness can buy money. Young people who describe themselves as happy typically earn higher incomes, years later, than those who said they were unhappy. It seems that a sense of well-being can make you more productive and more likely to show initiative and other traits that lead to a higher income. Contented people are also more likely to marry and stay married, as well as to be healthy, both of which increase happiness.

If more money doesn't buy more happiness, then the behavior of most Americans looks downright insane, as we work harder and longer, decade after decade, to fatten our W-2s. But what is insane for an individual is crucial for a national economy—that is, ever more growth and consumption. Gilbert again: "Economies can blossom and grow only if people are deluded into believing that the production of wealth will make them happy...Economies thrive when individuals strive, but because individuals will strive only for their own happiness, it is essential that they mistakenly believe that producing and consuming are routes to personal well-being." In other words, if you want to do your part for your country's economy, forget all of the above about money not buying happiness.

Discussion Starters

1. Evaluate the evidence provided in the essay that money does not by happiness unless it moves a person from poverty to the middle class. Beyond that, why does more money not translate to more happiness?
2. Why, according to the essay, have Americans bought into the false belief that making more and more money to buy more acquisitions leads to happiness?
3. Does the essay make you rethink the American obsession with money and materialism? What is your personal perspective on what makes people happy? What do you value most in life?

Ethical Relativism

By Manuel Velasquez, Claire Andre, Thomas Shanks, and Michael J. Meyer

Velasquez, Andre, Shanks, and Meyer are program directors and professors at the Markkula Center For Applied Ethics at the University of Santa Clara. In this essay, the authors explain the theory of ethical relativism, its universal ramifications, and why most philosophers don't adhere to it.

Cultures differ widely in their moral practices. As anthropologist Ruth Benedict illustrates in *Patterns of Culture*, diversity is evident even on those matters of morality where we would expect to agree:

> We might suppose that in the matter of taking life all peoples would agree on condemnation. On the contrary, in the matter of homicide, it may be held that one kills by custom his two children, or that a husband has a right of life and death over his wife or that it is the duty of the child to kill his parents before they are old. It may be the case that those are killed who steal fowl, or who cut their upper teeth first, or who are born on Wednesday. Among some peoples, a person suffers torment at having caused an accidental death; among others, it is a matter of no consequence. Suicide may also be a light matter, the recourse of anyone who has suffered some slight rebuff, an act that constantly occurs in a tribe. It may be the highest and noblest act a wise man can perform. The very tale of it, on the other hand, may be a matter for incredulous mirth, and the act itself, impossible to conceive as human possibility. Or it may be a crime punishable by law, or regarded as a sin against the gods.

Other anthropologists point to a range of practices considered morally acceptable in some societies but condemned in others, including infanticide, genocide, polygamy, racism, sexism, and torture. Such differences may lead us to question whether there are any universal moral principles or whether morality is merely a matter of "cultural taste." Differences in moral practices across cultures raise an important issue in ethics—the concept of "ethical relativism."

Ethical relativism is the theory that holds that morality is relative to the norms of one's culture. That is, whether an action is right or wrong depends on the moral norms of the society in which it is practiced. The same action may be morally right in one society but be morally wrong in another. For the ethical relativist, there are no universal moral standards—standards that can be universally applied to all peoples at all times. The only moral standards against which a society's practices can be judged are its own. If ethical relativism is correct, there can be no common framework for resolving moral disputes or for reaching agreement on ethical matters among members of different societies.

Most ethicists reject the theory of ethical relativism. Some claim that while the moral practices of societies may differ, the fundamental moral principles underlying these practices do not. For example, in some societies, killing one's parents after they reached a certain age was common practice, stemming from the belief that people were better off in the afterlife if they entered it while still physically active and vigorous. While such a practice would be condemned in our society, we would agree with these societies on the underlying moral principle—the duty to care for parents. Societies, then, may differ in their application of fundamental moral principles but agree on the principles.

Also, it is argued, it may be the case that some moral beliefs are culturally relative whereas others are not. Certain practices, such as customs regarding dress and decency, may depend on local custom whereas other practices, such as slavery, torture, or political repression, may be governed by universal moral standards and judged wrong despite the many other differences that exist among cultures. Simply because some practices are relative does not mean that all practices are relative.

Other philosophers criticize ethical relativism because of its implications for individual moral beliefs. These philosophers assert that if the rightness or wrongness of an action depends on a society's norms, then it follows that one must obey the norms of one's society and to diverge from those norms is to act immorally. This means that if I am a member of a society that believes that racial or sexist practices are morally permissible, then I must accept those practices as morally right. But such a view promotes social conformity and leaves no room for moral reform or improvement in a society. Furthermore, members of the same society may hold different views on practices. In the United States, for example, a variety of moral opinions exists on matters ranging from animal experimentation to abortion. What constitutes right action when social consensus is lacking?

Perhaps the strongest argument against ethical relativism comes from those who assert that universal moral standards can exist even if some moral practices and beliefs vary among cultures. In other words, we can acknowledge cultural differences in moral practices and beliefs and still hold that some of these practices and beliefs are morally wrong. The practice of slavery in pre-Civil war U.S. society or the practice of apartheid in South Africa is wrong despite the beliefs of those societies. The treatment of the Jews in Nazi society is morally reprehensible regardless of the moral beliefs of Nazi society.

For these philosophers, ethics is an inquiry into right and wrong through a critical examination of the reasons underlying practices and beliefs. As a theory for justifying moral practices and beliefs, ethical relativism fails to recognize that some societies have better reasons for holding their views than others.

But even if the theory of ethical relativism is rejected, it must be acknowledged that the concept raises important issues. Ethical relativism reminds us that different societies have different moral beliefs and that our beliefs are deeply influenced by culture. It also encourages us to explore the reasons underlying beliefs that differ from our own, while challenging us to examine our reasons for the beliefs and values we hold.

Discussion Starters

1. What is ethical relativism according to the essay? Why do most ethicists reject the concept despite the cultural differences among societies in the world?
2. Ethicists believe universal standards of right and wrong exist across all societies. How, then, are historical atrocities such as slavery in the U.S. or the Jewish genocide in Nazi Germany to be explained?
3. Do you agree that there are universal standards of right and wrong? What would some of these standards be? What international responses to unethical behavior provide examples?

Dusting Off GOD

By Tom Bartlett

Tom Bartlett is a senior writer for The Chronicle of Higher Education. In this essay, Bartlett ignores the question of whether God exists and focuses on the scientific evidence that religion produces positive behaviors among people.

When a moth flies at night, it uses the moon and the stars to steer a straight path. Those light sources are fixed and distant, so the rays always strike the moth's multilensed eyes at the same angle, making them reliable for nocturnal navigation. But introduce something else bright—a candle, say, or a campfire—and there will be trouble. The light radiates outward, confusing the moth and causing it to spiral ever closer to the blaze until the insect meets a fiery end.

For years Richard Dawkins has used the self-immolation of moths to explain religion. The example can be found in his 2006 best seller, *The God Delusion*, and it's been repeated in speeches and debates, interviews and blog posts. Moths didn't evolve to commit suicide; that's an unfortunate byproduct of other adaptations. In much the same way, the thinking goes, human beings embrace religion for unrelated cognitive reasons. We evolved to search for patterns in nature, so perhaps that's why we imagine patterns in religious texts. Instead of being guided by the light, we fly into the flames.

The implication—that religion is basically malevolent, that it "poisons everything," in the words of the late Christopher Hitchens—is a standard assertion of the New Atheists. Their argument isn't just that there probably is no God, or that intelligent design is laughable bunk, or that the Bible is far from inerrant. It's that religion is obviously bad for human beings, condemning them to ignorance, subservience, and endless conflict, and we would be better off without it. But would we?

Before you can know for sure, you have to figure out what religion does for us in the first place. That's exactly what a loosely affiliated group of scholars in fields including biology, anthropology, and psychology are working on. They're applying evolutionary theory to the study of religion in order to discover whether or not it strengthens societies, makes them more successful, more cooperative, kinder. The scholars, many of them atheists themselves, generally look askance at the rise of New Atheism, calling its proponents ignorant, fundamentalist, and worst of all, unscientific. Dawkins and company have been no more charitable in return.

While the field is still young and fairly small—those involved haven't settled on a name yet, though "evolutionary religious studies" gets thrown around—its findings could reshape a very old debate. Maybe we should stop asking whether God exists and start asking whether it's useful to believe that he does.

Let's say someone gives you $10. Not a king's ransom, but enough for lunch. You're then told that you can share your modest wealth with a stranger, if you like, or keep it. You're assured that your identity will be protected, so there's no need to worry about being thought miserly. How much would you give?

If you're like most people who play the so-called dictator game, which has been used in numerous experiments, you will keep most of the money. In a recent study from a paper with the ominous title "God Is Watching You," the average subject gave $1.84. Meanwhile, another group of subjects was presented with the same choice but was first asked to unscramble a sentence that contained words like "divine," "spirit," and "sacred."

The second group of subjects gave an average of $4.22, with a solid majority (64 percent) giving more than five bucks. A heavenly reminder seemed to make subjects significantly more magnanimous. In another study, researchers found that prompting subjects with the same vocabulary made some more likely to volunteer for community projects. Intriguingly, not all of them: Only those who had a specific dopamine receptor variant volunteered more, raising the possibility that religion doesn't work for everybody.

A similar experiment was conducted on two Israeli kibbutzes. The scenario was more complicated: Subjects were shown an envelope containing 100 shekels (currently about $25). They were told that they could choose to keep as much of the money as they wished, but that another member of the kibbutz was being given the identical option. If the total requested by the participants (who were kept separated) exceeded 100 shekels, they walked away with nothing. If the total was less than or equal to 100, they were given the money plus a bonus based on what was left over.

The kicker is that one of the kibbutzes was secular and one was religious. Turns out, the more-devout members of the religious kibbutz, as measured by synagogue attendance, requested significantly fewer shekels and expected others to do the same. The researchers, Richard Sosis and Bradley Ruffle, ventured that "collective ritual has a significant impact on cooperative decisions."

Another study that found that religious people were, in some instances, more likely to treat strangers fairly. Or the multiple studies suggesting that people who were prompted to think about an all-seeing supernatural agent were less likely to cheat. Or the study of 300 young adults in Belgium that found that those who were religious were considered more empathetic by their friends.

The results of other studies are less straightforward. A Harvard Business School researcher discovered that religious people were more likely to give to charity, but only on the days they worshiped, a phenomenon he dubbed the "Sunday Effect." Then there's the survey of how belief in the afterlife affected crime rates in 67 countries. Researchers determined that countries with high rates of belief in hell had less crime, while in those where the belief in hell was low and the belief in heaven high, there was more crime. A vengeful deity is better for public safety than a merciful one.

None of that research settles the value of belief, and much of it is based on assuming that certain correlations are meaningful or that particular techniques (like the one used in the dictator-game study) actually prime what researchers think they prime. And questions remain: How effective is religious belief, really, if it needs to be prompted with certain words? And is the only thing stopping you from robbing a liquor store really the prospect of eternal hellfire?

Still, a growing body of research suggests that religion or religious ideas, in certain circumstances, in some people, can elicit the kind of behavior that is generally good for society: fairness, generosity, honesty. At the very least, when you read the literature, it becomes difficult to confidently assert that religion, despite the undeniable evil it has sometimes inspired, is entirely toxic.

That is David Sloan Wilson's point, or one of them anyway. Wilson, a professor of biology and anthropology at Binghamton University, is an atheist (as was his father, the novelist Sloan Wilson) who is interested in finding out what religion does, from an evolutionary perspective, for individuals and societies. Why does belief in the supernatural cut across cultures, and why has it persisted for millennia? He took a crack at such dauntingly large questions in his book *Darwin's Cathedral*, arguing that religion bestows an array of evolutionary advantages on groups of believers.

Wilson is in his early 60s, thin, white-haired, excitable. You get the sense that he might bubble over at any moment, and sometimes he does, issuing a four-letter invective in the midst of a multisyllabic explication. His most recent book is *The Neighborhood Project: Using Evolution to Improve My City, One Block at a Time*. There isn't much Wilson thinks Darwin can't do. The professor's Skype handle is "evostud."

In two blog posts, one in March and one in May, Wilson questioned whether Richard Dawkins "might fail to qualify" as an evolutionist for, among other shortcomings, ignoring research on the evolution of religion. He has scolded the New Atheists for a militancy he sees as equivalent to religious fundamentalism. Firing shots at Dawkins is old hat for Wilson. When he reviewed *The God Delusion*, in 2007, he called Dawkins "deeply misinformed" on evolution. (Dawkins replied that the purpose of the book was not to discuss "religion's possible evolutionary advantages.") In a recent interview, Wilson declared that Dawkins and his fellow New Atheists "don't understand the nature of the beast" and yet still "go on and on in a very ignorant fashion."

Like Wilson, Scott Atran, an anthropologist at France's National Center for Scientific Research, is an atheist ("Yes!" he exclaimed when asked) and an evolutionist whose book *In Gods We Trust: The Evolutionary Landscape of Religion* was one of the first, along with *Darwin's Cathedral*, by Wilson, and *Religion Explained*, by Pascal Boyer, to chart a course for the field (the first two books were published in 2002 and Boyer's in 2001). In his book, Atran, who also teaches at the University of Michigan at Ann Arbor and the City University of New York's John Jay College of Criminal Justice, calls religion an evolutionary byproduct, a sort of cognitive accident. He's since modified his view to take into account the apparent culturally adaptive upside of faith. Atran, whose most recent book is about faith and terrorism, describes New Atheism as moronic. "I don't see anything in the New Atheists' work that tells us anything at all about religion," he says, "and I think their ad hominem attacks are ridiculous."

That view is echoed by Dominic Johnson, a professor of biopolitics at the University of Edinburgh, who has written about how the threat of supernatural punishment appears to enhance cooperation. The trouble, he says, is that the New Atheists have become the face of science. On one side, there is anti-science fundamentalism. On the other, there are pro-science New Atheists. "Whatever they say tends to be taken as the scientific perspective on religion, that it's representing the whole of science," Johnson says. "That's a problem."

The New Atheists have deemed Wilson not only wrong but dull. For Wilson, though, it's the New Atheists who have become a bore. If you've seen one video of Dawkins slaying a naïve believer, you've seen them all. If you've read one New Atheist anti-God tome, you know what the others will say. Wilson insists that trying to discover why we believe is more intriguing than the debate over whether anyone is up there looking down.

Discussion Starters

1. Evaluate the various studies presented in the essay that suggest that religious people are more generous, kinder, and more empathetic than non-religious people. How compelling do you find the studies? Why might religious people be more generous and kinder, assuming they are?
2. Scientists studying the effects of religion are not interested in whether a God actually exists. If a system of belief that produces virtuous behavior is based on a possible false premise (the existence of God), does it really matter? Is the behavior more important than its source?
3. While the existence of God has long been debated, how do you account for the pervasiveness of religious faith for thousands of years across all societies? Have the findings of modern science weakened the impact of religion?

A Nation of Promiscuous Prudes

By Victor Hanson

Victor Hanson is a noted historian, social critic, syndicated columnist, and author whose latest book is The Savior Generals. In this essay, Hanson explores the "schizophrenic" attitudes of Americans towards morality, providing multiple examples of how prudery and promiscuity exist side by side in our morally ambiguous society.

More than 500 people were killed in Chicago last year. Yet Chicago Mayor Rahm Emanuel still found time to berate the fast-food franchise Chick-fil-A for not sharing "Chicago values" apparently because its founder does not approve of same-sex marriage.

Two states have legalized marijuana, with more to come. Yet social taboos against tobacco smoking make it nearly impossible to light up a cigarette in public places. Marijuana, like alcohol, causes far greater short-term impairment than does nicotine. But legal cigarette smoking is now seen as a corporate-sponsored, uncool and dirty habit that leads to long-term health costs for society at large in a way homegrown, hip and mostly illegal pot smoking apparently does not.

Graphic language, nudity and sex are now commonplace in movies and on cable television. At the same time, there is now almost no tolerance for casual and slang banter in the media or the workplace. A boss who calls an employee "honey" might face accusations of fostering a hostile work environment, yet a television producer whose program shows an 18-year-old having sex does not. Many colleges offer courses on lurid themes from masturbation to prostitution, even as campus sexual-harassment suits over hurtful language are at an all-time high.

A federal judge in New York recently ruled that the so-called morning-after birth-control pill must be made available to all "women" regardless of age or parental consent, and without a prescription. The judge determined that it was unfair for those under 16 to be denied access to such emergency contraceptives. However, if vast numbers of girls younger than 16 need after-sex options to prevent unwanted pregnancies, will there be a flood of statutory rape charges lodged against older teenagers who had such consensual relations with younger girls?

Our schizophrenic morality also affects the military. When America was a far more traditional society, few seemed to care that Gen. Dwight Eisenhower carried on an unusual relationship at the front in Normandy with his young female chauffeur, Kay Summersby. As the Third Army chased the Germans across France, Gen. George S. Patton was not discreet about his female liaisons. Contrast that live-and-let-live attitude of a supposedly uptight society with our own hip culture's tabloid interest in Gen. David H. Petraeus' career-ending affair with Paula Broadwell, or in the private emails of Gen. John Allen.

What explains these contradictions in our wide-open but prudish society? Decades after the rise of feminism, popular culture still seems confused by it. If women should be able to approach sexuality like men, does it follow that commentary about sex should follow the same gender-neutral rules? Yet wearing provocative or inappropriate clothing is often considered less offensive than remarking upon it. Calling a near-nude Madonna onstage a "hussy" or "tart" would be considered crudity in a way that her mock crucifixion and simulated sex acts are not.

Criminal sexual activity is sometimes not as professionally injurious as politically incorrect thoughts about sex and gender. Former New York Gov. Eliot Spitzer, found to have hired prostitutes on a number of occasions during his time in office, was given a CNN news show despite the scandal. But when Miss California Carrie Prejean was asked in the Miss USA Pageant whether she endorsed same-sex marriage, she said no and thereby earned nearly as much popular condemnation for her candid defense of traditional marriage as Mr. Spitzer had for his purchased affairs.

Critics were outraged that talk-show host Rush Limbaugh grossly insulted birth-control activist Sandra Fluke. Amid the attention, Miss Fluke was canonized for her position that federal health care plans should pay for the contraceptive costs of all women. Yet in comparison to Miss Fluke's well-publicized victimhood, there has been a veritable news blackout for the trial of the macabre Dr. Kermit Gosnell, charged with killing and mutilating in gruesome fashion seven babies during a long career of conducting sometimes illegal late-term abortions. Had Dr. Gosnell's aborted victims been canines instead of humans—compare the minimal coverage of the Gosnell trial with the widespread media condemnation of dog-killing quarterback Michael Vick—perhaps the doctor's mayhem likewise would have been front-page news outside of Philadelphia.

Modern society also resorts to empty, symbolic, moral action when it cannot deal with real problems. So-called assault weapons account for less than 1 percent of gun deaths in America. Still, the country whips itself into a frenzy to ban them, apparently to prove that at least it can do something without wading into the polarized racial and class controversies of going after illegal urban handguns, the real source of the nation's high gun-related body count.

Not since the late 19th-century juxtaposition of the Wild West with the Victorian East has popular morality been so unbridled and yet so uptight. In short, we have become a nation of promiscuous prudes.

Discussion Starters

1. Hanson provides a number of examples that America is at the same time "prudish" and "promiscuous." Evaluate the validity of the comparison that he uses in each example.
2. If America is in fact both "up tight" and "unbridled" sexually, what do you think accounts for this "schizophrenic" attitude?
3. What are the consequences in a society that sends out mixed messages on what constitutes right-or-wrong behavior? What effect do these mixed messages have on younger people?

The Way of All Flesh

By Ted Conover

Ted Conover is an author, journalist, writer-in-residence in the Arthur L. Carter Journalism Institute of New York University, and contributor to numerous publications. In this essay, Conover relates his experience as an inspector in a high tech cattle slaughter house and details the process in a way that may make readers look at their next steak differently.

The cattle arrive in perforated silver trailers called cattle pots that let in wind and weather and vent out their hot breath and flatus. It's hard to see inside a cattle pot. The drivers are in a hurry to unload and leave, and are always speeding by. (When I ask Lefty how meat gets bruised, he says, "You ever see how those guys drive?") The trucks have come from feedlots, some nearby, some in western Nebraska, a few in Iowa. The plant slaughters about 5,100 cattle each day, and a standard double-decker cattle pot holds only about forty, so there's a constant stream of trucks pulling in to disgorge, even before the line starts up a little after six a.m.

First the cattle are weighed. Then they are guided into narrow outdoor pens angled diagonally toward the entrance to the kill floor. A veterinarian arrives before our shift and begins to inspect them; she looks for open wounds, problems walking, signs of disease. When their time comes, the cattle will be urged by workers toward the curving ramp that leads up into the building. The ramp has a roof and no sharp turns. It was designed by the livestock expert Temple Grandin, and the curves and penumbral light are believed to soothe the animals in their final moments. But the soothing goes only so far.

"Huele mal, no?" says one of the Mexican wranglers: "It stinks, doesn't it?" He holds his nose against the ammoniac smell of urine as I visit the pens with Carolina. We are new U.S. Department of Agriculture meat inspectors, getting the kitchen tour. The wrangler and his crew are moving cattle up the ramp. To do this, they wave sticks with white plastic bags tied to the ends over the animals' heads; the bags frighten the cattle and move them along. For cows that don't spook, the workers also have electric prods—in defiance, I was told, of company regulations—that crackle when applied to the nether parts. The ramp really does stink. "Yeah," I say in Spanish. "Why does it smell so bad?"

"They're scared. They don't want to die," the worker replies. But that's what they're here to do, and once on the ramp, they're just a few moments away from it.

While the inspectors work at Cargill Meat Solutions, we are not employed by them. Rather, you could say, we are embedded. The company accommodates us along the chain, at four special places on the kill floor. The kill floor, a singular circle of hell, is a hubbub of human and mechanical activity, something horrific designed by ingenious and no doubt well-meaning engineers. Herb, our immediate supervisor, shouts a few things, but the kill floor is so loud that I have no idea what he's saying—and little understanding, at first, of what I'm seeing.

Though it's called a floor, it's actually a room, about the size of a football field. It's filled with workers on their feet, facing some fraction of a cow as it passes slowly in front of them, suspended from the chain. Three workers are perched on hydraulic platforms fitted with electric saws, which they use to split hanging carcasses in half, right down the middle of the spinal column.

The key to comprehension is the chain, which moves the carcasses around the enormous room. It begins on the eastern wall, just beyond the area where the cows come in from the outside. This is the only section of the room hidden from view, behind a partition. But Herb takes us up onto a metal catwalk and through a heavy door. From there, grasping a railing, we can look down on the killing.

Passing one by one through a small opening in the wall, each animal enters a narrow, slightly elevated chute. On a platform just above the chute is a guy called the knocker. Suspended on cables in front of him is something that looks like a fat toaster oven with handles on either side: a captive-bolt gun. The knocker's job is to place the gun against the animal's forehead and pull the trigger. Most of the time, the cow immediately slumps forward, blood oozing from the circle where the thick steel bolt went in and came out. If one shot doesn't do the trick, the knocker does it again.

Meanwhile, down on floor level, a second worker wearing a helmet with a face mask and protective padding has reached into the chute from below and attached a cuff around the animal's left rear leg. Once the cow has been knocked, the chain hoists that leg and then the rest of the animal up into the air, and the body begins its journey around the room.

Carolina and I watch this for some time without talking. The knocker moves slowly, patiently waiting for his gun to achieve good contact with the animal's forehead. It usually takes more than one try, as the animals duck down or try to peer over the side of the chute, whose width the knocker can actually control with a foot pedal. One cow, unlike the others, lifts her head up high in order to sniff the knocking gun. *What could this thing be?* It's her last thought. The knocker waits until her wet nose goes down, then lowers the gun and *thunk*. She slumps, then gets hoisted aloft with the others. The knocked animals hang next to one another for a while, waiting for the chain to start moving—like gondolas at the base of a ski lift. From time to time an animal kicks violently, sporadically. "They're not really dead yet," says Carolina, which I can hear because she's close to my ear and it's slightly less loud in here. In most cases, apparently, what she says is true and intentional: the pumping of their hearts will help drain the blood from their bodies once their necks are sliced open, which will happen in the ensuing minutes. By the time the chain has made a turn or two, the kicking will stop.

Dismemberment proceeds by degrees. At different posts, workers make cuts in the hide, clip off the hooves, and clip off the horns, if any. The hide is gradually peeled from the body, until finally a big flap of loose skin is grasped by the "downpuller" machine, which yanks the whole thing off like a sweater and drops it through a hole in the floor. Here, for the first time, the cow no longer looks like a cow. Now it's a 1,200-pound piece of proto-meat making its circuit of the room.

Soon after, the heads, now dangling only by the windpipe, are detached from the body and go off on their own side chain. The huge tongues are cut out and hung on hooks adjacent to the heads: head, tongue, head, tongue. They turn a corner, pass through a steam cabinet that cleans them, make another quick turn, and meet their first inspectors.

I didn't eat beef at all during the time I worked at the pack. Seeing the knocker at work was part of the problem. So was standing near the cattle as they were herded up the doomsday ramp. And then there were the heads, eyeballs intact, and the highly rationalized industrial setting, the idea of a powerful enterprise devoted to wholesale killing. And if you believe that animals might have souls – sometimes I do – then you might relate to my mental picture of a spiritual highway spiraling upward from the knocking room, through the ceiling of Cargill Meat Solutions, and into bovine heaven, with a constant stream of cattle arriving every day.

Discussion Starters

1. What is your initial gut-level response to the essay? What details of the kill-and-dismember process, if any, do you find most disturbing?
2. Is there an ethical issue with killing animals for human consumption? Do you get a sense of the author's viewpoint? Does this essay make you think any differently about the next steak put before you?
3. People seldom if ever connect the meat they eat with the slaughtering of cattle presented in the essay. The essay makes us graphically aware of the connection. Is this a good thing, or does it really matter?

VI. Hot-Button Issues

Legalizing Marijuana: Why Citizens Should Just Say No

By Charles Stimson

Charles Stimson is a writer, an expert in national security and crime control, and senior legal fellow at The Heritage Foundation. In this essay, Stimson makes a detailed case against marijuana legalization in the U.S.

The scientific literature is clear that marijuana is addictive and that its use significantly impairs bodily and mental functions. Marijuana use is associated with memory loss, cancer, immune system deficiencies, heart disease, and birth defects, among other conditions. Even where decriminalized, marijuana trafficking remains a source of violence, crime, and social disintegration.

Marijuana advocates downplay the well-documented harms of marijuana trafficking and use while promising benefits ranging from reduced crime to additional tax revenue. In particular, supporters of the initiative make five bold claims:

1. "Marijuana is safe and non-addictive."
2. "Marijuana prohibition makes no more sense than alcohol prohibition did in the early 1900s."
3. "The government's efforts to combat illegal drugs have been a total failure."
4. "The money spent on government efforts to combat the illegal drug trade can be better spent on substance abuse and treatment for the allegedly few marijuana users who abuse the drug."
5. "Tax revenue collected from marijuana sales would substantially outweigh the social costs of legalization."

All five claims are demonstrably false or, based on the best evidence, highly dubious.

Further, supporters of legalization simply ignore the mechanics of decriminalization—that is, how it would directly affect law enforcement, crime, and communities. Among the important questions left unanswered are:

- Would decriminalization, especially if combined with taxation, expand market opportunities for the gangs and cartels that currently dominate drug distribution?
- Would existing zoning laws prohibit marijuana cultivation in residential neighborhoods, and if not, what measures would growers have to undertake to keep children from the plants?
- Would transportation providers be prohibited from firing bus drivers because they smoke marijuana?

No one knows the specifics of how marijuana decriminalization would work in practice or what measures would be necessary to prevent children, teenagers, criminals, and addicts from obtaining the drug.

The federal government shares these concerns. Gil Kerlikowske, Director of the White House Office of National Drug Control Policy (ONDCP), recently stated, "Marijuana legalization, for any purpose, is a non-starter in the Obama Administration." The Administration—widely viewed as more liberal than any other in recent memory and, for a time, as embodying the hopes of pro-legalization activists—has weighed the costs and benefits and concluded that marijuana legalization would compromise public health and safety.

Marijuana advocates have had some success peddling the notion that marijuana is a "soft" drug, similar to alcohol, and fundamentally different from "hard" drugs like cocaine or heroin. It is true that marijuana is not the most dangerous of the commonly abused drugs, but that is not to say that it is safe. Indeed, marijuana shares more in common with the "hard" drugs than it does with alcohol.

A common argument for legalization is that smoking marijuana is no more dangerous than drinking alcohol and that prohibiting the use of marijuana is therefore no more justified than the prohibition of alcohol. As Jacob Sullum, author of *Saying Yes: In Defense of Drug Use*, writes:

> Americans understood the problems associated with alcohol abuse, but they also understood the problems associated with Prohibition, which included violence, organized crime, official corruption, the erosion of civil liberties, disrespect for the law, and injuries and deaths caused by tainted black-market booze. They decided that these unintended side effects far outweighed whatever harms Prohibition prevented by discouraging drinking. The same sort of analysis today would show that the harm caused by drug prohibition far outweighs the harm it prevents, even without taking into account the value to each individual of being sovereign over his own body and mind.

At first blush, this argument is appealing, especially to those wary of over-regulation by government. But it overlooks the enormous difference between alcohol and marijuana. Legalization advocates claim that marijuana and alcohol are mild intoxicants and so should be regulated similarly; but as the experience of nearly every culture, over the thousands of years of human history, demonstrates, alcohol is different. Nearly every culture has its own alcoholic preparations, and nearly all have successfully regulated alcohol consumption through cultural norms. The same cannot be said of marijuana. There are several possible explanations for alcohol's unique status: For most people, it is not addictive; it is rarely consumed to the point of intoxication; low-level consumption is consistent with most manual and intellectual tasks; it has several positive health benefits; and it is formed by the fermentation of many common substances and easily metabolized by the body.

To be sure, there are costs associated with alcohol abuse, such as drunk driving and disease associated with excessive consumption. A few cultures—and this nation for a short while during Prohibition—have concluded that the benefits of alcohol consumption are not worth the costs. But they are the exception; most cultures have concluded that it is acceptable in moderation. No other intoxicant shares that status.

Alcohol differs from marijuana in several crucial respects. First, marijuana is far more likely to cause addiction. Second, it is usually consumed to the point of intoxication. Third, it has no known general healthful properties, though it may have some palliative effects. Fourth, it is toxic and deleterious to health. Thus, while it is true that both alcohol and marijuana are less intoxicating than other mood-altering drugs, that is not to say that marijuana is especially similar to alcohol or that its use is healthy or even safe.

In fact, compared to alcohol, marijuana is not safe. Long-term, moderate consumption of alcohol carries few health risks and even offers some significant benefits. For example, a glass of wine (or other alcoholic drink) with dinner actually improves health. Dozens of peer-reviewed medical studies suggest that drinking moderate amounts of alcohol reduces the risk of heart disease, strokes, gallstones, diabetes, and death from a heart attack. According to the Mayo Clinic, among many others, moderate use of alcohol (defined as two drinks a day) "seems to offer some health benefits, particularly for the heart." Countless articles in medical journals and other scientific literature confirm the positive health effects of moderate alcohol consumption.

The effects of regular marijuana consumption are quite different. For example, the National Institute on Drug Abuse (a division of the National Institutes of Health) has released studies showing that use of marijuana has wide-ranging negative health effects. Long-term marijuana consumption "impairs the ability of T-cells in the lungs' immune system to fight off some infections." These studies have also found that marijuana consumption impairs short-term memory, making it difficult to learn and retain information or perform complex tasks; slows reaction time and impairs motor coordination; increases heart rate by 20 percent to 100 percent, thus elevating the risk of heart attack; and alters moods, resulting in artificial euphoria, calmness, or (in high doses) anxiety or paranoia. And it gets worse: Marijuana has toxic properties that can result in birth defects, pain, respiratory system damage, brain damage, and stroke.

Further, prolonged use of marijuana may cause cognitive degradation and is "associated with lower test scores and lower educational attainment because during periods of intoxication the drug affects the ability to learn and process information, thus influencing attention, concentration, and short-term memory." Unlike alcohol, marijuana has been shown to have a residual effect on cognitive ability that persists beyond the period of intoxication. According to the National Institute on Drug Abuse, whereas alcohol is broken down relatively quickly in the human body, THC (tetrahydrocannabinol, the main active chemical in marijuana) is stored in organs and fatty tissues, allowing it to remain in a user's body for days or even weeks after consumption. Research has shown that marijuana consumption may also cause "psychotic symptoms."

Marijuana's effects on the body are profound. According to the British Lung Foundation, "smoking three or four marijuana joints is as bad for your lungs as smoking twenty tobacco cigarettes." Researchers in Canada found that marijuana smoke contains significantly higher levels of numerous toxic compounds, like ammonia and hydrogen cyanide, than regular tobacco smoke. In fact, the study determined that ammonia was found in marijuana smoke at levels of up to 20 times the levels found in tobacco. Similarly, hydrogen cyanide was found in marijuana smoke at concentrations three to five times greater than those found in tobacco smoke.

Marijuana, like tobacco, is addictive. One study found that more than 30 percent of adults who used marijuana in the course of a year were dependent on the drug. These individuals often show signs of withdrawal and compulsive behavior. Marijuana dependence is also responsible for a large proportion of calls to drug abuse help lines and treatment centers.

To equate marijuana use with alcohol consumption is, at best, uninformed and, at worst, actively misleading. Only in the most superficial ways are the two substances alike, and they differ in every way that counts: addictiveness, toxicity, health effects, and risk of intoxication.

Today, marijuana trafficking is linked to a variety of crimes, from assault and murder to money laundering and smuggling. Legalization of marijuana would increase demand for the drug and almost certainly exacerbate drug-related crime, as well as cause a myriad of unintended but predictable consequences.

To begin with, an astonishingly high percentage of criminals are marijuana users. According to a study by the RAND Corporation, approximately 60 percent of arrestees test positive for marijuana use in the United States, England, and Australia. Further, marijuana metabolites are found in arrestees' urine more frequently than those of any other drug.

Although some studies have shown marijuana to inhibit aggressive behavior and violence, the National Research Council concluded that the "long-term use of marijuana may alter the nervous system in ways that do promote violence." No place serves as a better example than Amsterdam.

Marijuana advocates often point to the Netherlands as a well-functioning society with a relaxed attitude toward drugs, but they rarely mention that Amsterdam is one of Europe's most violent cities. In Amsterdam, officials are in the process of closing marijuana dispensaries, or "coffee shops," because of the crime associated with their operation. Furthermore, the Dutch Ministry of Health, Welfare and Sport has expressed "concern about drug and alcohol use among young people and the social consequences, which range from poor school performance and truancy to serious impairment, including brain damage."

Theoretical arguments in favor of marijuana legalization usually overlook the practical matter of how the drug would be regulated and sold. It is the details of implementation, of course, that will determine the effect of legalization on families, schools, and communities. Most basically, how and where would marijuana be sold?

- Would neighborhoods become neon red-light districts like Amsterdam's, accompanied by the same crime and social disorder?
- If so, who decides what neighborhoods will be so afflicted—residents and landowners or far-off government officials?
- Or would marijuana sales be so widespread that users could add it to their grocery lists?
- If so, how would stores sell it, how would they store it, and how would they prevent it from being diverted into the gray market?
- Would stores dealing in marijuana have to fortify their facilities to reduce the risk of theft and assault?

Citizens also should not overlook what may be the greatest harms of marijuana legalization: increased addiction to and use of harder drugs. In addition to marijuana's harmful effects on the body and relationship to criminal conduct, it is a gateway drug that can lead users to more dangerous drugs. Prosecutors, judges, police officers, detectives, parole or probation officers, and even defense attorneys know that the vast majority of defendants arrested for violent crimes test positive for illegal drugs, including marijuana. They also know that marijuana is the starter drug of choice for most criminals. Whereas millions of Americans consume moderate amounts of alcohol without ever "moving on" to dangerous drugs, marijuana use and cocaine use are strongly correlated.

While correlation does not necessarily reflect causation, and while the science is admittedly mixed as to whether it is the drug itself or the people the new user associates with who cause the move on to cocaine, heroin, LSD, or other drugs, the RAND Corporation reports that marijuana prices and cocaine use are directly linked, suggesting a substitution effect between the two drugs. Moreover, according to RAND, legalization will cause marijuana prices to fall as much as 80 percent. That can lead to significant consequences because "a 10-percent decrease in the price of marijuana would increase the prevalence of cocaine use by 4.4 to 4.9 percent."

In addition to its direct effects on individual health, even moderate marijuana use imposes significant long-term costs through the ways that it affects individual users. Marijuana use is associated with cognitive difficulties and influences attention, concentration, and short-term memory. This damage affects drug users' ability to work and can put others at risk. Even if critical workers—for example, police officers, airline pilots, and machine operators—used marijuana recreationally but remained sober on the job, the long-term cognitive deficiency that remained from regular drug use would sap productivity and place countless people in danger. Increased use would also send health care costs skyrocketing—costs borne not just by individual users, but also by the entire society.

For that reason, among others, the Obama Administration also rejects supporters' economic arguments. In his speech, Kerlikowske explained that tax revenue from cigarettes is far outweighed by their social costs: "Tobacco also does not carry its economic weight when we tax it; each year we spend more than $200 billion and collect only about $25 billion in taxes." If the heavy taxation of cigarettes is unable even to come close to making up for the health and other costs associated with their use, it seems doubtful at best that marijuana taxes would be sufficient to cover the costs of legalized marijuana—especially considering that, in addition to the other dangers of smoking marijuana, the physical health effects of just three to four joints are equivalent to those of an entire pack of cigarettes.

Other claims also do not measure up. Many black-market dealers would rationally choose to remain in the black market to avoid taxation and regulation. Vibrant gray markets have developed throughout the world for many products that are legal, regulated, and heavily taxed. Cigarettes in Eastern Europe, alcohol in Scandinavia, luxury automobiles in Russia, and DVDs in the Middle East are all legal goods traded in gray markets that are wracked with violence. In Canada, an attempt at a $3 per pack tax on cigarettes was greeted with the creation of a black market that "accounted for perhaps 30 percent of sales."

In sum, legalization would put additional strain on an already faltering economy. In 2008, marijuana alone was involved in 375,000 emergency room visits. Drug overdoses already outnumber gunshot deaths in America and are approaching motor vehicle crashes as the nation's leading cause of accidental death. It is true that taxing marijuana sales would generate some tax revenue, but the cost of handling the influx of problems resulting from increased use would far outweigh any gain made by marijuana's taxation. Legalizing marijuana would serve only to compound the problems already associated with drug use.

The final two arguments of those favoring legalization are intertwined. According to advocates of legalization, the government's efforts to combat the illegal drug trade have been an expensive failure. Consequently, they argue, focusing on substance abuse and treatment would be a more effective means of combating drug abuse while reducing the violence and social ills stemming from anti-drug enforcement efforts.

There is no doubt that if marijuana were legalized, more people, including juveniles, would consume it. Consider cigarettes: While their purchase by people under 18 is illegal, 20 percent of high school students admit to having smoked cigarettes in the past 30 days. Marijuana's illegal status "keeps potential drug users from using" marijuana in a way that no legalization scheme can replicate "by virtue of the fear of arrest and the embarrassment of being caught." With increased use comes increased abuse, as the fear of arrest and embarrassment will decrease.

Legalization advocates attempt to create in the minds of the public an image of a typical "responsible" user of marijuana: a person who is reasonable and accountable even when under the influence of marijuana. And for those few that don't fit that image? Society will treat them and restore them to full health. The facts, however, are much uglier.

Keeping marijuana illegal will undoubtedly keep many young people from using it. Eliminate that criminal sanction (and moral disapprobation), and more youth will use the drug, harming their potential and ratcheting up treatment costs. Educators know that students using marijuana underperform when compared to their non-using peers. Teachers, coaches, guidance counselors, and school principals have seen the negative effect of marijuana on their students. The Rev. Dr. D. Stuart Dunnan, Headmaster of Saint James School in St. James, Maryland, says of marijuana use by students:

> The chemical effect of marijuana is to take away ambition. The social effect is to provide an escape from challenges and responsibilities with a like-minded group of teenagers who are doing the same thing. Using marijuana creates losers. At a time when we're concerned about our lack of academic achievement relative to other countries, legalizing marijuana will be disastrous.

If marijuana were legalized, violent, brutal, and ruthless Mexican DTOs will work to maintain their black-market profits at the expense of American citizens' safety. Every week, there are news articles cataloguing the murders, kidnappings, robberies, and other thuggish brutality employed by Mexican drug gangs along the border. It is nonsensical to argue that these gangs will simply give up producing marijuana when it is legalized; indeed, their profits will soar. Legalizing marijuana will only incentivize Mexican DTOs to grow more marijuana to feed the demand and exploit the black market. Thus, marijuana legalization will increase crime, drug use, and social dislocation—the exact opposite of what pro-legalization advocates promise.

Pro-marijuana advocates invite Americans to imagine a hypothetical and idyllic "pot market," but America's national approach to drug use, addiction, and crime must be serious, based on sound policy and solid evidence. In 1982, President Ronald Reagan adopted a national drug strategy that took a comprehensive approach consisting of five components: international cooperation, research, strengthened law enforcement, treatment and rehabilitation, and prevention and education. It was remarkably successful: Illegal drug use by young adults dropped more than 50 percent.

Reagan was right to make drug control a major issue of his presidency. Illegal drugs such as marijuana are responsible for a disproportionate share of violence and social decline in America. Accordingly, federal law, representing the considered judgment of medical science and the nation's two political branches of government, takes the unequivocal position that marijuana is dangerous and has no significant beneficial uses.

There is strong evidence to suggest that legalizing marijuana would serve little purpose other than to worsen the nation's drug problems—addiction, violence, disorder, and death. While long on rhetoric, the legalization movement, by contrast, is short on facts.

Discussion Starters

1. Analyze and evaluate the evidence provided in the essay regarding the negative effects of marijuana legalization. How compelling do you find the evidence?
2. Analyze and evaluate the arguments that counter the reasons that advocates support marijuana legalization. How successfully are the reasons refuted?
3. What is your opinion on the legalization of marijuana? How did the essay influence your opinion, if at all? How does your own experience, or those of others, influence your opinion?

Decriminalizing Marijuana Usage

By Maria Navarro

Maria Navarro is a free-lance writer and textbook author. In this essay, Navarro makes a case for the legalization of marijuana in the U.S. based on comparative data from other countries where marijuana usage has been decriminalized.

Should marijuana usage be decriminalized in the U.S.? Millions of marijuana users certainly think so, claiming that smoking marijuana is no different than drinking alcohol. What would happen if marijuana usage was decriminalized in the U.S.? Would usage, particularly among younger Americans, increase dramatically? Looking at what has happened in states and countries that don't put people in jail for using marijuana gives us some indication.

Although recreational marijuana usage is illegal in the U.S., in 1973, Oregon became the first state to decriminalize cannabis possession. By 1978, Alaska, California, Colorado, Mississippi, New York, Nebraska, North Carolina, and Maine had some form of cannabis decriminalization, meaning that possessing small amounts of marijuana, one ounce being the most common maximum, was not a misdemeanor or felony. At worst, the possession of marijuana, if detected by police, would result in a fine.

What impact did the decriminalization of marijuana have on usage rates in states where the fear of arrests and prison sentences for users no longer existed? Studies conducted in California, Oregon, and Maine within a few years of decriminalization found little increase in cannabis use compared to the rest of the country. In 1997, the Connecticut Law Revision Commission examined states that had decriminalized cannabis and found any increase in cannabis usage was *less* than the increase in states that had not decriminalized cannabis, and that the largest proportionate increase of marijuana use occurred in those states with the most severe penalties. The Commission recommended that Connecticut decriminalize the possession of one ounce or less of marijuana for adults 21 years and older.

Enough countries in different parts of the world have decriminalized marijuana usage to give a good picture of the impact of decriminalization. In South Australia, marijuana usage has been decriminalized, and Australians who are caught in possession either receive a warning or pay a small fine. In Western Australia, however, marijuana possession remains a felony and jail sentences are the norm. A two-year study conducted by the Drug and Alcohol Council of South Australia found no difference in levels of marijuana use between Western Australia with its harsh anti-marijuana laws and South Australia with its decriminalization of marijuana usage.

The Netherlands is known for the most liberal marijuana laws in the world, where people can actually smoke marijuana legally in "shops" around the city of Amsterdam. However, according to a 2010 study by The European School Survey Project on Alcohol and Other Drugs (ESPAD), marijuana use among teens in the Netherlands is actually lower than in the United States. The survey found 28% of Dutch teens have smoked marijuana as compared with 41% of American teens, and 23% of American teens have experimented with other illicit drugs as compared with only 6% of Netherlands' teens.

According to American decriminalization advocate Kevin Zeese of Common Sense for Drug Policy, the lure of the "forbidden" attracts American teens to marijuana. Zeese added, "It is worth pointing out that the Dutch, when they made marijuana available for purchase, said one reason they were doing so was to make marijuana boring." The Netherlands eliminated the forbidden lure of marijuana usage that Zeese contends attracts American teens, who are in the most rebellious, risk-taking phase of their lives.

According to a *Times Science* article "Drugs in Portugal: Did Decriminalization Work?" decriminalization has been a great success. Following decriminalization, according to a Cato Institute Report, Portugal had the lowest rate of lifetime marijuana use in people over 15 years of age in Europe: 10%. The most comparable figure in America is in people over 12 years of age: 39.8%. In fact, proportionally, more Americans have used cocaine than Portuguese have used marijuana. Might decriminalization of marijuana in the U.S. lead to similar positive effects? Mark Kleiman, director of the drug policy analysis program at UCLA says, "I think we can learn that we should stop being reflexively opposed when someone else does decriminalize and should take seriously the possibility that anti-user enforcement isn't having much influence on our drug consumption."

In the article "The Drug Problem: Europe Tolerance vs. U.S. Criminalization," world-travel expert and author Rick Steves offers some compelling anecdotal evidence. Steves talked with locals, researched European drug policies and visited marijuana "coffee shops" in Amsterdam, getting a close look at the alternative to America's war on drugs. "While the Netherlands' policies are the most liberal," says Steves, "across Europe no one is locked away for discreetly smoking a joint. The priority is on reducing abuse of such hard drugs as heroin and cocaine. The only reference to marijuana I found among the pages of the European Union's drug policy was a reference to counseling for 'problem cannabis use.'"

Meanwhile, according to FBI statistics, in recent years about 40 per cent of the roughly 80,000 annual drug arrests in the U.S. were for marijuana, and the majority of marijuana arrests - 80 per cent - were for possession. Treating marijuana users the same as hard drug users is like treating parking ticket offenders like drunk drivers. It just doesn't make a lot of sense.

Comparisons between states in the U.S. that have decriminalized marijuana usage and those that haven't and between countries where marijuana possession has been decriminalized and the U.S. appear to confirm that decriminalization doesn't lead to increased marijuana usage and that it may even cause a decrease in use. But is the fact that decriminalizing marijuana possession doesn't lead to increased usage enough to warrant changing America's punitive marijuana laws? Perhaps not by itself.

However, consider the other effects if America decriminalized marijuana. The 64,000 drug arrests for marijuana possession in recent years would not have occurred. The millions of dollars and tremendous amount of police time spent on the arrest and prosecution of recreational marijuana users could have been much better spent on reducing the usage of hard drugs such as heroin and cocaine. The millions of taxpayer dollars wasted on incarcerating marijuana users could have been spent on much more important concerns such as reducing violent crime. Our prisons would not be overcrowded with marijuana users, and the continual need to build more prisons would disappear.

It is clear that America's criminal drug law against marijuana usage doesn't work. Marijuana is used as much if not more in states where possession is a felony than in states where users receive a small fine. Despite its punitive marijuana law, marijuana usage in America is significantly higher than in European countries, where no one is arrested for possession. It is also clear that the tremendous amount of time and money spent on arresting and prosecuting marijuana users could be put to much better use, and that America's huge prison population would diminish significantly, as would the great expense to incarcerate marijuana users.

If marijuana usage did in fact lead conclusively to harder drug use, that would be a concern in its decriminalization, but no credible study has ever proven marijuana to be a "gateway" drug to heroin, cocaine, or other dangerous drugs. Apparently, marijuana smokers are no more apt to use cocaine or heroin than beer drinkers, and anyone can see the ludicrousness of criminalizing beer drinking. There are some very good reasons for decriminalizing marijuana usage in America and little reason for maintaining the current unworkable law. If enough states lead the way in decriminalizing marijuana possession, the Federal government will eventually follow. That appears to be the only way that America will one day have a sensible nationwide law that doesn't treat recreational marijuana users like criminals.

Discussion Starters

1. Analyze and evaluate the evidence provided in support of decriminalizing marijuana. How compelling do you find the evidence?
2. The essay does not address the effects of marijuana usage on the health or intellectual performance of marijuana users. Does this weaken the impact of the essay in any way?
3. Compare this pro-legalization essay with the previous anti-legalization essay. Which do you think provided the strongest case for its position and why?

Gun Control Doesn't Work

By Kristie Snyder

Kristie Snyder is the editor of Discerning the Times Digest. In this essay, Snyder makes a case against gun control based on what she considers its negative consequences.

Anyone familiar with statistical analysis knows that statistics can be twisted to say almost anything. Take for example the number of deaths caused by medical mishaps: 120,000 per year in the U.S., which has approximately 700,000 physicians. That's 171 deaths per doctor each year. Compare that with the number of gun owners, which is around 80,000,000, with 1,500 accidental gun deaths each year. That means that the number of accidental, gun related deaths each year per gun owner is .0000188. Nevertheless it would be ludicrous to say that doctors are 9,000 times more dangerous than gun owners. The comparison between gun owners and physicians just makes no sense. So let's look at some statistics that really that do make sense.

Advocates of gun control want us to believe that banning private gun ownership will reduce violent crime. In 1996, in the wake of a mass shooting, the Australian government seized more than 640,000 guns from its citizens. According to the Australian Bureau of Statistics, in the next two years, armed robbery rose by 73%, unarmed robbery by 28%, kidnaping by 38%, assault by 17% and manslaughter by 29%.

Following the trend from down under, the government in the U.K. also imposed new gun controls after a mass shooting. Again violent crime did not decrease. According to the U.S. Justice Department Bureau of Justice Statistics, although the rates of murder and rape are higher in the U.S., England has surpassed us in its rate of robberies, assaults, burglaries and motor vehicle thefts. And the English crime rate has been rising while the U.S. rate has been falling. In 1998 the mugging rate in England was 40% higher than in the U.S.; furthermore, assault and burglary rates were nearly 100% higher in England than in the United States.

Another rate that will strike terror in the heart of every woman is the rate of hot burglaries, which are burglaries that take place when people are home. I think one of my worst nightmares would be to wake up in the dead of night to find an intruder in my room. Yet, most criminals in this country know that breaking in with people home is a good way to get shot. In fact, if someone were to break into my home when we are home, that is exactly what will happen. The hot burglary rate in the U.S. is 13%. However, in countries with strict gun control, such as England and Canada, the hot burglary rate is closer to 50%. The criminals know that their victims, having been rendered helpless by their governments, cannot defend themselves.

If the facts show that gun control legislation does not lower crime rates, then why is there such a push to take guns away from law abiding people? What happened to our Constitutional right to bear arms? The founding fathers knew that a well-armed citizenry would not easily be taken over by a tyrannical government. Those pushing for a global government are keenly aware of this fact as well. To control a people, first you must disarm them.

U.S. Code Title 22 section 2551, which was passed as Public Law 87-297 by President

Kennedy in 1961, lays out the plan to completely disarm both citizens and governments of the world. Section 2552 defines disarmament this way: *"identification, verification, inspection, limitation, control, reduction, or elimination, of armed forces and armaments of all kinds under international agreement including the necessary steps taken under such an agreement to establish an effective system of international control, or to create and strengthen international organizations for the maintenance of peace."*

Every president since Kennedy has worked to implement this agenda. The United States has been systematically emasculating its military for more than a decade. The Russians and Chinese are supposed to be reducing their military in the same manner, but as DTT has previously reported, that is just not happening. The final outcome of this plan is that the armies of the world will be centrally controlled, becoming a global force, and that only the military will be armed. Our national sovereignty has been traitorously undermined.

Gun control finds its greatest success in keeping guns out of the hands of ordinary, law abiding citizens. The government will always be armed. And the criminal mind will always find a means of acquiring weapons. That will leave you and me stuck somewhere in the middle between criminal corruption and government tyranny. It's getting harder and harder to tell the difference.

Discussion Starters

1. Analyze and evaluate the evidence provided against gun control. How effectively does the essay makes its case?
2. What, if any, arguments in favor of gun control are not addressed in the essay? Does this lessen the essay's impact in any way?
3. What is your opinion on gun control? What impact, if any, did the essay have on your viewpoint?

Gun Control and Metal Detectors: The Failure of Congress

By Larry Womack

Larry Womack is the founder of 1450 Media and former Associate News Editor of the Huffington Post. In this essay, Womack makes a case for stronger gun control laws in the U.S. and the abject failure of Congress to take action.

The last major gun control effort passed by Congress was the 1994 Federal Assault Weapons Ban, a largely toothless effort it has since allowed to expire. Since that came and went, there have been more firearm massacres in the U.S. than we care to count. Through all of those, the federal government has sat silently by while states passed laws allowing people to carry guns onto playgrounds and into movie theaters, schools, bars and churches. Vermont even allows 16-year-olds to purchase and carry concealed handguns legally, without so much as a permit. So long as that 16-year-old isn't carrying it into a bar or *R-rated* movie, of course.

Or into the U.S. Capitol. Members of Congress, it seems, are very much in favor of controlling the flow of deadly weapons into *their* workplace. And by "controlling," I mean completely barring the entry of guns into the building—unless they are worn by someone paid to protect them. If you or I visit the U.S. Capitol or any congressional office building, we can expect to pass through a metal detector.

In fact, it's almost as if the U.S. Congress believes that someone without a gun would have a harder time murdering people. The city surrounding their place of work banned handguns in 1975, too (I'm going to guess that the reason was Virginia), but the courts overturned that law in 2007. Still, you can rest assured that while they're hard at work not doing anything about the flow of guns into your workplace, or your children's school, your local movie theater or even your house of worship, your legislators will be well protected from the threat of gun violence. Unless they happen to be working outside your local supermarket that day, of course.

It's easy to see why they would be so concerned for their own safety. The United States currently has, by a wide margin, the highest number of gun-related deaths of any highly developed country. In fact, our number of firearm-related deaths is nearly three times that of any other nation ranked as "very high" on the Human Development Index. (Or perhaps merely 40 percent higher—we'll get to that soon.) Just three nations share the distinction of being ranked "very high" in human development *and* having unusually high rates of gun-related death: The United States, Canada and Switzerland. You might also note that since the mass shooting on Friday, Switzerland's rate of gun-related death (as listed on Wikipedia) has been updated to a number that cut its previously listed level in half.

The timing is no coincidence. The sudden interest in controlling information about gun violence in Switzerland probably has something to do with the fact that opponents of gun control actually point to Switzerland as evidence that gun proliferation prevents crime. Because of the way its militia is organized, nearly every Swiss household has a gun. Switzerland offers the second highest quality of life on planet Earth. Just 3% of its population is working poor and a mere 3.3 percent is dependent on some form of social welfare. So, opponents of gun control are asking us to believe that the easy availability of guns is what's *keeping crime down*...in an otherwise idyllic nation with none of the markers we associate with violent crime that still *somehow* manages to generate *three and a half to seven times* the gun-related deaths of, say, Ireland. Makes perfect sense, right? Guns for all! Frankly, it doesn't matter which number is correct. Both stink.

It turns out that guns, outside the hands of the military or law enforcement, just aren't any good at preventing crime and, in fact, their presence is associated with an increase in the likelihood of tragedy. Stepping briefly outside the statistics and into the realm of anecdote, we might be wise to remember that access to seven firearms did nothing to save Kassandra Perkins. Access to one, however, was enough to facilitate the murder of Phil Hartman in a moment of rage. That is, it seems, how guns too often equalize power between victim and perpetrator.

That's probably because guns aren't *made* to shield you from someone else's bullets. Nor are they made to deter, catch or frighten criminals. Guns are made to kill. Some are designed to kill one thing at a time. In the right hands, these can be pretty useful, because some Americans live in areas in which they face genuine threats from dangerous animals. Even more live in areas where there used to be dangerous animals which have now been driven out by man. That removal of natural predators leaves some animals (like deer) to multiply unchecked and, without the relatively more humane option of allowing hunters to fill that void, can leave entire populations literally starving in the streets come winter. Some people in this country need these guns.

Some also just enjoy them, because they can be used for other things, too—like punching holes in far away objects, relieving stress and making you feel like a big man. Most people in favor of gun control have no problem with people owning these.

Unfortunately, there are also guns and magazines designed for killing *many* things quickly and easily. The availability of these weapons outside of the military is something that should bother any sane person a great deal. It doesn't seem to bother our representatives on the other side of the metal detector so much, but I assure you that some of us are pretty concerned.

An AR-15 is "just a tool," they say as if it were designed for gardening, rather than killing as many people as possible, in as little time as possible, with as little effort as possible. "Cars kill people, too," they say, as if the efficient extermination of humans is exactly what a Ford Focus was designed for, or you didn't need a license to operate and a registration to own one. "Guns don't kill people, people kill people," they might even say. Like how high speed rail doesn't move people from central to southern China in under three hours, people move people from central to southern China in under three hours. It turns out that having a device specifically designed to do something you could not otherwise achieve *kinda helps* when you have an urge to do that thing.

And then there is, "criminals will just find another way to do it," which, well, *is total baloney*. (There will be more on that later.) Eventually, people resort to, "If we start banning guns, they'll ban everything! We will have *no freedom*!" Because responsible levels of gun control will make us just like the totalitarian state of...*almost every other free, developed society on planet Earth*!

What's especially painful about the slippery slope fallacy is that it's being employed by people who seem fairly oblivious to the fact that they are living in a nation that bans pretty much any object designed to perform an illegal task that *does not happen to also be a gun*. If the server at your favorite restaurant legally owns a device that can store your credit card information, it is an outrage. If he has one that could kill you and your entire family in a matter of seconds, why that is *freedom*.

And, finally, there is the truly absurd suggestion that, "If guns are outlawed, only outlaws will have guns." (Oh no! That means only outlaws have hand grenades!) The people who parrot this ask us to believe that the twenty-year-old suburbanites who tend to carry out these mass shootings have easy access to black market gun runners and that it is simply an astonishing coincidence that the wealthy, industrialized nations with the lowest levels of gun violence also happen to be the ones that most tightly control the ownership and operation of firearms.

The left is nearly as bad when it comes to swallowing the lie that limiting availability is not a staggeringly obvious solution. Michael Moore—who I am quite certain is very much in favor of reasonable gun control—made Canada his model of responsible gun ownership in *Bowling for Columbine*. Yet, you are nearly five times more likely to die of a gunshot wound in Canada than in the UK. This is what we are to aspire to? Thanks, but no thanks. (To be fair, I haven't seen this film in years and he may well have pointed out that Canada's death-by-gun numbers are pretty atrocious, too.)

If we are to believe that the correlation between strict gun control and low rates of gun violence in other industrialized nations really is some sort of incredible coincidence, events in Australia must be taken for nothing short of a miracle. In the 18 years prior to 1996 gun control reforms, that nation saw 13 mass shootings. In the 16 since, they have seen one—which usually isn't even counted, because the shooter was only able to kill two people before he had to stop to reload (because: gun control) and was apprehended. That wouldn't even count as a mass shooting in America. Still, after that incident, Australia reviewed and tightened its gun laws again. Ten years later, there hasn't been another.

Before the gun fetishists start freaking out (as if they hadn't already): it didn't take some sort of total authoritarian prohibition in Australia to achieve this kind of result. It just took common sense gun laws. In fact, there are more guns in Australia now than there were before the 1996 reforms. But, magazine size is limited, weapons designed for war zones can only be owned (in a non-operational state) by collectors, and people who own any gun need to be over 18, have a license and keep them stored safely. Exactly what part of that sounds so unreasonable to the average sportsman?

And if you're a gun enthusiast still clinging to the based-on-nothing belief that people will just find other ways of committing gun homicides, here's a little something more from our friends down under. After the introduction of gun laws, a significant downward trend was evident in total homicides, and the ratio of pre-law to post-law trends differed statistically from "no effect" ($p = 0.01$, table 33).). We conclude that the data do not support any homicide method substitution hypothesis. In short: when gun homicides declined, all homicides declined. People did not simply commit them another way.

I actually disagree when they conclude that *no* method substitution occurs, however. There is some evidence to suggest that people who want to go on a violent rampage do *try* to find other ways when guns are not available. Of course these people do not, in fact, slyly poison 20 school children when a Glock isn't handy or mix up some kind of crazy Joker laughing gas. When guns aren't handy, they seem to use the next best thing: a knife. We've seen this over and over again in China lately. The major difference is that, even when a knife-wielding maniac is able to reach dozens of victims, often every single victim survives. These events aren't showing up as homicides perhaps because homicide wasn't achieved, because it wasn't as easily achievable. Ever hear that expression about taking a knife to a gunfight? It exists for a reason.

Still, too many Americans—including our lawmakers—insist on remaining astonishingly obstinate when it comes to any suggestion of responsible firearm regulations. Instead of common sense solutions, they repeat bizarre myths and offer idiotic distractions. It's as if every time a white suburbanite picks up a gun, half the country suddenly becomes your crazy grandfather, claiming that the same violent films and video games that kids in Australia, Ireland and Britain are watching and playing are somehow compelling *only Americans* to go on shooting sprees. It's an unique idea, to say the least. (Let's not even *talk* about what they're watching in Japan, which has—through strict gun control efforts—virtually eliminated gun violence altogether.)

Not that it would matter if these things *were* somehow magically compelling only Americans to shoot up their local malls. Contrary to popular belief, sometimes the most effective solution is not, actually, attempting to remove every underlying motive or eliminate every contributing factor. Sometimes it's just using the most effective solution at your disposal. What I am saying is that by far the most effective, proven solution at our disposal is a major, common sense reform of our gun control laws, and that there is no good reason not to do it.

So I have a challenge for members of Congress: if you truly believe that gun proliferation, not gun control, is the best way to combat gun violence, remove the metal detectors from the Capitol entrances and don't bring them back until you've changed your mind. If criminals will just find another way, they're nothing but a waste of taxpayer money and visitor time. If gun control gives criminals all the power, then those metal detectors are threats to the safety of everyone behind them. If reasonable, common sense security measures are violations of our civil liberties, then those metal detectors, located at the heart of our democracy, are an affront to the personal liberty of every American.

After all, it seems only right that members of Congress should be as safe as the average child they represent.

Discussion Starters

1. Analyze and evaluate the arguments presented in support of gun control. How compelling do you find them?
2. Evaluate how well the essay refutes each argument that opponents of gun control use. Which do you find more sensible: the refutations or the arguments?
3. Which essay do you think made the best case for its position on gun control and why? What is your own opinion on gun control? Did either essay influence your viewpoint?

Executioner's New Song

By Justine Sharrock

Justine Sharrock is a freelance writer, West Coast editor of BuzzFeed, and author of the book Tortured: When Good Soldiers Do Bad Things. In this essay, Sharrock reveals that former San Quentin warden Jeanne Woodford, who was in charge of all of California's executions, was always against the death penalty, why she opposes it, and her new role as a spokesperson for Death Penalty Focus, an anti-capital punishment organization.

Every morning, Jeanne Woodford would wake up at dawn and think over her to-do list for what she calls the "planning process to murder someone." As the San Quentin warden from 1999 to 2004, she was in charge of all of California's executions.

It was her job to meet with the death row inmates—many of whom she had gotten to know over her twenty-six years at the prison—during their last days. She made sure they were able to call their families and their lawyers. She listened to them talk about their lives and childhoods. And she answered their questions: "Will it hurt?" and "What will happen to my body?"

"I really brought the pain of the job home with me," says Woodford, now fifty-eight. "Reading through a file, I would break down crying because I can't even imagine how any human being can do that to another human being. There were four or five years when I was a single parent, when I didn't turn the lights off at my house at night."

Families of the victim had to be prepared for watching the executions, too. Some resisted but their lawyers insisted; otherwise the governor could doubt their seriousness and grant clemency. Some asked, "Will this make me feel better?" She knew the answer was most likely no, but all she'd say was, "I don't know."

Some of the other corrections officers involved in the executions would seek religious counseling. They never discussed their feelings about what it was like to help kill someone on the job, but Woodford says that afterward they would say to each other, "Did we really make anyone safer?"

During her thirty years in corrections—climbing the ranks from San Quentin guard to the prison's first female warden, and eventually leading the California Department of Corrections—Woodford was silently but adamantly opposed to the death penalty. She was renowned for a progressive approach to criminal justice reform, stressing rehabilitation, reentry, and prevention, but she never addressed capital punishment.

That changed last May, when she became the executive director of Death Penalty Focus, one of the nation's largest anti-death-penalty advocacy groups. "I don't want anyone to think that I took this job because in my mind it makes up for everything I've been involved in," she says. "I don't want to be let off the hook so easily. But I do think that it will help end the death penalty because I have seen it from every point of view, and I can articulate it in ways that other people can't."

"Having a conversation about the death penalty is very different when you aren't responsible for doing it," says Roderick Hickman, the secretary of the California Department of Corrections while Woodford was warden. "A lot of different people say, 'I'm for it.' I say, 'OK, then you come on down and execute them.' " He says being a warden at San Quentin is an exercise of applied ethics: "Everyone involved has some sort of personal ethical dilemma that they have to resolve within themselves."

Woodford has the potential to become one of the most powerful voices in the abolition movement, given her unique position.

"This isn't a bleeding heart do-gooder," says Elaine Leeder, dean of Sonoma State's School of Social Sciences, who has worked with lifers at San Quentin. "She has actually done these painful things like killing someone for the state. Having lived it and walked it means she will have a great impact."

"We have been on the outside looking in, and she provides inside connections," says Mike Farrell, the former *M.A.S.H.* star who is president of Death Penalty Focus. "We have had governors and former wardens we could draw on before, but never one saying, 'I'm not just with you, but I want to be part of the organization.' "

I met Woodford in Death Penalty Focus's San Francisco office, which is so cramped we had to move around the folding chairs in order to close the door. To the constant bing of her overflowing e-mail inbox, Woodford made the usual arguments against the death penalty: the exorbitant cost, the fact it isn't a true deterrent, the wrongful executions. But she proceeded to make new ones related to her own experience.

"Very few people really understand how complicated death row issues are," she says. Her first claim is that the inmates she executed had changed a lot since they had committed their crimes. "I knew that at the point of execution they weren't the same person," she says. Second, "they clearly can't make it in society, but within the prison they weren't a problem; they weren't a threat to anyone," she says. And third, criminologists could have studied these inmates: "Some were mentally ill, low-functioning individuals who we should want to know a lot more about if we ever want to figure out how to prevent these kinds of horrific crimes."

Soon after starting the job, Woodford reread a book by a former San Quentin warden, Clinton T. Duffy. The book's title, 88 Men and 2 Women, comes from the number of executions that happened under Duffy's watch. Duffy is a famed prison reformer, having ended corporal punishment and having established vocational training, an Alcoholics Anonymous program, and a prison newspaper. He also protested the death penalty while still at the helm.

"It must have been hard for his staff to know they were doing something the leadership didn't believe in," says Woodford. "I did what I thought was right for the staff. I told myself they are looking to you and you can't break down or talk about whether it's right or wrong."

When I pressed Woodford on why she didn't refuse to carry out the executions, she responded, "I was just a body. If I left, another body would be brought in to carry it out. When you are in corrections, you are really trained not to think about the sentences of people and that you aren't the judge of anybody." Instead, she tried to bring a level of dignity and empathy to the process. "Maybe it was my rationale, but I tried to be kind to everyone, and told myself that was important," she says.

Under her watch, San Quentin put four men to death:

Mannie Babbit, whose brother had testified against him with the promise that Mannie wouldn't get the death penalty, was executed in May 1999;

Darrell Rich, a.k.a. the Hilltop Rapist, whose last word was "peace," was killed in 2000; Stephen Wayne Anderson was executed in 2002 for murdering an eighty-one-year-old at close range during a burglary;

Robert Lee Massie volunteered to be executed in 2001 for a murder he committed while on parole in the 1970s. Woodford, who knew Massie well and had seen him transform himself into a better person, says his volunteering actually made it harder since he had given up all the will to fight.

"I don't consider myself a murderer," says Woodford. "There are others who probably would, but I do view myself as someone who was asked to carry out a law that really is so inappropriate for our society and so inconsistent with our values as a nation."

Woodford followed in Duffy's footsteps by bringing extensive rehabilitation and reform programs to San Quentin. It was famous for its 3,000 volunteers who helped run prison programs, ranging from an inmate-run newspaper to sports teams, gardening, yoga, creative writing, art, and parenting classes. Inmates could earn their GED and college degrees. Even the 600-odd inmates on death row who were only allowed out of their cells for ten hours a week for exercise in cage-like pens were able to take correspondence courses.

"We send people away to prison for indeterminate sentences and expect nothing from them other than to do their time," says Woodford. "People could be working, giving back in some way, however little it is, to our society and in other ways paying restitution to the victims. A system that doesn't have accountability for people to change and to improve who they are is just unacceptable."

When she started, Death Penalty Focus had forty-seven current and former judges, prosecutors, police, and corrections officers sign a petition against the death penalty. With her connections, Woodford has brought that number up to more than 100, including Gil Garcetti, the former Los Angeles district attorney.

She has worked out better than Death Penalty Focus could have imagined. At her job interview, one board member asked her how she would feel about attending a vigil outside of San Quentin if there were another execution. According to Farrell, she said she was worried about being in an adversarial position with people she has known and liked over the years. But after giving it a lot of thought, Woodford decided she could help keep protesters respectful, and reach sympathizers among those who work inside the prison walls. Farrell praises Woodford's contributions: "Her willingness to stand up in such a public way and help strategize is a magnificent lesson for everyone about humanity on both sides of the issue."

Discussion Starters

1. How did being responsible for carrying out death sentences influence Woodford's viewpoint on the death penalty? How, according to the essay, does the perspective of those involved with the actual executions differ from other people? Should we care about their perspective?

2. Evaluate the arguments Woodford makes against the death penalty. How effectively do they make her case?

3. What is your opinion about the death penalty? Did the essay influence your viewpoint in any way?

If Same-sex 'Marriage' is Legalized, Why Not Polygamy?

By Michael Foust

Michael Foust is a writer and associate editor for Baptist Press. In this essay, Foust argues against the legalization of same-sex marriage by comparing it to the legalization of polygamy.

Late last year, months after the landmark Lawrence v. Texas decision striking down anti-sodomy laws, two Utah polygamists filed suit in state court, asking that their relationships with multiple wives be validated by the government. Laws against polygamy, they said, are unconstitutional.

"Everyone should be free unless there's a compelling state interest that you shouldn't be," John Bucher, one of the lawyers, told The Salt Lake Tribune. "The state is not able to show that there's such an evil to polygamy that it should be prohibited."

As the nation continues to debate same-sex "marriage," some have begun examining the logical extension of its legalization. If the legal benefits of marriage are awarded to homosexual men, then why aren't they also given to, say, three polygamists?

"There isn't a single argument in favor of same-sex marriage that isn't also an argument in favor of polygamy –- people have a right to marry who they love, these relationships already exist...we have no right to deny the children of their protections," columnist Maggie Gallagher, an outspoken supporter of a federal marriage amendment, told Baptist Press.

Jennifer Marshall, director of domestic policy studies at The Heritage Foundation, said she sees no "logical stopping point" if same-sex "marriage" is legalized. "This is the dissolution of the parameters around marriage," she said. "You'd be hard-pressed to say, 'Why not any other kind of arrangement?'"

Conservatives and traditionalists say the debate over same-sex "marriage" is the result of marriage being separated from its religious roots and from procreation. If marriage is not tied to childbearing, traditionalists warn it literally could mean anything.

In its landmark ruling on same-sex "marriage" last year, the Massachusetts high court ruled that marriage's purpose is not procreation, but instead the commitment of two people to one another for life. That argument troubles Gallagher, who asserts that government benefits are awarded to married couples because they, in turn, benefit society by raising the next generation of adults. "If marriage is only about private love, why is the government involved?" she asked, rhetorically. "Why does the government care? Why is the [government] involved if you have this view of marriage that's just kind of a private, emotional lover's vow? But for some reason, you record it in law and it changes your tax status."

The issue of polygamy has been one that has frequently stumped supporters of same-sex "marriage." During a January debate, University of Louisville law professor Sam Marcosson, a supporter of homosexual "marriage," called the polygamy argument a "red herring." Candice Gingrich, a homosexual activist, made the same assertion during an appearance on Sean Hannity's radio program.

Last November on ABC's "This Week," conservative columnist George Will asked two homosexual men—Rep. Barney Frank and columnist Andrew Sullivan—to give him a "principle" as to why polygamy should be banned in light of the Lawrence and Massachusetts decisions.

"Some distinctions are hard to draw," Frank answered. "But the difference between two people and three people is almost always clear. It is responsible for a society to say, 'Look, you can do what you want personally. If three people want to have sex together, that's not against the law. But when it comes to being married and institutionalizing these legal relationships with regards to the ownership of property and children, then we believe a three-way operation is likely to cause difficulty, friction with the children.'" Sullivan responded: "I don't want the right to marry anyone. I just want the right to marry someone."

Sociologist Glenn Stanton of Focus on the Family said one reason same-sex "marriage" has made advances is because marriage itself is viewed as a means of receiving legal benefits. "If we have to honor the relationship that two guys have, then we have to honor the relationship that a guy and his three wives have," Stanton said. "We have to honor the relationship that two heterosexual single moms have. If we are going to offer health benefits and government benefits to other configurations, why keep anybody from joining together and saying, 'Our relationship is significant, too,' regardless of what that relationship is?" Gallagher said there is "no logical reason" for not awarding benefits to polygamists if they are given to same-sex couples.

The irony of the current debate is that polygamy is rooted far deeper in human history—and is accepted in far more cultures today—than is same-sex "marriage." Polygamy once dominated the Mormon church, and Utah was not given statehood until it outlawed the practice. The church officially disavows it now, although estimates say that up to 100,000 people in the West still practice it. Worldwide, polygamy is legal in some countries and is common among Muslims. Islam's founder, Muhammad, had multiple wives.

The United Nations allows employees to divide their benefits among multiple wives, as long as they come from a country where polygamy is practiced, The Washington Post reported.

Seeing the logical extension from same-sex "marriage," some in America have begun to argue for the legalization of polygamy, too. Anthropologist Robert Myers wrote in a USA Today editorial March 14 that the United States has a "narrow view" of marriage. "[W]e will allow marriage to any number of partners, as long as it is to only one at a time," he wrote.

Gallagher said she believes that polygamy is less of a departure from traditional marriage than is same-sex "marriage." After all, she said, it involves procreation. Of course, Gallagher and other traditionalists aren't arguing for polygamy's legalization. They're showing the logical inconsistency of same-sex "marriage."

"The argument in the 19th century that Congress made is that polygamy is associated with despotic forms of government, because basically the most powerful men start hogging all the women," Gallagher said. "There is something to be said for that. I think it's also associated with less investment by fathers in their children. Some children get subordinated in polygamous marriage systems. The attention of the father and the family tends to focus on the heir."

Other arguments against polygamy include an increase in child and spousal abuse, welfare fraud and forced marriages. Christians say Scripture has an answer for both polygamy and homosexual "marriage"—in Matthew 19 Christ points to Old Testament law as limiting marriage to one man, one woman.

Marshall, of The Heritage Foundation, said the onus must be placed on same-sex "marriage" supporters as to why marriage should not include polygamy and other forms of relationships. The polygamy question is not a "red herring," she said. "It seems to me," she said, "that those who are trying to argue for the redefinition of marriage should have to answer the question, 'What is the logical stopping point after this?' It seems to me that that question should be turned around, and the ones who are answering it should be the ones who are proposing the redefinition of marriage."

Discussion Starters

1. The essay argues that if same-sex marriage is legalized, it opens the door for the legalization of other marriage "arrangements" such as polygamy. Do you agree with the basic premise? Why?
2. The essay draws a comparison between same-sex marriage and polygamy. Do you find this a legitimate comparison? Why?
3. What is your viewpoint on the legalization of same-sex marriage? Did the essay influence your viewpoint in any way?

Sentencing Children As Adults

By Terence Gorski

Terence Gorski, an internationally recognized expert on substance abuse, mental health, violence and crime, has published several books including Straight Talk about Addiction and Freedom from Suffering. In this essay, Gorski argues against trying and sentencing minors as adults for violent crimes, contending that it does more harm than good.

Should children and adolescents who have not reached legal age be sentenced as adults when they commit serious crimes such as murder? It is my position that they should not. Here's why.

According to Amnesty International, a human rights watch dog organization, the United States is the only western democracy that sends youthful offenders to adult court and sentences them to adult prisons. According to amnesty international the imprisonment of youthful offenders in adult prisons violates United States international treaty obligations prohibiting cruel and inhumane treatment of children and adolescents.

Is this an unwarranted or extreme position to take? I don't believe that it is. Most youthful offenders will be physically and/or sexually assaulted within seventy-two hours of admission to adult correctional facilities. Such abuse will continue to occur on a regular basis for the duration of their incarceration. The effects of this abuse are horrific and include suicides, suicide attempts, severe personality damage, and the development of severe and permanent psychiatric symptoms. These effects make youthful offenders sentenced as adults more dangerous, not less. Our willingness to do this to our children sends a strong message that the level of moral development of elected officials, judges, prosecutors and the general public is rapidly and dangerously declining.

We need to ask ourselves an important question: *Are we the kind of people who are capable of inflicting cruel and inhumane punishment upon our children and adolescents?*

As a nation, we answered that question decades ago with an emphatic no. At that time we recognized that most kids deserve a second chance and can turn their lives around with proper no-nonsense treatment in rehabilitation oriented juvenile correction centers. We backed up our answer up by developing a Juvenile Justice System that protects kids from cruel and inhumane punishment while providing rehabilitation, and teaching the skills necessary to become a productive member of society.

We did all this because it's the right thing to do. We did it because to do less would have been beneath us as one of the most moral nations in the civilized world.

We built our Juvenile Justice System around three critical principles:

- It is wrong to hold children and adolescents who have not reached legal age to adult standards. They are developmentally immature and often unclear about the nature of right and wrong and without proper adult supervision can have problems with judgment and impulse control causing them to act out impulsively without forethought.
- With appropriate treatment most children who commit crimes, even the most violent crimes, can be rehabilitated and become responsible adults.

- A moral society feels obligated to give kids a second chance whenever possible by having a Juvenile Justice System designed to help kids change rather than punish them for past offenses.

Our Juvenile justice system is based upon the recognition that moral societies value their children and seek to help rather than hurt, treat rather than punish, and rehabilitate rather than destroy.

Of course, not all youthful offenders can be rehabilitated. Some pose a real and present danger and need to be segregated from society. The period of confinement, however, should be designed to give youthful offenders a chance to learn, grow, and change. If long-term protective segregation is required, it should be done in adolescent correctional facilities which protect the children from harm.

It is important to remember that *punishment does not work*. The threat of punishment is an ineffective deterrent to crime, especially for children and adolescents. Punishment is a failed a strategy for changing behavior, teaching new skills, or developing new and more positive attitudes and beliefs. The only justification for inflicting harsh punishment is to deliver vengeance in accord with the Old Testament standard of an eye-for-an-eye.

Loved ones of victims may feel justified in crying out for vengeance. The result is tragic. Vengeance does not relieve the grief and loss. It also instills a sense of inner conflict and guilt. On a deep level most human beings intuitively know that vengeance breeds more vengeance and violence breeds more violence. When people mature to higher levels of moral development they recognize the obligation to break the cycle of vengeance and retribution.

The following two children are both victims. One is a victim of lethal violence inflicted by a twelve year old playmate. The other is a victim of a legal system that is rapidly declining into Old Testament morality or retribution.

Tiffany Eunick, age 6, was the victim of violence perpetrated by an unsupervised twelve year old, Lionel Tate. Lionel thought he was playing when he emulated the moves and tactics of the professional wrestlers who were his heroes and role models. He watched professional wrestling week after week. He witnessed hundreds if not thousands of savagely brutal acts perpetrated by professionally wrestlers assuming the personas of theatrical psychopaths. He watched as they savagely body slammed, knee-dropped, and kicked each other.

In his immaturity, he couldn't see that it was all a show. He had inadequate adult supervision. There was no one to point out the dangerousness and immorality of the violent displays he was witnessing. There was no adult present to impress upon his immature mind the dangerous of using such savage tactics on others.

Lionel, an immature 12 year old, assumed he could do to other kids what these heroic wrestlers did to each other. He assumed the outcome would be the same – no one would really get hurt. Tragically, the showmanship of professional wrestlers can become lethal when inflicted by one child upon another. Thinking he was playing, Lionel body-slammed, head kicked, and knee dropped Tiffany. It was over quickly. Lionel was shocked and traumatized to see that he killed Tiffany.

Is Lionel a hopeless psychopath who should be locked away for the rest of his life? He doesn't appear to be. Will throwing away Lionel's life bring back Tiffany or sooth the grief of her parents and friends? Probably not. Will Lionel be helped to become a better person as a result of his life-long imprisonment? Definitely not. He will be physically and sexually abused and psychiatrically damaged in deep and profound ways by his prison experiences. There is a strong possibility he will attempt suicide to try and escape the torturous consequences of his imprisonment.

So why are we as a nation allowing this to happen? Part of the reason is because our adolescent treatment professionals, the experts trained and educated to know better, are standing silently on the sidelines. The clinical professionals who are obligated to advocate for our youth and to protect our juvenile justice system from destruction have failed to act decisively and effectively. As a result the safety of all children is progressively going at risk.

How many children need to be tried, convicted, and imprisoned in adult facilities before it becomes wrong? How many children must be destroyed by a criminal justice system going out of control before we do something?

Discussion Starters

1. Evaluate the arguments presented in the essay against the incarceration of juveniles as adults. How compelling do you find them?
2. Is the example in the essay involving Tiffany and Lionel typical of the type of violence that juveniles are tried for as adults? How strongly does the example support Gorski's viewpoint?
3. If adult prisons have such devastating effects on juvenile offenders, why do you think most states have legalized the practice? What is your opinion on trying juveniles who commit violent crimes as adults? Did the essay influence your viewpoint in any way?

Back to 18? Reconsidering the Minimum Drinking Age

By Radley Balco

Radley Balco is a senior writer and investigative reporter for the Huffington Post. In this essay, Balco presents arguments supporting changing the minimum drinking age to 18, citing the advocacy of a number of college educators.

It's been almost 30 years that America has had a minimum federal drinking age. The policy began to gain momentum in the early 1980s, when the increasingly influential Mothers Against Drunk Driving added the federal minimum drinking age to its legislative agenda. By 1984, it had won over a majority of the Congress. President Reagan initially opposed the law on federalism grounds but eventually was persuaded by his transportation secretary at the time, Elizabeth Dole.

Over the next three years every state had to choose between adopting the standard or forgoing federal highway funding; most complied. A few held out until the deadline, including Vermont, which fought the law all the way to the U.S. Supreme Court (and lost).

Thirty years later, the drawbacks of the legislation are the same as they were when it was passed. The first is that the age set by the legislation is basically arbitrary. The U.S. has the highest drinking age in the world (a title it shares with Indonesia, Mongolia, Palau). The vast majority of the rest of the world sets the minimum age at 17 or 16 or has no minimum age at all.

Supporters of the federal minimum argue that the human brain continues developing until at least the age of 21. Alcohol expert Dr. David Hanson of the State University of New York at Potsdam argues such assertions reek of junk science. They're extrapolated from a study on lab mice, he explains, as well as from a small sample of actual humans already dependent on alcohol or drugs. Neither is enough to make broad proclamations about the entire population.

If the research on brain development is true, the U.S. seems to be the only country to have caught on to it. Oddly enough, high school students in much of the rest of the developed world—where lower drinking ages and laxer enforcement reign—do considerably better than U.S. students on standardized tests.

The second drawback of the federal drinking age is that it set the stage for tying federal mandates to highway funds, enabling Congress to meddle in all sorts of state and local affairs it has no business attempting to regulate—so long as it can make a tortured argument about highway safety. Efforts to set national speed limits, seat belt laws, motorcycle helmet laws and set a national blood-alcohol standard for DWI cases have rested on the premise that the federal government can blackmail the states with threats to cut off funding.

The final drawback is pretty straightforward: It makes little sense that America considers an 18-year-old mature enough to marry, to sign a contract, to vote and to fight and die for his country, but not mature enough to decide whether or not to have a beer.

So for all of those drawbacks, has the law worked? Supporters seem to think so. Their primary argument is the dramatic drop in the number of alcohol-related traffic fatalities since the minimum age first passed Congress in 1984. They also cite relative drops in the percentage of underage drinkers before and after the law went into effect.

But a new chorus is emerging to challenge the conventional wisdom. The most vocal of these critics is John McCardell Jr., the former president of Middlebury College in Vermont. McCardell's experience in higher education revealed to him that the federal age simply wasn't working. It may have negligibly reduced total underage consumption, but those who did consume were much more likely to do so behind closed doors and to drink to excess in the short time they had access to alcohol. McCardell started the organization Choose Responsibility, which advocates moving the drinking age back to 18.

McCardell explains that the drop in highway fatalities often cited by supporters of the 21 minimum age actually began in the late 1970s, well before the federal drinking age set in. What's more, McCardell recently explained in an online chat for the "Chronicle of Higher Education," the drop is better explained by safer and better built cars, increased seat belt use and increasing awareness of the dangers of drunken driving than in a federal standard. The age at highest risk for an alcohol-related auto fatality is 21, followed by 22 and 23, an indication that delaying first exposure to alcohol until young adults are away from home may not be the best way to introduce them to drink.

McCardell isn't alone. Kenyon College President S. Georgia Nugent has expressed frustration with the law, particularly in 2005 after the alcohol-related death of a Kenyon student. And former *Time* magazine editor and higher ed reporter Barrett Seaman echoed McCardell's concerns in 2005. The period since the 21 minimum drinking age took effect has been "marked by a shift from beer to hard liquor," Seaman wrote in Time, "consumed not in large social settings, since that was now illegal, but furtively and dangerously in students' residences. In my reporting at colleges around the country, I did not meet any presidents or deans who felt the 21-year age minimum helps their efforts to curb the abuse of alcohol on their campuses."

The federal drinking age has become somewhat sacrosanct among public health activists, who've consistently relied on the accident data to quell debate over the law's merits. They've moved on to other battles, such as scolding parents for giving their own kids a taste of alcohol before the age of 21 or attacking the alcohol industry for advertising during sporting events or in magazines aimed at adults that are sometimes read by people under the age of 21.

But after 30 years, perhaps it's time to take a second look—a sound, sober (pardon the pun), science-based look—at the law's costs and benefits, as well as the sound philosophical objections to it.

McCardell provides a welcome voice in a debate too often dominated by hysterics. But beyond McCardell, Congress should really consider abandoning the federal minimum altogether, or at least the federal funding blackmail that gives it teeth. State and local governments are far better at passing laws that reflect the values, morals and habits of their communities.

Discussion Starters

1. Evaluate the arguments in the essay supporting lowering the drinking age to 18. How strongly do they make the case?
2. Evaluate the counter arguments in the essay that address the main points of support for keeping the drinking age at 21. How successfully does the essay refute those points?
3. What is your own opinion on lowering the drinking age to 18? How does your experience and the experience of others inform your opinion?

VII. Health and Well-Being

A Healthy Bottom Line: Profits or People?

By Claire Andre and Manuel Velasquez

Andre and Velasquez are professors and program directors at the Markkula Center for Applied Ethics At Santa Clara University. In this essay, the authors compare the practices of for-profit and non-profit health care facilities and the arguments supporting the advantages of each, and raise questions regarding whether the health care profession has a moral obligation to provide affordable health care for all.

In Alameda County, a private hospital turned away a woman in labor because the hospital's computer showed that she didn't have insurance. Hours later, her baby was born dead in a county hospital.

In San Bernardino, a hospital surgeon sent a patient who had been stabbed in the heart to a county medical center after examining him and declaring his condition stable. The patient arrived at the county medical center moribund, suffered a cardiac arrest, and died.

These two hospitals shifted these patients to county facilities not for medical reasons, but for economic ones—the receiving hospitals feared they wouldn't be paid for treating the patient. These patients simply weren't "good business."

With little public warning, a concern for "good business" has moved to the heart of health care, a sector once relatively insulated from the pursuit of profit that drives the rest of the U.S. economy. Throughout our history, medical institutions have largely been "charitable," nonprofit establishments existing primarily to serve the community. But during the past 20 years, the number of for-profit health care facilities, ranging from national hospital chains affiliated with major academic institutions to local dialysis centers, has grown at a rate exceeding even that of the computer industry.

The ethical implications of the growing commercialization of health care have become a matter of heated controversy. Those favoring the trend toward health care for profit claim that an increased role for entrepreneurs and competition in the delivery of health care will result in a more efficient and effective health care system. For others, the pursuit of profit is antithetical to the values central to medicine.

Opposing the commercialization of health care are those who base their arguments on considerations of justice. They argue that a society as wealthy as ours has a moral obligation to meet the basic needs of all of its members. Every American, rich or poor, should have access to the health care he or she needs. The escalating costs of care and a growing unwillingness of insurance companies to cover these costs, along with government budget cutbacks, have severely restricted access to health care for the poor, the aged, and those with catastrophic health problems. The rise of for-profit health care only exacerbates the growing problem of access to care.

Studies show that the growth of for-profits decreases the availability of health care for "unprofitable" patients. Traditionally, non-profits have financed care for the poor by overcharging paying patients to subsidize services for the poor. For-profits, by refusing to serve nonpaying patients while at the same time taking a great share of paying patients, leave non-profits with more of the poor to serve but with fewer paying patients to subsidize their care. Furthermore, by serving only profitable patients and offering only profitable services, for profits are able to generate high revenues, which enables them to charge lower prices for their services and to invest in attractive facilities located in areas convenient to paying patients, both of which create substantial competition for non-profits. As a result, it has become increasingly difficult for non-profits to continue to serve those who can't pay.

Opponents of commercialized health care also argue that for-profit health care institutions do not contribute their "fair share" to society. In view of the benefits health care institutions derive from society, it is unfair for them to refuse to help society serve those who can't afford care or are too costly to treat. All hospitals benefit from government subsidized programs like Medicare and Medicaid. They also profit from medical research and medical education paid for by taxpayers' money. In fairness, hospitals have an obligation to serve society's needy. Investor-owned corporations that turn away patients who can't afford to pay fail to discharge this obligation. Moreover, by not taking their fair share of unprofitable patients, for-profits place an undue burden on nonprofit and public hospitals. It's unjust that the costs of serving these patients should fall more heavily on nonprofit institutions.

Further, critics of health care for profit maintain that all persons have a right to live their lives with dignity. Mixing business with medicine will inevitably lead to abuses that violate patient dignity. A patient is in a vulnerable position, necessarily trusting that the doctor's decisions about his or her medical care will be guided solely by the patient's best interests. But in a system of for-profit health care, doctors will become subject to the control of lay managers accountable to share-holders whose primary aim is making a profit. Such hospitals will encourage doctors to promote profit-producing drugs, surgeries, tests and treatments. And, medical treatments and counseling lacking profit potential, however effective, will be discouraged. Even more worrisome are physicians who themselves own the facilities they operate. Doctors owning dialysis centers, for example, have been accused of putting patients on dialysis sooner than necessary and putting off kidney transplants that would eliminate the need for dialysis altogether.

In a system of for-profit health care, the opportunities for patient manipulation and exploitation are endless. Society must not allow the motive of economic gain to enter so directly into the practice of medicine, placing the well-being of patients in serious jeopardy, and undermining the trust so essential to the physician-patient relationship.

It is also argued that commercialized medicine will harm society, yet produce little in the way of benefits. Nonprofit hospitals undertake costly, but needed, research and maintain services which are not economically viable but which provide doctors with the training experiences necessary to medical education. Where profits rule, however, such necessary, but unprofitable, research and services important to medical education will be neglected. Furthermore, as for-profits come to dominate the health care sector, society will suffer a severe shortage of unprofitable, but critical, services, such as emergency rooms. Meanwhile, scarce resources will be squandered to produce and aggressively market lucrative, but unnecessary, services, such as cosmetic surgery.

While for-profits promise to harm society, critics continue, they fail to deliver any of the promised benefits, such as controlling health care expenditures, reducing the costs of care, and lowering the price of care. How will for-profits help control health care expenditures and the overuse of health services when, by definition, they are in the business of increasing total sales? For-profits are also unlikely to reduce the costs of care. Studies show that the rise of investor-owned hospitals has increased rather than lowered costs. Moreover, studies show that the prices charged by for-profit hospitals to paying patients, as well as the per-day expense of providing care, are higher than those of non-profits. The economic benefits promised by for-profits have not been demonstrated.

Finally, some critics of for-profit health care claim that the commercialization of medicine will lead to the abandonment of certain virtues and ideals that are necessary to a moral community. Most non- profits continue to uphold an ideal of service to humankind. The virtues of caring, compassion, and charity, and a sense of community have guided their decisions about the range of services to provide and the kinds of research or education to support. The ideal of altruism has been perpetuated by physicians whose primary concern has been the alleviation of human suffering and the restoration of health. Society must not allow such important and fragile virtues and ideals to be extinguished by the self-interest that drives for-profit enterprise.

Those favoring the growing commercialization of health care argue that society ought always to follow that course of action that will bring about the greatest benefits at the least cost. A health care system run by for profits will provide the greatest benefits at the least cost. First, for-profit health care will lower the costs of care. The amount we spend on health care every year has grown from $75 billion in 1980 to nearly $500 billion today. If this rate continues, by the year 2020, we will be spending 40 cents of every dollar we make on health care. Commercialized health care is our only hope for controlling the soaring costs and over-utilization of health services. Only the businesslike efficiency and the discipline that accompanies the drive to maximize profits can cure the ills of a system plagued by inefficiency and waste.

Under the present system, administrators and physicians have no incentives to operate in a cost-efficient manner. More concerned with institutional prestige than with the bottom line, administrators of non-profit organizations acquire sophisticated equipment and highly trained personnel, without regard for their need or likely use. Costly technologies are adopted and services added that are only marginally beneficial. Physician's themselves are offered little incentive to concern themselves with the cost of care, and go about ordering treatments that yield little or no benefit. Moreover, the nonprofit health care system is rife with costly, under-used facilities. Cardiac operations are performed in 100 different hospitals. Millions of dollars could be saved if these 15,000 procedures could be done in 30 centers specifically built for that purpose.

As the number of for-profit health care facilities increase, we can expect to see an end to such gross inefficiency. Aiming to maximize profits, for profits will invest only in the equipment and the personnel necessary to provide services that patients actually need. Decisions about what technologies should be adopted will be based on whether the benefits of these technologies outweigh their costs. The entrepreneurial spirit will give rise to innovation in the delivery and management of services, leading to more efficient methods of production and treatment. Doctors will be forced to come to terms with what will really benefit patients, resulting in fewer unnecessary hospitalizations, shorter hospital stays, and fewer needless tests.

Lower costs also can be expected from the economies of scale achieved by for-profit corporations. Unlike nonprofit health care institutions which often operate independently of each other, for-profits are often linked together as chains, allowing for economies in financing and management, and for centralized services and shared equipment, all resulting in lower costs.

Second, society will benefit from the enhanced access to care promised by for-profits. Currently, 37 million people are without the coverage needed to afford care. For-profits can pass on savings they achieve through more cost-efficient operations by lowering the price of care, so more people are able to afford it.

Third, for-profit health care enterprises produce benefits for society because for-profits have greater and quicker access to capital at lower costs than do non-profits. At a time when massive investments of capital are needed to keep up with the state of the art in medicine, non-profits are experiencing increasing difficulty in attracting funding. For-profits, on the other hand, can lure investors by issuing stocks, securing the money sorely needed to build and renovate facilities and to replace and modernize outdated equipment.

Proponents of for-profit enterprise in health care also support their position by maintaining that all persons have a basic right to freedom and thus a right to use their property in ways they freely choose. They argue that owners of for-profits have no special obligation to provide free services to the poor. While public funds may indeed subsidize research and medical education, it is patients and doctors who benefit from this education and research, not the owners of hospitals. If there is any obligation to serve the community in return for such subsidies, it is with patients and doctors that it lies. Nor does the possibility that hospitals have profited from an expanded market for services generated by government-subsidized programs oblige their owners to provide free care to the poor. Defense contractors profit greatly from the business generated by public funds. Yet, they are under no obligation to provide free public services. Nor can it be said that for-profits unfairly impose a burden on non-profits by not assuming a fair share of the costs of caring for the poor. For-profits, unlike non-profits, pay taxes, and in doing so, can be said to pay their share in serving the poor through tax-supported public programs. To impose on owners of for-profits a social obligation over and above an obligation to pay taxes is to impose an obligation on them that is not imposed on owners of other businesses.

Finally, it is argued, health care is like food, clothing and shelter. Just as these "basic needs" are sold on the market and distributed according to ability to pay, so too should health care. If some cannot afford to pay for such basic needs, it is up to the government or voluntary agencies to see that they secure it.

What is the moral response to the increasing commercialization of health care? The arguments in favor of for-profits appeal to the values we place on the freedom of free enterprise and the economic benefits that may flow from a more efficient health care system. But are we willing to uphold these values at the cost of other important values, including a concern for justice, the dignity of persons and a community-centered ethics that places the needs of people before profits? What is a "healthy" bottom line?

> "I swear by Apollo Physician and Asclepius and Hygieia and Panaceia and all the gods and goddesses, making them my witness, that I will fulfill according to my ability and judgment this oath and this covenant...I will apply...(treatment) for the benefit of the sick according to my ability and judgment; I will keep them from harm and injustice." —Hippocratic oath

Discussion Starters

1. Evaluate the arguments in the essay on both sides of the issue of whether for-profit medical institutions are a good thing. Which arguments do you find most compelling and why?
2. Discuss the viewpoint underlying for-profit health care that health care is a privilege, not an entitlement, and that a society does not have an "obligation" to provide health care for all.
3. What is your own opinion on for-profit health care? What if anything did you learn from the essay that informed your opinion?

STDs Still a Growing Problem with Young Adults

By Paul Skrickus

Paul Strickus is a former reporter for The Pendulum, Elon University's student newspaper. In this essay, Strickus offers evidence that contracting STDs remains a serious problem among young adults and reveals the most common STDs, their effects, and their treatments, and how best to avoid contracting them.

Young adults in this country put themselves in high-risk situations all too frequently. One of the worst risks is participating in unprotected sex, which puts all involved in danger of acquiring a sexually transmitted disease or causing an unwanted pregnancy.

"People aged 15-25 don't think it's going to happen to them," said Dr. William Hawkins, Elon University physician and medical director. "That's why they drive too fast, drink too much and that's why they jump over fires after their school wins a basketball game. They think nothing will happen to them even though they know the risks and dangers of their actions." Injuries can heal and the effects of drugs and alcohol can pass, but the consequences of having unprotected sex and acquiring STD's can stay with an individual forever.

Although there has been a strong push over the past few decades to educate the youth of America and increase awareness about STD's, it is still a problem. According to the American Social Health Association, two-thirds of all STDs occur in people 25 years of age or younger. The Society for Adolescent Medicine recently released a national survey that found about 56 percent of college students living away from home are sexually active and of that, 73 percent reported having unprotected sex.

Although the most commonly known and the most life threatening of all STDs, AIDS is not the most prevalent in the United States or on college campuses. "We see more chlamydia, occasional gonorrhea and I really can't remember the last time I've seen a positive syphilis test here," Hawkins said.

Chlamydia is a bacterial sexually transmitted disease and is the most common STD among college-aged people. There are an estimated 3 million people in the U.S. who have the disease, and as many as one in 10 sexually active women would test positive for it, according to the American Social Health Association.

Chlamydia bacteria are passed from one person to another through contact during sexual intercourse; it is uncommonly passed through oral-genital contact.

Once a person has contracted chlamydia there could be anywhere from one to three weeks before that person starts to see symptoms. Some people have been known not to show any symptoms at all.

A second kind of STD plaguing college campuses is the human papillomavirus, the most common STD in the U.S. today. Some types of HPV cause genital warts. "HPV is the most common STD I see here on campus," Hawkins said. "It's the fastest growing STD in the country over the past few years." There are more than 100 known strands of HPV, more than 30 of them being known to cause genital warts. The warts can take anywhere from three weeks to three months to appear. This makes HPV dangerous because a person might not know he or she has contracted the disease for some time, meanwhile continuing to be sexually active.

A third STD prevalent among college-aged students is gonorrhea, a bacteria disease that in some cases is also called "the clap." Gonorrhea can be passed from one person to another through all types of sexual contact. According to the ASHA, the gonorrhea bacteria thrives on soft skin, usually mucous membranes including the urethra, vagina, cervix, anus, lining of ones eyelid and throat. Symptoms for gonorrhea become visible in men two to five days after exposure; most women will remain asymptomatic but if women do show symptoms they will be visible within 10 days of contracting the disease, according to the ASHA. Like chlamydia, gonorrhea can cause very serious complications down the road if left untreated.

A common misconception for young people learning about STD's is there is no cure for any of them. Many of the bacterial STD's such as chlamydia and gonorrhea are curable with antibiotics. The viral diseases, like HIV and HPV, while incurable, are still treatable. "Chlamydia and gonorrhea can both be silent and both are totally curable," Hawkins said. "The bacteria are treatable, and there are even several options depending on response and allergies." He added that it is important for patients to take these prescriptions as directed and to halt all sexual activity until the disease is gone, usually within a week according to the ASHA.

HPV, a viral infection, is not curable; however, there are treatments that can minimize the effects. The symptoms are sometimes dormant, making it impossible for those people to know if they have been infected. This is why doctors encourage all sexually active women to get pap smears regularly. "We see a growing number of pap smears every week," Hawkins said. "I always encourage women to come and get checked out because it is the only way to really know what's going on." For those people who have visible symptoms, genital warts, there are special medications that can dissolve the warts; if the warts are big enough the doctor can freeze them or use a chemical or laser treatment, similar to how warts are dealt with on other parts of your body.

Many young people are still too ashamed to talk to their doctors about STD's and ask to get tested. Because STD's aren't discussed, many myths remain out there that give young people false hopes and lead them to make dumb decisions. Young adults are notorious for engaging in sexual activity with several partners, both men and women. "It is very possible for myself or one of my friends to get an STD here at Elon, without a doubt," said Caity C., an Elon University sophomore. "I was very sheltered in high school, and it was amazing to come here and see how many girls hook up with the same guys, and it's completely possible for someone I know to get an STD." Elon student Shepard S. agreed. "Sure it's possible," he said. "It's not something you want to think about but definitely possible. I have seen multiple guys be with the same girl. It's scary how possible it is."

It is a big step for anyone to get tested for an STD. If you consider the worst-case consequence of getting tested, you are stuck with an incurable disease that will severely affect the rest of your life; even still it is the responsibility of anyone who is sexually active to know if they have a disease. Everybody should also know about any prospective partner and take the precautionary steps necessary to protect themselves.

"It's a personal decision and I just want to let all the young people out there know that no matter what choice they make be sure to take all the possible steps to keep themselves safe," Hawkins urged.

Discussion Starters

1. What if anything did you learn from the essay about STD's? Are they a topic of discussion at your school?
2. What are the best ways to ensure that a person doesn't contract an STD? Are most college students in your opinion mindful of the dangers of contracting an STD?
3. What is your own experience or that of persons you know with STD's? What advice can you offer others?

My Personal Experience with Schizophrenia

By Kurt Snyder

Kurt Snyder devotes his website SchizoWorld to helping people who may suffer from schizophrenia. In this essay, readers enter the world of a schizophrenic, view the increasingly debilitating symptoms of the illness, and discover how Snyder over time was able to control his schizophrenia through medication and begin living a normal life.

I have paranoid schizophrenia. I developed schizophrenia gradually over a period of nine years, with the most severe symptoms appearing when I was twenty–eight years old. For most of those years, my family, friends, and colleagues were unaware that I was experiencing any mental problems.

My illness, as is true with all mental illnesses, started in the privacy of my own mind. My thoughts slowly wandered away from the normal range–I began to think less and less about daily life and more about a fantasy created in my mind. I cannot think of anything physical or psychological that could have triggered a change in my mental state. I had wonderful, supportive parents, relatives, and friends, and I had a wonderful childhood.

Somewhere between the ages of nineteen and twenty–one, I was exposed to the mathematical idea of fractals. I began to think obsessively about fractals and infinity. I thought I was going to discover some incredible and fabulous mathematical principle that would transform the way we view the universe. This delusion occupied my thoughts all day long, every day. I couldn't concentrate on my regular university studies, and my academic career eventually ended in failure. Still, I thought I was going to become famous. I was a genius just waiting to be discovered by the world. Soon everyone would know who I was because I was going to solve the riddle of the universe. I was having grandiose ideation.

I thought about fractals and infinity for many years. I always told myself I was on the verge of discovery, but I simply had to think a little bit harder about it. I just wasn't thinking hard enough. The reality is that the problems I was trying to solve were far beyond my mental abilities, but I didn't recognize this fact. Even though I had no evidence to substantiate my self–image, I knew in my heart that I was just like Einstein, and that someday I would get a flash of inspiration. I didn't recognize the truth–that I am not a genius. I kept most of my mathematical ideas to myself and spoke to very few people about them. I was paranoid that someone else would solve the riddle first if I provided the right clues.

At about the age of twenty–two, I had my first significant paranoid episodes. The first episode happened when I was on vacation with my girlfriend, my brother, and his wife in the mountains. We had rented a cabin together. For some reason, I started to think about images from horror movies where an insane man breaks into the house and kills everyone. I actually started to believe this was going to happen to us. I created a fantasy in my mind that we were very vulnerable and helpless, and that someone was going to kill us. It did not occur to me that this scenario was unlikely. The more I thought about it, the more I believed it was going to happen. I remember that I tried to reinforce the doors of the cabin with chairs. Everyone else seemed bewildered by my behavior. Eventually, however, I calmed down and went to bed.

Later that year, I had two more minor paranoid episodes. The first one happened when I hurt my leg and had to go to the university clinic. I was again feeling very vulnerable. I began to imagine that the nurse might try to hurt me in some way. I thought she might try to infect me with the AIDS virus by injecting me with a tainted needle. Of course, this idea was completely irrational, but I thought somehow that it could be true. A few weeks later, I became paranoid again–I thought the police were following me. But this idea only lasted a few hours. It would be several more years before any other symptoms of paranoia returned.

At about the age of twenty–four, I started to become preoccupied with the idea that people were watching me. I wondered about this several times a day. This idea began occurring to me more and more frequently, and the feeling that I was being watched became more intense. By the age of twenty–six, the thought that I might be under observation was occurring to me more than a hundred times a day. I became severely self–conscious in public places. I also became very sensitive to security cameras. They made me think I was being watched all the time. Oftentimes I thought the security cameras were watching me exclusively. At the age of twenty–seven, I took a job at a high–security facility where there were cameras in every room, every hallway, and all over the exterior of the building. I did not anticipate how this environment would affect me. During my first day on the job there, I could not escape the feeling that I was being constantly watched. The idea took on a life of its own. THEY were watching me. THEY could see everything I was doing. Long after I left the building to go home, I wondered if THEY were still watching me—somehow. Soon, THEY, whoever THEY were, were now watching me—all the time.

As one becomes more insane, rational thought fades away, but it happens gradually. In the midst of irrational thought, there still exists some rational thinking. I knew that no single individual could be watching me all the time, so I thought, "It must be a group of them. THEY are watching me, collectively."

The idea that THEY were watching me was irrational but persistent. The idea of who exactly THEY were, and why THEY were watching me, was an idea that evolved. My concept of THEM grew and began to color every experience I had. After a few months, everything that happened to me was somehow related to THEM, or was caused by THEM. When I started experiencing problems with my home computer, I blamed THEM. When I got a parking ticket, it was THEIR influence with the police that got me in trouble. Every thought I had was somehow associated with THEM.

I can understand now why some schizophrenics believe other people are controlling their thoughts. THEY were a concept in my mind that expanded beyond my own control. The concept of THEM was taking over all my thought processes, in every way possible. I could not think about anything or anyone without making some type of association with THEM. THEY were everywhere, involved with everything. THEY became the national intelligence agencies. THEY were random people I saw on the street. THEY were friends and relatives. THEY were people sitting next to me in the movie theater. THEY were observing me, 24 hours a day.

Even as my mental illness worsened, some part of my rational mind was still active. I tried to reconcile my new perception of reality with the reality I had known in earlier years. This new concept of THEM even infiltrated my memories. Experiences I had had years ago were now colored by this new perceptual filter. I wondered if THEY had caused certain things to happen to me in the past. I wondered if THEY had been following me for many years. I relived past experiences in new ways because of my delusion. I invented various scenarios to explain how THEY had been affecting or influencing my whole life.

At the age of twenty–eight, I suddenly started to become psychotic. I am using the word psychotic to mean that my understanding and perception of the real world diverged sharply from reality. I could no longer work. At one point, I wondered whether my whole existence and everything I experienced was manufactured by a virtual reality machine and whether my whole life was spent in a laboratory run by some type of alien creatures. This initial psychotic episode lasted for a few days. Then the most bizarre thoughts seemed to dissipate. However, the delusions involving THEM were persistent and continued for the next year, through two more psychotic episodes.

In my second psychotic episode, I experienced for the first time what I can confidently say were auditory and visual hallucinations. Only three months after that, I had another psychotic episode where I experienced another visual hallucination. At the time, these hallucinations seemed real to me, absolutely real. I could not distinguish them from reality. They came from some part of my brain that had never been activated before.

During each psychotic episode, my family tried to get me medical help. Medications were prescribed, but I refused to take them. I didn't believe anything was wrong with me. I thought I was just having an unusual experience. I didn't want to take anything that altered my brain–those pills were for crazy people!

After several months I finally decided to take the medication (Geodon), but my decision was based in part on a delusion. Thankfully, I took the medication regularly. Approximately two months after I started taking Geodon, I developed a severe case of depression. This depression lasted for at least one month, perhaps two. I wanted to die rather than continue to experience this feeling. I remained in bed for most of every day. My doctor prescribed an antidepressant, and my situation improved.

It took a long time for me to admit to myself that I had been mentally ill, and that I needed to take some type of psychiatric medication for the rest of my life. At first I wanted to hide this fact from other people, but eventually I accepted the fact that I couldn't have done anything differently, and I couldn't blame myself for being sick.

I continued to take Geodon for two years. My progress was very gradual, but I noticed a steady reduction in positive symptoms for that entire period. Eventually I was able to go back to work. At the end of my second year of taking Geodon, I began to experience severe akisthesia. This unusual type of anxiety is the worst emotional feeling I have ever experienced in my entire life, even more disturbing than the severe depression I had felt. I wanted to escape from existence. My doctor switched my medication to Zyprexa, and the akisthesia gradually diminished.

I have now been taking Zyprexa for three years, and it seems to be working beautifully, except for the extra twenty pounds of fat I'm carrying around. However, I wouldn't change it for anything. I have continued to notice steady improvement in my condition over the last three years, both for positive and negative symptoms. I now believe that I have fully recovered from schizophrenia, and I realize that my recovery is owed entirely to medication. I now experience no delusions, no paranoia, and I do not have bizarre thoughts. To get better, I did not perform any mental gymnastics (such as meditation or positive thinking), nor did I pursue any type of psychoanalysis. I simply took the medication, and I improved. Most people I know would never suspect that I ever had a mental illness, and many people are surprised when I tell them I have schizophrenia.

I have actually had quite a lot of success in recent years. I joined my local volunteer fire department, and I was elected vice president this past year. My illness has abated, I am productive again, and I plan on having a normal existence for the rest of my life.

Discussion Starters

1. What if anything did you learn about schizophrenia from the essay? Based on the essay, in what ways does untreated schizophrenia debilitate a person?
2. Why do you think that the author remained untreated for so many years? Do you think this may be common among people with mental illness?
3. What is your experience or those of others you know with mental illness? What should people understand about the mentally ill?

What Pregnant Women Won't Tell You - Ever

By Elyse Anders

Elise Anders is a regular poster on StepChick.com. In this essay, Anders, with a good dash of humor, reveals the significant downside of pregnancy that women seldom share.

Are you pregnant? Know someone who is? Might you become pregnant in the future? Do you have a uterus and engage in sexual intercourse with a man(s)? Are you a man(s) who engages in sexual intercourse with uterus owner(s)? Are you exposed to people who engage in sexual intercourse? Have you ever seen or heard of a baby? Have you or any of your friends ever expressed interest in creating a human being from scratch?

If you've answered "yes", "maybe", "perhaps", "I'd like to", or "Does this site contain any content relevant to anyone anywhere?" to any of the above questions, this post is for you!

While the human-baking process has been going on for like at least 6000 years or so, it's hardly a process that's been perfected. And shockingly, a good portion of the process is not discussed. Really. If you think that being pregnant is anything like what you've seen in the movies or heard from your friends or co-workers, you might be surprised to hear that normal uncomplicated pregnancies can suck.

So I made a list of things no one tells you about pregnancy until you're already sucked in. Not everyone experiences all of these. Some women experience none of these. Some women experience all of these and more. And these do not include any of the things no one tells you about complications, miscarriages, infertility or unwanted pregnancy. So this list is only for the lucky ones.

You must be happy!

You're pregnant with a baby you want and you and your husband planned for! Congrats! You must be thrilled! Everyone else is! Don't you love being pregnant? Everyone else does! It's magical! It's wonderful!

Except...you're not. Don't try to talk about it with anyone. It's like explaining mustard to a frog. Women who are already parents will explain to you that you're just dealing with some stress, and that everything will be fine. Everyone who is not a mother will just be confused or think you're joking.

Reality: Pregnancy is terrifying. You don't know what's going on with your body. No one tells you what's normal and what's not. And suddenly, no matter how excited and prepared you thought you were, you realize you are totally and completely not ready to be responsible for another human being. You're filled with doubt. You're sure you're making a mistake...and you know what? You might be. No one will tell you that either (unless you're not married, in which case you are not to be happy at all and any mention of being happy will be met with feigned congratulations and followed up with lectures to your face and whispers behind your back about how naive/stupid/irresponsible you are.) But really, parenting isn't for everyone. And even if you once thought it was for you, it might not be. For you, it is entirely possible that you made a mistake.

But even if it's not a mistake (BTW, it *probably* isn't), it can sure feel like it. And it's not only okay, but normal to feel overwhelmed and confused…even angry. On top of being one of the biggest life changing events you will ever experience, you're uncomfortable and your hormones are messing with your mind…and your body. And on top of that is the fact that it's hard to find sympathy from anyone other than women who are currently pregnant and women who are dealing with their newborns.

Morning sickness

Ok, everyone talks about morning sickness. But I don't think it gets proper credit for being as awful as it is. Somehow, barfing endlessly for months has gained a reputation as being a romantic rite of passage. It's not. It's like being hungover with the flu for 6 weeks – 9 months.

People will think they're laughing along with you as you struggle to keep anything down. They will either be completely unsympathetic or think it's an amusing practical joke to expose you to smells that will bring on your nausea. They will even insist that you're wrong that the smell of chicken a block away will keep you sick for days because "but you *love* chicken!"

Then there's the morning sickness fetishists. They love hearing stories about morning sickness because it means that your pregnancy is going well. It's true, kind of. There is a correlation between the severity of morning sickness and pregnancy outcomes. But really, when you have 7 months to go, and haven't held down more than water and saltines for weeks, you don't give a shit. Also, morning sickness does not necessarily mean that you will have a healthy, full term pregnancy either. You can puke for eight weeks straight and still miscarry.

Don't be fooled into thinking "morning sickness" has anything to do with mornings. Noon doesn't change anything. "Morning" sickness is better termed "all the damn time" sickness. It's sweet that Hollywood is naive enough to believe that preggos throw up three times before 9 am then go on to have a normal day. And by "sweet" I mean that it makes me want to puke.

Staying awake

The first trimester, it's not even worth it to try. You will not stay awake. You can't fight it. You can't sleep your way into more energy. You will feel narcoleptic. The second trimester you won't be able to sleep. You will be full of energy. Anything that can be done, must get done now! Before bed! Who needs sleep! You will feel like a manic on meth. The third trimester you will be motivated but exhausted. You will want to sleep all the time but will not be able to. You will not be able to get comfortable. Once you are comfortable and dozing off, your baby will decide that it's time to throw a uterus rave. You will feel like a narcoleptic with a conjoined manic-meth-head twin.

Aches

Everything will hurt. Your head, your boobs, your teeth, your back, your belly, your thighs, your feet.

If nothing hurts, something is probably wrong. If everything hurts too much, something is probably wrong. If everything hurts the right amount, that is a great sign and it means that everything is going perfectly. How do you know the right amount? You don't. And every day, the "right amount" can change. Good luck. You can take Tylenol (paracetamol for the foreigners), but don't expect it to work for anything ache-related.

Cervix kicks

Oh your sweet little baby is healthy and moving around and kicking. You can feel him bumping around. It's magical. HOLY SHIT! WHAT WAS THAT? That? That crazy sudden pain that almost made you collapse? That feeling that someone just sent an electric fireball down your vagina and through your legs? That, my dear, was your sweet little baby kicking you in the cervix. You can't prepare for it. You can't stop it. You can only hope that each time it happens, you are near something to break your fall. Or that you are in a place where no one cares if you scream.

Bladder kicks

It's probably unfair to say no one talks about this one. But I don't think it's talked about enough.

Once your kid starts kicking hard enough to feel it on the outside, it's time to go to the pharmacy and pick up some Poise pantyliners. Do it. Do not be embarrassed. Do not wait to see if I am making this up.

At this point, your kid can kick with some force. Your bladder lives next to her feet. Think of your bladder as a crudely fastened water balloon. A quick punch aaaaand......hopefully you have access to new pants. Otherwise you have to start yelling at invisible people about Zeus to get away with walking around smelling like pee.

Gaining sympathy

Don't expect anyone to ever be sympathetic to any of the things you are going through. Maybe this is why no one talks about these things. Your friends who want kids don't want to hear this. Your friends who don't want kids will want you to shut up and snap, "You're the one who wanted kids." (Because wanting a family means that you want to be kicked in the cervix while urinating on yourself with a back that aches so bad you can hardly move...that's what YOU GET!) Your partner might try to be sympathetic, but is going through all this for the first time, too. He won't have much advice, and will pretty much feel helpless.

With the exception of women with newborns, everyone who doesn't fall into the first three groups just wants to tell you how great it will be when the kid comes out. Yeah, it is worth it in the end...but that doesn't change anything you're going through right now. Even though you're literally never alone, pregnancy can be a very lonely time.

Swelling junk

Everyone knows things swell when you're pregnant. Your hands swell. Your feet swell. Your face swells. Your boobs enter a room 5 minutes before you, and 10 minutes after your belly. But no one tells you that your genitals swell. No one. And once they start, there's nothing you can do to stop them. And it hurts. It feels like someone punched you in the crotch with brass knuckles. Sitting hurts. Standing makes the blood rush down. Laying down keeps the pressure off, which feels better, but also helps everything engorge for when you do sit or stand. And as the baby gets heavier, it acts like a tourniquet, trapping your entire blood supply inside your labia. At some point, you may think you've grown giant infected testicles. Nope. Those are your girl parts.

At this point you'll probably stab anyone who looks like they may even be thinking about sex. If you're not ready to stab anyone, try having sex...a little more blood rushing down there will undoubtedly get you stabbing within minutes!

Feet

New moms always talk about how they want to get back into their pre-pregnancy jeans. This is their way of coping with the loss of every pair of shoes they ever loved. By the middle of your 3rd trimester, none of your shoes will fit. Your feet will be swollen and all the muscles and ligaments in your feet will have relaxed, spreading your feet out. The swelling does go away once you've pushed your little doll out. The spreading does not. I hope you didn't buy your dream Manolos to celebrate your growing family. Now, the only place they're going to fit is the donation bin. Bright side: some hobo out there is gonna look FABulous!

Pooping

You will poop during child birth. There is nothing you can do about this. Pushing is pushing. Your doctor and husband (or other coach) will tell you that you didn't so that you're not too embarrassed to keep going. You'll assume they're being honest. You'll brag to everyone that you didn't. Then your husband will get drunk a year and a half later and laugh at you for dooking yourself...then laugh at you for thinking you didn't. You'll punch him in the balls, but it won't change anything because he's right. You did. You pooped your bed while a room full of people were staring at your bloody gaping vagina.

Bloody gaping vagina

Yeah. That's where the baby comes out. People will be staring at it intently. I have nothing else to add.

Alcohol

If you choose not to drink alcohol while pregnant, be prepared for After School Special levels of peer pressure to drink. It is apparently unacceptable to say to anyone ever that you feel safer abstaining completely. You can argue whatever facts you want. Everyone has a sister/aunt/cousin who drank and smoked through her entire pregnancy and gave birth to a healthy 13 lb baby. Your friends, family and co-workers will be annoyed by the fact that you choose not to drink...because for some reason an increased risk of raising a child with ADHD is no reason to stop kicking back with a 6 pack once (or seven times) a week. You need to stop being such a pretentious sober bitch.

The people who applaud your choice to be a pretentious sober bitch will freak out if anyone drinks in your vicinity. Do not offer to mix up some of your signature cocktail for everyone at a party. Forget it. You're pregnant. For 9 months, the world is to act as if alcohol never existed. If you mention that you're really missing margaritas, or take half a sip of one, your friends will call DCFS on you.

Using TP

After giving birth, you will be instructed to stop using toilet paper. Not forever, but for a while. You will be sent home with a little squirt bottle to use to clean yourself after you pee. Eventually your doctor will clear you to wipe yourself again. But really, it's not like the TP thing matters. You'll be too bloody down there for it to really make a difference. Every time you pee, you'll want to jump into the shower to wash your unusable bloody sexy parts...and your bloody thighs...even your bloody calves and ankles, too, at least for a few days.

Advice

Everyone you meet who has ever met another pregnant woman is an expert on your pregnancy. Everything they will tell you defies logic, and is likely the opposite of anything your OB would ever tell you. The longer ago and the farther away they gave birth, the more advice they will have and the more they will insist your doctor is wrong. Example: 95 year old woman who birthed her youngest 80 years ago in Siberia knows more than your doctor, and will terrify you while going on for hours about what the best way to be pregnant is (using vodka to douche every hour is important for a healthy fetus! You don't need prenatal care! Birth defect screening is rubbish; try a dowsing rod for your answers! Pickled fish make the best pantyliners!). Your 25 year old friend next door with a 3 month old daughter will not impose her advice on you.

Your husband will give you advice based on what he remembers from his aunt being pregnant in 1989. Everyone else will ask you questions, benign questions compared to the stuff I've listed here, and will be horrified by your answers. "OMG YOU HAVE TO DO WHAT ON THE PREGNANCY TEST STICK? OOOOOOOH YUCK!" "Transvaginal ultrasound? What's that? OOOOOOOOH YUCK!" "They look THERE? On the BABY? To find out what sex it is? OOOOOOH YUCK!" "Wait, it's moving right NOW? Like while we talk? OOOOOOOOOOOH YUCK!" "Can you still have sex? OOOOOOOOH YUCK!"

So there you have it. Everything you may or may not have wanted to know about being pregnant that no one would have ever told you anyway. Now, I need to go ice my crotch and change my Poise pad.

Discussion Starters

1. What is your overall reaction to the essay? Did you find it enlightening, amusing, somewhat sickening, all of the above, or something else?
2. What did you learn about being pregnant that you didn't already know? After reading the essay, how do you view pregnancy differently, if at all?
3. While the information in the essay was perhaps sobering for women who haven't experienced pregnancy, the tone of the essay was light. Why do you think the author juxtaposed the "heavy" information with the light, humorous tone?

The End of Football

By John Kass

John Kass is a columnist for the Chicago Tribune. In this essay, Kass explains why he believes that professional football is a dying sport.

With all that college beef on parade this week, the NFL draft is a wonder of sports marketing, a televised pageant for the multibillion-dollar American football industry. But there's something football fans should know: Football is dead in America.

Even through all the chatter and cheerleading and media hype, football as an American cultural institution lies in final spasm. It's as dead as the Marlboro Man. And if the professional game survives at all, it will be relegated to the pile of trash sports, like mixed martial arts or whatever is done in third-rate arenas with monster trucks and mud. It won't be as American as apple pie. Instead, football will become the province of people with face tattoos.

Lawyers are circling football now. For years they've had their wings locked, cruising overhead, but lately they've swooped in low, landing and hopping over to take chunks out of the great billion-dollar beast. But it's not the lawyers who are the death of football. Blaming lawyers misses the point. Like their counterparts in nature, lawyers are merely the cleanup crew. What finishes football are the parents of future football players.

The NFL desperately needs American parents. Not as fans, but as suppliers of young flesh. The NFL needs parents to send their little boys into the football feeder system. And without that supply of meat for the NFL grinder—first youth teams, then high school and college—there can be no professional football. And yet every day, more American parents decide they're finished with football. Why? Because parents can no longer avoid the fact that football scrambles the human brain.

In cultural terms, parents who send their 10-year-olds to play football might as well hold up signs saying they'd like to give their children cigarettes and whiskey.

Make no mistake. I loved football. I loved it desperately. Even now, four decades later, I remember endlessly damning myself for being too small to play it at a big-time college. I ached for it, for the violence of it, for the training, the salt pills and no water on hot August fields, the helmet scabs on the forehead, but mostly the collisions. And I still love it, but I can't shake the guilt of supporting the physical ruin of great athletes. My wife and I wouldn't let our sons play. We just couldn't.

Future historians may explain all this in terms of cultural change, of more information about concussions, spinal cord injuries, paralysis and brain damage, and another football killer, taxpayer liability. Some 4,000 former NFL players have joined lawsuits against the league for allegedly hiding the dangers to the brain. This follows a rash of depression-related suicides, with some players shooting themselves in the chest so that their brains could be studied after their deaths. One of these was the great Chicago Bears safety Dave Duerson. He left a suicide note, asking that doctors examine what was in his skull after a lifetime of bashing it. College players have also filed suit.

Eventually, lawsuits will overwhelm the high schools. And high school superintendents won't be able to increase property taxes to pay for the additional cost of subsidizing the game.

"The idea that five years ago I would have forbidden my kids to play football is hard to imagine," said Joseph Siprut, a lawyer representing former Eastern Illinois University player Adrian Arrington and other athletes in federal court over the long-term effects of head injuries. "It never would have occurred to me. Now, given what I know about the concussion issue—first as a lawyer who has litigation, but also as someone who reads the papers—for me as a parent, I don't think I would ever let my kids set foot on a football field. Ever."

Football may hang on for a few years, hang on desperately like a cat dying under a backyard deck, hissing as it goes. There are billions of dollars at stake, feeding owners, players, agents, advertisers, journalists, and most importantly, bookies. The NFL is about gambling.

The game is not just a contact sport—it's a high-impact collision sport. It is about exploding into your opponent, refusing to break, while breaking others to your will and knocking them senseless. For young players on the field and old spectators remembering, there is still joy in it. But expressing that joy has become culturally taboo.

Fans have been led to pretend that the violence is merely ancillary. But to say that violence isn't at the heart of football is a lie. Remove the violence, and you remove what is great about the game, what is awe-inspiring and guilt-inspiring at the same time. All sports can be dangerous. They involve physical and spiritual risk. But football is different from other team sports. It is designed to slam body against body, and often, head slams against head. There is no way to alter this fact, no way to spin it.

So if you're wondering about the future of football during the NFL draft, try this experiment: Ask the parents of a little boy about tackle football, about concussions, and look into their eyes when they speak.

Discussion Starters

1. What is the author's thesis – that professional football is dying – predicated on? Do you agree with him?
2. Cass believes that the very violence of football is one of its greatest attractions. Why are fans attracted to such violence, to players "exploding" into their opponents?
3. Would you let your child (or future child) play football, knowing what you know about the physical risks?

Marked for Mayhem

By Chuck Hustmyre and Jay Dixit

Chuck Hustmyre is an author, journalist and screenwriter with over 700 published articles. Jay Dixit is a psychology writer whose work has appeared in The New York Times, The Washington Post, Rolling Stone, and Psychology Today. In this essay, the authors reveal the mannerisms and behavior that assailants look for in their potential victims and offer advice to help people from being targeted.

Midnight in New Orleans. Lisa Z. was walking home from the French Quarter hotel where she works when three men stepped around a corner and stopped in front of her. When she tried to cross the street to get away, the men charged after her. "One guy clotheslined me," she recalls, "then choked me, threw me on the sidewalk, and jammed a chrome, snub-nosed .38 revolver against my cheekbone." Lisa was kicked, robbed, and then told not to move or she'd be shot in the face.

The men who robbed her likely chose Lisa because she unknowingly sent out signals that marked her as a "soft" target. Alone and encumbered by a backpack, she appeared to be a vulnerable person who could be easily controlled. "Some of these guys concentrate on people who are easy to overcome," says Volkan Topalli, a psychologist and criminologist at Georgia State University. "They'll target females, they'll target older people, but they're also looking for cues of weakness or fear."

Criminals, like their victims, come in all varieties, but researchers have found that they don't choose their victims randomly. There's a reason FBI agents begin crime investigations by creating profiles of victims. It's because the identity of victims—particularly if there are several victims with differing characteristics—helps investigators determine whether a criminal is targeting a specific kind of person or choosing victims opportunistically.

In the field of victimology, one of the central concepts is that of the "risk continuum"—there are degrees of risk for a type of crime based on your career, lifestyle, relationships, movements, and even personality, aspects of which are manifest in your behavior and demeanor. Some factors that make people potential victims are obvious—flashing wads of cash, wearing expensive jewelry, walking alone on back streets. Others are subtler, including posture, walking style, even the ability to read facial expressions.

The cues add up to what David Buss terms "exploitability." An evolutionary psychologist at the University of Texas, Buss is examining a catalogue of traits that seem to invite some people to exploit others. There's cheatability (cues you can be duped in social exchange), sexual-exploitability (cues you can be sexually manipulated), as well as mugability, robability, killability, stalkability, and even sexual-assaultability. "As adaptations for exploitation evolved, so did defenses to prevent being exploited—wariness toward strangers, cheater-detection sensitivities, and possibly anti-rape defenses," explains Buss. "These defenses, in turn, created selection pressure for additional adaptations for exploitation designed to circumvent victim defenses. This co-evolutionary arms race can continue indefinitely."

Nowhere does victimology imply that people who stand out as easy targets are to blame for becoming victims. Predators bear sole responsibility for the crimes they commit—and should be held accountable and punished accordingly. Moreover, many attacks are random, and no amount of vigilance could deter them. Whether victims are selected randomly or targeted because of specific characteristics, they bear no responsibility for crimes against them. But by being aware of which cues criminals look for, we can reduce the risk of becoming targets ourselves.

In a classic study, researchers Betty Grayson and Morris I. Stein asked convicted criminals to view a video of pedestrians walking down a busy New York City sidewalk, unaware they were being taped. The convicts had been to prison for violent offenses such as armed robbery, rape, and murder. Within a few seconds, the convicts identified which pedestrians they would have been likely to target. What startled the researchers was that there was a clear consensus among the criminals about whom they would have picked as victims—and their choices were not based on gender, race, or age. Some petite, physically slight women were not selected as potential victims, while some large men were.

The researchers realized the criminals were assessing the ease with which they could overpower the targets based on several nonverbal signals—posture, body language, pace of walking, length of stride, and awareness of environment. Neither criminals nor victims were consciously aware of these cues. They are what psychologists call "precipitators," personal attributes that increase a person's likelihood of being criminally victimized.

The researchers analyzed the body language of the people on the tape, and identified several aspects of demeanor that marked potential victims as good targets. One of the main precipitators is a walking style that lacks "interactional synchrony" and "wholeness." Perpetrators notice a person whose walk lacks organized movement and flowing motion. Criminals view such people as less self-confident—perhaps because their walk suggests they are less athletic and fit—and are much more likely to exploit them.

Just like predators in the wild, armed robbers often attack the slowest in the herd. People who drag their feet, shuffle along, or exhibit other unusual gaits are targeted more often than people who walk fast and fluidly. That criminals are attuned to cues of vulnerability makes sense given that most criminals, especially murderers, are looking for people who will be easy to control. Even rape is motivated less by sex and more by the desire for control and power.

Sexual predators in particular look for people they can easily overpower. "The rapist is going to go after somebody who's not paying attention, who looks like they're not going to put up a fight, who's in a location that's going to make this more convenient," says Tod Burke, a criminologist at Radford University in Virginia.

"If I had the slightest inkling that a woman wasn't someone I could easily handle, then I would pass right on by. Or if I thought I couldn't control the situation, then I wouldn't even mess with the house, much less attempt a rape there," says Brad Morrison, a convicted sex offender who raped 75 women in 11 states and who's quoted in *Predators: Who They Are and How to Stop Them*, by Gregory M. Cooper, Michael R. King, and Thomas McHoes.

"Like, if they had a dog, then forget it. Even a small one makes too much noise. If I saw a pair of construction boots, for example, out on the porch or on the landing, I walked right on by. In fact, I think if women who live alone would put a pair of old construction boots—or something that makes it look like a physically fit manly-type of guy lives with them—out in front of their door, most rapists or even burglars wouldn't even think about trying to get into their home."

Distraction is another cue criminals look for. Some people think talking on a cell phone enhances their safety because the other person can always summon help if there's trouble—but experts disagree. Talking on a phone or listening to an iPod is a distraction, and armed robbers are casting about for distracted victims. "Not paying attention, looking like a tourist—having the map out, looking confused—absolutely makes people more vulnerable," Burke says.

Being aware of your surroundings, however, may not help much if you don't know what to pay attention to. James Giannini of Ohio State University discovered something shocking: Women who are the victims of rape tend to be less able than average to interpret nonverbal facial cues— which may render them oblivious to the warning signs of hostile intent and more likely to enter or stay in dangerous situations.

The same team also found that rapists tend to be more able than average to interpret facial cues, such as a downward gaze or a fearful expression. It's possible this skill makes rapists especially able to spot passive, submissive women. One study even showed that rapists are more empathetic toward women than other criminals—although they have a distinct empathy gap when it comes to their own victims. A highly attuned rapist and a woman who's oblivious to hostile body language make a dangerous combination.

Even personality plays a role. Conventional wisdom holds that women who dress provocatively draw attention and put themselves at risk of sexual assault. But studies show that it is women with passive, submissive personalities who are most likely to be raped—and that they tend to wear body-concealing clothing, such as high necklines, long pants and sleeves, and multiple layers. Predatory men can accurately identify submissive women just by their style of dress and other aspects of appearance. The hallmarks of submissive body language, such as downward gaze and slumped posture, may even be misinterpreted by rapists as flirtation.

Drinking and drug use, not surprisingly, also mark a person as a potential victim. "It's a robber's dream to knock a drunk down and take what they've got," says former Ohio detective Stacy Dittrich. That goes double for sexual assault. Drunken people not only appear more vulnerable, they're also especially likely to place themselves in dangerous situations. Alcohol decreases people's ability to evaluate the consequences of their actions and distorts their ability to predict how others perceive them. And women who are intoxicated, studies show, tend to be animated, giving off signals sexual offenders may misinterpret as sexual interest.

Many armed robbers have a chip on their shoulders and view life as inherently unfair, says criminologist Richard Wright, a professor at the University of Missouri at St. Louis and co-author of *Armed Robbers in Action: Stickups and Street Culture*. As a result, they often see someone else's success as a reminder of their own failure and inferiority. Worse still, they interpret outward signs of another's prosperity as a personal affront. "When they see people flaunting their wealth or driving fancy cars, they see that as an attempt to put them down," Wright says.

For this reason, robbers are especially apt to target people who are flaunting material possessions or even just displaying a cocky, superior attitude. Street predators have their own word for such behavior—"flossing"—and it infuriates them. "It's a very visible reminder of their situation," Wright adds, "of being poor, that they've got nothing in their pockets. From the perspective of the perpetrator, the robbery balances the scales, at least temporarily. "It's a restoration of justice," Wright explains. "'You were putting me down. Now guess what? I'm going to put you down. You've got all that. I'm going to take it away.'"

Sometimes, however, indignation may be just moral flimflam robbers use to justify their own behavior. "In some cases, offenders need to manufacture motivation to commit the crime," Topalli says. Somehow, they need to justify their actions. "It's better to rob people who deserve it." In the inverted universe that resentment builds in the brain, many armed robbers view themselves as the real victims in the world, a world in which the rich take their wealth from the poor.

Grayson, co-author of the classic study on body language and exploitability, believes people can be taught how to walk in a confident way that reduces their risk of assault. To reduce the chances of becoming a victim, you can't look like a victim. "Walk in an alert fashion, walk with purpose, with your shoulders held back," advises Topalli.

Even better, avoid placing yourself in dangerous situations and stay aware of your surroundings at all times. Location is a key factor in street crime, particularly in cases of sexual assault. Criminals prefer sites that are likely to serve up few witnesses and little chance of being caught. Plan routes that avoid such locations.

And while you're at it, don't even talk to strangers on the street in isolated locations. One warning sign that you may be about to be robbed or attacked is the approach of a stranger on the street. The person may try to engage you in conversation. He may ask for the time, directions, bus fare, or try to tell you about a nice club or restaurant just around the corner. Calvin Donaldson, who's been in prison in Louisiana for the last 28 years after robbing a couple in the French Quarter who asked him for directions, offers some advice: "Once you stop and let this guy engage you in conversation, you're opening yourself up," he says. "Some people you don't talk to. You just keep going."

How do you survive unharmed if you find yourself targeted? Cooperate. "They're not going to hurt you unless they need to," says New Orleans Police Department psychologist James Arey. Convicted armed robber Darryl Falls, who admits to committing more than 100 robberies, agrees. "The quicker you comply and give them your goods," he says, "the quicker they're out of your face."

Some of Falls' victims tried to conceal jewelry to which they had an emotional attachment—wedding rings, for example. "I understand the sentimental value," he says. "But you can get that back. You can't get your life back."

Discussion Starters

1. What did you learn from the essay about how criminals target their victims? What if anything surprised you about whom they targeted?
2. Based on the essay, what things can you do, and not do, to makes yourself less likely to be a victim? Might the essay change in any way your behavior, dress, or routine?
3. Have you or anyone you know ever been the victim of a crime? Did any of the criminal targeting factors presented in the essay play a possible role in the crime?

Living with the Mystery of Headache

By Sallie Tisdale

Sallie Tisdale has written several books including Women of the Way, and her essays have appeared in the New Yorker, Harper's, and Esquire. In this essay, Tisdale details the physical and mental anguish of living with an extreme, chronic headache, her journey through the medical corridors in hopes of finding relief, and how she is coping today with her life-changing condition.

My headache began on a Monday afternoon around three o'clock. The pain centered on my left temple and eye, constant, gnawing, broken only by sudden waves of sharper pain. My doctor was on vacation, but after several days I decided I couldn't wait and took the next available appointment. By the time I made it to her office I could hardly walk across the room in a straight line.

The physician's assistant was attentive, working down the neurological checklist: reflexes, balance, gait, grip strength, and cranial-nerve function, which affects swallowing, eye movement, sensation, facial expression, and more. Everything was normal, except for the pain. Finally, with a grunt of satisfaction, she decided that I must be dehydrated. I knew that I was dehydrated because I couldn't eat, and that I couldn't eat because I had a headache that would not stop. By then the headache had so eroded my ability to think that I didn't even comment; I just waited in a darkened room while she wrote a prescription for Vicodin.

When my doctor returned a week later, she was also attentive, and took her time: reflexes, balance, gait, grip strength, cranial-nerve function. The Vicodin had given me no relief. I was tremulous, ill defined. The feeling was hard to describe; my words failed, trailing off.

"I'm sure it's not migraine," she told me. Migraines rarely last more than a few days. "But I'm not sure what it is." Although severe headaches are only rarely a sign of something dire, like a ruptured aneurysm or a brain tumor, she recommended an MRI to be sure.

"There is a medication that sometimes works for headaches like these," she said, and suggested I try indomethacin, an anti-inflammatory drug in the same class as ibuprofen. Usually reserved for arthritis, it's a nasty medication, known for causing stomach ulcers and gastrointestinal bleeding, cardiac arrhythmia and heart failure. I started taking twenty-five milligrams twice a day—started as soon as the pharmacist handed me the bottle—along with a daily dose of omeprazole, an acid-reducing drug, to protect my gut. The pain retreated but didn't disappear. I complained in private but mostly I kept my headache to myself, shivering my way through conversations. I had work and a class to teach and my son was getting married in a month.

Headaches are nothing special. They grant one only brief and local respite. That this one endured, that it buffeted my every step, was hard to explain. I wasn't sure anyone would believe me; after all, I hadn't really believed in such a thing, either. Another person's pain, writes Elaine Scarry, is "vaguely alarming yet unreal," and the inability to truly sympathize with another's suffering is a sign of "pain's triumph." She adds, "Whatever pain achieves, it achieves in part through its unsharability."

Headache is a peculiar insult, an intrusion into the mind; it is inherently emotional. The pain makes it hard to think and destroys equanimity, but so does the accompanying neuronal storm. Headaches trigger a response in the emotional centers of the brain; your head is making you lose your temper, making you cry. I'm not trying to claim that the pain from a headache is worse than the pain of a broken bone or the gnaw of tumor and infection—though certain types of headache cause profound pain—but there is something fundamentally different about it, a pain benign in a technical sense, malignant in an existential one. The sufferer is oddly contracted and reduced. The word is almost unbearably banal for the metaphysical jolt and psychic crisis engendered; what we call a headache is a neurological event encompassing every part of a person: body, mind, feeling, and that ephemeral construct we call *self.*

The indomethacin tamped down my constant pain, but every hour or so I had sudden tides of sharp pain that I began to call surges. They were always on the left side of my head above the eye and in the temple, with swells of tingling and electrical sensations. They made my eye squint and blink; sometimes my jaw ached, or I found myself leaning to the left in my chair.

Indomethacin is singularly diagnostic for an uncommon headache I had never heard of called hemicrania continua. Indomethacin reduces intracranial pressure, but how this relates to the pain of hemicrania is unclear. Other drugs in the same class don't help; opiates don't help, and neither do the triptans, drugs that reduce the constriction of blood vessels in the brain and help treat migraine. (No other severe headache is relieved by indomethacin alone.) So, ipso facto, hemicrania is a headache that responds to indomethacin—"responds absolutely" is the classic description; an "exquisite response" isanother.

The pain of hemicrania continua centers around the eye and forehead. (A number of people with HC experience "foreign body" syndrome, the sense that there is something in the eye.) HC may seem to wax and wane, but it never disappears; in fact it is layered: the moderate, relentless foundation, a kind of water torture of headache, overlaid with bursts of sharp, even blinding, pain. Many people with hemicrania (and "many" is the wrong word; it is rarely diagnosed, though some researchers think it is less rare than once believed) also have "migrainous" symptoms, like my occasional nausea and sensitivity to light.

How quickly I was willing to take on the risks of indomethacin! I felt dizzy, clumsy, weak, but whether this was the medication or the headache is hard to say. The continual pain faded into the background, turning into a kind of internal pressure, as though the headache were pushing on the inside of my head, trying to get out. The surges diminished in frequency, and then in intensity, but didn't cease. Beneath the business of preparing for my son's wedding, a monotone of dull pain; on top of the happiness and cheer, the faint perfume of indomethacin. After a few weeks, I found myself sinking to the bottom of Maslow's hierarchy of needs: in danger. One night my heart began to skitter and twitch; I lay in bed and hoped they wouldn't take my medicine away.

I didn't tell my doctor about my heart, but still she refused to increase my dose, instead referring me to Dr. N., a neurologist with a weeks-long waiting list. Together they decided to start me right away on a low dose of gabapentin, an anticonvulsant.

Almost immediately, my heart settled down. But that week of weaning myself off the indomethacin gave me a headache that seemed to fill the world. When I woke each morning, I couldn't think clearly. *What time is it?* I would wonder. *What's going on?* Eventually I would rise, going straight for the morning dose, then dip my head under the faucet before climbing into the shower, pulling on clothes, and careening into the kitchen to line my stomach for the pills. Within an hour of each dose, I'd feel better. I've never needed medication in this acutely timed way before; it seemed the first sign of a fatal erosion. I resented the needing of it.

I waited three weeks for the next appointment and went back to Dr. N., who was not smiling. "I've reached my limit on headaches," he told me. "I'm a general neurologist. If you had Parkinson's disease? Multiple sclerosis, epilepsy—that's what I do."

Having reached the mountaintop of his exam table again, I was not willing to relinquish it so quickly. "Do you think it's possible this really is a persistent headache?" I asked. NDPH: the headache that never goes away, never gets diagnosed beyond its own description, with few treatments. He nodded. "Yes, perhaps." Precise syllables, a cock of the head.

In order to see a headache specialist, I had to get authorization from my insurance provider to go out of network. I have good insurance, but I was into this for thousands of dollars by then. As the bills began to arrive, I could see why people delayed treatment, or gave up. More time on the phone, more voicemails, explaining myself to the point of crying, head in hand, letters, more calls, more waiting. How do people who don't know how to work the system navigate it? How do people *with headaches* navigate it?

I had reached a point of feeling almost infinitely strange. I still had a headache all the time, though it was masked; I was depersonalized. Something almost like an aura ebbed and flowed away—the feeling of a crucial piece broken wild and loose, the cotter pin of control. After a particularly bad day, when my skin felt like fuzzy wool and I was afraid to drive and I couldn't get an appointment with anyone, I cut back on my medication; I had plenty now, and I had reached the point of prescribing for myself. Soon my thinking cleared up, but the surges renewed—pain, and a frisson of electricity around the eye, into the cheek, a vague tingle. I found myself getting used to it.

Dr. P.'s headache clinic was just off a busy freeway exit at the junction of two overgrown suburbs of Portland, a cheap second-story office with a few small rooms and cardboard boxes piled in one corner next to a few chairs near the secretary's desk.

First we talked: the entire history of the headache, my family medical history, the medications I'd taken, how I felt right then. When I tried to explain that I sometimes felt like I had a headache without actually having pain, she knew what I meant. She heard this a lot—that something feels wrong in the head in an uncertain way. All she does is headaches; the only patients she sees are patients like me, struggling to explain the way it feels inside our heads, stumbling over words because each thought is work. It was only after we had talked for forty-five minutes that she examined my reflexes, balance, gait, grip strength, cranial-nerve function.

Finally, she pressed on my shoulders for a moment and stepped back. "I'm quite sure this is hemicrania. The indomethacin didn't work perfectly because you couldn't take a high enough dose." She had seen it before. We discussed alternative drugs, one of which, topiramate, is known to cause memory and speech problems. She suggested lamotrigine, another anticonvulsant, instead, noting that I would have to increase the dose very slowly. Lamotrigine has interesting side effects—behavioral changes, nausea, double vision, and the rare Stevens–Johnson syndrome, a widespread inflammatory reaction in which large sections of skin blister and slough off. Lamotrigine can also cause headaches.

I winced at her description. "How long do I need to take it?" "I hope I can talk you into a year," she answered. "Sometimes hemicrania just burns itself out. Sometimes it doesn't." The quiet paring of disease, the fraying at the edges of liver and heart, the vision slowly blurring, the cough that sticks around. Sometimes we can only rely on a kind of maladaptation. We get used to it.

All along, I have written about *my* headache, as though it were a possession, something I could grasp. This headache has been my close companion for a while now; we are intimate. Perhaps hemicrania is not that uncommon, but I've never met anyone else who has it. That my doctor even knew enough to suspect it is to her credit; most doctors and nurses I know have never heard of it. Most have never heard of chronic daily headache, and several have asked me, "So when someone tells me they've had a headache for years, maybe I should believe them?" Yes, I say. Believe them.

I'm on a drug that is not benign; I've gained some weight, and my blood pressure has gone up a bit. I am still occasionally dizzy, and, for the first time in my life, I'm sensitive to the sun. Only months after I began taking lamotrigine did I suddenly remember that it is sometimes used for mood disorders; now and then I wonder how much of my sense of well-being is just the chemical. But it helps.

Reading my journal from the spring, I find it hard to accept my fragile handwriting, the daily recording of what felt like slow destruction. I don't have a headache most of the time now, and not having a headache is like being twenty years younger. I have energy and good cheer and I can hike and travel. I can write again, at last. Then the surge comes. I stop, hold my hand against my temple, cupping my eye. I stand still for a moment, feeling the pain scrape across the bone above my eye and fade. And then I forget again.

Discussion Starters

1. How according to Tisdale does the pain of an excruciating headache differ from other physical pains? Does that differentiation make sense to you?
2. Based on Tidale's experiences with doctors and medications as she sought out help, how do you view the process of medical diagnosis and prescription?
3. Have you had personal experience or know of others who have experienced severe headaches? How is your experience different from or similar to Tisdale's?

VIII. Jobs and the Economy

Tough Job Outlook for College Grads

By Catherine Rampell

> *Catherine Rampell writes about economics for The New York Times. In this essay, Rampell reveals the difficult job situation for recent college graduates, how they are coping, and how best to survive in a tight job market.*

The individual stories are familiar. The chemistry major tending bar. The classics major answering phones. The Italian studies major sweeping aisles at Wal-Mart. Now evidence is emerging that the damage wrought by the sour economy is more widespread than just a few careers led astray or postponed. Even for college graduates—the people who were most protected from the slings and arrows of recession—the outlook is rather bleak.

Employment rates for new college graduates have fallen sharply in the last two years, as have starting salaries for those who can find work. What's more, only half of the jobs landed by these new graduates even require a college degree, reviving debates about whether higher education is "worth it" after all.

"I have friends with the same degree as me, from a worse school, but because of who they knew or when they happened to graduate, they're in much better jobs," said Kyle Bishop, 23, a 2009 graduate of the University of Pittsburgh who has spent the last two years waiting tables, delivering beer, working at a bookstore and entering data. "It's more about luck than anything else."

The median starting salary for students graduating from four-year colleges in 2009 and 2010 was $27,000, down from $30,000 for those who entered the work force in 2006 to 2008, according to a study released on Wednesday by the John J. Heldrich Center for Workforce Development at Rutgers University. That is a decline of 10 percent, even before taking inflation into account.

Of course, these are the lucky ones—the graduates who found a job. Among the members of the class of 2010, just 56 percent had held at least one job by the spring, when the survey was conducted. That compares with 90 percent of graduates from the classes of 2006 and 2007. (Some have gone for further education or opted out of the labor force, while many are still pounding the pavement.)

Even these figures understate the damage done to these workers' careers. Many have taken jobs that do not make use of their skills; about only half of recent college graduates said that their first job required a college degree.

The choice of major is quite important. Certain majors had better luck finding a job that required a college degree, according to an analysis by Andrew M. Sum, an economist at Northeastern University, of 2009 Labor Department data for college graduates under 25. Young graduates who majored in education and teaching or engineering were most likely to find a job requiring a college degree, while area studies majors—those who majored in Latin American studies, for example—and humanities majors were least likely to do so. Among all recent education graduates, 71.1 percent were in jobs that required a college degree; of all area studies majors, the share was 44.7 percent.

An analysis by the *New York Times* of Labor Department data about college graduates aged 25 to 34 found that the number of these workers employed in food service, restaurants and bars had risen 17 percent in 2009 from 2008, though the sample size was small. There were similar or bigger employment increases at gas stations and fuel dealers, food and alcohol stores, and taxi and limousine services.

This may be a waste of a college degree, but it also displaces the less-educated workers who would normally take these jobs.

"The less schooling you had, the more likely you were to get thrown out of the labor market altogether," said Mr. Sum, noting that unemployment rates for high school graduates and dropouts are always much higher than those for college graduates. "There is complete displacement all the way down."

Meanwhile, college graduates are having trouble paying off student loan debt, which is at a median of $20,000 for graduates of classes 2006 to 2010. Mr. Bishop, the Pittsburgh graduate, said he is "terrified" of the effects his starter jobs might have on his ultimate career, which he hopes to be in publishing or writing. "It looks bad to have all these short-term jobs on your résumé, but you do have to pay the bills," he said, adding that right now his student loan debt was over $70,000. Many graduates will probably take on more student debt. More than 60 percent of those who graduated in the last five years say they will need more formal education to be successful.

"I knew there weren't going to be many job prospects for me until I got my Ph.D.," said Travis Patterson, 23, a 2010 graduate of California State University, Fullerton. He is working as an administrative assistant for a property management company and studying psychology in graduate school. While it may not have anything to do with his degree, "it helps pay my rent and tuition, and that's what matters."

Going back to school does offer the possibility of joining the labor force when the economy is better. Unemployment rates are also generally lower for people with advanced schooling. Those who do not go back to school may be on a lower-paying trajectory for years. They start at a lower salary, and they may begin their careers with employers that pay less on average or have less room for growth. "Their salary history follows them wherever they go," said Carl Van Horn, a labor economist at Rutgers. "It's like a parrot on your shoulder, traveling with you everywhere, constantly telling you 'No, you can't make that much money.' "

And while young people who have weathered a tough job market may shy from risks during their careers, the best way to nullify an unlucky graduation date is to change jobs when you can, says Till von Wachter, an economist at Columbia. "If you don't move within five years of graduating, for some reason you get stuck where you are. That's just an empirical finding," Mr. von Wachter said. "By your late 20s, you're often married, and have a family and have a house. You stop the active pattern of moving jobs."

Discussion Starters

1. What evidence is provided in the essay that the job market for college graduates is rather bleak? Do you find the evidence convincing?

2. How does the reality of college grads having to take lower-paying jobs to make ends meet affect those in the job market with a high school degree or less? Is a college degree still worth the cost?

3. How does the knowledge of a tough job market affect your own college plans if at all? Do you take into account the job market in deciding on a major?

What is Wrong with Capitalism?

By Thomas Storck

Thomas Storck is the author of three books relating Catholic social teaching and political principles, and his essays appear in many publications including the New Oxford Review. In this essay, Storck details what he considers the problems with capitalism and its negative impact and offers a better alternative.

Since at least the first half of the nineteenth century one of the main causes of strife in our civilization has been our capitalist economic system. Capitalism has had many bitter opponents, socialists of all kinds, to be sure, but many also who while they disdained any affinity with socialism, nevertheless rejected capitalism or at least called for major reforms in its workings. Supporters of capitalism seem not to understand such criticism, sometimes even resorting to psychological explanations for hostility to capitalism, as if by positing a subjective reason for their hostility they could somehow dismiss their opponents' arguments without refuting them. But why is capitalism so hated? What, if anything, is wrong with it that evokes such animosity?

Since it is important that disputes about ideas be separated from mere verbal quarrels, it is necessary to state exactly what capitalism is before a serious discussion of its merits or demerits can take place. I realize that there is no generally accepted definition of capitalism. Although most people would agree that our present economic system is capitalistic, few would agree about why this was so. Is it because of private property, because most economic decisions are made by non-state actors, because there is relative freedom of legal competition?

Although all of these are likely to characterize a capitalist economy, I do not think that any of them gets to the essential note of capitalism. This essential note I put in the separation of capital from labor, the fact that in a capitalist economy the most usual situation is for those with capital to hire others to work for them, making use of the means of production owned by the employers. Thus what I mean by capitalism is an economy whose distinguishing mark is the employer/employee divide, where the majority of economic activity is carried on not by owners of small property working for themselves, but by capitalists who employ others to work for them for wages.

Although such an economic arrangement is not in itself unjust, nevertheless it is nearly always productive of great mischief, injustices, evils whose consequences extend far beyond the economy itself. Why is this so? The shortest answer is one given by the English historian, social theorist, poet and novelist, Hilaire Belloc.

> But wealth obtained indirectly as profit out of other men's work, or by process of exchange, becomes a thing abstracted from the process of production. As the interest of a man in *things* diminishes, his interest in abstract wealth – money – increases. The man who makes a table or grows a crop makes the success of the crop or the table a test of excellence. The intermediary who buys and sells the crop or the table is not concerned with the goodness of table or crop, but with the profit he makes between their purchase and sale. In a productive society the

superiority of the things produced is the measure of success: in a Commercial
society the amount of wealth accumulated by the dealer is the measure of success.

Let us look at this further. All proper human activity exists for an end. Eating, for example,
has the primary end of sustaining human life and health, although it has several secondary ends,
such as fostering fellowship. Now the production and use of all external goods also has its purpose,
the sustaining of human life so that we can pursue what is most characteristic and most important
for mankind, our family and social life, our intellectual life, our spiritual life. Economic activity of
its nature is subordinated to those higher ends and when it forgets or rejects those ends, it begins
to dominate and distort human society. This natural subordination is most easily perceived when
economic activity is directly tied to production for use. In the past when craftsmen usually worked
only because a customer had put in an order for an item, it was difficult to forget the essential
orientation of economic activity to its end.

The separation of ownership from work, however, meant that the owners of capital, in some
degree at least, became removed from actual production for meeting mankind's needs. As a result
these capitalists tended to become preoccupied not in serving man's needs for goods, but in simply
amassing wealth itself. "As the interest of a man in *things* diminishes, his interest in abstract wealth
– money – increases." And when goods began to be produced in mass, goods which then needed to
be sold, buyers had to be found – or an artificial demand had to be created by advertising. Owners
cared little if their products were well-made or useful, so long as they could be sold, often by making
consumers think they needed the product to be happy.

But although this was evil enough, the logic of capitalism did not stop here. For if one's interest
is in wealth, why produce a product at all? Why not spend one's time manipulating surrogates for
real wealth, such as currencies, stocks and bonds, peddling junk securities, engineering mergers and
buyouts? This was often an easier way to make money, and although it bore almost no relation to
supplying mankind's need for goods and services, it certainly served to make some people very rich.
Nor did these capitalists hesitate to gain and use political power, when they could, to further their
ends, using their money to buy politicians in order to make the legal system more favorable to their
aims and remove whatever restraints on their activities existed in the law.

Capitalism, however, has done more than pervert the purpose of economic activity. It has
turned our society into a commercial society, a society inclined to measure everything by a money
standard. Thus education is valued chiefly as the ticket to a better job, the number of those studying
the liberal arts declines, and business professors generally command much higher salaries than
philosophy professors.

Moreover, since under capitalism the economy is no longer tied to a fulfillment of man's real
needs, but rather to what can be sold, it no longer has any natural limit. As St. Thomas Aquinas
wrote, "...the appetite of natural riches is not infinite, because according to a set measure they
satisfy nature; but the appetite of artificial riches [i.e. money] is infinite, because it serves inordinate
concupiscence...."

Under capitalism the economy has become unhinged, as it were, disconnected from its
purpose, a purpose which both limits it and gives it direction. As a result, a corporation is not
satisfied if its sales remain stable; they must increase from quarter to quarter. This attitude has
infected society as a whole, so that few are happy unless they acquire newer and better gadgets,

regardless of whether these serve human life as a whole. Although we are not determined by our economic relations, as Marx erroneously believed, society can be influenced by how it conducts economic activity, and when such activity is disoriented from any rational goal, it tends to disorient all of society.

Probably all religions and all serious philosophies have recognized that human life is not about the mere acquisition of wealth. Indeed, they have often warned of the dangers that riches pose to cultivation of human virtue. Our modern world, and especially the United States, has elevated the acquisition of wealth to such a point that it tends to distort almost all social relations. Capitalism, the separation of ownership from work, of economic activity from serving man's needs, is at the root of this. It is true that not all critics of capitalism have a vision of man that corresponds to truth in all respects. But nearly all of them, even those most confused, sense something fundamentally wrong with a system in which "the appetite of artificial riches" and "inordinate concupiscence" reign supreme and almost unhindered.

There is a better way. Our ancestors understood the need for curbing and guiding our powerful appetite for gain, just as we curb and guide our appetite for sexual pleasure. Opposition to capitalism does not equate with socialism. We need to recover the approaches to economics represented by distributism, by solidarism. Otherwise we will continue to destroy our social order, deform our environment, both within and outside us, and spend our time on earth in pursuit of things unworthy of human persons.

Discussion Starters

1. What are the "evils" of capitalism presented in the essay? Do you agree with the author? How would supporters of capitalism respond?
2. Stoerk calls up a long-past economy where small business people created products based on customer need. Would it be possible to return to such an economy today? What other options may be available to the capitalist system described by Stoerk?
3. Do you agree with Stoerk that due to our capitalist system, Americans are obsessed with making money and acquiring things they often don't need?
6. Do you feel our capitalist system has badly distorted American values?

Retails Hidden Potential

By Catherine Ruetschlin

Catherine Ruetschlin is an economic policy analyst and writer for Demos.org. In this essay, Ruetschlin argues that improving the compensation of retail employees would provide a living wage for millions of Americans currently living below the poverty line and also provide a boost to the economy and the companies they work for.

With more than 15 million workers in the sector, and leverage over workplace standards across the supply chain, retail wields enormous influence on Americans' standard of living and the nation's economic outlook. It connects producers and consumers, workers and jobs, and local social and economic development to the larger US economy. And over the next decade, retail will be the second largest source of new jobs in the United States.

Given the vital role retail plays in our economy, the question of whether employees in the sector are compensated at a level that promotes American prosperity is of national importance. According to the Bureau of Labor Statistics, the typical retail sales person earns just $21,000 per year. Cashiers earn even less, bringing home an annual income of just $18,500.

The continued dominance of low wages in this sector weakens our nation's capacity to boost living standards and economic growth. Retail's low-wage employment means that even Americans who work full-time fail to make ends meet, and growth slows because too few families have enough remaining in each paycheck to contribute to the broader economy.

This study assumes a new wage floor for the lowest-paid retail workers equivalent to $25,000 per year for a full-time, year-round retail worker at the nation's largest retail companies—those employing at least 1,000 workers. For the typical worker earning less than this threshold, the new floor would mean a 27 percent pay raise. Including both the direct effects of the wage raise and spillover effects, the new floor will impact more than 5 million retail workers and their families.

This study examines the impact of the new wage floor on economic growth and job creation, on consumers in terms of prices, on companies in terms of profit and sales, and for retail workers in terms of their purchasing power and poverty status.

Effect on Workers and Their Families

More than 700,000 Americans would be lifted out of poverty, and more than 1.5 million retail workers and their families would move up from in or near poverty. Retail jobs are a crucial source of income for the families of workers in the sector, yet currently more than 1 million retail workers and their family members live in or near poverty. More than 95 percent of year-round employees at large retail firms are ages 20 and above. More than half (54.2 percent) of workers in this group contribute at least 50 percent of their family's total income. A large number of them – almost 1 in 5 – are the sole earner for their family. Our study finds:

A wage standard equivalent to $25,000 for a full-time, year-round employee would lift 734,075 people currently in poverty – including retail workers and the families they support – above the federal poverty line.

An additional 769,191 people hovering just above poverty would see their incomes rise to above 150 percent of the poverty line.

The Effect on Economic Growth and Job Creation

The economy would grow and 100,000 or more new jobs would be created. Families living in or near poverty spend close to 100 percent of their income just to meet their basic needs, so when they receive an extra dollar in pay, they spend it on goods or services that were out of reach before. This ongoing unmet need makes low-income households more likely to spend new earnings immediately – channeling any addition to their income right back into the economy, creating growth and jobs. This "multiplier effect" means that a higher wage standard for retail workers will also generate new jobs.

Our estimates of the job creation effect are derived from widely accepted multipliers on consumer spending. It includes the benefits of a raise on disposable income and accounts for the impact of any additional costs to the firm and the potential for businesses to pass-through the cost of decent wages onto their customers through higher prices. In order to account for uncertainty regarding the firm's willingness to pay for the raise out of profits, we offer both low and high measures of the total impact of the raise. Estimating both low- and high-end estimates, our study finds that:

A wage standard at large retailers equivalent to $25,000 per year for full-time, year-round workers would increase GDP between $11.8 and $15.2 billion over the next year.

As a result of the economic growth from a wage increase, employers would create 100,000 to 132,000 additional jobs.

Effects on Retail Sales

Increased purchasing power of low-wage workers would generate $4 to $5 billion in additional annual sales for the sector. Much of the increased consumer spending by low-wage workers after the raise will return to the very firms that offered the raise. The average American household allocates 20 percent of their total expenditures toward retail goods, but for low-income households that proportion is higher. A raise for workers at large stores would bring billions of dollars in added retail spending back to the sector. Our study finds that:

> Assuming that workers do not save money out of their wage income, the additional retail spending by employees and their families generated by the higher wage would result in $4 to $5 billion in additional sales across the retail sector in the year following the wage increase.

Effects on Companies

The additional payroll costs would represent a small fraction of total sales. Our study measures the total cost of the higher wage standard with generous assumptions by accounting for the likely effects of wages on those workers currently earning just above the wage floor. We assume that every worker earning less than $17.25 will receive additional compensation as firms adjust pay scales in order to preserve their internal wage structures or to reward workers with long tenures or supervisory positions. That assumption probably overstates the indirect cost of raising wages at the bottom, since it extends to workers earning well above the cutoff for spillover effects that have been observed in empirical research. Yet the cost of the increase under these assumptions is just a small percentage of payroll or sales. Our study finds that the cost of the wage increase amounts to $20.8 billion, or just 1 percent of the $2.17 trillion in total annual sales by large retailers. Alternatively, it represents 6 percent of payroll for the retail sector overall, or 10 percent for those firms with more than 1000 employees.

Using profits to pay for the wage increase would be a more productive use than the current trend towards stock repurchases. In the first half of 2012, large retailers earned over $35 billion in profits and paid out $12.8 million in dividends. Though unlikely, companies could choose to pay the full cost of a higher wage standard out of profits alone. Our study suggests that this use of profits would be more economically productive than the increasingly common practice of "stock buybacks": retailers repurchasing public shares of company stock in order to boost earnings per share. Buybacks allow the firm to consolidate earnings; shareholders benefit by receiving higher earnings without paying taxes on dividends, and where compensation is tied to performance, executives get a hike in their paychecks. But share repurchases do not contribute to the productivity of the industry or add to economic growth, in contrast to a raise that benefits over 5 million workers and the firms where they are employed. In 2011, the top 10 largest retailers alone spent $24.8 billion on stock repurchases, billions more than the $20.8 billion all large retailers could have productively invested in their workers.

Effects on Prices

The potential cost to consumers would be just cents more per shopping trip on average. If retail firms were to pass the entire cost on to consumers instead of paying for it by redirecting unproductive profits, shoppers would see prices increase by only 1 percent. But productivity gains and new consumer spending associated with the raise make it unlikely that stores will need to generate 100 percent of the cost. More plausibly, prices will increase by less than the total amount of the wage bill, spreading smaller costs across the entire population of consumers. The impact of rising prices on household budgets will be negligible, while the economic benefits of higher wages for low paid retail workers will be significant. Our study finds that:

- If retailers pass half of the costs of a wage raise onto their customers, the average household would pay just 15 cents more per shopping trip—or $17.73 per year.
- If firms pass on 25 percent of the wage costs onto their customers, shoppers would spend just 7 cents more per shopping trip, or $8.87 per year.
- Higher income households, who spend more, would absorb a larger share of the cost. Per shopping trip, high income households would spend 18 cents more, for a total of $36.80 per year. Low-income households would spend just 12 additional cents on their shopping list, or $24.87 per year.

Large Retailers Can Afford It

If the nation's biggest retailers raised the floor on wages to the equivalent of $25,000 per year for full-time, year-round work, the cost would be just 1 percent of total sales and would generate $4 to $5 billion of additional retail revenue.

The cost of increasing the living standards of more than 5 million Americans, adding $11.8 to $15.2 billion to GDP, and creating no less than 100,000 jobs amounts to just a small portion of total earnings among the biggest firms. The retail sector takes in more than $4 trillion annually and firms with 1000 or more employees account for more than half of that. At the same time labor compensation in the sector contributes only 12 percent of the total value of production, making payroll just a fraction of total costs. Large retailers could pay full-time, year-round workers $25,000 per year and still make a profit – satisfying shareholders while rewarding their workers for the value they bring to the firm. A raise at large retailers adds $20.8 billion to payroll for the year, or less than 1 percent of total sales in the sector. At the same time it is very likely the firm will experience benefits that offset the cost of the wage increase—in the form of productivity gains and higher sales per employee—making the net cost of the new wage even lower.

Elephant in Living Room

Walmart is the elephant in the retail living room. Operating 4,500 stores nationwide (including Sam's Club locations) and employing 1.4 million U.S. workers, Walmart is not only the nation's largest retail employer, it is America's largest private employer of any kind, and among its most profitable corporations. With one in every ten American retail employees working at Walmart, the company has an unparalleled capacity to reshape the landscape for retail work.

So far, Walmart has used this power to lower wages, cut hours, and deny benefits to its workforce, reducing the quality of retail jobs as a whole. The company's history of using extreme methods to push down the cost of labor stretches back at least to the 1960s, when founder Sam Walton set up shell companies to dodge federal minimum wage laws that would have forced him to pay employees $1.15 an hour. While Walton was ultimately forced by federal courts to drop the scheme, Walmart's continued practice of paying poverty-level wages and operating at the limits of the law to discourage unemployment and workers' compensation claims and deter employees from working overtime has been well documented.

A 2005 study from New York University found that Walmart employees earn 28 percent less, on average, than workers employed by other large retailers. At the same time, Walmart's sheer size and competitive influence exert a downward pressure on wages at other retailers. A study from the University of California Berkeley finds that Walmart store openings in communities lead to the replacement of better paying jobs with jobs that pay less. As a result of this dynamic, average wages for retail workers were 10 percent lower, and their job-based health coverage rate was 5 percentage points less in an area than it would be if Walmart did not exist. The study concludes that in 2000, retail employees nationwide would have taken home $4.5 billion more in their total paycheck if Walmart had not been around.

Yet Walmart could easily afford to set a different pattern for the retail sector—and, as the country's most profitable retailer whose shareholders are among the wealthiest people on Earth, do so without passing any of the costs to customers. The six heirs to the Walmart fortune have more wealth than the bottom 42 percent of American families combined, with holdings of almost $90 billion. Since last year, they've received more than $1.8 billion in dividend payments from their Walmart shares.

By raising wages and putting more than $4 billion into the hands of it underpaid workers, Walmart could have a significant impact on retail employment and the overall economy, while taking the lead as a trailblazer for the industry as a whole.

Conclusion

America's largest retailers play an important role in our nation's economy and in the well-being of millions of their workers' lives. It has become conventional wisdom that retail workers must be paid low wages. Yet our study, adding to a growing body of research, demonstrates that retailers could provide the nation a needed economic boost by paying higher wages, while remaining profitable and continuing to offer low prices. After years of slow economic growth and income stagnation or decline, retail can help put America back on track, creating meaningful gains for household budgets, GDP, employment, and their own outlook for growth.

Discussion Starters

1. Evaluate the positive results presented in the essay that raising the base salary for retail workers to $25,000 would have. Do you find the results plausible?
2. Large retailers argue that wage increases (like the minimum wage) would be passed on to and harm consumers. How does the essay refute this claim?
3. What would it take for large retailers to increase their employees' wages to the level suggested in the essay? Is the retail wage increase a realistic way of helping family's living at or below the poverty line?

The End of Middle Class Growth

By Jonathan Rauch

Jonathan Rauch is a guest scholar at the Brookings Institution in Washington and the author of six books and many articles on public policy, culture, and government. In this essay, Rauch paints a rather depressing picture of the condition of America's dwindling middle class and subsequent growing lower class and what must be done to reverse the trend.

If the American economy were an automobile, you would say the transmission is failing. The engine works, but not all wheels are getting power. To put the matter less metaphorically: The economy no longer reliably and consistently transmits productivity gains to workers. The result is that many millions of Americans, in particular less-skilled men, are leaving the workforce, a phenomenon the country has never seen before on the present scale.

Well. That was a mouthful. It certainly bites off more than Washington's polarized politicians can handle at the moment. In the next few months, they need to worry about the so-called fiscal cliff, the round of automatic tax increases and spending cuts that, if not averted, might start a recession. Plus a politically vexing debt-limit bill, which will need to be passed early in 2013. Plus a recovery that, for many Americans, feels more like a recession. (The median family income fell as much during the first two years of the recovery as it did during the two years of the recession itself, according to the Pew Research Center.) Plus a debt crisis and downturn in Europe. Isn't that enough?

Sadly, no. The U.S. economy has weakened, and much needs fixing—beyond the fiscal cliff—if it's to regain its strength. A reelected President Obama and a still-divided Congress face a lengthy To Do list for the economy. We've chosen eight entries: innovation, jobs, rising health care costs, entitlement programs, college-completion rates, infrastructure, housing, and retirement security. None of them will be easy to fix.

But first, let's consider a nexus of troubling economic trends that seem to be driving and deepening many of the specific problems—and may prove to be the most intractable problem of all. If *economic strength* means anything, it is that the economy can make almost everyone better off, thereby strengthening the country's social fabric as well as its balance sheet. Such an economy unites rather than divides us.

Today's economy, by that standard, is struggling. Its ability to deliver rising living standards across the income spectrum is in decline, and perhaps also in question. "This is a fundamental problem," says Robert J. Shapiro, the chairman of Sonecom, an economic consultancy in Washington. "This is America's largest economic challenge. People can no longer depend on rising wages and salaries when the economy expands."

A number of policy responses are on the agenda already, such as creating jobs, helping more students finish college, and reducing wage-denuding health care inflation. Others, such as reforming the federal disability program, have yet to attract much notice. In truth, however, the extent of Washington's ability to repair the economy's gearbox is an open question, because the problem is complex. It implicates not just one slipped gear but many: disruptions in long-established connections between productivity and earnings, between labor and capital, between top earners and everyone else, between men and work, between men and marriage. Together, they are bringing the economy to a place where a large and growing group of people—indeed, whole communities—are isolated from work, marriage, and higher education. That place might look like today's America, only with a larger welfare state. But it might just as easily bring social unrest and class resentment of a magnitude the country hasn't known before.

For decades, productivity and compensation rose in tandem. Their bond was the basis of the social compact between the economy and the public: If you work harder and better, you and your family will be better off. But in the past few decades, and especially during the past 10 years or so, the lines have diverged. This is slippage No. 1: Productivity is rising handsomely, but compensation of workers isn't keeping up.

True, compensation is still rising, on average. But the improvements are spotty. Production and nonsupervisory workers—factory, retail, and clerical workers, for example—saw productivity gains disappear from their paychecks much earlier and got hit harder than did supervisors and professionals. Over the past 30 years or so, their compensation has hardly risen at all.

"This is something that has been happening and building for years and is now really rooted in the economy, and it's vicious," said Lawrence Mishel, president of the Economic Policy Institute, a liberal think tank in Washington. "There's a remarkable disconnect. The problem isn't a lack of the economy producing sufficient income to make everybody's living standards improve—it's that the economy is structured so that the majority don't benefit." Or, to state the point more cautiously, the majority doesn't benefit from productivity gains very much—certainly, less than our parents and grandparents did.

The higher you stand on the income ladder, the better you are doing; the highest-paid 1 percent of earners soared above and away from everyone else, practically occupying an economy of their own. By contrast, the bottom 90 percent of earners—which is to say, almost everyone—saw barely any increase, and much of what they did see came in the boom years of the late 1990s.

So, productivity is rising, but it isn't being evenly allocated; the top is effectively disconnected from the rest of the spectrum—slippage No. 2. One reason, especially pronounced in the past decade or so, is that fewer of the productivity gains are flowing to workers, and more are flowing to investors. From the end of World War II through about 1980, almost two-thirds of every dollar of income generated by the economy flowed to workers in the form of wages and benefits. Beginning around 1980, workers' share began to slide and, in the past decade or so, has nose-dived, to about 58 percent. The difference went to shareholders and other investors—who provide capital rather than labor—in the form of higher returns on their holdings.

Why would workers be receiving a smaller share of output, and why would the share they do receive be skewed toward the top? No one is sure, but Sonecom's Shapiro tells a plausible story. First, globalization has reduced American companies' ability to raise prices, and thus to increase their workers' pay, without losing competitiveness against companies in, say, China and India. Second, a smaller share of the value that companies produce today comes from the physical goods made by people like factory workers, and a larger share comes from ideas and intangible innovations that people like software designers and marketers develop. Between the early 1980s and the mid-

2000s, Shapiro says, the share of a big business's book value accounted for by its physical assets fell by half, from 75 percent to only 36 percent. "So the basis for value shifts," Shapiro explains. "This is the full flowering of the idea-based economy." Which is great if you are a brain worker or an investor; otherwise, not so much.

As a result, less-educated workers are in trouble, and men are in trouble, and less-educated men are in deep trouble. The problem has become more serious than most people realize. "It has reached a very extreme point," said David Autor, a labor economist at the Massachusetts Institute of Technology.

Only a minority of Americans obtain four-year college degrees, and yet the economy offers ever-fewer well-paying jobs for men with nothing more than a high school diploma. Since 1969, the weekly earnings of the median full-time male worker have stagnated, according to economists Michael Greenstone of MIT and Adam Looney of the Brookings Institution's Hamilton Project on economic growth. Stagnation is disappointing, to put it mildly, given that the per capita gross domestic product has more than doubled (adjusted for inflation) since 1969. But men with only high school diplomas have faced worse than stagnation: Their earnings have dropped by around a fourth. And men who didn't finish high school have fared worse still: Their incomes sank by more than a third, leaving their inflation-adjusted earnings stranded in the 1950s.

In effect, the economy is telling less-educated men: Get lost. And they are doing just that. Forty years ago, virtually all men with at least a high school degree held jobs. Most high school dropouts worked, too. Most men, regardless of education, could make a decent living, and holding a job was the unquestioned norm. Any man who didn't work for years at a stretch was known as a bum. Since then, men have been steadily withdrawing from the workforce—but, again, not uniformly. Ninety percent of college-educated men are still working. But a fifth of men with only a high school degree weren't working in 2008, before the recession struck; today, a fourth of them don't hold a job. Among men who didn't finish high school, a third aren't working. As a result of these trends, America today is pockmarked with neighborhoods where nonwork is the male norm. Men's withdrawal from work isn't cyclical; it doesn't recover after downturns. Here, then, is slippage No. 3, arguably the most consequential: the decoupling of less-skilled men from jobs.

If you are out of the workforce, economic growth can't reach you, at least not directly. You might live off a girlfriend, receive welfare or disability payments, or dip in and out of the underground economy. But the performance of the economy as a whole becomes largely irrelevant. "A lot of these people will never work again," said Looney at Brookings. "Less-skilled workers are falling so far behind that they are going to place a huge strain on the social safety net in the coming decades."

Most measures of earnings look only at the incomes of men who work; their earnings have gone nowhere for the past 40 years. That measure, however, overlooks the large and growing population of men who don't work. If you add them to the mix and thereby look at the earnings of all American men, including nonworkers with zero income, you get a misery index for the male population. The median man in America, by this measure, is almost 20 percent worse off than he was four decades ago. The misery line sinks still lower, of course, for all men (working or not) with a high school degree but no college; their median earnings have fallen 40 percent.

Harder to quantify, but probably at least as important, are the social consequences of the broken link between less-educated men and work. Work, for men, means more than money: It connects them to their communities, makes them more attractive as mates and more successful as spouses, and is a linchpin of their self-esteem. When they don't work, their role in the community tends to wither, harming the places where they live as well as themselves. Their family lives suffer, too. More and more often, less-educated men are strangers to marriage.

It seems promising that scholars of left, right, and center are fastening onto the failure to transmit productivity gains to workers and starting to agree on its magnitude and importance. True, these scholars differ on causes and implications. Liberals emphasize economic forces that are eroding less-skilled workers' ability to make a decent living; conservatives emphasize cultural changes and government programs that make it easier to get by without working. Both views, actually, are probably correct: Economic *and* cultural forces are at work—and remedies to both can and arguably should be tried. Among the sorts of measures that experts are discussing:

- Get more people, especially men, through high school and college. The agenda includes an increase in financial aid and loans, a push for states to require that students stay in high school (as Obama has proposed), and encouragement of online learning.
- Expand federal support for job training and consolidate the tangle of programs. Obama wants to do this, too, as do many politicians in both parties—which doesn't make it a bad idea.
- Expand and improve vocational education for those not suited to college. Apprenticeship, in particular, can help prepare young men for the kinds of jobs that the economy increasingly creates. The United States does far less of this than, say, Germany does.
- Change Social Security disability benefits so that the program helps people keep working (and helps employers accommodate disabilities) instead of encouraging them to leave the workforce, as it does now. An analogous overhaul of welfare in the 1990s was a notable success.
- Liberals talk about increasing wage subsidies for low-skill jobs, raising the minimum wage, or both. Although such measures can be expensive, they may be worth it if they keep men working.
- Conservatives talk about nudging the culture back toward stigmatizing nonwork among men. "Don't prettify the way you talk about it," said AEI's Murray. "It is never rational not to take a job." Liberals may be squeamish about stigmatizing nonwork, but some men may need tough love.

The answer, of course, may be some or all of the above. In truth, another point of agreement is this: No one is sure what might work, because the country is in unexplored territory. "There's pretty much no precedent" for today's double detachment from work and marriage among low-earning men, Murray said. In any case, in the current political climate, before the fiscal cliff and after, most or all of the pricey ideas under discussion are probably a stretch.

And if nothing changes, what then? What will be the effect—on families, on kids, on neighborhoods, on politics and public spending—as millions of less-skilled Americans, and then entire neighborhoods and demographic groups, slip beyond the reach of economic growth? No one really knows, because the experiment hasn't been tried. Until now.

Discussion Starters

1. Evaluate the points of "slippage" the essay claims are responsible for the faltering economic situation for the majority of Americans. Which do you find most disturbing and intractable?
2. What effects, according to the essay, does the high unemployment rate and stagnant wages have on the social fabric of the country? Do you agree?
3. Evaluate the "solutions" presented in the essay to improve the economic conditions of most Americans. Which do you feel are most important?

Marriage Shows the Way Out of Poverty

By Jennifer A. Marshall

> *Jennifer A. Marshall is the Director of Domestic Policy Studies at The Heritage Foundation and contributor to The Daily Standard. In this essay, Marshall points to marriage as a cornerstone for economic success that is often overlooked.*

For years, the slogan "Stay in School" has communicated an anti-poverty message to young people. Now it's time for an even more important poverty-fighting theme: "Get Married." Every student knows that dropping out of high school will hurt her chances of succeeding in life. Major media, public education campaigns and government programs have told her so.

But does she know that having a baby outside marriage will put her and her child at serious risk of living in poverty? Last year, poverty in America grew more than ever before in the 51 years that the U.S. government has tracked the poor, the Census Bureau reported Sept. 16. The total climbed by 3 million to 44 million—or one in seven Americans.

The search is on for solutions. Regrettably, too little of the conversation is turning to the principal cause of child poverty: the collapse of marriage. Waiting until marriage to have children is the second of three "golden rules" for avoiding poverty that researchers identified over the years: (1) graduate from high school; (2) marry before having children; and (3) get a job.

Actually, being married is even more significant than graduating from high school for avoiding poverty. Robert Rector, a senior research fellow at The Heritage Foundation, shows this in a new paper, "Marriage: America's No. 1 Weapon Against Child Poverty." By contrast, typical responses to poverty call for more spending on government programs. Far from helping poor Americans escape dependency, however, massive increases in welfare spending over the past four decades have entrenched poverty across generations.

Proponents of a government solution also cite lack of quality education and decent-paying jobs. True, inner-city schools often are appallingly sub-par, but ever-increasing spending hasn't significantly improved educational quality and opportunity for those who need it most.

And although the bad news on poverty in part reflects increased joblessness during the recession, the economy doesn't explain the undercurrents trapping millions in persistent poverty. Three of every four Americans defined as poor—35 million of the 44 million total—are poor during economic booms, Rector notes.

Government anti-poverty programs fail because such persistent poverty is not primarily material. It's about relationships and behavior. Even in good times, fatherlessness and lack of work trap the underclass. Unwed childbearing has risen from 6.3 percent of all births in 1964, when President Lyndon Johnson launched the War on Poverty, to more than 40 percent today. As Rector shows, these single-parent families with children are six times more likely to be poor than are married couples with kids. Put differently, marriage lowers the probability of child poverty by 82 percent.

So why have we ignored the obvious? After all, marriage has been the standard in every human society. "Marriage is the way societies provide a map of life and norms about behavior," researcher Kay Hymowitz says. Role models and explicit messages create norms in society. That's why it's troubling to see the emergence of a "pattern of family non-formation," as scholar Heather MacDonald describes it.

Hymowitz and MacDonald, both affiliated with the Manhattan Institute, were among leaders invited by the U.S. Commission on Civil Rights to participate in a conference recently in Washington, by addressing the topic of "The Role of Family Structure in Perpetuating Racial and Ethnic Disparities." In minority communities, the collapse of marriage has become especially acute. More than half of Hispanic children are born to single mothers, as are seven out of 10 black children.

Among Hispanics, families headed by unmarried parents are three times more likely to be poor. For blacks, these families are five times more likely to be poor. Meanwhile, the growing trend is "multi-partner fertility"—an antiseptic term to describe the relational mess of women having children by more than one man. The Commission on Civil Rights deserves credit for tackling a subject too long considered off-limits. With lives at stake, America cannot afford to ignore these plain facts any longer.

How can we restore a cultural consensus on marriage and reduce child poverty? Rector suggests seven ideas. Among them: Policymakers should reduce anti-marriage penalties in welfare programs. Welfare offices and federally funded birth control clinics should provide facts about the value of marriage in fighting poverty. And, in low-income neighborhoods and schools with a high proportion of at-risk youth, public education campaigns should teach the benefits of marriage.

If we're asking fathers not to walk away from their children, Americans must not walk away from the difficult task of restoring a culture of marriage.

Discussion Starters

1. The essay draws a direct cause-and-effect relationship between getting married and staying out of poverty. Do you agree that such a relationship exists? Might there be other complicating factors?
2. The essay doesn't touch on *how* marriage keeps people out of poverty. If there is a connection between marriage and economic success, what do you think the causes are?
3. Do you agree with the essay that "restoring the culture of marriage" is important in our country? If so, how can it be restored?

U.S. Workers in a Global Job Market

By Ron Hira

Ron Hira is a professor of public policy at Rochester Institute of Technology and co-author of the book Outsourcing America. In this essay, Hira reveals the growing disconnect between the economic success of corporations and the hiring of American employees in the STEM (science, technology, engineering math) fields and what must be done to enhance the job opportunities for STEM majors in a global job market.

Among the many changes that are part of the emergence of a global economy is a radically different relationship between U.S. high-tech companies and their employees. As late as the 1990s, a degree in science, technology, engineering, or mathematics (STEM) was a virtual guarantee of employment. Today, many good STEM jobs are moving to other countries, reducing prospects for current STEM workers and dimming the appeal of STEM studies for young people. U.S. policymakers need to learn more about these developments so that they can make the critical choices about how to nurture a key ingredient in the nation's future economic health, the STEM workforce.

U.S. corporate leaders are not hiding the fact that globalization has fundamentally changed how they manage their human resources. Craig Barrett, then the chief executive officer (CEO) of Intel Corporation, said that his company can succeed without ever hiring another American. In an article in Foreign Affairs magazine, IBM's CEO Sam Palmisano gave the eulogy for the multinational corporation (MNC), introducing us to the globally integrated enterprise (GIE): "Many parties to the globalization debate mistakenly project into the future a picture of corporations that is unchanged from that of today or yesterday....But businesses are changing in fundamental ways—structurally, operationally, culturally—in response to the imperatives of globalization and new technology."

GIEs do not have to locate their high-value jobs in their home country; they can locate research, development, design, or services wherever they like without sacrificing efficiency. Ron Rittenmeyer, then the CEO of EDS, said he "is agnostic specifically about where" EDS locates its workers, choosing the place that reaps the best economic efficiency. EDS, which had virtually no employees in low-cost countries in 2002, had 43% of its workforce in low-cost countries by 2008. IBM, once known for its lifetime employment, now forces its U.S. workers to train foreign replacements as a condition of severance. In an odd twist, IBM is offering U.S. workers the opportunity to apply for jobs in its facilities in low-cost countries such as India and Brazil at local wage rates.

Policy discussions have not kept pace with changes in the job market, and little attention is being paid to the new labor market for U.S. STEM workers. In a time of GIEs, advanced tools and technology can be located anywhere, depriving U.S. workers of an advantage they once had over their counterparts in low-wage countries. And because technology workers not only create new knowledge for existing companies but are also an important source of entrepreneurship and startup firms, the workforce relocation may undermine U.S. world leadership as game-changing new companies and technologies are located in low-cost countries rather than the United States.

The new corporate globalism will make innovations less geographically sticky, raising questions about how to make public R&D investments pay off locally or even nationally. Of course, scientists and engineers in other countries can generate new ideas and technologies that U.S. companies can import and put to use, but that too will require adjustments because this is not a strategy with which U.S. companies have much experience. In short, the geographic location of inputs and the flow of technology, knowledge, and people are sure to be significantly altered by these changes in firm behavior.

As Ralph Gomory, a former senior vice president for science and technology at IBM, has noted, the interests of corporations and countries are diverging. Corporate leaders, whose performance is not measured by how many U.S. workers they employ or the long-term health of the U.S. economy, will pursue their private interests with vigor even if their actions harm their U.S. employees or are bad prescriptions for the economy. Simply put, what's good for IBM may not be good for the United States and vice versa. Although this may seem obvious, the policy and political processes have not fully adjusted to this reality. Policymakers still turn to the CEOs of GIEs for advice on what is best for the U.S. economy. Meanwhile, STEM workers have yet to figure out that they need to get together to identify and promote what is in their interest.

Most STEM workers have not embraced political activism. Consider employees in the information technology (IT) industry, one of the largest concentrations of STEM workers. They have by and large rejected efforts by unions to organize them. One might expect a professional organization such as the Institute of Electrical and Electronics Engineers (IEEE) to represent their interests, but IEEE is an international organization that sees little value in promoting one group of its members over another.

Because STEM workers lack an organized voice, their interests are usually neglected in policy discussions. There was no worker representative on the National Academies committee that drafted the influential report Rising Above the Gathering Storm. And although the Council on Competitiveness, which prepared the National Innovation Initiative, has representatives of labor unions in its leadership, they did not participate in any significant way on the initiative. Both studies had chairs who were CEOs of GIEs. It should come as no surprise, therefore, that neither of these reports includes recommendations that address the root problem of offshoring: the misalignment of corporate and national interests, in which firms compete by substituting foreign for U.S. workers. Instead, the reports diagnosed the problem as a shortage of qualified STEM workers and therefore advocated boosting R&D spending, expanding the pool of STEM workers, and recruiting more k-12 science and math teachers.

The emerging opportunities for GIEs to take advantage of high-skilled talent in low-cost countries have markedly increased both career uncertainty and risk for the U.S. STEM workforce. Many U.S. STEM workers worry about offshoring's impact on their career prospects and are altering career selection. For instance, according to the Computing Research Association, enrollment in bachelors programs in computer science dropped 50% from 2002 to 2007. The rising risk of IT job loss, caused in part by offshoring, was a major factor in students' shying away from computer science degrees.

Offshoring concerns have been mostly concentrated on IT occupations, but many other STEM occupations may be at risk. Princeton University economist Alan Blinder analyzed all 838 Bureau of Labor Statistics standard occupation categories to estimate their vulnerability to offshoring. He estimates that nearly all (35 of 39) STEM occupations are "offshorable," and he described many as "highly vulnerable." By vulnerable, he is not claiming that all, or even a large share, of jobs in those occupations will actually be lost overseas. Instead, he believes that those occupations will face significant new wage competition from low-cost countries. Further, he finds that there is no correlation between vulnerability and education level, so simply increasing U.S. education levels, as many have advocated, will not slow offshoring.

The National Science Foundation should work with the appropriate agencies such as the Bureaus of Economic Analysis, Labor Statistics, and the Census to begin collecting more detailed and timely data on the globalization of innovation and R&D. Workers need to know which jobs will be geographically sticky and which are vulnerable to being offshored so that they can make better choices for investing in their skills. But there is a great deal of uncertainty about how globalization will affect the level and mix of domestic STEM labor demand. The response of some workers appears to be to play it safe and opt for occupations, often non-STEM, that are likely to stay. Further, most employers, because of political sensitivities, are very reluctant to reveal what jobs they are offshoring, sometimes going to great lengths to mask the geographic rebalancing of their workforces. The uncertainty introduced by offshoring aggravates the already volatile job market that is characteristic of the dynamic high-tech sector.

STEM offshoring has created a pessimistic attitude about future career prospects for incumbent workers as well as students. To make STEM career paths more reliable and resilient, the government and industry should work together to create programs for continuing education, establish a sturdier safety net for displaced workers, improve information about labor markets and careers, expand the pool of potential STEM workers by making better use of workers without a college degree, and provide assistance for successful reentry into the STEM labor market after voluntary and involuntary absences. Some specific steps are:

- The government should encourage the adoption and use of low-cost asynchronous online education targeted at incumbent STEM workers. The program would be coordinated with the appropriate scientific and engineering professional societies. A pilot program should assess the current penetration rates of online education for STEM workers and identify barriers to widespread adoption.
- The Department of Labor should work with the appropriate scientific and engineering professional societies to create a pilot program for continuous education of STEM workers and retraining of displaced mid-career STEM workers. Unlike prior training programs, these should be targeted at jobs that require at least a bachelor's degree. Funding could come from the H-1B visa fees that companies pay when they hire foreign workers.
- The National Academies should form a study panel to identify on-ramps to STEM careers for students who do not go to college and recommend ways to eliminate barriers and identify effective strategies for STEM workers to more easily reenter the STEM workforce.

- Congress should reform immigration policy to increase the number of highly skilled people admitted as permanent residents and reduce the number of temporary H-1B and L-1 work visas. Rules for H-1B and L-1 visas should be tightened to ensure that workers receive market wages and do not displace U.S. citizens and permanent resident workers.

As workers in other countries develop more advanced skills, U.S. STEM workers must develop new skills and opportunities to distinguish themselves. They should identify and pursue career paths that are geographically sticky, and they should acquire more entrepreneurship skills that will enable them to create their own opportunities. The National Academies could help by forming a study panel to identify necessary curriculum reforms and best practices in teaching innovation, creativity, and entrepreneurship to STEM students. NSF should encourage and help fund study-abroad programs for STEM students to improve their ability to work in global teams.

The public sector—federal, state, and local government—is 19% of the economy and is an important mechanism that should be used by policymakers. There is a long, strong, and positive link between government procurement and technological innovation. The federal government not only funded most of the early research in computers and the Internet but was also a major customer for those new technologies. U.S. taxpayers have a right to know that government expenditures at any level are being used appropriately to boost innovation and help U.S. workers. The first step is to do an accounting of the extent of public procurement that is being offshored. Then the government should modify regulations to keep STEM intensive-work at home.

We are at the beginning of a major structural shift in global distribution of R&D and STEM-intensive work. Given the critical nature of STEM to economic growth and national security, the United States must begin to adapt to these changes. The responses that have been proposed and adopted so far are based on the belief that nothing has changed. Simply increasing the amount of R&D spending, the pool of STEM workers, and the number of k-12 science and math teachers is not enough. The nation needs to develop a better understanding of the new dynamics of the STEM system and to adopt policies that will advance the interests of the nation and its STEM workers.

Discussion Starters

1. How, according to the essay, has "offshoring" affected the STEM job market? What does it mean that "the interests of corporations and countries are diverging?"
2. Do you think that "offshoring" jobs is a permanent situation? What might it take to keep jobs in the U.S. and get corporations to bring "offshored" jobs back?
3. Might the "offshoring" of STEM jobs affect your future employment goals or those of others you know? What might be the best ways for a STEM college graduate to ensure best his/her chances of getting a job?

IX. Education

With Their Whole Lives Ahead of Them

By Jean Johnson and Jon Rochkind

> *Johnson is a Senior Fellow and Rochkind the Research Director at Public Agenda, a non-profit organization engaged in research projects in subjects ranging from education to government leadership. In this essay, the authors present the myths and the reality of why students drop out of college and what can be done to reduce the drop-out rate.*

According to the U.S. Department of Education, only 20 percent of young people who begin their higher education at two-year institutions graduate within three years. There is a similar pattern in four-year institutions, where about 4 in 10 students receive a degree within six years. And these bleak statistics on national college completion rates are averages. In some institutions, the numbers are even gloomier.

This is clearly a personal disappointment for the students and their families, but increasingly, experts and leaders see it as a threat to U.S. international competitiveness and a phenomenon that perpetuates economic insecurity and inequality. The question bedeviling many of those concerned about higher education and the economy is why so many college students drop out. Some 2.8 million students enroll in some form of higher education each fall, in two- and four-year programs and in public, private, online, and for-profit institutions. These young people are motivated enough to start college, and somehow they manage to find sufficient resources to enroll, but getting a college ID card, buying the books and showing up for class doesn't mean they are poised to complete a degree. What exactly goes wrong?

This study asks young Americans why so many college students drop out. It is designed to test the assumptions many of us make about college students today and why so many of them fail to graduate. It also helps to identify solutions that young people themselves say would help most. We surveyed more than 600 young adults, ages 22 to 30, who had at least some higher education coursework. We asked those who started college but did not complete a degree why they left, and we compared their views, experiences and responses with those of students who had successfully completed a two- or four-year college program.

Many of us envision young people living in college dorms, going to school full-time, attending ball games and fraternity parties, maybe working a few hours a week or in the summer to bring in a little spare cash. In high school, perhaps, they dreamed about going to a particular school, filled out application after application and waited eagerly for the acceptance letter to arrive. The facts, though, show quite a different picture:

- Among students in four-year schools, 45 percent work more than 20 hours a week.
- Among those attending community colleges, 6 in 10 work more than 20 hours a week, and more than a quarter work more than 35 hours a week.

- Just 25 percent of students attend the sort of residential college we often envision.
- Twenty-three percent of college students have dependent children.

The findings here reveal gaps in the higher education system that serve to undercut the efforts of students who need to work and go to school at the same time. They raise serious questions about long-standing policies that seem profoundly ill-suited to students who simply cannot afford to go to school full-time for several years. They powerfully suggest the need for innovative responses that would help more young Americans continue their education, but in better-organized and more cost-effective programs. The results of this research pose a challenge.

MYTH NO. 1: *Most students go to college full-time. If they leave without a degree, it's because they're bored with their classes and don't want to work hard.*

REALITY NO. 1: *Most students leave college because they are working to support themselves and going to school at the same time. At some point, the stress of work and study just becomes too difficult.*

The number one reason students give for leaving school is the fact that they had to work and go to school at the same time and, despite their best efforts, the stress of trying to do both eventually took its toll. More than half of those who left higher ed before completing a degree or a certificate say that the "need to work and make money" while attending classes is the major reason they left. Balancing work and school was an even bigger barrier than finding money for tuition. Those who dropped out are almost twice as likely to cite problems juggling work and school as their main problem as they are to blame tuition bills (54 percent to 31 percent). The problem often begins in the first year. Of those who fail to graduate, more than 6 in 10 report that the statement "I had to work as well, and it was too stressful trying to do both" described their first year of school; more than a third say it describes their first year "a lot."

In contrast, nearly half of those who graduated (48 percent) say this statement doesn't describe their first year in school at all. Few former students say they left college because they were bored or found that college "just isn't for them." Only about 1 in 10 students who have left college say a major reason they quit was that they didn't like sitting in class or thought the classes were too difficult.

More than a third (36 percent) of those who left school say that even if they had a grant that fully paid for tuition and books, it would be hard to go back. And twice as many of them say the need "to work full-time" (56 percent) and "family commitments" (53 percent) are major reasons they can't go back, compared with 26 percent who say they would "not be able to afford college." In the focus groups, young people often described their predicaments.

A young woman in Seattle said, "Yeah, I think [working and going to school] was hard. You want to work so that you can help pay off [your tuition and loans] so you don't have this accumulating debt. I think, for me, it always got in the way. I didn't have enough time in the day to get everything done." A young woman from the Phoenix area who had dropped out but recently returned to classes told us, "It's very hard because I go to school three nights a week. I work from 8 to 5. I don't get home until 9:30, 10 at night…I also think my dedication to my classes could be better if I didn't work as much."

A young man in Erie, Pennsylvania, who hoped to return to school described his fears that he might never get a diploma: "The reason why I'm set back is because I got a wife, kids. My wife's doing her thing. Once she's done with that then she can stay at home and take the side job, whatever that she's doing. Then I can do my thing at school, and then once I'm done we'll have the jobs."

Many of the young people we interviewed believed that they could not afford not to work for the time it would take to complete a degree. They had to have a paying job to make ends meet. Far from being slackers, as some people imagine, they were often assuming responsibilities and financial burdens that traditional full-time college students do not have to shoulder. It is a test of maturity and perseverance that more affluent students are usually not required to face.

Such responses to our survey are a bracing reminder that the world of higher education has changed markedly over the years. For many students today, the experience of "going to college" is a far cry from that of the stereotypical "Joe College" so often seen in the movies and on television. For these students, the balancing act is not between going to class and attending football games and frat parties; it's more likely between going to class and punching a clock in order to pay the rent. Theirs is a dilemma that relatively few government or higher education programs readily address.

MYTH NO. 2: *Most college students are supported by their parents and take advantage of a multitude of available loans, scholarships, and savings plans.*

REALITY NO. 2: *Young people who fail to finish college are often going it alone financially. They're essentially putting themselves through school.*

According to one recent analysis, college costs have risen more than 400 percent in the last 25 years, while the median family income has increased less than 150 percent. And even though the pressure of having to balance the demands of a job and school is the major reason young people say they drop out of college, it would be misleading to dismiss the role of rising college costs and stagnant family incomes. National statistics show that young people who leave college without a degree are more likely than their peers to come from less privileged backgrounds and to live in more precarious economic circumstances. This study revealed that these students often bear the full responsibility of paying for school: Nearly 6 in 10 students in our study who left higher education without graduating say that they had to pay for college costs themselves, rather than being able to count on help from their families. In contrast, more than 6 in 10 of those who completed their degrees say they had help from parents or other relatives to cover the costs of school.

Young people who fail to finish college are also substantially less likely to have received scholarships or financial aid, loans or even good advice about how to get help. About 7 in 10 of those who leave school report that they did not have scholarships or financial aid, compared with about 4 in 10 of those who graduate. The majority of students (62 percent) who told us that they alone were responsible for paying for college (regardless of whether they dropped out) report that their high school guidance counselors did a poor or only fair job of helping them to understand the college application process. Among students who had financial support from their parents, less than half said the same.

Unfortunately, about 3 in 10 of those young people who leave school without getting a diploma report that they have college loans—money that has to be repaid even though they do not have the financial leg up that a college degree affords. In many respects, they have the worst of both worlds—no diploma, but college loans to repay.

MYTH NO. 3: *Most students go through a meticulous process of choosing their college from an array of alternatives.*

REALITY NO. 3: *Among students who don't graduate, the college selection process is far more limited and often seems happenstance and uninformed.*

In recent years, the media have been awash with "can you believe it?" stories about the college selection and application process and the stress it engenders in affluent families. According to the coverage, families are organizing summer vacations around visiting colleges. High school students are filling out dozens of applications, sometimes with a "coach" whose job it is to help them present themselves at their best. A cottage industry of publications, Web sites and experts offers advice on selecting the right college and getting into it. But according to this survey, many young Americans—and especially those who fail to get a diploma—barely go through any college selection process at all. Their options may be quite limited because they do not have the financial resources to go away to school and/or they are able to consider only those options that mesh with their job schedules and family responsibilities.

In many instances, college selection is more constrained and happenstance than deliberate choice. Among those who did not complete college, two-thirds say they selected their school primarily for its convenient location, nearly 6 in 10 because its schedule worked with theirs and 57 percent because the tuition and fees were affordable. A third based their choice on the academic reputation of the school and only a quarter on recommendations from friends and family.

Given that students who drop out of college are far more likely to come from families in which neither parent has a college degree, the minimal role played by recommendations from friends and family may not be surprising. Perhaps most notable is that when respondents who dropped out of college were asked about the most important reason they chose their school, a third named convenience or proximity to their home.

In Seattle, a woman who had left college said, "I just picked [the school] that was close to where I lived and that a couple of my friends were going to." In Phoenix, a man told us, "It was ASU [Arizona State University] that I chose, partly because of cost and partly just because of proximity, because ASU is really the easiest school for me to get to from where I live." For students who successfully complete their degrees, the selection process is dramatically and substantively different: Their top reasons for choosing their school include that the school offered a desired program or major, the belief that going to the school will help them secure a good job and the school's academic reputation. Tuition and fees are important considerations for any college student today, but among those who dropped out, the selection process seems more a matter of chance or location, not the pursuit of a specific goal or future career.

MYTH NO. 4: *Students who don't graduate understand fully the value of a college degree and the consequences and trade-offs of leaving school without one.*

REALITY NO. 4: *Students who leave college realize that a diploma is an asset, but they may not fully recognize the impact dropping out of school will have on their future.*

This survey leaves little doubt that young Americans who dropped out of college often faced the double-edged challenge of working to make a living and going to school at the same time. What's more, many seem to have drifted into college without a specific goal or purpose beyond hoping for a "better job" or a "better future." But do those who fail to graduate have the same urgency about getting a degree as those who do graduate? Do they see the attainment of a degree as something essential to their future, something that requires whatever sacrifice and effort may be required?

This study and others have shown persuasively that most young people acknowledge that having a college degree will pay off in the end. Most also say they have received a fair amount of encouragement to go to college from family, school and other sources. Yet the findings here suggest that young people who leave college before finishing are somewhat less likely to hold these views passionately. That is, as a group they are less likely to strongly agree that their parents always instilled in them the importance of college, less likely to strongly agree that people who have a college degree make more money and less likely to say they would still go to college if they knew they could get a good job without a degree.

And, again, although most young people who drop out say that going to college was their plan even in high school, the numbers are slightly weaker than for those who successfully completed their degrees. Students who fail to graduate are 16 percentage points less likely to say that they always knew they would continue to college and 15 points less likely than those who completed college to say that their teachers and counselors probably thought they would go to college immediately after high school.

The differences here are subtle. Students who drop out of college are only slightly less likely to endorse the benefits of higher education or to say that attaining a degrees has always been their plan. In some respects, this may be a natural outcome of having left college – after all, one needs to believe that he or she still has a good future ahead.

Nevertheless, though these response variations are relatively small, they may play a role in a student's ultimate decision to leave school. For someone who is scrambling to work and attend classes at the same time and has taken on the burden of paying part or all of his or her own way, even a small amount of uncertainty could be the tipping point. Or, as an old Spanish expression has it, it could be the drop of water that finally makes the glass overflow.

Conclusion

Much of the broad national discussion about raising college completion rates has focused on making loans more available and keeping tuition costs in line. But the vast majority of young people who made the decision to leave college without a degree (or, in effect, had the decision made for them by circumstances) point first to options that would give them more flexibility in schedules and help them mitigate the challenge of working and going to school at the same time. Eight in

10 of those who did not complete college supported two proposals that they believe would make college graduation feasible: 1) making it possible for part-time students to be eligible for more financial aid (81 percent said this would help "a lot"); and 2) offering more courses in the evening and on weekends so that they could continue working while taking classes (78 percent said this would help "a lot").

Of course, there's little doubt that changes in costs and an expansion of the availability of financial aid would be enormously helpful to nearly all college students—those who complete their programs as well as those who struggle to do so. When young adults were asked to name which among our list of proposals would be most likely to help them and people like them, 25 percent of those who dropped out and 40 percent of those with degrees suggest as their top priority cutting the cost of college by a quarter.

Nearly two-thirds of young Americans who left college without finishing say that they have given a lot of thought to returning. In the focus groups, almost to a person, these young people talked about their aspirations and the hopes for their lives. A woman in Erie, Pennsylvania, described her dream: "I want the 8 to 5 [job], no weekends. I want the set schedule. I want the job that's indoors, nicer, and the majority of the time, if you want to move up in a job like that, you got to have a degree." A young woman in Seattle who aspired to become a teacher but had left school before getting her degree said, "I have to finish school. I'm already working with kids. I've worked in a day care for over six years. I have the experience. I just need to go back to school." Nearly every young person we talked to shared his or her desire to do more in life. Yet despite their dreams, many were working in jobs that didn't seem to offer any way to get where they want to go.

This study revealed some eminently practical steps that schools could take to benefit this group, beyond simply offering more and bigger loans to help pay tuition costs. Having enough money for tuition and books is step one, to be sure, but by itself that step may not provide the breathing space that many of these young people need to stay the course. Numerous responses suggest that one set of solutions might revolve around making part-time attendance more viable by giving those students better access to loans, tuition assistance and health care—benefits and services that are frequently available only to full-time students.

There may also be implications for employers. Are there ways that businesses can help part-time workers to pursue higher education, perhaps by providing access to health benefits or by offering more predictable working hours so that would-be students can more easily schedule their classes? Part-time work is often seasonal or otherwise vulnerable to the business cycle and other economic ups and downs. Would more secure part-time employment options be a game changer for some students?

In a focus group in Erie, Pennsylvania, several young women gasped in disbelief when the moderator listed child care as one of many possibilities for solutions to the college dropout problem. Of course that would help, several immediately agreed. "Would a college ever do that?" most of them asked. A woman in Seattle who had dropped out of college said, "The one [school] I was at, they have a huge waiting list for the day care. It was just really difficult to get in....It was all really complicated to get it subsidized, at least where you weren't paying $300 a week, plus whatever you're paying for tuition."

What is clear from these results is that it would be a mistake of the highest order to write off these young people because they dropped out of college. Nearly all young adults understand the value of knowledge and know-how in today's world. Even though many hedge their bets, given what's happened in their own lives, most do grasp the economic facts of life: Attaining a college degree can change your life. Most strive to complete school; most would like to return to school, but the realities of their lives become insurmountable obstacles.

Perhaps the most poignant evidence of how these young people really feel about college is this: Even though they themselves left before finishing—and chances are that many of those we spoke to will never return to higher education—fully 97 percent of young American parents who dropped out of college say that they will encourage their own children go to college. Given their aspirations and their clear message that some distinctly practical and attainable changes could genuinely enhance their prospects, the ball is now in our court. As a society, are we willing to act on what they have to say?

Discussion Starters

1. As a college student, do you find any of the reasons that the survey group of drop-outs gave for leaving college surprising? Are you more in tune with the four "realities" regarding college students than the four "myths?"
2. Evaluate the solutions suggested by the survey group: financial aid for part-time students, more flexible class schedules (e.g. weekends, nights), child care. Do you agree that such solutions would keep more students in college?
3. Discuss your own college/work/family responsibility situation. What if any roadblocks to your graduation do you see? How will you overcome them?

First-Generation College Graduates: Their Stories

By Luz Gonzalez

Luz Gonzales is Dean of the College of Social Sciences, Fresno State University. In this essay, Gonzales chronicles her story of going from a migrant fieldworker to a university dean.

My journey from fieldworker to educator took prayer, courage and hard work—lots of it. I never had the opportunity to attend high school and I began college at a third grade level in reading and mathematics.

I grew up following the harvest from state to state. As migrant farm workers, we traveled from Mexico to California to Oregon to Montana and back to Mexico, picking strawberries, tomatoes, grapes and sugar beets. Consequently, I received minimal schooling both in Mexico and in the U.S. During the winter months in Mexico, student teachers would come and leave quickly. From February to April we went to school in the U.S. Even then, we were often called out to help with the crop. Being a good farm worker isn't about how strong you are, it's about how fast you are. So there is always something kids can do in the fields to help the adults make more money.

After finishing the eighth grade at El Monte School in Orosi, CA, I started working full- time in the fields with my parents. With only a fifth grade education in Mexico, they knew just enough English to talk to the farmers and survive. But in his early twenties, my father got diabetes. In his thirties, he started developing complications in his toes and ankles and his eyesight deteriorated. At times, he was hospitalized as long as two months. I'm the oldest of six children, and the load on my mother was tremendous. She worked in the fields with six kids to care for, paid the bills, did the laundry, sat with my dad in the hospital and kept him up-to-date on everything so he could stay an involved, empowered member of the family. She kept it all together.

The bulk of what Latinos do is for family and community. We do some things for ourselves, and we're competitive in the fields, but we're raised to be cooperative within the family and to keep others in mind. It's just second nature that if you're done with your homework, mom would say, "help your brother or your sister." Or if you're going outside to play, she'd say, "don't go without your friend." I was an excellent fieldworker and could have made a lot of money, but my dad was the center of my life. When I thought about what would help him most I realized that I needed to speak the language the doctors and nurses spoke so I could protect him and assure that he got good medical care.

For many years my father wasn't happy about me going to college. It took awhile to convince him to let me attend. He was afraid I'd lose my culture, values and traditions, and afraid something would happen to me driving to school. In the 1960s and 70s, girls didn't have cars. They didn't go to college. They were supposed to get married, find a good farmer to work for, have kids and follow the crops and maybe finish the eighth grade. If they didn't take on these roles, they risked bringing shame on the family. But my mother backed me up all the way. "If I can get one of my six children out of the fields, I'll be happy," she said.

When I was 18, my father relented. I decided to become a missionary and, while still working in the fields, I enrolled at West Coast Bible College in Fresno. I had to learn everything I never got in elementary and secondary school and learn it fast. I shared a dorm with six English-speaking women who became my friends. Living with them, and listening to their conversations, was how I learned to speak English. I remember sitting under a tree with my text book in one hand and a dictionary in the other, struggling over every word. If I failed, I believed, everybody behind me would fail. If I went back home and said I couldn't do it, it would be the end of women trying. My mother's strength carried me for many years. It was from her that I learned not to give up and to dream bigger dreams.

After college, I taught a year and a half at a private Baptist school. That was when I realized teaching is my calling. I completed a second baccalaureate degree, a teaching credential, and a master's degree at California State University-Fresno. After earning a doctorate in teacher education at the University of Arizona, I returned to Fresno State as a full-time lecturer in 1989. Until then, at age 32, I continued to spend my summers picking tomatoes and working in the table grapes in the San Joaquin Valley. I couldn't stand the thought of my mom and sisters picking grapes and tomatoes while I was sleeping in. It was my mother who finally told me it was time to leave the fields behind and focus on education.

Across the years, as my father's health worsened, I studied every medical condition he developed. I was forced at times to request, and often demand, the best medical treatment for him. He spent a lot of time in the hospital, but we were always with him. When he needed a kidney transplant in 1996, I donated one to him. Unfortunately, he died 18 hours after the surgery. Despite his initial resistance to my getting an education, he was proud of me and my accomplishments. He could see in me that education doesn't mean losing the values you were raised with.

As a Latina educator, recruiting and enrolling Latinos is important to me. Through my own experience, I not only helped my parents, but the Latino community to understand the U.S. educational system. When I look into the eyes of worried parents, especially farmworkers, and I get to tell them in Spanish not to worry that their child will be well taken care of at our university, it makes me proud of my accomplishments. Seeing parents relax and feel comfortable about letting their children out of their nest and into ours is my reward.

By Mui Vuong

Mui Vuong is Director of Student Affairs at Fresno State University. In this essay, Vuong reveals the numerous obstacles she overcame as an uneducated immigrant on her road to becoming a respected educator.

"Ho.c Va^~n," — "education" is a privilege. Even in America, where education is an integral part of the culture, being educated makes you privileged. In third world countries like Vietnam where few educational institutions exist, people cannot even get an education unless they are already privileged. There, only the children of parents who hold important official positions can attend college, and many natives are fighting for equal access.

I was nine years old when my family and I left Vietnam for the United States. We were refugees in a small boat headed for a land we'd heard about but never seen. After six days at sea, we were rescued by the U.S. Navy. My family was sponsored by two American families from Utah. I was placed in the third grade in a school where my siblings and I were the only minority students. We spoke limited English. Despite this language barrier, however, I graduated from middle school as the valedictorian. Being recognized in this way made me realize I truly enjoy learning.

As the oldest child in my family, I was the one to pave the way. It was expected. I became multilingual, speaking Chinese, Vietnamese and English. Because my parents spoke so little English, I had to translate for them. One of the funniest experiences happened when I accompanied my dad to the doctor. I was in the seventh grade. My dad and I sat in the doctor's office and as the doctor spoke, I translated. Examining my dad, the doctor asked, "How is your dad's stool?" I must have had the most puzzling expression on my face because I was looking at the chair my dad was sitting on thinking it looked fine but wondering why the doctor would ask about his stool. Clearly, the doctor realized I didn't know the meaning of the medical term "stool." So he turned to me and said, "How is his shit?" I knew what that word meant!

Throughout high school, I was an eager student. But I was very lucky to have incredible teachers. I graduated seventh in my high school class. Even so, I had difficulty filling out the applications for admission and scholarships. My Math teacher helped me and so did my AP Chemistry teacher. She was a new teacher and very caring. Every day, she brought scholarship applications to class and helped us apply.

People from my culture and background knew very little about the social sciences, but I discovered a deep passion for psychology. I think, because of my experience as a refugee, I wanted to understand why people behave the way they do. I received a full scholarship from the Psychology Department at the University of Utah and graduated after four years. During that time, I accepted a part-time job as a math tutor working with the Upward Bound Program. Until then, I hadn't met students who were like me, students whose backgrounds were similar to my own. I was excited by meeting them and realizing I could help, and they were thrilled to work with me. So my start in working with low-income and first-generation college students was accidental. The experience spurred me on to pursue a Master's degree in Educational Psychology and eventually to enroll in the joint doctorate program with University of California, Davis and California State University, Fresno.

Although my family is proud of my academic achievement, I do not have support from them. The courage and determination it took for them to leave their native country for a place unknown to them with the hope that they and their children could live a better life inspires me. They never questioned whether I should go to college. That was a MUST. But my parents are still very traditional. They believe a woman's main role and responsibilities should be her family. It's very important to them that I have a family of my own. I'm not married yet, so in their view I haven't achieved the most critical thing in life. My career and academic achievement are perceived as secondary.

In 1998, I had an opportunity to visit Vietnam for the first time since my family and I left twenty years ago. There were many social and economic changes, but one critical factor, the reason we escaped, remains the same: the lack of educational support and opportunities. Even today, there are only a few educational institutions and only the most socially privileged can attend. Youth from poor family backgrounds or whose parents have limited political affiliations have no educational opportunity.

Consequently, hundreds of children beg in the street for food, money and whatever they can get to make ends meet. Often, these children stand outside restaurants and wait. As soon as the patrons finish their meal and stand up to leave, the kids rush to the table and eat whatever is left. This disturbing sight brought back sad memories. At the same time it reinforces and strengthens my conviction to pursue higher education and help others along the way.

By James E. Walton

James E. Walton is an English Professor at Fresno State University. In this essay, Walton tells the story of growing up in poverty with an uncaring step-father, his chance encounter with a man who would forever change his life, and their unlikely reconnection over thirty years later.

As a city champion in the 880-yard run in Canton, Ohio, in 1960, I always thought that athletics would be my ticket to college. I had wrestled varsity in high school and, sometime later, held my college's record in the mile run. In addition to my athletic ability, my grades were excellent, yet a partial scholarship to a local college was the only offer I received. So I gave up the idea of going to college.

Growing up in poverty with a stepfather who cared nothing about my siblings and me and who saw us as a burden, I knew he would not support the idea of my attending college nor would he provide any financial assistance. I'd heard it often enough. "Boy, when you turn 16 years old, there are 18 ways to get out of my house," he'd say, irritably. He was counting all of the windows along with the front and back doors.

So like my brother one year before, I graduated from high school at age 16 with no job prospects, no plan for further education and my allotted time to live at home had expired. The U.S. military offered the only hope, so I signed up for the Navy.

Two weeks prior to shipping out to Cleveland and eventually Viet Nam, I agreed to take my pastor's place in a church play performed across town at a "white" church. After the play, I was downstairs trying to arrange a ride home when a foreigner who I didn't know congratulated me on my role in the play and innocently asked, "How's school going?" "School?" I responded with some indignation. "I graduated!" "Well, why aren't you in college then?" the stranger shot back. I had no response to that impossibility.

A week later I received a phone call. "You have been on my mind," the stranger I'd met at the church said, "so I looked up your number." We talked for several minutes, then he asked to speak to my mother. As I feared, my mother mentioned to the stranger that I had signed up to join the Navy. This news spurred the caller into action. Reminding me that Seventh-day Adventists did not volunteer for the military (Seventh-day Adventists, as a matter of faith, only go to the military if drafted and only as conscientious objectors, at that), the caller tried to talk me out of going. He had no way of knowing the hateful and abusive ways of my stepfather, so I could only promise that I would try.

Even though I had not officially taken the military oath, I had given my birth certificate to a stern-faced local military recruiter and I didn't want to face him again. After some begging, my sister agreed to retrieve my birth certificate from the recruiter.

One week later, the stranger—having only met me once—called again to ask directions to my home. "I think I can get you into the college in Michigan that I attended," he told me. "I'll be at your house in about one hour. Can you be packed by then?"

I quickly tossed my few personal items in a pillow case, slung it over my shoulder, and was standing, waiting, by the time the stranger arrived. My stepfather only had discouraging words as the stranger approached our house. The Navy, he told me, was still my best option. "I won't be giving you a damn dime to go to no school," he said.

In sub-freezing temperatures and tall, drifting snow gusts, the stranger and I headed into the darkness toward a private university hundreds of miles away from Canton, Ohio in Berrien Springs, Michigan. I had not applied to attend the university. I hadn't even taken the SAT or the ACT. Three dollars, left over from the five-dollar bill a relative had given me for graduation, was all I had to cover room, board and tuition.

On the long, treacherous drive to Michigan, I learned that the stranger's name was Dr. Joseph Nozaki, a young physician serving out his residency in a local hospital. He hadn't slept for three days and was having difficulty staying awake. We stopped the car several times and ran in the snow to stay awake. During one of our runs around the car, he lost his wallet, but we decided to continue on to the university anyway.

Many challenges awaited me: working half days, going to class half days, living on government-surplus peanut butter at times, surviving without adequate clothes in frigid Michigan winters, and being saved once by the financial intervention of Dr. Nozaki when the college threatened to suspend me for lack of funds. Somehow, scratching my way and generally depending on the kindness of strangers, I graduated from Kent State University where I'd transferred during my third year.

Unfortunately during this time, I lost all contact with Dr. Nozaki, even though I visited the alumni office of his alma mater several times for updated addresses. The letters I sent to China, to Singapore, and to Hong Kong always came back a few months later stamped "address unknown."

After teaching high school in Canton for three years, earning a doctorate, then teaching at a liberal arts college for 20 years, my family and I moved 3,000 miles away from Ohio to Fresno where I began teaching at Fresno State. Miraculously, through a series of improbable events, I rediscovered Dr. Nozaki, who at age 79 is still a practicing surgeon. He had spent many years as a missionary on several continents before returning to his practice in Fresno. Dr. Nozaki and I had lunch together just yesterday—as we do weekly—at the church where we both are now members: Fresno Asian and Community Seventh-day Adventist Church. After 40 years I rediscovered my education angel.

Discussion Starters

1. What do the lives of the three first-generation graduates have in common? What obstacles did each have to overcome to get an education?
2. What did you find most inspiring about each of the personal stories? How did their experiences contribute to the people they are today?
3. Compare your own family and educational experiences to those of Gonzales, Vuong, and Walton. Do you share any similarities with them? How much easier, or more difficult, was your road to higher education than theirs?

The End of Men

By Hanna Rosin

Hanna Rosin is a writer for The Atlantic and has also has written for the Washington Post, The New Yorker, and GQ. In this essay, Rosin chronicles the depletion of men from the college ranks, its causes, the consequences for both men and women, and what can be done about the problem.

If you really want to see where the world is headed, of course, looking at the current workforce can get you only so far. To see the future—of the workforce, the economy, and the culture—you need to spend some time at America's colleges and professional schools, where a quiet revolution is under way. More than ever, college is the gateway to economic success, a necessary precondition for moving into the upper-middle class—and increasingly even the middle class. It's this broad, striving middle class that defines our society. And demographically, we can see with absolute clarity that in the coming decades the middle class will be dominated by women.

We've all heard about the collegiate gender gap. But the implications of that gap have not yet been fully digested. Women now earn 60 percent of master's degrees, about half of all law and medical degrees, and 42 percent of all M.B.A.s. Most important, women earn almost 60 percent of all bachelor's degrees—the minimum requirement, in most cases, for an affluent life. In a stark reversal since the 1970s, men are now more likely than women to hold only a high-school diploma. "One would think that if men were acting in a rational way, they would be getting the education they need to get along out there," says Tom Mortenson, a senior scholar at the Pell Institute for the Study of Opportunity in Higher Education. "But they are just failing to adapt."

This spring, I visited a few schools around Kansas City to get a feel for the gender dynamics of higher education. I started at the downtown campus of Metropolitan Community College. Metropolitan is the kind of place where people go to learn practical job skills and keep current with the changing economy, and as in most community colleges these days, men were conspicuously absent. One afternoon, in the basement cafeteria of a nearly windowless brick building, several women were trying to keep their eyes on their biology textbook and ignore the text messages from their babysitters. Another crew was outside the ladies' room, braiding each other's hair. One woman, still in her medical-assistant scrubs, looked like she was about to fall asleep in the elevator between the first and fourth floors.

When Bernard Franklin took over as campus president in 2005, he looked around and told his staff early on that their new priority was to "recruit more boys." He set up mentoring programs and men-only study groups and student associations. He made a special effort to bond with male students, who liked to call him "Suit." "It upset some of my feminists," he recalls. Yet, a few years later, the tidal wave of women continues to wash through the school—they now make up about 70 percent of its students. They come to train to be nurses and teachers—African American women, usually a few years older than traditional college students, and lately, working-class white women from the suburbs seeking a cheap way to earn a credential. As for the men? Well, little has changed.

"I recall one guy who was really smart," one of the school's counselors told me. "But he was reading at a sixth-grade level and felt embarrassed in front of the women. He had to hide his books from his friends, who would tease him when he studied. Then came the excuses. 'It's spring, gotta play ball.' 'It's winter, too cold.' He didn't make it."

It makes some economic sense that women attend community colleges—and in fact, all colleges—in greater numbers than men. Women ages 25 to 34 with only a high-school diploma currently have a median income of $25,474, while men in the same position earn $32,469. But it makes sense only up to a point. The well-paid lifetime union job has been disappearing for at least 30 years. Kansas City, for example, has shifted from steel manufacturing to pharmaceuticals and information technologies. "The economy isn't as friendly to men as it once was," says Jacqueline King, of the American Council on Education. "You would think men and women would go to these colleges at the same rate." But they don't.

In 2005, King's group conducted a survey of lower-income adults in college. Men, it turned out, had a harder time committing to school, even when they desperately needed to retool. They tended to start out behind academically, and many felt intimidated by the schoolwork. They reported feeling isolated and were much worse at seeking out fellow students, study groups, or counselors to help them adjust. Mothers going back to school described themselves as good role models for their children. Fathers worried that they were abrogating their responsibilities as breadwinner.

The student gender gap started to feel like a crisis to some people in higher-education circles in the mid-2000s, when it began showing up not just in community and liberal-arts colleges but in the flagship public universities—the UCs and the SUNYs and the UNCs. Like many of those schools, the University of Missouri at Kansas City, a full research university with more than 13,000 students, is now tipping toward 60 percent women, a level many admissions officers worry could permanently shift the atmosphere and reputation of a school.

In February, I visited with Ashley Burress, UMKC's student-body president. (The other three student-government officers this school year were also women.) Burress, a cute, short, African American 24-year-old grad student who is getting a doctor-of-pharmacy degree, had many of the same complaints I heard from other young women. Guys high-five each other when they get a C, while girls beat themselves up over a B-minus. Guys play video games in each other's rooms, while girls crowd the study hall. Girls get their degrees with no drama, while guys seem always in danger of drifting away. "In 2012, I will be Dr. Burress," she said. "Will I have to deal with guys who don't even have a bachelor's degree? I would like to date, but I'm putting myself in a really small pool."

UMKC is a working- and middle-class school—the kind of place where traditional sex roles might not be anathema. Yet as I talked to students this spring, I realized how much the basic expectations for men and women had shifted. Many of the women's mothers had established their careers later in life, sometimes after a divorce, and they had urged their daughters to get to their own careers more quickly. They would be a campus of Tracy Flicks, except that they seemed neither especially brittle nor secretly falling apart.

Victoria, Michelle, and Erin are sorority sisters. Victoria's mom is a part-time bartender at a hotel. Victoria is a biology major and wants to be a surgeon; soon she'll apply to a bunch of medical schools. She doesn't want kids for a while, because she knows she'll "be at the hospital, like,

100 hours a week," and when she does have kids, well, she'll "be the hotshot surgeon, and he"—a nameless he—"will be at home playing with the kiddies."

Michelle, a self-described "perfectionist," also has her life mapped out. She's a psychology major and wants to be a family therapist. After college, she will apply to grad school and look for internships. She is well aware of the career-counseling resources on campus. And her fiancé?

Michelle: He's changed majors, like, 16 times. Last week he wanted to be a dentist. This week it's environmental science.

Erin: Did he switch again this week? When you guys have kids, he'll definitely stay home. Seriously, what does he want to do?

Michelle: It depends on the day of the week. Remember last year? It was bio. It really is a joke. But it's not. It's funny, but it's not.

Among traditional college students from the highest-income families, the gender gap pretty much disappears. But the story is not so simple. Wealthier students tend to go to elite private schools, and elite private schools live by their own rules. Quietly, they've been opening up a new frontier in affirmative action, with boys playing the role of the underprivileged applicants needing an extra boost. In 2003, a study by the economists Sandy Baum and Eban Goodstein found that among selective liberal-arts schools, being male raises the chance of college acceptance by 6.5 to 9 percentage points. Now the U.S. Commission on Civil Rights has voted to investigate what some academics have described as the "open secret" that private schools "are discriminating in admissions in order to maintain what they regard as an appropriate gender balance."

Jennifer Delahunty, the dean of admissions and financial aid at Kenyon College, in Ohio, let this secret out in a 2006 *New York Times* op-ed. Gender balance, she wrote back then, is the elephant in the room. And today, she told me, the problem hasn't gone away. A typical female applicant, she said, manages the process herself—lines up the interviews, sets up a campus visit, requests a visit with faculty members. But the college has seen more than one male applicant "sit back on the couch, sometimes with their eyes closed, while their mom tells them where to go and what to do. Sometimes we say, 'What a nice essay his mom wrote,'" she said, in that funny-but-not vein.

To avoid crossing the dreaded 60 percent threshold, admissions officers have created a language to explain away the boys' deficits: "Brain hasn't kicked in yet." "Slow to cook." "Hasn't quite peaked." "Holistic picture." At times Delahunty has become so worried about "overeducated females" and "undereducated males" that she jokes she is getting conspiratorial. She once called her sister, a pediatrician, to vet her latest theory: "Maybe these boys are genetically like canaries in a coal mine, absorbing so many toxins and bad things in the environment that their DNA is shifting. Maybe they're like those frogs—they're more vulnerable or something, so they've gotten deformed."

Clearly, some percentage of boys are just temperamentally unsuited to college, at least at age 18 or 20, but without it, they have a harder time finding their place these days. "Forty years ago, 30 years ago, if you were one of the fairly constant fraction of boys who wasn't ready to learn in high school, there were ways for you to enter the mainstream economy," says Henry Farber, an economist at Princeton. "When you woke up, there were jobs. There were good industrial jobs, so you could have a good industrial, blue-collar career. Now those jobs are gone."

Since the 1980s, as women have flooded colleges, male enrollment has grown far more slowly. And the disparities start before college. Throughout the '90s, various authors and researchers agonized over why boys seemed to be failing at every level of education, from elementary school on up, and identified various culprits: a misguided feminism that treated normal boys as incipient harassers (Christina Hoff Sommers); different brain chemistry (Michael Gurian); a demanding, verbally focused curriculum that ignored boys' interests (Richard Whitmire). But again, it's not all that clear that boys have become more dysfunctional—or have changed in any way. What's clear is that schools, like the economy, now value the self-control, focus, and verbal aptitude that seem to come more easily to young girls.

Researchers have suggested any number of solutions. A movement is growing for more all-boys schools and classes, and for respecting the individual learning styles of boys. Some people think that boys should be able to walk around in class, or take more time on tests, or have tests and books that cater to their interests. In their desperation to reach out to boys, some colleges have formed football teams and started engineering programs. Most of these special accommodations sound very much like the kind of affirmative action proposed for women over the years—which in itself is an alarming flip.

Whether boys have changed or not, we are well past the time to start trying some experiments. It is fabulous to see girls and young women poised for success in the coming years. But allowing generations of boys to grow up feeling rootless and obsolete is not a recipe for a peaceful future. Men have few natural support groups and little access to social welfare; the men's-rights groups that do exist in the U.S. are taking on an angry, anti-woman edge. Marriages fall apart or never happen at all, and children are raised with no fathers. Far from being celebrated, women's rising power is often perceived as a threat.

Discussion Starters

1. What do you think the long-term societal effects will be of girls graduating from college at significantly higher rates than boys?
2. In the essay, several possible reasons are presented as to why boys don't perform as well as girls in school. Do you agree with the reasons?
3. Does your own college reflect a similar female/male ratio as that presented in the essay? What effects, if any, do you think that has on students?

Giving Students Room to Run

By Lorna Green

Lorna Green is an instructor at Front Range Community College and contributor to Teaching Tolerance magazine. In this essay, Green reveals how she was inspired to become a teacher by how her elementary-school teacher treated a "special" child in her class.

In the third grade, near the end of World War II, I learned why I wanted to be a teacher. Mrs. Wright, a woman in her late 50s (or so it seemed to an 8-year-old) taught me what every child needs to know. And I don't mean grammar or multiplication tables or how to sit quietly in our chairs, which were bolted to the floor.

Mrs. Wright was austere in appearance, wearing beige two-piece suits, sensible shoes and a white blouse with a jabot fluff held securely by an oval cameo pin. She was a gentle, supportive and knowledgeable person who was obviously born to be a teacher. Her voice never rose in anger or frustration. Her pleasant, plain face, framed by bobbed silver hair, never displayed anger or disappointment

And in the back of the room, in seat seven of row six, sat Joel, an active 7-year-old with dark unruly hair, lopsided glasses and fidgeting hands. He spoke with a decided lisp, although he did not speak to the rest of us often. Joel was in our classroom, but he was not in our "class." A mathematical genius, he was a long-time member of a national quiz show featuring children with exceptional intellectual ability. Joel's aptitude for mathematics was amazing, even to those of us who didn't know what calculus or trigonometry meant. He was taking math classes through the local high school and some college-level classes as well. But he was taking those classes while sitting in our third-grade classroom.

Today, Joel would be identified as ADHD, or perhaps even as autistic. Back then he followed a peculiar ritual. He would look at his "homework," whisper something to himself, get up, run around the perimeter of the classroom at full speed two or three times and then slide into his seat and write down the answer. With 10 to 15 problems on the page, Joel spent most of his time running around the classroom. Meanwhile, we sat quietly, participating in reading groups or individual work.

Finally, after three or four weeks, one of the children apparently had had enough, either of sitting quietly or of watching Joel whiz around the room. "Mrs. Wright," she asked, "why is it that we have to stay in our seats to do our work, and we have to mostly not talk to our friends, but Joel gets to run around and around and around and talk to himself even when he is supposed to be doing his seat work? Why? How come he gets to do that?"

Without even a pause Mrs. Wright replied, "Well, remember how we talked about how some of us learn to read very quickly, and some of us take a little longer, and some of us have very small voices and some of us have very big voices—because we are different, but we are all special. You know that Joel is very special in doing things with numbers. He is doing many things we don't even understand, things like calculus and trigonometry. Joel can do those things because his mind works very, very fast. In fact, his mind works so fast that sometimes he has to hurry so that his body can keep up with his mind. That's why he runs around the classroom when he is thinking. So he can help his body to keep up with his very fast mind." "Oh," the little girl said. "I get it—sort of like singing really fast when you are jumping rope really fast." "Yes," replied Mrs. Wright, "something like that." And everyone went back to work while Joel ran frantically around the room.

Today, a student like Joel would have an IEP, but it's unlikely he'd have a more accommodating classroom. Six decades ago, special education was in its infancy. Special needs students were often shuffled off to private schools, kept at home or shunted into separate rooms. A few unusual savants, like Joel, awkwardly made their way in general ed classrooms. Joel was different in how he worked, but we respected his differences because Mrs. Wright respected them.

I knew then that if I could make one child feel as comfortable with "specialness" as Joel was made to feel with his, and if I could help one child accept another who was "different" in any way, I would do something really wonderful. And so that is why I teach.

Discussion Starters

1. The Joels of today are usually put in special classes of some sort. Do you think this is better than the "mainstreaming" of Joel sixty years ago? Why?
2. What did you think of Mrs. Wright's explanation for why she let Joel run around the room? Was there perhaps some scientific support for her response or was it just a clever explanation that children could understand?
3. Mrs. Wright was no doubt a very special teacher. What teachers if any would you regard as special in your life and what impact did they make?

Colleges Confront a Gender Gap in Student Engagement

By Libby Sander

Libby Sander is a staff writer for The Chronicle of Higher Education. In this essay, Sander explores the differences between how men and women navigate the college experience, the post-graduate effects of those differences, and what each gender can learn from the other.

For decades, women have enrolled in college in greater numbers than men, and, by many measures, have outperformed them in the classroom. But in recent years, as social scientists and student-affairs offices have focused on other differences between the genders, they have documented patterns that could explain how engagement influences student development.

The focus on gender is leading some colleges to try new approaches to interacting with their students. And it is also providing some fascinating—if often maddening—hints at how differently male and female students experience college.

Women tend to study abroad, volunteer in the community, and spend longer hours preparing for class, some experts have noted. Men spend more time playing video games, relaxing, and watching television. But men have more substantive engagements with their professors, are more likely to do undergraduate research, and tend to major in fields that steer them into better-paying jobs. And although women do many of the things that researchers have identified as positive influences on a college experience, they also report higher levels of stress and lower levels of confidence than men.

Researchers continue to wrestle with those contrasts. How, they wonder, do such differences shape the way men and women experience college? The patterns prompt complex questions about the expectations that men and women internalize long before they even set foot on a campus.

"It's not necessarily that men are not engaged and that's bad, and women are very engaged and that's good. The real story is much more nuanced than that," says MaryAnn Baenninger, a scholar of gender and cognition and president of the College of Saint Benedict, a women's college in Minnesota. Saint Benedict has close ties to the all-male Saint John's University, sharing a curriculum and extracurricular activities with the institution six miles down the road.

Girls and boys are treated differently from the day they're born, Ms. Baenninger says, and the disparities playing out on college campuses say as much about how men and women are socialized before they get to campus as they do about what happens once they're there." They're different," she says. "But there is probably something to be learned from both the women and the men in terms of how they navigate in college."

Looking at student-engagement trends in the aggregate—men and women together—can mask some important differences between the genders, researchers say. Men and women, it turns out, tend to view college differently—and those differences often shape their willingness to get invested in academic pursuits and other activities.

Some colleges are trying to learn from the patterns. At Saint Benedict and Saint John's, academic awards used to be split evenly between women and men. (Women make up 52 percent of the two institutions' combined enrollment.) Then Ms. Baenninger advocated a survival-of-the-fittest approach. Now, she says, slightly fewer men receive awards: Phi Beta Kappa, for instance, is roughly 60 percent female.

"When left to their own devices in an academic environment, women are excelling," Ms. Baenninger says. But she's noticed that that doesn't always translate into professionally oriented tasks like career fairs, where men often schmooze more readily with prospective employers. The disconnect makes her wonder if the ideal lies somewhere between the women's academic gusto and the men's more laid-back approach. "What good is Phi Beta Kappa if you don't know how to go through that job interview?" she asks. "And suppose you know how to go through that job interview—wouldn't it be great if you had Phi Beta Kappa on your résumé?"

When Demetri Morgan was a student at the University of Florida, he observed that his female friends were active on the campus and excelled academically as a way to assert themselves and find their footing at the large institution. Not so for the guys. "That wasn't how they were defining themselves," he says. "Their social capital came from how many women they were sleeping with or how good they were at sports or what job they were aspiring to."

Today, Mr. Morgan, who graduated in 2011 and is now pursuing a master's degree in higher education and student affairs at Indiana University at Bloomington, sees a conflict between what he has learned from research on student engagement and what he has seen in his own life. "I know plenty of guys who were only involved in the fraternity—and they weren't even really involved in that—and they're doing fine," he says. On many occasions, he'd get deep into discussions with other men about why it was important to get involved. They'd often meet his pleas with a pragmatic comeback: "If I'm here to get a degree, why are you talking to me about involvement?" he recalls them saying. "Sometimes I try to argue back about all the positive outcomes about engagement," he says. Other times, he felt they had a point: "I'm like, 'Yeah, you are here to get a degree.'"

The gender differences tend to become evident early on, usually during students' first year of college, says Jillian Kinzie, associate director at the National Survey of Student Engagement, based at Indiana. At that time, survey results have shown, female students are participating at very different levels than male students are. The women are volunteering in the community, spending more time each week preparing for class, and caring for dependents; male students, meanwhile, spend more time relaxing and playing intramural sports.

Many of those trends equalize over time, Ms. Kinzie says. But she is troubled by other contrasts. Women work harder to meet expectations, spending more time on drafts of papers, say, before turning them in. But men spend more time interacting with faculty on research projects and other serious academic endeavors.

"Women are doing more of the things that are beneficial for them in college," says Linda J. Sax, a professor of higher education at the University of California at Los Angeles and one of the authors of The Gender Gap in College (Jossey-Bass, 2008). But the fact that men spend more time on leisure is "not necessarily a bad thing."

The diligence and motivation that many female students display, though, often belies a complicated vision of their own skills and abilities. Women appear to be harsher—or perhaps just more realistic—critics of themselves than men are.

In the 2011 freshman survey, administered each year by UCLA's Higher Education Research Institute, men claimed to be above average at certain skills at rates higher than women—in some cases, much higher. They saw themselves as above average in academic ability, popularity, mathematical ability, physical and emotional health, and in negotiating controversial issues, to name a few. In some cases, the gender disparities were more than 15 percentage points. (Women viewed themselves as "above average" more than men did in only a handful of categories, including artistic ability and "drive to achieve.")

Men and women also respond differently in academic settings. Women may spend more time revising papers and hitting the books, but the impact of academic engagement on students' overall success tends to be stronger for men, Ms. Sax says.

"We know that men spend less time studying. But we know that if we can increase their homework time, they're going to reap greater benefits," she says. "There's something about the academic engagement that's a bit more eye-opening for men than for women when it comes to their thinking about their place in the larger world."

Ms. Sax has found that interacting with professors is a powerful influence on how women view themselves. It can cut both ways, though. If women feel that faculty are taking them seriously, they tend to feel better about themselves. But if they think they're not being taken seriously, that impression can undermine their confidence.

With growth in female enrollment attributed in large part to an influx of women from previously underrepresented minority groups, it's men of color, researchers say, who are least likely to engage. Mr. Morgan, the Indiana graduate student, has found that to be true. As an undergraduate at Florida and a self-described "involved guy," he wanted to understand why his fellow African-American male students held back. Under the auspices of his fraternity, he organized a group of black men to get together and talk about their experiences at the university.

The reason that black men didn't get involved, he learned, was that they didn't want to be seen as "gay" or nerdy. They also didn't want to seem white. After the discussion, Mr. Morgan says, he was angry. But he didn't know where to lay blame: On men, for hanging back? On the university, for not engaging them? On the women, whose energy the men saw as emasculating? "I was just confused," he says.

Some scholars and campus officials are grappling with similar dilemmas. But they do acknowledge that in other respects, the gender gap favors men. They still earn more than women, and they tend to dominate positions of power and prestige in government and the private sector. But Frank Harris III, an associate professor of postsecondary education at San Diego State University who has studied engagement among male college students for a decade, says that such eventual success doesn't let colleges off the hook now. "Men are absolutely still more advantaged in society than are women," Mr. Harris says. "But I don't think that should be a reason for us not to do the work necessary to help men become better people."

The work that colleges do with men in their college years, he believes, could help them make better decisions later in life. But first, colleges need men to show up.

Discussion Starters

1. What are some of the major differences cited in the essay for how "engaged" men and women are in college? What do you think the main reasons are for this "gender gap?"
2. How do you reconcile the contradictory contention that women work harder and are more successful in college but that men get the better jobs upon graduation?
3. The essay suggests that women and men approach college differently because they are raised differently. What differences in upbringing would lead to the educational disparities that reveal themselves in college (and before)?

Good Silences, Bad Silences, Unforgivable Silences

By Angela Onwuachi-Willig

Angela Onwuachi-Willig is a professor at the College of Law, University of Iowa, and author of According to Our Hearts: Lessons on Race, Family, and Law. In this essay, Onwuachi-Willig relates her experiences as a black woman in a white male-dominated profession and how remaining silent is sometimes wise and other times unforgiveable.

For an untenured faculty member, perception is everything. How should this young "lamb" signal to all that she is a dedicated teacher, a brilliant scholar, and a wonderful colleague? For outsiders, such as women of color, this task of negotiating and performing identity can prove rather burdensome because of the need to counter negative stereotypes based on race, gender, and class. For many junior faculty members, a recurring conflict is the longstanding tension between voice and no voice: to speak or not to speak becomes the question. How, then, can women of color, especially those from poor or working-class backgrounds, draw the line between following advice for survival and resisting their own subjugation?

The tenure process is an exhausting one, and each individual must do what allows her to sleep at night. We all have to strive to be like Sister Pollard, who proclaimed during the Montgomery bus boycott, "My feets is tired, but my soul is rested." Although I went through the tenure process recently and emerged relatively unscathed, I constantly struggled with the issue of silence, and continue to do so now. Through it all, I have learned that there are good silences, bad silences, and unforgivable silences.

Silence as Action

As an untenured professor, I learned firsthand about the power of silence by observing the conduct of a senior male colleague of color at the first law school where I worked. I recall my initial surprise at his silence during most faculty meetings, especially given his stature as a highly respected faculty member. His silence stood in stark contrast to the frequent speech of many of our white, male senior colleagues, some of whom voiced their opinions on every matter—repeatedly. I wanted to learn from my colleague's opinions, but, in the end, I learned more from his silence. As I watched him throughout the year, I understood that his silences were, at least in part, strategic. They gave him a powerful voice when he spoke in public settings. I later learned that he did much of his speaking outside of the public faculty eye—in private.

Through him, I learned that we have to become comfortable enough with silences to know when to read them and nurture them into spoken voice. As the legal scholar Dorothy Roberts said in her article "Paradox of Silence": "One possibility is that by employing silence, the professor subverts the dominant style of speech in law-school classrooms. By breaking through the fast-paced aggressive banter, typically dominated by white, male students, silence allows less aggressive students of color to compose their thoughts and to participate." Undoubtedly, silence can be powerful. But when are the silences harmful? And how can such harm be prevented?

The Harmful Effects of Silence

We—female faculty of color—can be silenced in many aspects of our job. We can be silenced through our difficulties in saying no to extra service burdens that involve diversity, especially where we know our voices will not otherwise be represented; or through our shame in talking about the daily biases we face in the classroom, biases that are often invisible to white colleagues; or through our feelings that we are impostors in the academic world. We have to ask ourselves, How can we balance the act of not speaking without losing self and yet speak without losing the game?

Most recently, I struggled with these issues when I taught employment discrimination for the first time. Little did I know that I was in for a surprise as I covered the law regarding workplace-appearance codes and discrimination—in particular, those cases concerning the hairstyles of black women. I presented the class with a hypothetical case based upon an actual one (Rogers v. American Airlines), in which a black female airline employee had filed a discrimination lawsuit. She argued that the airline discriminated against "her as a woman, and more specifically, a black woman" through a grooming policy that prohibited certain employees from wearing all-braided hairstyles.

I was pleasantly surprised by my students' initial reaction. My students—none of whom were black, and many of whom came from small, rural towns—argued fervently that the prohibition on braided hairstyles was a form of race discrimination. I then revealed that my hypothetical was based on an actual case, which a court had dismissed on the grounds that the appearance provision did "not regulate on the basis of any immutable characteristic" and that the policy applied equally to both races and sexes. My students slowly began to nod their heads in agreement. Their challenges ended. I pressed them briefly, but I never really dove into complex criticisms of the case. I later questioned my silence during this classroom discussion. Why had I remained on the sidelines?

I began to understand how Paulette Caldwell, a black legal scholar who wrote 20 years ago about her reluctance to discuss the Rogers case, had felt. I had remained silent because I was nervous about voluntarily making myself both a subject and an object. But my silences in that class hurt not only me but also my students.

A few weeks later, I had another chance in that course to address the hair issue. This time I spoke openly, explaining my theory about how braids, locks, and twists—in light of the gender ideal for women with long, straight hair—should be understood as natural hairstyles and thus a marker of race. The students were receptive, nodding this time with me instead of the Rogers court. Only rarely, though, do we get second chances to make up for our silences. There are times when we have no choice but to speak.

Unforgivable Silences

I had just moved to a new school, where I was scheduled to come up for review for tenure the following fall. During a meeting to discuss my file, one associate dean, a white, senior male, remarked, "What we really care about are your teaching evaluations here, not the ones at your previous institution." I was in my first semester of teaching at my new school. I had no evaluations to speak of yet and—at least until that moment—had not been too preoccupied with them. I immediately thought, "Really? My record does not matter much?" I wanted to explain to him that—unlike him and many of my white, male colleagues—I did not walk into a classroom with a presumption of competence; that students judged me more harshly than they did my white peers; that I effectively had to work twice as hard to get good evaluations; that it could take at least two semesters to build up the same credibility that my white peers so often automatically received; and that this struggle would be particularly arduous because of the overwhelmingly white student body.

I then thought back to the pretenure meeting at my first school, a meeting that had gone completely differently. In that meeting, the dean, a white, senior male, told me, "You should know that I am fully aware of the challenges that women of color face in the classroom. We fully consider these challenges as we evaluate your teaching." I remembered how soothing I had found his words at that time. Struck by the stark differences at my new school, I remained silent in that pretenure meeting.

When I later had a chance to speak about my classroom challenges in my tenure file, I limited my words. I had previously planned to discuss these challenges at length—to educate others from what I hoped would be a position of relative privilege. However, my evaluations in one course were not as strong as my prior ones, and I was worried that my discussion of those challenges, including studies of proven bias against women of color, would sound too much like I was making excuses. My silences before had affected my freedom to speak later.

Although I went through the tenure process—as others repeatedly tell me—easily and unscathed, that incident and others continue to haunt me. But they have also taught me much about unforgivable silences—about the times when we must speak up.

I refer primarily to the tenured voices that helped the dean at my first school understand the classroom challenges faced by people of color. My silent senior male colleague of color and a senior female colleague of color had often met privately with that dean to discuss such challenges over the years. They had used status to create understanding for those who came after them.

It is my thoughts of these colleagues that often remind me that it is time to stop being a lamb, that it is my duty now to educate and speak up, that the silences reserved for the young lambs are no longer my own.

Discussion Starters

1. What distinctions does Onwuachi-Willig make among "good," "bad," and "unforgiveable" silences? Do you agree with her?
2. Onwuachi-Willig contends that women of color face discrimination and have to work harder to be successful than others. What experiences of your own or others you know confirm this contention?
3. Discuss your own comfort in "speaking out" in the classroom or other settings. What if anything keeps you quiet? Are there times you would like to speak out when you don't? How does someone overcome such silences?

X. Arts and Entertainment

Is Rap Music Dead?

By Nekesa Mumbi Moody

Nekesa Mumbi Moody is Global Entertainment & Lifestyles Editor at The Associated Press who has written numerous essays on the cultural impact of music. In this essay, Moody contends that rap music is fading in popularity due to its degradation of women, "gansta" persona, and vulgar language, and presents varied voices in the black community to support his contention.

Maybe it was the umpteenth coke-dealing anthem or soft-porn music video. Perhaps it was the preening antics that some call reminiscent of Stepin Fetchit. The turning point is hard to pinpoint. But after 30 years of growing popularity, rap music is now struggling with an alarming sales decline and growing criticism from within about the culture's negative effect on society. Rap insider Chuck Creekmur, who runs the leading Web site Allhiphop.com, says he got a message from a friend recently "asking me to hook her up with some Red Hot Chili Peppers because she said she's through with rap. A lot of people are sick of rap...the negativity is just over the top now."

Rapper Nas, considered one of the greats, challenged the condition of the art form when he titled his latest album "Hip-Hop is Dead." It's at least ailing, according to recent statistics: Though music sales are down overall, rap sales slid a whopping 21 percent from 2005 to 2006, and for the first time in 12 years no rap album was among the top 10 sellers of the year.

A recent study by the Black Youth Project showed a majority of youth think rap has too many violent images. In a poll of black Americans by The Associated Press and AOL-Black Voices last year, 50 percent of respondents said hip-hop was a negative force in American society.

Nicole Duncan-Smith grew up on rap, worked in the rap industry for years and is married to a hip-hop producer. She still listens to rap, but says it no longer speaks to or for her. She wrote the children's book "I Am Hip-Hop" partly to create something positive about rap for young children, including her 4-year-old daughter.

"I'm not removed from it, but I can't really tell the difference between Young Jeezy and Yung Joc. It's the same dumb stuff to me," says Duncan-Smith, 33. "I can't listen to that nonsense....I can't listen to another black man talk about you don't come to the 'hood anymore and ghetto revivals.... I'm from the 'hood. How can you tell me you want to revive it? How about you want to change it? Rejuvenate it?"

Hip-hop also seems to be increasingly blamed for a variety of social ills. Studies have attempted to link it to everything from teen drug use to increased sexual activity among young girls. Even the mayhem that broke out in Las Vegas during last month's NBA All-Star Game was blamed on hip-hoppers. "(NBA Commissioner) David Stern seriously needs to consider moving the event out of the country for the next couple of years in hopes that young, hip-hop hoodlums would find another event to terrorize," columnist Jason Whitlock, who is black, wrote on AOL.

While rap has been in essence pop music for years, and most rap consumers are white, some worry the black community is suffering from hip-hop - from the way America perceives blacks to the attitudes and images being adopted by black youth.

But the rapper David Banner derides the growing criticism as blacks joining America's attack on young black men who are only reflecting the crushing problems within their communities. Besides, he says, that's the kind of music America wants to hear.

"Look at the music that gets us popular - 'Like a Pimp,'" says Banner, naming his hit.

"What makes it so difficult is to know that we need to be doing other things. But the truth is at least us talking about what we're talking about, we can bring certain things to the light," he says. "They want (black artists) to shuck and jive, but they don't want us to tell the real story, because they're connected to it."

Criticism of hip-hop is certainly nothing new. It's as much a part of the culture as the beats and rhymes. Among the early accusations were that rap wasn't true music, its lyrics were too raw, its street message too polarizing. But those complaints rarely came from the youthful audience itself, which was enraptured with genre that defined them as none other could. "As people within the hip-hop generation get older, I think the criticism is increasing," says author Bakari Kitwana, who is part of a lecture tour titled "Does Hip-Hop Hate Women?" "There was a more of a tendency when we were younger to be more defensive of it," he adds.

During her 1990s crusade against rap's habit of degrading women, the late black activist C. Dolores Tucker certainly had few allies within the hip-hop community, or even among young black women. Backed by folks like conservative Republican William Bennett, Tucker was vilified within rap circles. In retrospect, "many of us weren't listening," says Tracy Denean Sharpley-Whiting, a professor at Vanderbilt University and author of the new book "Pimps Up, Ho's Down: Hip-Hop's Hold On Young Black Women." "She was onto something, but most of us said, 'They're not calling me a ——-, they're not talking about me, they're talking about THOSE women.' But then it became clear that, you know what? Those women can be any women."

One rap fan, Byron Hurt, made the searing documentary "Hip-Hop: Beyond Beats and Rhymes," which debuted on PBS last month. Hurt addresses the biggest criticisms of rap, from its treatment of women to the glorification of the gangsta lifestyle that has become the default posture for many of today's most popular rappers. "I love hip-hop," Hurt, 36, says in the documentary. "I sometimes feel bad for criticizing hip-hop, but I want to get us men to take a look at ourselves."

Even dances that may seem innocuous are not above the fray. Last summer, as the "Chicken Noodle Soup" song and accompanying dance became a sensation, Baltimore Sun pop critic Rashod D. Ollison mused that the dance - demonstrated in the video by young people stomping wildly from side to side - was part of the growing minstrelization of rap music.

"The music, dances and images in the video are clearly reminiscent of the era when pop culture reduced blacks to caricatures: lazy (and) sexually super-charged," he wrote.

And then there's the criminal aspect that has long been a part of rap. In the 1970s, groups may have rapped about drug dealing and street violence, but rap stars weren't the embodiment of criminals themselves. Today, the most popular and successful rappers, such as the Lil' Wayne, boast about who has murdered more foes and rhyme about dealing drugs as breezily as other artists sing about love. The lyrics of Wayne and others regularly talk of gang-style wars and sexual escapades that involve not just explicit descriptions of intercourse but also a concurrent domination of the women involved.

Creekmur says music labels have overfed the public on gangsta rap, obscuring artists who represent more positive and varied aspects of black life, like Talib Kweli, Common and Lupe Fiasco. "It boils down to a complete lack of balance, and whenever there's a complete lack of balance people are going to reject it, whether it's positive or negative," Creekmur says.

Yet Banner says there's a reason why acts like KRS-One and Public Enemy don't sell anymore. He recalled that even his own fans rebuffed positive songs he made - like "Cadillac on 22s," about staying away from street life - in favor of songs like "Like a Pimp." "The American public had an opportunity to pick what they wanted from David Banner," he says. "I wish America would just be honest. America is sick....America loves violence and sex."

Discussion Starters

1. Do you agree with the essay's thesis that rap music is dying or fading dramatically in popularity? How convincing is the evidence provided in the essay?
2. The essay contends that the negative images of rap – sexually explicit, degrading characterizations of women and "gangsta" violence – are responsible for its demise. Do you agree? How do you respond to such images?
3. The essay was written a few years ago. Has rap changed in any ways in recent years? Do you feel it has continued to decline? Why?

Poetry Makes You Weird

By Eric G. Wilson

Eric G. Wilson is a professor of English at Wake Forest University and the author, most recently, of Everyone Loves a Good Train Wreck. *In this essay, Wilson responds to the common student query of "What's the point of reading poetry?" by relating his own poetry-reading experiences and how they changed him and how he viewed the world.*

In my first semester as a tenure-track English professor, my chairman asked me to represent our department at a weekend recruiting fair for high-school seniors. My job would be to court prospective majors. Knowing that "yes" was the right pre-tenure answer, I agreed, and so found myself that next Saturday morning standing behind a folding table, cheap brochures littered on its brown surface. I was irritable, hung over, and resentful.

A father and son immediately appeared, in virginal Wake Forest T-shirts and blond crew cuts. They smiled at me as if I had just praised their promptness. The younger looked up at dad, and father nodded to son, and son blurted: "Sell me the English major!" Through my brain's murk, I searched for the hype. Failing to find it, I confessed: "It makes you weird."

After a confused "OK," the two looked down, backed away, and were gone. They shouldn't have been so hasty. I had revealed to them, though I didn't know it then, the great payoff of literary study: It estranges us from our normal habits of thought and perception, nullifies old conceptual maps, and so propels us into uncharted regions, outlandish and bracing, where we must create, if we are to thrive, coordinates more capacious, more sublime than the ones we already know. The uncanny—not truth, beauty, or goodness—is literature's boon.

Like most English professors, I endure the grumbling of undergraduates subjected to literature requirements. "What's the use?" they ask. "Why must I study complicated, densely worded fictions that have little to do with the real world?" In the past, I had my elevated answers ready. What Aristotle says of poetry is true of all great literature. It is "more philosophical and a higher thing than history: for poetry tends to express the universal, history the particular." Wordsworth believes that the literary—which is mainly, for him, verse—also invigorates our emotions, issuing from the "spontaneous overflow of powerful feelings," thus arousing us from "savage torpor." He would have heartily concurred with Matthew Arnold: Poetry teaches us "how to live."

The students I pelted with this rhetoric would squint into the "I'm thinking" expression, and, brown-nosing, say, "I see." If they'd read Plato, they could have countered that poetry is an irrational fomenting of lies. Or they could have invoked Auden, who admitted that poetry "makes nothing happen."

But I now no longer unleash the literary giants. I simply tell my disgruntled students about the first time I read, as an undergraduate, these lines:

> There's a certain Slant of light,
> Winter Afternoons—
> That oppresses, like the Heft
> Of Cathedral Tunes—

I had often witnessed beams of dull December light with a melancholy I didn't understand. Dickinson's flash clarified my feelings: In the impoverished glow of the cold time were heavy reminders of brightness I desired but couldn't possess. But this affliction had fever, intimations of future heat that was luminous, like hymns.

Dickinson's verse spelled out the abstruse, made the strange familiar. In this new intimacy, however, was a novel astonishment: The chilly light from that day onward exposed the enigmas of longing, both tormenting and radiant. Her poetry left me amazed—caught in wonderment as well as labyrinth.

Other epiphanies followed. What I had taken for granted was shattered; the marvelous erupted amid the fragments. In Whitman I saw ordinary grass morph into the "uncut hair of graves." In Eliot's "Prufrock," I watched twilight transmogrify into "a patient etherized upon a table." The grass, the evening—in these metaphors, they grew more lucid than before, and more cryptic.

Shelley articulates literature's invigorating disorientation: "Poetry lifts the veil from the hidden beauty of the world, and makes familiar objects be as if they were not familiar." But the result of that alienation is not only an aesthetic rush; it is also a moral life. In shocking us into awareness, poetry urges us to relate to the world in fresh ways. The problem is, How do I connect my own mind, relatively familiar, with what is before me, enticingly bizarre?

Shelley answers: Imagine what it's like to be what you perceive. To accomplish that connection requires "a going out of our nature, and an identification of ourselves with the beautiful which exists in thought, action, or person, not our own." I take that to mean that the more distinctly we imagine the plight of another, the more empathy we feel, and the more beauty we appreciate. As Shelley put it, "The great instrument of moral good is the imagination; and poetry administers to the effect by acting upon the cause."

Literary study propels us into uncharted regions, where we must create coordinates more sublime than the ones we know. The poet most likely to practice and evoke ethical imagination is not "poetical," in the sense of flamboyant or opinionated. Thinking of Shakespeare, Keats, who was Shelley's contemporary, claimed that the most powerful versifier "has no identity" at all, for "he is continually...filling some other body." He inhabits shade as much as light, Iago as much as Imogen.

The chameleonesque Keats had a preternatural talent for this "negative capability," his phrase describing the ability to be "in uncertainties, mysteries, doubts, without any irritable reaching after fact and reason." Adept at suspending the prejudices that so often accompany dogmatic surety, especially in moral contexts, he could adapt to myriad perspectives, and relished doing so.

As a close friend once reported, Keats, while describing his appreciation of Spenser's description of a whale, "hoisted himself up, and looked burly and dominant, as he said, 'what an image that is—sea-shouldering whales!'" Keats could expand into a leviathan; he could also contract, telling another friend that he was able to imagine a billiard ball delighting in "its own roundness, smoothness and rapidity of its motion." He felt himself transmuted in other instances into a tormented bear, a sparrow picking at gravel, and a woman whose leopardlike seductiveness caused him to "forget [him]self entirely" and "live in her."

Neither Keats's nor Shelley's ethics of identification justifies nefarious behavior, of course. True, the empathetic imagination, as Keats claims, can shock the "virtuous philosopher." But just because a poet occupies an Iago or a Robespierre doesn't mean that she endorses the villain's actions. The purpose of suspending stereotypes is to make one more sensitive to the irreducible intricacies of the real, and so be better able to forge informed judgments about what is right and wrong.

Those slantwise lines of Keats's disciple, Dickinson, likely arose from her mind's blending with the light. Electrified by her language, I tried to become more empathetic. Seeing in the winter's oppressive beams revelations of my own melancholy, I grew more sensitive to the troubles of others. I thought freshly, and with more kindness, about the anxieties (usually irritating) of my girlfriend at the time. I told myself that I would treat her more gently in the days to come, and I did. My charity fizzled out pretty quickly, though, as my ego again took charge and redeployed its agents: blame, resentment, self-righteousness.

Still, even though my will faltered, I learned the ethics of standing where another is and saying, in earnest, "yes." My moments of affirmative identification enable me to be more gracious, though less often than I'd like. Perhaps Dickinson's poetry affected me as nature did Wordsworth, arousing "little, nameless, unremembered, acts / Of kindness and of love."

I no longer show up at recruiting fairs—a perk of tenure—and so have fewer opportunities to spout haze-induced aphorisms on the use of the English major. But I do teach Keats and Shelley, Wordsworth and Dickinson, and work hard to initiate my students into these poets' transformative strangeness. I fail more than I succeed, even on days when my brain is as brisk as a new recruit's.

Walker Percy once wrote that our educational system has lost the "creature," treating specimens, whether Shakespearean sonnets or dissected frogs, merely as "examples" of ideas—of Poetry or Anatomy. We don't see the particular for the general, the trees for the forest. Percy recommends that biology teachers bring sonnets to class, and English professors, frogs: to stun abstraction, ignite the concrete.

I'm too cowardly to tote amphibians down the hall. But I continue to hope that during a Monday-morning class, when the weather and the mood are right, I can chant Keats's reverie of the "murmurous haunt of flies on summer eves" and a drowsy student will jerk awake. Green-blue bugs will buzz eerily in his head. Suddenly nothing is right. Something has happened.

Discussion Starters

1. In Wilson's viewpoint, how can poetry affect the reader? In what ways can it change his or her perspective?
2. How according to Wilson does poetry make one more "empathetic?" Do you agree with him?
3. What is your own experience with poetry as reader or writer? What impact if any has it had on you?

The Science of Heartbreak and How Music Heals

By Christie Wilcox

Christie Wilcox is a freelance science writer and PhD student at the University of Hawaii majoring in evolutionary biology. In this essay, Wilcox explains the biological connection between emotional and physical pain, her own experience with heartache, and how music and writing can ease the pain.

I know I'm not physically hurt. Though it feels like I've been kicked in the stomach with steel-toed boots, my abdomen isn't bruised. Spiking cortisol levels are causing my muscles to tense and diverting blood away from my gut, leading to this twisting, gnawing agony that I cannot stop thinking about. I can't stop crying. I can't move. I just stare at the ceiling, wondering when, if ever, this pain is going to go away.

It doesn't matter that my injuries are emotional. The term heartache isn't a metaphor: emotional wounds literally *hurt*. The exact same parts of the brain that light up when we're in physical pain go haywire when we experience rejection. As far as our neurons are concerned, emotional distress is physical trauma.

Evolutionary biologists would say that it's not surprising that our emotions have hijacked the pain system. As social creatures, mammals are dependent from birth upon others. We must forge and maintain relationships to survive and pass on our genes. Pain is a strong motivator; it is the primary way for our bodies tell us that something is wrong and needs to be fixed. Our intense aversion to pain causes us to instantly change behavior to ensure we don't hurt anymore. Since the need to maintain social bonds is crucial to mammalian survival, experiencing pain when they are threatened is an adaptive way to prevent the potential danger of being alone.

Of course, being able to evolutionarily rationalize this feeling doesn't make it go away. I lie flattened, like the weight of his words has literally crushed me. I need to do something, anything to lessen this ache. The thought crosses my mind to self-medicate, but I quickly decide against that. Mild analgesics like ibuprofen would be useless, as they act peripherally, targeting the pain nerves which send signals to the brain. In this case, it is my brain that is causing the pain. I would have to take something different, like an opioid, which depresses the central nervous system and thus inhibits the brain's ability to feel. Tempting as that might be, painkillers are an easy—and dangerous—way out. No, I need to deal with this some other way.

Slowly, I sit up and grab the guitar at the foot of my bed. Where music comes from, or even why we like and create music, is still a mystery. What we do know is that it has a powerful effect on our brains. Music evokes strong emotions and changes how we perceive the world around us. Simply listening to music causes the release of dopamine, a neurotransmitter linked to the brain's reward system and feelings of happiness. But even more impressive is its effect on pain. Multiple studies have shown that listening to music alters our perception of painful stimuli and strengthens feelings of control. People are able to tolerate pain for longer periods of time when listening to music, and will even rate the severity of the sensation as lower, suggesting that something so simple as a melody has a direct effect on our neural pathways.

So, too, does self-expression. Expressive writing about traumatic, stressful or emotional events is more than just a way to let out emotion—college students told to write about their most upsetting moments, for example, were found to be in remarkably better health four months later than their counterparts who wrote on frivolous topics. These positive results of self-expression are amplified when the product is shared with others. While negative emotions may have commandeered our pain response, art has tapped into the neurochemical pathways of happiness and healing.

So, I begin to write. At first, it is just a jumble of chords and words, haphazardly strung together. But, slowly, I edit and rewrite, weaving my emotions into lyrics. I play it over and over, honing the phrasing, perfecting the sound. Eventually, it begins to resemble a song.

The rush of dopamine loosens the knot in my stomach ever so slightly. For now, the agony is dulled. Still, I can't help but think that I'm never going to really feel better—that the memory of this moment will be seared into my brain, and a mental scar will always be there, torturing me with this intense feeling of loss.

Scientifically, I know I'm wrong. As I close my eyes, I am comforted by the thought that the human brain, though capable of processing and storing ridiculous amounts of information, is flawed. The permanence of memory is an illusion. My memory of this moment will weaken over time. It will be altered by future experiences, until what I envision when I try to recall it will be only a faint reflection of what I actually feel. Eventually, this pain won't overwhelm me, and I will finally be able to let go.

Discussion Starters

1. According to Wilcox, how do music and writing ease emotional pain? What scientific explanation does she provide?
2. Wilcox contends that emotional and physical pain are much alike, originating in the same area of the brain. Do you agree with her? Why?
3. Does music have a similar effect on you as it does on Wilcox? What role does music play in your life? What role does writing play if any?

Why Arts Education Is Crucial

By Fran Smith

Fran Smith is a contributing editor for Edutopia.org. In this essay, Smith makes the case for education in the arts being a central part of educational curriculum, revealing its numerous positive effects on children.

"Art does not solve problems, but makes us aware of their existence," sculptor Magdalena Abakanowicz has said. Arts education, on the other hand, does solve problems. Years of research show that it's closely linked to almost everything that we as a nation say we want for our children and demand from our schools: academic achievement, social and emotional development, civic engagement, and equitable opportunity.

Involvement in the arts is associated with gains in math, reading, cognitive ability, critical thinking, and verbal skill. Arts learning can also improve motivation, concentration, confidence, and teamwork. A 2005 report by the Rand Corporation about the visual arts argues that the intrinsic pleasures and stimulation of the art experience do more than sweeten an individual's life—according to the report, they "can connect people more deeply to the world and open them to new ways of seeing," creating the foundation to forge social bonds and community cohesion. And strong arts programming in schools helps close a gap that has left many a child behind.

From Mozart for babies to tutus for toddlers to family trips to the museum, the children of affluent, aspiring parents generally get exposed to the arts whether or not public schools provide them. Low-income children, often, do not. "Arts education enables those children from a financially challenged background to have a more level playing field with children who have had those enrichment experiences," says Eric Cooper, president and founder of the National Urban Alliance for Effective Education.

It has become a mantra in education that No Child Left Behind, with its pressure to raise test scores, has reduced classroom time devoted to the arts (and science, social studies, and everything else besides reading and math). Evidence supports this contention—we'll get to the statistics in a minute—but the reality is more complex. Arts education has been slipping for more than three decades, the result of tight budgets, an ever-growing list of state mandates that have crammed the classroom curriculum, and a public sense that the arts are lovely but not essential.

This erosion chipped away at the constituencies that might have defended the arts in the era of NCLB—children who had no music and art classes in the 1970s and 1980s may not appreciate their value now. "We have a whole generation of teachers and parents who have not had the advantage of arts in their own education," says Sandra Ruppert, director of the Arts Education Partnership (AEP), a national coalition of arts, business, education, philanthropic, and government organizations.

Yet against this backdrop, a new picture is emerging. Comprehensive, innovative arts initiatives are taking root in a growing number of school districts. Many of these models are based on new findings in brain research and cognitive development, and they embrace a variety of approaches:

using the arts as a learning tool (for example, musical notes to teach fractions); incorporating arts into other core classes (writing and performing a play about, say, slavery); creating a school environment rich in arts and culture (Mozart in the hallways every day) and hands-on arts instruction. Although most of these initiatives are in the early stages, some are beginning to rack up impressive results. This trend may send a message to schools focused maniacally, and perhaps counterproductively, on reading and math.

"If they're worried about their test scores and want a way to get them higher, they need to give kids more arts, not less," says Tom Horne, Arizona's state superintendent of public instruction. "There's lots of evidence that kids immersed in the arts do better on their academic tests."

Education policies almost universally recognize the value of arts. Forty-seven states have arts-education mandates, forty-eight have arts-education standards, and forty have arts requirements for high school graduation. The Goals 2000 Educate America Act, passed in 1994 to set the school-reform agenda of the Clinton and Bush administrations, declared art to be part of what all schools should teach. NCLB, enacted in 2001, included art as one of the ten core academic subjects of public education, a designation that qualified arts programs for an assortment of federal grants.

In a 2003 report, "The Complete Curriculum: Ensuring a Place for the Arts and Foreign Languages in American's Schools," a study group from the National Association of State Boards of Education noted that a substantial body of research highlights the benefits of arts in curriculum and called for stronger emphasis on the arts and foreign languages. As chairman of the Education Commission of the States from 2004 to 2006, Mike Huckabee, then governor of Arkansas, launched an initiative designed, according to commission literature, to ensure every child has the opportunity to learn about, enjoy, and participate directly in the arts.

Top-down mandates are one thing, of course, and implementation in the classroom is another. Whatever NCLB says about the arts, it measures achievement through math and language arts scores, not drawing proficiency or music skills. It's no surprise, then, that many districts have zeroed in on the tests. A 2006 national survey by the Center on Education Policy, an independent advocacy organization in Washington, DC, found that in the five years after enactment of NCLB, 44 percent of districts had increased instruction time in elementary school English language arts and math while decreasing time spent on other subjects. A follow-up analysis, released in February 2008, showed that 16 percent of districts had reduced elementary school class time for music and art—and had done so by an average of 35 percent, or fifty-seven minutes a week.

Some states report even bleaker numbers. In California, for example, participation in music courses dropped 46 percent from 1999-2000 through 2000-04, while total school enrollment grew nearly 6 percent, according to a study by the Music for All Foundation. The number of music teachers, meanwhile, declined 26.7 percent. In 2001, the California Board of Education set standards at each grade level for what students should know and be able to do in music, visual arts, theater, and dance, but a statewide study in 2006, by SRI International, found that 89 percent of K-12 schools failed to offer a standards-based course of study in all four disciplines. Sixty-one percent of schools didn't even have a full-time arts specialist.

In many districts, the arts have suffered so long that it will take years, and massive investment, to turn things around. New York City mayor Michael Bloomberg has made arts education a priority in his school reform plans, and the city has launched sweeping initiatives to connect more students with the city's vast cultural resources. Nearly every school now offers at least some arts instruction and cultural programming, yet in 2007-08, only 45 percent of elementary schools and 33 percent of middle schools provided education in all four required art forms, according to an analysis by the New York City Department of Education, and only 34 percent of high schools offered students the opportunity to exceed the minimum graduation requirement.

Yet some districts have made great strides toward not only revitalizing the arts but also using them to reinvent schools. The work takes leadership, innovation, broad partnerships, and a dogged insistence that the arts are central to what we want students to learn.

In Dallas, for example, a coalition of arts advocates, philanthropists, educators, and business leaders have worked for years to get arts into all schools, and to get students out into the city's thriving arts community. Today, for the first time in thirty years, every elementary student in the Dallas Independent School District receives forty-five minutes a week of art and music instruction. In an op-ed piece in the *Dallas Morning News*, Gigi Antoni, president and CEO of Big Thought, the nonprofit partnership working with the district, the Wallace Foundation, and more than sixty local arts and cultural institutions, explained the rationale behind what was then called the Dallas Arts Learning Initiative: "DALI was created on one unabashedly idealistic, yet meticulously researched, premise—that students flourish when creativity drives learning."

The Minneapolis and Chicago communities, too, are forging partnerships with their vibrant arts and cultural resources to infuse the schools with rich comprehensive, sustainable programs—not add-ons that come and go with this year's budget or administrator.

In Arizona, Tom Horne, the state superintendent of public instruction, made it his goal to provide high-quality, comprehensive arts education to all K-12 students. Horne, a classically trained pianist and founder of the Phoenix Baroque Ensemble, hasn't yet achieved his objective, but he has made progress: He pushed through higher standards for arts education, appointed an arts specialist in the state Department of Education, and steered $4 million in federal funds under NCLB to support arts integration in schools throughout the state. Some have restored art and music after a decade without them.

"When you think about the purposes of education, there are three," Horne says. "We're preparing kids for jobs. We're preparing them to be citizens. And we're teaching them to be human beings who can enjoy the deeper forms of beauty. The third is as important as the other two."

Discussion Starters

1. What evidence does the essay provide to support the need for arts education in the schools? How compelling do you find the evidence?
2. What is your viewpoint on the K-12 emphasis on math and reading to boost students' standardized test scores at the expense of arts education and other curricula? Is there an educationally sound balance that could be achieved?
3. What was your own experience with the arts – choir, drama, orchestra/band, painting/drawing, writing poetry – in K-12? How did it affect your education and enjoyment of school? What kinds of opportunities were available?

The Case for Reality TV

By Michael Hirschorn

Michael Hirschorn is a contributing editor for The Atlantic and founder and Chief Creative Officer at IconicTV. In this essay, Hirschorn argues that reality TV not only is not harmful to viewers but superior to other forms of television programming.

This past January, I had the pleasure of serving as official spear-catcher for a *CBS Evening News* report on the increasing levels of humiliation on *American Idol* and other reality-TV shows, including some on my channel, VH1. The segment featured snippets of our shows *I Love New York* (a dating competition with an urban vibe) and *Celebrity Fit Club* (which tracks the efforts of overweight singers and actors to get back in shape, and, by extension, reignite their careers). "VH1, among other things, showcases faded celebrities who are fat," said the CBS correspondent Richard Schlesinger.

In between shots of me fake working at my computer and fake chatting with the amiable Schlesinger while fake strolling down our corporate-looking hallway, I took my best shot at defending the alleged horrors of *AI* and *CelebrityFit Club*. But it was clear that CBS News was set on bemoaning what it saw as yet another outrage against the culture. The central complaint, per Katie Couric's intro to the report, was that more people had watched *American Idol* the previous week than watched the State of the Union address on all the broadcast networks combined. When the segment ended, Couric signed off with an extravagant eye roll. "We're doing our part here at CBS News," she seemed to be saying, "but the barbarians are massing at the gates, people."

A line had been drawn in the sand, as if the news were now akin to an evening at the Met. Is there an easier position to take in polite society than to patronize reality TV? Even television programmers see the genre as a kind of visual Hamburger Helper: cheap filler that saves them money they can use elsewhere for more-worthy programming. Reality shows cost anywhere from a quarter to half as much to produce as scripted shows. The money saved on *Extreme Makeover: Home Edition*, the logic goes, allows ABC to pay for additional gruesome medical emergencies and exploding ferries on *Grey's Anatomy*; NBC's crappy *Fear Factor* pays for the classy *Heroes*.

As befits a form driven largely by speed and cost considerations, reality TV is not often formally daring. Fifteen years after MTV's *The Real World* set the template for contemporary reality TV by placing seven strangers in a downtown Manhattan loft, reality television has developed its own visual shorthand: short doses of documentary footage interspersed with testimonials (often called OTFs, for "on-the-fly" interviews) in which the participants describe, ex post facto, what they were thinking during the action you are watching.

The current boom may be a product of the changing economics of the television business, but reality TV is also the liveliest genre on the set right now. It has engaged hot-button cultural issues—class, sex, race—that respectable television, including the august *CBS Evening News*, rarely touches. And it has addressed a visceral need for a different kind of television at a time when the Web has made more traditionally produced video seem as stagey as Molière.

Reality TV may be an awkward admixture of documentary (with its connotations of thousands of hours of footage patiently gathered, redacted by monk-like figures into the purest expression of truth possible in 90 to 120 minutes) and scripted (with its auteurs and Emmys and noble overtones of craft). But this kludge also happens to have allowed reality shows to skim the best elements of scripted TV and documentaries while eschewing the problems of each. Reality shows steal the story structure and pacing of scripted television, but leave behind the canned plots and characters. They have the visceral impact of documentary reportage without the self-importance and general lugubriousness. Where documentaries must construct their narratives from found matter, reality TV can place real people in artificial surroundings designed for maximum emotional impact.

Scripted television is supposedly showing new ambition these days, particularly in the hour-long drama form. *Studio 60 on the Sunset Strip* was going to bring the chatty intelligence of *The West Wing* back to prime time. *Lost* was going to challenge network audiences like never before, with complex plots, dozens of recurring characters, and movie-level production values. Shows are bigger now: On *24* this season, a nuclear bomb exploded. But network prime-time television remains dominated by variants on the police procedural (*Law & Order*, *CSI*, *Criminal Minds*), in which a stock group of characters (ethnically, sexually, and generationally diverse) grapples with endless versions of the same dilemma. The episodes have all the ritual predictability of Japanese Noh theater: Crimes are solved, lessons are learned, order is restored.

Reality shows have leaped into this imaginative void. Discovery's *Deadliest Catch*, which began its third season in April, is an oddly transfixing series about...crab fishermen in the Bering Sea. As a straightforward documentary, *Catch* would have been worthy fodder, but the producers have made it riveting by formatting the whole season as a sporting event, with crab tallies for each of the half dozen or so boats and a race-against-the-clock urgency that, for all its contrivance, gives structure and meaning to the fishermen's efforts.

Narrative vibrancy is not the only thing that electrifies these shows. Reality TV presents some of the most vital political debate in America, particularly about class and race. Fox's *Nanny 911* and ABC's *Supernanny* each offer object lessons on the hazards of parenting in an age of instant gratification and endless digital diversion. ABC's *Extreme Makeover: Home Edition* features intensely emotional tales of people who have fallen through the cracks in America—often blue-collar families ravaged by disease, health-care costs, insurance loopholes, layoffs, and so forth. My channel's *The (White) Rapper Show* turned into a running debate among the aspiring white MCs over cultural authenticity—whether it is more properly bestowed by class or race.

Class realities are plumbed to remarkable effect on *The Real Housewives of Orange County*, a "docu soap" that completed its second season on Bravo this spring. The show is inspired by a trio of suburban dramas: *The O.C.*, *Desperate Housewives*, and the 1999 movie *American Beauty*. Lacking the visual panache, or the budgets, of its scripted forebears, *Real Housewives* nonetheless goes deeper, charting the spiritual decay of life in gated communities, where financial anxieties, fraying families, and fear of aging leave inhabitants grasping for meaning and happiness as they steer their Escalades across Southern California's perfectly buffed, featureless landscape. *Crash*, the 2006 Oscar winner, trafficked in similar white California dread, but with all the nuance of a two-by-four to the face.

Value systems are smashed into each other, like atoms in an accelerator, on ABC's *Wife Swap*, where the producers find the most extreme pairings possible: lesbian mommies with bigots, godless cosmopolites with Bible thumpers. On one February show, a Pentacostal family, the Hoovers, was paired with the family of a former pastor, Tony Meeks, who has turned from God to follow his rock-and-roll dreams (mom Tish rocks out as well). "I feel by being there," Kristin Hoover said, "I was able to remind Tony that God still loves him and is not finished with him." The episode took seriously the Hoovers' commitment to homeschooling and their rejection of contemporary culture (a rejection not taken to the extreme of declining an invitation to appear on reality TV). Compare this with the tokenism of "born-again Christian" Harriet Hayes on NBC's dramedy *Studio 60 on the Sunset Strip*. Harriet's but a cipher, a rhetorical backboard against which ex-boyfriend Matt Albie can thwack his heathen wisecracks.

The competitions and elimination shows are latter-day Milgram experiments that place real people in artificial situations to *see what happens*. *The Apprentice* is Darwinism set loose inside an entrepreneurial Habitrail. Post-9/11, *Survivor* became less a fantasy and more a metaphor for an imagined postapocalyptic future. What happens on these shows might be a Technicolor version of how we behave in real life, but so is most fiction. Creative endeavors—written, scripted, or produced—should be measured not by how literally they replicate actual life but by how effectively they render emotional truths.

For all the snobbism in the doc community, reality TV has actually contributed to the recent boom in documentary filmmaking. The most successful docs of recent vintage have broken through in part by drawing heavily from reality television's bag of tricks, dropping the form's canonical insistence on pure observation. In *Fahrenheit 9/11*, Michael Moore brings an Army recruiter with him to confront legislators and urge them to enlist their children in the Iraq War effort. In *Bowling for Columbine*, Moore takes children who were shot at Columbine to a Kmart, where they ask for a refund on the bullets that are still lodged in their bodies.

Of course, Moore's never been a doc purist. *TV Nation*, his short-lived 1994 television series, prefigured a long line of gonzo reality, from *Joe Millionaire* to *Punk'd*. Having the Serbian ambassador sing along to the Barney theme song ("I love you, you love me") while statistics about the number of Bosnians killed during the breakup of Yugoslavia appeared on the screen was not only ur-reality; it was ur-Borat. And speaking of talking animals, *March of the Penguins* turned stunning footage of mating and migrating penguins into an utterly contrived Antarctic version of *Love Story*.

The resistance to reality TV ultimately comes down to snobbery, usually of the generational variety. People under 30, in my experience, tend to embrace this programming; they're happy to be entertained, never mind the purity of conception. As an unapologetic producer of reality shows, I'm obviously biased, but I also know that any genre that provokes such howls of protest is doing something interesting. Try the crab.

Discussion Starters

1. Evaluate the arguments that Hirschorn makes in defense of reality TV. Which if any do you find most convincing? Do you agree with his viewpoint?

2. What comparisons does Hirschorn make among reality TV, scripted shows, and documentaries to help make his case? Are the comparisons convincing?

3. What is your opinion of reality TV? What shows do you enjoy watching? Why do you think reality TV is so popular? Is there both good and bad reality TV?

The Professor Lady Spits Rhymes

By Kristin Van Tassel

Kristin Van Tassel is an English Professor at Bethany College and contributor to AlterNet.org and CommonDreams.org. In this essay, Van Tassel relates how she went far outside her comfort zone and expertise to create a rap-centered course to try and attract more male students.

The problem was, I didn't have enough guys in my elective English classes. I teach at a small Lutheran college in central Kansas, and 75 percent of the male students are athletes (many of them attending on scholarship from other parts of the country), majoring in business, criminal justice, athletics training, or pre-med. With a few exceptions, these young men never voluntarily enroll in writing or reading courses.

One of the exceptions, a student-athlete named James, suggested a solution. "If you want guys in your class," he said, "offer a class about rap."

I am a middle-aged white woman who lives on a 40-acre farm. I don't have a television. My college is in Lindsborg, population 3,500, a town founded by Swedish immigrants. On holidays the townspeople don clogs and ruffled shirts and do Swedish folk dances. Imagine the least-qualified candidate in the least-suitable place offering a rap class, and you will see me clutching a loaf of homemade rye bread and a well-worn copy of Willa Cather's *O Pioneers*!

But James was unwavering. "You can analyze anything," he said, handing over his iPod full of Nas, 50 Cent, and Bone Thugs-N-Harmony. "I guarantee guys will take the class." So, despite my misgivings, I cooked up a January course called "The Poetics and Politics of Rap: From Run DMC to Lil Wayne."

I tackled course preparations in my usual way: I started reading. By the last week of December, however, I could see that I had wandered into deeply unfamiliar territory. I was in the wrong neighborhood with nothing but a pile of library books and thousands of unwatched YouTube videos. After several days of dull panic, I seized on the only way out of my predicament: The students would have to teach the course.

Q's brother had his own hip-hop recording studio in Florida. Charlie, a 300-pound offensive lineman—a white kid from LA—fiercely admired the late Biggie Smalls. Emmanuel kept talking about Drake like I was supposed to know who he was. I required students to buy one text, Adam Bradley's *Book of Rhymes: The Poetics of Hip Hop*, which argues that hip-hop's rhyming, metered lyrics resonate with us in ways that contemporary poetry does not. The students were expected to provide all of the songs we would listen to and analyze.

Any illusions that I was in charge of the class ended on the day Trey announced that it was time to practice freestyling, a concept I did not fully comprehend at the time. The notion of just winging it, making rhymes the instant they occurred to you, was several city boroughs away from my understanding of how careful language production works. But Trey insisted that freestyling would help us understand the way flow works in rapping. Scanning the classroom computer for samples, he cued a beat loop and started rhyming, his words rolling over and over into the "pocket" of the beat, smooth and consistent.

Q went next, and then, as I looked at the students sitting between him and me, terror leapt under my rib cage. We were all expected to join in the freestyling. Wait: What about the brainstorming? The peer-review workshops? Delicia was freestyling now. I looked at the door. How could I leave gracefully? What would I say? That I was about to throw up? That I'd just remembered an urgent meeting with the academic dean regarding the cancellation of this class?

Darren freestyled his rhymes, and the class turned to me. Two, four, six pockets of the beat came and went. "I have two boys," I faltered. The words missed each pocket, skidding down the slope of the beat like loose scree. "They no longer play with toys." I blushed, humiliated, but the students didn't seem to care. Trey smiled encouragingly; Ashley jumped in on the next downbeat.

Later that week, Darren, Jordan, and Sarah walked into class and announced that their group—LBK Swag (LBK as in Lindsborg, Kansas)—had mixed some beats and written a rap. They gave an informal rehearsal, and by the time they'd finished, the class agreed that we needed a more ambitious goal for our final exam than the in-class performance described in the syllabus. Within minutes, the class had approved a new plan: All of us—including me—would perform in the college's main auditorium; the entire campus would be invited. By the following week, the students had secured an evening slot, reserved a sound system, and distributed announcements via campus mail and social media.

I was scared. I possessed neither the competence nor the confidence to write and perform a rap. But it was my assignment. Encouraged by how much every rapper seems to love his mama, I decided to write about how we recognize the rhythm of rap in utero, from our mothers' heartbeats; how even our first word, "mama," is a rhyme. "We reach across the breach, we climb into speech / On the fly, all the while, there's a beat, life beats, it beats, like a heartbeat." I practiced it at home, to the horror of my sons, ages 9 and 11, who implored me never to perform it, ever. In this moment of crisis, I turned to my students. I admitted that what I'd written didn't feel like a rap.

"This is you," Jordan told me. "You have to be true to yourself and perform it because that's what rap is about. Keeping it real." The others nodded their heads.

During the hour before the performance, my students were as nervous as I was. Charlie paced up and down the auditorium aisle, running his lines. Emmanuel kept swinging his arms and rolling his head from side to side, like he was warming up for the discus. Delicia, who'd nailed her rap beautifully in practice, was close to tears.

The show began, and we went onstage. More than 200 students and faculty—a third of the campus population—had shown up. Between each song, even during pauses within the songs, the audience hooted and cheered. Charlie's football teammates were so loud that by the last stanza we couldn't hear him. "Big Chucky P!" they chanted. My performance was easily the worst of the night, but the audience yelled and whistled at my shout-out to mamas. LBK Swag closed the set. Darren, Jordan, and Sarah had rehearsed their steps and moved together as they rapped their verses and sang their chorus. The crowd gave them a standing ovation.

Later in the week, I sat in my office and read the students' rhetorical analyses. It was clear that they'd been thinking about who would be listening—roommates, teammates, coaches, teachers. The songs were about friends, competitors, home, place, love lost and found. My students were thinking about the form of their poetry, too. The chain rhymes, slant rhymes, perfect rhymes, rhyme leashes, forced rhymes—the play with sound, repetition, speed.

This final writing task revealed, in ways the performances could not, the students' planning and worries—the thoughtfulness required for writing and performing poems they were deeply invested in, the challenges of participating in a community of artists they cared about.

Rap did bring male students to my classroom, but more important, it delivered a freestyle remix of the classroom dynamic in which students choreograph their own learning. It also reminded me what learning feels like. I wonder if sometimes teaching what we don't know carries value for us, the professors. Maybe genuine discovery helps us keep things real.

Discussion Starters

1. Do you feel that Van Tassel created a legitimate English course or merely catered to the students to fill her class? Why?
2. The course was obviously a learning experience for Van Tassel. What do you think the students learned? What academic or artistic value was there?
3. Van Tassel provided a rather unique learning experience: the students taught the course rather than the students. In your viewpoint, what are the strengths and weaknesses of such an approach for student learning?

XI. International Perspectives

Sewing Her Way Out of Poverty

By Nicholas Kristof

Nicholas Kristof is a journalist, op-ed columnist for The New York Times and winner of two Pulitzer Prizes. In this essay, Kristof reveals how among the poorest people in the world can dig their way out of poverty by relating the story of a former prostitute from a Nairobi slum who created her own successful business with a helping hand.

I came to Kenya partly to help make a PBS documentary about empowering women as a way to lift families and communities—men included—out of poverty. And I promptly met a prostitute-turned-businesswoman who epitomizes that theme.

Jane Ngoiri is a 38-year-old single mom who grew up in a slum and dropped out of school after the eighth grade. She married at age 18, but when she was pregnant with her second child, her husband informally took a second wife (polygamy is common for Christians here as well as Muslims), and she was nudged out. Jane soon found herself with small children, no home and no money.

To survive, she sold her body for the next five years. It was a perilous existence in Mathare, a collection of dangerous slums in Nairobi. The area, a warren of winding, muddy alleys, is consumed by crime and despair.

Regular jobs are rare, and many men self-medicate in ways that perpetuate self-destructive cycles of hopelessness. Social workers estimate that one-third of the slum's men get drunk every night—spending about $1.50 an evening, which could otherwise finance their children's education. Poverty becomes self-replicating.

Then in 1999, Jane joined an antipoverty organization called Jamii Bora, which means "good families" in Swahili. The group, founded by 50 street beggars with the help of a Swedish woman, Ingrid Munro, who still lives in Nairobi, became Kenya's largest microfinance organization, with more than 300,000 members. But it also runs entrepreneurship training, a sobriety campaign to reduce alcoholism, and a housing program to help slum-dwellers move to the suburbs.

In Jamii Bora, Jane was pushed to save for the future, to lean forward. There is growing evidence that the most powerful element of microfinance is not microlending, but microsavings, and that's how Jamii Bora starts: it encourages members to save small amounts, perhaps just 50 cents a week. Then members are coached to use those savings, coupled with loans and training, to start tiny businesses.

Jane learned to sew, left prostitution and used her savings and a small loan to buy a sewing machine. She began buying secondhand wedding gowns and bridesmaid dresses for about $7 each, and then cutting them up to make two or three smaller dresses.

Jane's business flourished, and she used her profits to buy a small home in a safe suburb and to keep her children in school. Her eldest daughter, Caroline, became the first child in the family to graduate from high school and is now taking computer classes.

The intellectual star of the family is Anthony, the second child, who is ranked No. 1 in his class of 138 pupils at a good boarding school with much richer students. Anthony, a star soccer player even though he has no soccer shoes, hopes to go to college and become an engineer. He told me that when he gets his first paycheck, he's going to buy something beautiful for his mom—and his eyes glistened as he spoke.

Another child, Cynthia, a seventh grader, has just been chosen by teachers to become head girl of her school next year, a tribute to her grades and leadership. Jane hopes to send Cynthia, who dreams of being a lawyer, to a good boarding school as well, but it's difficult to see how she will pay all these tuition costs.

Careful research by Professor Esther Duflo of M.I.T. and other economists suggests that microfinance can chip away at poverty but is not a panacea. You see that in Jane's life. After I finished my interviews, catastrophe struck. Cynthia's big toe was mangled in a traffic accident, and ultimately it was amputated—a disfigurement in a country where people routinely wear sandals. Jane devoted every scrap of savings to medical costs—leaving Anthony unable to return to school.

Our documentary team took up a collection, and Anthony is now back in class. But the crisis was a reminder of how fragile the family's gains are. Jane's life reflects the lesson of mountains of data: overcoming poverty is a tumultuous and uncertain task, but it can be done.

There's a tendency these days to give up on poverty, to dismiss it as a sad but inevitable feature of humanity, particularly at a time when we have deep economic problems of our own. But if a former prostitute in a Nairobi slum can build a dressmaking business, buy a home in the suburbs and produce over-achievers like Caroline, Anthony and Cynthia, then it's worth remembering that sheer grit, and a helping hand, can sometimes blaze trails where none seem possible.

Discussion Starters

1. How according to the essay can "microfinancing" help people escape poverty? Why do you think that encouraging savings is a more "powerful element" of microfinancing than "microlending?"
2. How does Jane's story reflect both great success and the fragility of remaining out of poverty? What types of "safety net" programs for poorer residents are in place in the U.S. that obviously don't exist in countries such as Kenya?
3. Do you think it is possible for microfinancing organizations to lift entire communities out of poverty in parts of the world where poverty is stark and persistent? Is poverty a "sad but inevitable feature of humanity?"

The Roots of Brazil's Success

By Jeffrey Rubin

Jeffrey Rubin is Professor of Latin American History at Boston University and Co-Director of The International Consortium on Social Movements in the Americas. In this essay, Rubin chronicles the economic and democratic successes of modern-day Brazil, the roots of those successes, and how Brazil can serve as a model for other Latin American countries.

The strong Presidential victory for Dilma Rousseff confirms Brazil's unique trajectory from military dictatorship in the 1970s to thriving democracy today. With booming exports, competitive and transparent elections, and diminishing poverty rates, Brazil appears well on the path to world power status. That Brazil's new president is a woman, ex-guerrilla, and leader of the leftist Worker's Party makes Brazil's success story of development in the age of globalization rich in political inspiration and compelling historical lessons.

A hemisphere with more countries like Brazil would change the geopolitical map of the world. If Latin America were to demonstrate that democracy and deepening respect for human rights produced growing economies that included poor people and minorities, then the project of development, in its more secular and non-violent form, would gain renewed traction globally.

And if this were to occur without US dominance, but rather with a complementary base of political power and economic cooperation south of the Panama Canal, then the project of secular modernity might be rescued from its association primarily with the US and Europe. And indeed, in his promotion of Unasur, the Union of South American Nations, and his economic support for neighboring Bolivia and Paraguay, Rousseff's predecessor Luiz Inácio Lula da Silva has taken impressive steps in this direction, including laying the groundwork for a Brazilian seat on the UN Security Council.

Yet as President Rousseff looks ahead to booming trade with China, the World Cup in 2014, and the Olympics in 2016, she also looks out on one of the most unequal societies in the world. In Brazil's major cities, including Rio de Janeiro and São Paulo, drug gangs rule sprawling and violent shantytowns with sky-high homicide rates. Daily life in Brazil's impoverished Northeast, where growing GNP does not translate into well-being, has been improved by small income transfers in the form of the popular *bolsa familia*, or family grants, but not by land reform, sustainable agriculture, or innovative regional industry.

Brazil's Amazon continues to disappear at lightning speed, with agribusiness gaining land and profits at the expense of indigenous groups and sustainable agriculture, while a tipping point of destruction may produce unstoppable dry-out, fires, and declines in rainfall. Education, a mere half day of schooling for Brazil's burgeoning student population, does not meet the private sector's needs for skilled workers or contribute to the development of an engaged citizenry to face democracy's twenty-first century challenges.

Many veteran democracy-watchers rightly say it takes time to produce reforms that lesson inequality, improve education, and grapple with environmental destruction. Economic growth, meanwhile, has contributed to improving living standards and bolstering the capacity of government to address key problems. As a result, economists, politicians, and policy experts in Brazil and the US tend to extrapolate today's successes into the future. They take from Brazil's experience the reassuring lesson that globalization can be steered—by sensitive technocrats in democracies—to produce measurable gains in export revenue and electoral stability.

But it is naïve to assume that any economy has long to grow before the next economic crisis. And it is equally misguided to imagine that any newly democratic system has decades to alleviate deprivation and violence before the next popular uprising, wave of violence, or need for military intervention to quell unrest. That's why understanding the origins of Brazil's success is key to forging policies that will enable the country's economic and political reforms to endure.

Brazil stands out as a Latin American success story for reasons that are often overlooked. First, Brazil's transition to democracy was accompanied by a broad and long-lasting surge of radical grassroots activism. This activism shaped the writing of Brazil's new constitution in 1988, providing for both decentralization of resources and for grassroots participation in policymaking. The broad range of feminist, environmental, land, agricultural, gay and lesbian, and urban shantytown movements that spread across Brazil in the 1980s and 1990s also shaped profoundly the way Brazilians became democratic citizens, making clear that politics occurred in the streets as well as in formal institutions and that to be a citizen was to act in both locations.Second, Brazil's transition was shaped from the get-go, even while the military still held power, by the emergency of a new political party, the Workers Party (PT). Significantly, the PT defined itself as a radical leftist party but squarely rejected the Leninism and vanguardism of the Soviet Union and Cuba . Since its inception, the PT has emphasized democratic procedures - debate followed by voting - in its internal affairs and municipal policies, as well as in Brazil's multi-level electoral arena.

Third, in the economic realm, Brazil's democracy has been strengthened by the government's role in promoting infrastructure, industry, and agricultural commodities, as well as in fostering the ethanol and oil production that have made the country energy self-sufficient. In fact, the Brazilian government has consistently played a central role in economic planning and investment since the 1930s, when Brazilians jump-started industrialization and sought economic autonomy in response to worldwide depression.

This state role in the economy has repeatedly produced far-sighted benefits, albeit with some wrong turns. Under military rule, the generals at the top promoted both the construction of infrastructure and industrial partnerships between government, private sector, and foreign investors. These active interventions in Brazil's economy brought the boom years of the so-called "Brazilian miracle," but also the pitfalls inherent in basing *grandeza*, or visions of greatness, on imported oil and foreign loans. In turn, recent Presidents have responded by forging energy independence and bringing the foreign debt to near zero.

Thus supporters of democracy might note that in Brazil's success story, widespread grassroots mobilizations and the prominence of a radical leftist party played key roles, from the years preceding democratic transition though nearly three decades of elections. Equally noteworthy, the path of local grassroots activism and political party development moved from the streets to the institutions and from anti-capitalist positions to acceptance of markets without insisting that everyone assume this stance. Brazil's democracy is marked by ongoing tension over where to do politics and how to balance economic and social welfare goals.

Supporters of democracy might similarly note that government economic planning, with a key role for the state in investment and ownership, produced benefits in both economy and politics in Brazil. Long-range commitment and expertise in state planning laid the groundwork for and continue to undergird today's economic boom. This stance shifted to a degree under President Fernando Henrique Cardoso, an ex-Marxist professor who in the 1990s embraced free markets and privatized many sectors of the Brazilian economy. And it may shift again as President Rousseff seeks energy partnerships to fund ambitious education or environmental programs. As with grassroots mobilization and political party radicalism, Brazilians are likely to pursue a changing mixture of economic policies, maintaining the tension between private sector and government initiative.

It is this tension that makes democracy strong. It also provides lessons for the future. The inclusion of ordinary citizens—poor, female, Afro-Brazilian, indigenous, middle class, private sector—in multiple forms of political participation and economic production has deepened Brazilian democracy. These citizens, in turn, expect the kind of reform that improves their lives in the short run, but does not come from elections or markets alone.

Enduring reform in the developing world needs active social movements *and* adherence to democratic procedures, state economic planning and investment *and* commitment to markets. President Rousseff would be wise to continue to challenge political and economic orthodoxies as she promotes equality and inclusion in what could continue to be a pioneering global success story.

Discussion Starters

1. How is Brazil's democracy and economic approach similar to and different from that of the U.S.? How are Brazil' leftist politics different from those of Cuba?
2. What are the primary factors underlying Brazil's economic success? How does this set them apart from most Latin American nations?
3. Brazil is energy independent and has almost "zero" foreign debt. How can Brazil achieve these enviable goals when the U.S. is not close to achieving either?

10 Things Most Americans Don't Know

By Mark Manson

Mark Manson is a writer and world traveler who writes social commentary at PostMasculine. com. In this essay, Manson draws from his extensive international travels to give his perspective on how other countries view America and on what is wrong with Americans.

Imagine you have a brother and he's an alcoholic. He has his moments, but you keep your distance from him. You don't mind him for the occasional family gathering or holiday. You still love him. But you don't want to be around him.

This is how I lovingly describe my current relationship with the United States. The United States is my alcoholic brother. And although I will always love him, I don't want to be near him at the moment. I know that's harsh, but I really feel my home country is not in a good place these days. That's not a socio-economic statement (although that's on the decline as well), but rather a cultural one.

We don't really get perspective on what's close to us until we spend time away from it. Just like you didn't realize the weird quirks and nuances of your family until you left and spent time with others, the same is true for country and culture. You often don't see what's messed up about your country and culture until you step outside

I've lived in different parts of the US, both the deep South and the Northeast. I have visited most of the U.S.'s 50 states. I've spent the past three years living almost entirely outside of the United States. I've lived in multiple countries in Europe, Asia and South America. I've visited over 40 countries in all and have spent far more time with non-Americans than with Americans during this period. I speak multiple languages. I'm not a tourist. I don't stay in resorts and rarely stay in hostels. I rent apartments and try to integrate myself into each country I visit as much as possible.

From my international experience, here are 10 things Americans don't know about America.

Few People Are Impressed By Us

Unless you're speaking with a real estate agent or a prostitute, chances are they're not going to be excited that you're American. It's not some badge of honor we get to parade around. Yes, we had Steve Jobs and Thomas Edison, but unless you actually *are* Steve Jobs or Thomas Edison (which is unlikely) then most people around the world are simply not going to care. There are exceptions of course, and those exceptions are called English and Australian people.

As Americans, we're brought up our entire lives being taught that we're the best, we did everything first and that the rest of the world follows our lead. Not only is this not true, but people get irritated when you bring it to their country with you. So don't.

Few People Hate Us

Despite the occasional eye-rolling and complete inability to understand why anyone would have voted for George W. Bush, people from other countries don't hate us either. In fact—and I know this is a really sobering realization for us—*most people in the world don't really think about us or care about us*. I know, that sounds absurd, especially with CNN and Fox News showing the same 20 angry Arab men on repeat for ten years straight. But unless we're invading someone's country or threatening to invade someone's country (which is likely), then there's a 99.99% chance they don't care about us. Just like we rarely think about the people in Bolivia or Mongolia, most people don't think about us much. They have jobs, kids, house payments—you know, those things called lives—to worry about. Kind of like us.

Americans tend to assume that the rest of the world either loves us or hates us (this is actually a good litmus test to tell if someone is conservative or liberal). The fact is, most people feel neither. Most people don't think much about us.

Remember that immature girl in high school, who every little thing that happened to her meant that someone either hated her or was obsessed with her; who thought every teacher who ever gave her a bad grade was being totally unfair and everything good that happened to her was because of how amazing she was? Yeah, we're that immature high school girl.

We Know Nothing About The Rest Of The World

For all of our talk about being global leaders and how everyone follows us, we don't seem to know much about our supposed "followers." They often have completely different takes on history than we do. Here were some brain-stumpers for me: the Vietnamese believe the Vietnam War was about China (not us), Hitler was primarily defeated by Russia (not us), Native Americans were wiped out largely by disease and plague (not us), and the American Revolution was "won" because the British cared more about beating France (not us). Notice a running theme here? (Hint: It's not all about us.)

We did not invent democracy. We didn't even invent modern democracy. There were parliamentary systems in England and other parts of Europe over a hundred years before we created government. In a recent survey of young Americans, 63% could not find Iraq on a map (despite being at war with them), and 54% did not know Sudan was a country in Africa. Yet, somehow we're positive that everyone else looks up to us.

We Are Poor At Expressing Gratitude And Affection

There's a saying about English-speakers. We say "Go screw yourself," when we really mean "I like you," and we say "I like you," when we really mean "Go screw yourself."

Outside of getting shit-housed drunk and screaming "I LOVE YOU, MAN!", open displays of affection in American culture are tepid and rare. Latin and some European cultures describe us as "cold" and "passionless" and for good reason. In our social lives we don't say what we mean and we don't mean what we say.

In our culture, appreciation and affection are implied rather than spoken outright. Two guy friends call each other names to reinforce their friendship; men and women tease and make fun of each other to imply interest. Feelings are almost never shared openly and freely. Consumer culture has cheapened our language of gratitude. Something like, "It's so good to see you" is empty now because it's expected and heard from everybody.

In dating, when I find a woman attractive, I almost always walk right up to her and tell her that

a) I wanted to meet her, and b) she's beautiful. In America, women usually get incredibly nervous and confused when I do this. They'll make jokes to defuse the situation or sometimes ask me if I'm part of a TV show or something playing a prank. Even when they're interested and go on dates with me, they get a bit disoriented when I'm so blunt with my interest. However, in almost every other culture, approaching women this way is met with a confident smile and a "Thank you."

The Quality of Life For The Average American Is Not That Great

If you're extremely talented or intelligent, the US is probably the best place in the world to live. The system is stacked heavily to allow people of talent and advantage to rise to the top quickly.

The problem with the US is that *everyone* thinks they are of talent and advantage. As John Steinbeck famously said, the problem with poor Americans is that "they don't believe they're poor, but rather temporarily embarrassed millionaires." It's this culture of self-delusion that allows America to continue to innovate and churn out new industry more than anyone else in the world. But this shared delusion also unfortunately keeps perpetuating large social inequalities and the quality of life for the average citizen lower than in most other developed countries. It's the price we pay to maintain our growth and economic dominance.

In my "Guide to Wealth," I defined being wealthy as, "Having the freedom to maximize one's life experiences." In those terms, despite the average American having more material wealth than citizens of most other countries (more cars, bigger houses, nicer televisions), their overall quality of life suffers in my opinion. American people on average work more hours with less vacation, spend more time commuting every day, and are saddled with over $10,000 of debt. That's a lot of time spent working and buying crap and little time or disposable income for relationships, activities or new experiences.

The Rest Of The World Is Not A Slum-Ridden Shithole Compared To Us

In 2010, I got into a taxi in Bangkok to take me to a new six-story cineplex. It was accessible by metro, but I chose a taxi instead. On the seat in front of me was a sign with a wifi password. Wait, what? I asked the driver if he had wifi in his taxi. He flashed a huge smile. The squat Thai man, with his pidgin English, explained that he had installed it himself. He then turned on his new sound system and disco lights. His taxi instantly became a cheesy nightclub on wheels...with free wifi.

If there's one constant in my travels over the past three years, it has been that almost every place I've visited (especially in Asia and South America) is much nicer and safer than I expected it to be. Singapore is pristine. Hong Kong makes Manhattan look like a suburb. My neighborhood in Colombia is nicer than the one I lived in in Boston (and cheaper).

As Americans, we have this naïve assumption that people all over the world are struggling and way behind us. They're not. Sweden and South Korea have more advanced high speed internet networks. Japan has the most advanced trains and transportation systems. Norwegians make more money. The biggest and most advanced plane in the world is flown out of Singapore. The tallest buildings in the world are now in Dubai and Shanghai. Meanwhile, the US has the highest incarceration rate in the world.

What's so surprising about the world is how unsurprising most of it is. I spent a week with some local guys in Cambodia. You know what their biggest concerns were? Paying for school, getting to work on time, and what their friends were saying about them. In Brazil, people have debt problems, hate getting stuck in traffic and complain about their overbearing mothers. Every country thinks they have the worst drivers. Every country thinks their weather is unpredictable. The world becomes, err...predictable.

We're Paranoid

Not only are we emotionally insecure as a culture, but I've come to realize how paranoid we are about our physical security. You don't have to watch Fox News or CNN for more than 10 minutes to hear about how our drinking water is going to kill us, our neighbor is going to rape our children, some terrorist in Yemen is going to kill us because we didn't torture him, Mexicans are going to kill us, or some virus from a bird is going to kill us. There's a reason we have more guns than people. In the US, security trumps everything, even liberty. We're paranoid.

I've probably been to 10 countries now that friends and family back home told me explicitly not to go to because someone was going to kill me, kidnap me, stab me, rob me, rape me, sell me into the sex trade, give me HIV, or whatever else. None of that has happened. I've never been robbed and I've walked through some of the "roughest" parts of Asia, Latin America and Eastern Europe.

In fact, the experience has been the opposite. In countries like Russia, Colombia or Guatemala, people were so friendly it actually scared me. Some stranger in a bar would invite me to his house for a bar-b-que with his family, a random person on the street would offer to show me around and give me directions to a store I was trying to find. My American instincts were always that, "Wait, this guy is going to try to rob me or kill me," but they never did. They were just insanely friendly.

We're Status-Obsessed and Seek Attention

I've noticed that the way we Americans communicate is usually designed to create a lot of attention and hype. Again, I think this is a product of our consumer culture: the belief that something isn't worthwhile or important unless it's perceived to be the best (BEST EVER!!!) or unless it gets a lot of attention (see: every reality-television show ever made).

This is why Americans have a peculiar habit of thinking everything is "totally awesome," and even the most mundane activities were "the best thing ever!" It's the unconscious drive we share for importance and significance, this unmentioned belief, socially beaten into us since birth that if we're not the best at something, then we don't matter.

We're also status-obsessed. Our culture is built around achievement, production and being exceptional. Therefore comparing ourselves and attempting to out-do one another has infiltrated our social relationships as well. Who can slam the most beers first? Who can get reservations at the best restaurant? Who knows the promoter to the club? Who dated a girl on the cheerleading squad? Socializing becomes objectified and turned into a competition. And if you're not winning, the implication is that you are not important and no one will like you.

We Are Very Unhealthy

Unless you have cancer or something equally dire, the health care system in the US sucks. The World Health Organization ranked the US 37th in the world for health care, despite the fact that we spend the most per capita by a large margin.

The hospitals are nicer in Asia (with European-educated doctors and nurses) and cost a tenth as much. Something as routine as a vaccination costs multiple hundreds of dollars in the US and less than $10 in Colombia. And before you make fun of Colombian hospitals, Colombia is 28th in the world on that WHO list, nine spots higher than us.

A routine STD test that can run you over $200 in the US is free in many countries to anyone, citizen or not. My health insurance the past year? $65 a month. Why? Because I live outside of the US. An American guy I met living in Buenos Aires got knee surgery on his ACL that would have cost $10,000 in the US...for free.

But this isn't really getting into the real problems of our health. Our food is killing us. I'm not going to go crazy with the details, but we eat chemically-laced crap because it's cheaper and tastes better (profit, profit). Our portion sizes are absurd (more profit). And we're by far the most prescribed nation in the world AND our drugs cost five to ten times more than they do even in Canada (ohhhhhhh, profit, you sexy bitch). In terms of life expectancy, despite being the richest country in the world, we come in a paltry 38th. Right behind Cuba, Malta and the United Arab Emirates, and slightly ahead of Slovenia, Kuwait and Uruguay. Enjoy your Big Mac.

We Mistake Comfort For Happiness

The United States is a country built on the exaltation of economic growth and personal ingenuity. Small businesses and constant growth are celebrated and supported above all else—above affordable health care, above respectable education, above everything. Americans believe it's your responsibility to take care of yourself and make something of yourself, not the state's, not your community's, not even your friend's or family's in some instances.

Comfort sells easier than happiness. Comfort is easy. It requires no effort and no work. Happiness takes effort. It requires being proactive, confronting fears, facing difficult situations, and having unpleasant conversations.

Comfort equals sales. We've been sold comfort for generations and for generations we bought: bigger houses, separated further and further out into the suburbs; bigger TV's, more movies, and take-out. The American public is becoming docile and complacent. We're obese and entitled. When we travel, we look for giant hotels that will insulate us and pamper us rather than for legitimate cultural experiences that may challenge our perspectives or help us grow as individuals.

In Conclusion

Depression and anxiety disorders are soaring within the US. Our inability to confront anything unpleasant around us has not only created a national sense of entitlement, but it's disconnected us from what actually drives happiness: relationships, unique experiences, feeling self-validated, achieving personal goals. It's easier to watch a NASCAR race on television and tweet about it than to actually get out and try something new with a friend.

Unfortunately, a by-product of our massive commercial success is that we're able to avoid the necessary emotional struggles of life in lieu of easy superficial pleasures.

Throughout history, every dominant civilization eventually collapsed because it became TOO successful. What made it powerful and unique grows out of proportion and consumes its society. I think this is true for American society. We're complacent, entitled and unhealthy. My generation is the first generation of Americans who will be worse off than their parents, economically, physically and emotionally. And this is not due to a lack of resources, to a lack of education or to a lack of ingenuity. It's corruption and complacency. The corruption from the massive industries that control our government's policies, and the fat complacency of the people who sit around and let it happen.

There are things I love about my country. I don't hate the US and I still return to it a few times a year. But I think the greatest flaw of American culture is our blind self-absorption. In the past it only hurt other countries. But now it's starting to hurt ourselves.

So this is my lecture to my alcoholic brother—my own flavor of arrogance and self-absorption, even if slightly more informed—in hopes he'll give up his wayward ways. I imagine it'll fall on deaf ears, but it's the most I can do for now. Now if you'll excuse me, I have some funny cat pictures to look at.

Discussion Starters

1. What did you find surprising or interesting about Manson's perspective on what other countries outside the U.S. are like? Did it change your own perspective of other countries in any way?
2. How in Manson's opinion do people from most other countries view the U.S.? Do you agree with his perspective?
3. Manson finds much to find fault with in the U.S., his "alcoholic brother." Discuss the various flaws that he presents and whether some or all have merit. Did the essay change your perspective in any way towards the U.S., other countries, or the American lifestyle presented in the essay?

Egypt Paves the Way for Revolution of Consciousness

By Marwan Bishara

> *Marwan Bishara is Al Jazeera English's senior political analyst and the editor & host of Empire, which examines global powers and their agendas. In this essay, Bishara views the recent revolution in Egypt in a positive light, contending that Egypt's future is in the hands of the youthful protesters, not the military or radical Islamists.*

There's nothing's like walking alongside the Nile to give one a historical perspective on the momentous changes sweeping through Egypt and the Arab region. Watching this ancient nation react to the dramatic developments since the downfall of Hosni Mubarak is sobering.

The latest drama was caused by the recently elected president, Mohammed Morsi, who granted himself broad new powers under the pretext of protecting the revolution from counterrevolutionary forces and of breaking the deadlock over writing a new constitution.

The move set off a political storm. The opposition condemned Morsi as "dictatorial," and Egypt's Supreme Judicial Council denounced him for putting the presidency above the law. Public pressure forced Morsi to rescind the controversial decree over the weekend.

The escalation reinforced the long-held belief among observers of the Arab world that success always carries with it the seeds of failure, and good news is just a precursor to bad.

But realism shouldn't be confused with cynicism. Needless to say, Egypt faces countless political, social and economic challenges. The Arab revolution has just started. Like Cairo's traffic, it is chaotic, boisterous and frequently congested, and yet it continues to flow. And like traffic, it will ultimately be measured by how effectively it allows people to reach their desired destinations.

Beyond general demands for regime change, a unifying political agenda or revolutionary philosophy has so far been absent. Bringing down Mubarak was swift, but building democracy and modern nationhood is a generational challenge.

However, Egypt, along with Tunisia, has paved the way for a revolution of consciousness. This has produced new realities with long-term consequences.

First, the revolution fomented the notion of an Arab "public opinion," which will slowly but surely replace the "Arab street." Long denied access to the corridors of power, people have historically voiced their pent-up political frustrations through intermittent outbursts. Today, elected leaders are wary of public criticism and try hard to win support in an effort to secure renewed mandates. Citizens now realize their political weight and will vote for those who best represent their aspirations.

Second, Egyptians have underlined an overwhelmingly popular wish to embrace the civil state, having rejected the notion of a military republic or a theocratic state. The bulk of Islamists who won election have accepted the principles of a state where civil law – not sharia – is the modus operandi and where religion is neither distanced nor enforced by law. Any attempt by Morsi and the Muslim Brotherhood to reverse that will be met with popular opposition.

The third major reality is the embrace of constitutional democracy as a system of government.

As Egypt, like other Arab countries, faced the postcolonial challenges of war, sovereignty and nation-building, democracy was hardly a national priority, let alone the regime's wish. Today, democracy's advocates include those who, until recently, denounced it as "un-Islamic" and those unable even to fully define the notion of democracy and what it entails.

Meanwhile, the forces that caused a great deal of the tumult after January 2011 continue to either drive or inhibit change. The security apparatus, military echelon, bureaucracy and old oligarchy have mounted a desperate comeback, but the future does not belong to them. While these reactionary forces continue to exploit the popular dissatisfaction with the lack of change and persistent chaos, authoritarian development has been discredited as a model.

The revolution has also unleashed Islamist and other long repressed primordial furies. Considering the terrible condition of the Egyptian economy and state institutions, the Islamists don't have specific Islamic solutions to the problems they've inherited. But people expect their leaders, once in power, to deliver results, not religious slogans.

Enter the young democrats, liberals and feminists who spearheaded the Arab revolutions in Tahrir Square, as well as countless other public spaces in Egypt and the Arab world, from Sanaa to Tunis. They have been fighting an uphill battle against counterrevolutionary and conservative religious forces since Mubarak's downfall, and now there is a growing concern that their revolution is being reversed. Perhaps they left the squares too early, without following through with the process they started. However, they continue to gain experience and build coalitions with other progressive, secular and liberal groups.

The youth leaders I meet are determined activists who, despite the killings, harassment and arrests over the last two years, continued to organize and take their cause directly to the public. Wherever and whenever I meet them, it is clear to me that in their minds and hearts, the revolution continues. They are the future.

Discussion Starters

1. How is "public opinion" replacing the "Arab Street" in Egypt? How does the rise of democracy change the political role of Egyptian residents?
2. Why does Bishara believe that Egypt will become a civil state rather than an Islamic theocracy? Do you agree with him?
3. What role, if any, do you feel the U.S. should play in countries such as Egypt where popular revolutions are overturning dictatorial rule?

Our 'Africa' Lenses

By Chimamanda Ngozi Adichie

Chimamanda Ngozi Adichie is a prominent Nigerian writer, the author of four novels including Purple Hibiscus and Half of a Yellow Sun. In this essay, Adichie educates readers on their misperceptions of Africa and how those misperceptions can drive wrong-headed American policy.

Growing up in Nsukka, a small university town in eastern Nigeria, I often had malaria. It was so commonplace that when you went to the medical center, a nurse would say, "Malaria has come again, hasn't it?" Because I know how easily treatable malaria is, I was surprised to learn that thousands of people die from it each year. People like the relatives of David Banda, Madonna's adopted son from Malawi.

But of course most American media do not say "Malawi"; they just say "Africa." I realized that I was African when I came to the United States. Whenever Africa came up in my college classes, everyone turned to me. It didn't matter whether the subject was Namibia or Egypt; I was expected to know, to explain.

I reject this facile compression of a varied continent into a monolithic country, but I have also come to accept that African nations do have much in common with one another. Most have a history of European colonization. Most also have a failure of leadership, a long line of presidents and prime ministers and heads of state all intent on the plunder of the state.

And so I was wearing my "African" lenses as I watched Madonna on television, cautiously, earnestly explaining the media circus around her adoption. I did not think it my place to wonder what her motivation for adoption was. I did cringe, however, when she said that her greatest disappointment was that the media frenzy would discourage people who wanted to do the same thing that she had done: adopt an African child. She wanted people to go to Africa and see what she had seen; she wanted them, too, to adopt.

Later, watching David Banda's biological father speak about being grateful that she would give David a "better life," I could not help but look away. The power differential was so stark, so heartbreakingly sad; there was something about it that made Africa seem terribly dispensable.

Madonna will give David a better life, at least a materially better life: better food, housing, books. Whether this will make him a happier and normatively better human being is open to debate. What really matters is not Madonna's motivation or her supposed flouting of Malawian adoption laws (as though non-celebrities would not also hasten adoption processes if they could). Rather, it is the underlying notion that she has helped Africa by adopting David Banda, that one helps Africa by adopting Africa's children.

It is easy to romanticize poverty, to see poor people as inherently lacking agency and will. It is easy to strip them of human dignity, to reduce them to objects of pity. This has never been clearer than in the view of Africa from the American media, in which we are shown poverty and conflicts without any context.

If I were not African, I would, after watching the coverage, think of Africa as a place of magnificent wild animals in which black Africans exist as tour guides, or as a place of desperately poor people who kill or are killed by one another for little or no reason.

I once watched CNN's Anderson Cooper, who is undoubtedly well-meaning, interview a Belgian (who, we were told, was a "Congo expert") about the conflict in that country, while Congolese people stood in the background and watched. Surely there was a Congolese who was qualified to speak about Congo. Surely there are Congolese who are working just as hard as the foreigners and who don't fit into the category of either killer or killed. Surely the future for Africa should be one in which Africans are in a position to raise their own children.

Which brings me back to Madonna. I applauded her funding of orphanages in Malawi. I wish, however, that instead of asking television viewers to go to Africa and adopt, she had asked them to send a check to malaria-eradication organizations. I wish she had added, after one of those thoughtfully dramatic pauses, that Africa cannot depend on aid alone, that aid is like salted peanuts: The more failed leaders got, the more they wanted. I wish she had said that she was setting up an organization to use donations as micro-credit and that this organization, by the way, would be run by locals rather than expatriate staff whose expatriate salaries raise the rent in the cities.

I wish she had pointed out, with suitable celebrity-style rage, that Western countries need to stop appeasing and propping up hopeless African leaders, that Western banks must stop enabling and accepting stolen money from these leaders, that Western donors who insist on the free movement of capital across borders must also insist on the free movement of labor, that Western trade subsidies make it impossible for Africans to compete. I wish she had then shown, with graphs on the screen, how these things affect the father and relatives of David Banda.

Of course this isn't really about Madonna. It is about a formula that well-meaning people have adopted in looking at Africa, a surface-only, let's-ignore-the-real-reasons template that African experiences have all been forced to fit in order to be authentically "African."

If I were not African, I wonder whether it would be clear to me that Africa is a place where the people do not need limp gifts of fish but sturdy fishing rods and fair access to the pond. I wonder whether I would realize that while African nations have a failure of leadership, they also have dynamic people with agency and voices. I wonder whether I would know that Africa has class divisions, that wealthy Africans who have not stolen from their countries actually exist. I wonder whether I would know that corrupt African countries are also full of fiercely honest people and that violent conflicts are about resource control in an environment of (sometimes artificial) scarcity.

Watching David Banda's father, I imagined a British David visiting him in 2021 and I wondered what they would talk about.

Discussion Starters

1. According to Adichie, what distorted picture of Africa do Americans get from the press and television? How is the true picture significantly different?
2. How does Madonna's adopting an African child reflect the American attitude towards Africa and Africans? Do you think African children are better off being adopted and raised by well-intentioned Americans?

3. What does Adichie mean that African people "do not need limp gifts of fish but sturdy fishing rods and fair access to the pond?" How would this translate into the type of American involvement in Africa that could be most helpful?

Living with Terrorism

By Bjorn Staerk

Bjorn Staerk is a Norwegian blogger whose posts can be found at essay.bearstrong.net. In this essay, Staerk offers his viewpoint that world-wide terrorism will always be a part of our lives and that we need to learn the best ways to live with it.

No matter where we live in the world, terrorism will be in our lives for a long time. When and if it ends, it will end because the terrorists grow tired of it, not because we somehow find a permanent way to protect ourselves.

Why would terrorists grow tired of terrorism? Who knows? Perhaps, embarrassed by the naivety of today's terrorists, who thought they could destroy their way to an Islamist utopia, tired after decades of fruitless effort, a new generation of Islamist fanatics will decide that pragmatism is a smarter road after all. They wouldn't be the first movement of violent radicals to do this.

Or maybe they won't. Whatever happens, I do not believe we can *make* the threat go away with outside force. Not with police work, not by invading terrorist states, not by solving any social problems, nor by making the world more peaceful and wealthy, and not - certainly not! - by giving them what they want. We can reduce the threat, we can make it difficult for terrorists to succeed, but the threat is not going away. The *risk* of terrorism will always be there, until *they* choose to remove it.

And if the Islamists do give up terrorism, others will pick it up. Islamists are not the first to use this tactic - anarchists used it in the 19th century, radical leftists in the 1970's - and they won't be the last. It is a very odd idea to be infected with, that the world is evil and must be put right with explosives, but the world is full odd ideas, and people who will believe them. The internet and the new global culture will help the crazy fringes more than it helps the rest of us, it will help them to discover each other and maintain their closed little worldviews - and then it will help them to plan and carry out their attacks.

Do you think surveillance will put an end to terrorism? Read up on cryptography. Today's terrorists may not have understood the potential of information technology, but the next generation will. It will never be easy to carry out a spectacular terrorist attack, and there are many things we can do to make it more difficult, but there will always be a risk of success. Do what you like, our fight against terrorism will always have a component of luck. Flip a coin: Heads, a neighbor sees something suspicious and reports it, tails, they don't, and a bus gets blown up.

When we talk about terrorism, it is usually to say how horrible it is, and to ask what we can do to fight it. A lot of people died! Or they could have died! What are we going to do about it? Who's to blame? Is there a law we could pass? Should we give more money to somebody, or maybe invade some place?

This is useful. There are many things we can do, and there's no reason to make it easy for terrorists to kill us. New laws can be useful, and so can money, and even sometimes invasions. But there is another thing I believe we should *also* talk about, and think about, which we usually forget, and that is how to live with terrorism. How to deal with terrorism as a part of our lives.

What?! Live with terrorism? What are you, a defeatist? We must fight it! We must end the terror threat once and for all! Fight everyone who supports it and makes it possible, teach everyone the futility and immorality of terrorism, until no one is left alive and free who would even want to be a terrorist.

Right, so let us do all this. Whatever it is you have in mind, imagine it done. And then what? Have we now eradicated terrorism? Unless your solution is a police state, walled in and trigger-happy and suspicious of everyone and everything, afraid of strangers and obedient to the state, (and maybe not even then), I believe the answer is no. Let us do all that we can do without becoming something we despise, and there is still a terrorist threat to worry about.

So we need to learn how to live with terrorism. It is a part of our lives that no power we have (or want) can fully take away. No matter how you want to fight terrorism, you also need to find a way to *live with it*. Live with the possibility of hijackings and plane bombings, of suicide bombers on trains and buses, of snipers killing random people in the street. Terrorism is here to stay; *deal* with it.

And we are dealing with it, in our own different ways. In the years since September 11, several strategies have come up. One is to pretend that there is no threat. "Of course it could happen *there*, but never here!" Or "terrorism is really scary, I'm so glad we have police and airport security to protect us!" Or "it's all a conspiracy anyway, it just crazy to think that Muslims would be evil enough to blow themselves up!" Denial is an effective strategy, but it is not for me. I like to keep my brain free from lies; I have this funny obsession.

Denial is often combined with another popular strategy: Retreat. Pretend that the threat is concentrated in certain places, and then stay away from those places. If bombs go off in London, cancel your London vacation. If they go off on Bali, stay away from Indonesia. If a plot to blow up airplanes is uncovered, avoid flying for a couple of months - or at least get off the plane if you see any Arabs on it.

Legislation is a popular strategy, well in keeping with our political culture: If Something Bad happens, pass a law. Don't think, don't ask if it will work, don't ask what it will cost, just write it, pass it, and sign it. In fact, the more expensive it is and the more it hurts, the more it feels like we're doing something.

Others deal with terrorism by distracting themselves with the *fight* against terrorism, thus avoiding the question of how to live with it. Be very angry about terrorism, write about it on your blog, blame your political enemies for helping the terrorists - do anything but face the inevitability of terrorism. These are usually the people who go furthest in losing their sense of proportion, to a point where they embrace autocratic ideas. "No trial for terror suspects? Torture, unaccountable surveillance, and harebrained identity schemes? Fine, I don't care! Just do whatever it takes to protect me!"

I have a different strategy. It is not for everyone, but I believe it is honest and politically safe. Let us take away the most powerful weapon the terrorists have: Fear. Be less afraid of terrorism. Make it your personal project not to fear terrorism, and not to let the fear that remains influence your life. Don't panic over newspaper headlines. Don't cancel your vacation because of terror alerts. Don't hold back your plane because there are some Arabs on it. Don't support hasty laws and careless political decisions, simply because we "have to do something."

Accept that there is a threat, but don't exaggerate it. Don't trust your instinct to guide you; our instincts are notoriously bad at risk assessment. Use reason and facts instead. When people are afraid of flying, they remind themselves that they're much more likely to die in their car on the way to the airport than on the plane itself. Do the same with terrorism. Fight your fears with facts. I don't believe in denial, and it is not denial to say that terrorism is one of the smallest threats that any of us face. It is simply *irrational* to fear terrorism more than traffic.

When you have reduced your fear to a rational level as much as you can, face what remains of it with open eyes. Don't let the fear influence your behavior, except after careful thought. Life is full of risks, and terrorism is no different from all the others. So there's a tiny risk you might die today. That's no excuse to act like a fool or a coward. Death is a part of life.

Terrorism is *naturally* more frightening than, say, car accidents or natural disasters. Accidents are impersonal and random, terrorism is personal, it is *evil*. But that is precisely why we have to think rationally about it, so that terrorists *cannot* exploit the irrational fear that their actions create in us.

After all, what other weapons do terrorists have to harm us with than fear? They have some guns and explosives. They can kill a few people, once in a while, at high cost and high chance of failure. That is all they have. Measured in terms of pure damage to people and property, the terrorist threat is small. Only with nuclear weapons might terrorists come close to the threat posed to us by cars. It is the fear of it that makes terrorism uniquely dangerous. The killing is only a means, a way to trigger the destruction of their enemies. Make us angry, make us fearful, make us do something stupid.

There is an overlap between what terrorists want and what terrorism actually makes us do - excessive retribution and suspicion is a useful recruitment tool - but on the whole we should not spend much time thinking about what terrorists want, and how to avoid it. They live in their own crazy little world, a world where their enemies are weak and ready to break, and all that is needed is a push in in the right place. It is the world Alan Moore imagines in V for Vendetta, where an authoritarian government is brought down through surgical use of terrorism. A small cut here, another there, and down it all falls, and come now everyone and embrace our truth, let us build a new world together in the name of our God/ideology.

This is not the real world. Terrorists have a different reality, and it is silly to obsess about what they really "want" with their attacks. Whatever it is it has little relation to our reality. "Victory" for an Islamist terrorist is the submission of the globe to their form of Islam, not that we introduce some bad laws.

But it is bad for *us* when terrorism makes us do this. Islamist terrorists will never succeed at whatever it is they're aiming for, but they often make us do foolish things. The fear makes us stupid. It makes us want to throw out centuries of experience with democracy and rule of law, it makes us consider identity cards and massive surveillance, it makes us treat all Muslim immigrants as suspects, it makes us take hasty and clumsy decisions in foreign policy, and give massive powers to the state, and bog our airports down with pointless security measures. And that's just the mainstream - consider the fringes, as they prepare for The Great War With The Muslims, dismissing liberal democracy as weak and inefficient, branding moderation as treason, and creating a new nationalism.

Dangerous ideas like these will always be with us, but hystericism makes them more appealing. So. Remove the fear, or reduce it to a rational level, and we will have changed terrorism from a major disruptive force to a minor physical threat, far below the level of accidents and disease. Take away the panic, and then we can think rationally of how to balance our efforts against terrorism against other things that are important to us. Things such as political freedom, human rights, decent behavior, and not acting like panicked chickens.

The irony is that the ones who want to go furthest in placating their own fears, have succeeded in presenting themselves as "brave", and their opponents, who worry about civil rights and discrimination, as "cowardly." I don't see much bravery anywhere, but least of all among the loudest of the anti-terror warriors. It's not brave to scream on your blog for even more anti-terror laws. It's not brave to be willing to torture innocent people because there's a chance they might be guilty.

Brave is sitting down calmly on a plane behind a row of suspicious-looking Arabs, ignoring your own fears, because you know those fears are irrational, and because even if there's a chance that they are terrorists, it is more important to you to preserve an open and tolerant society than to survive this trip. Brave is insisting that Arabs not be searched more carefully in airport security than anyone else, because you believe that it is more important not to discriminate against people based on their race than to keep the occasional terrorist from getting on a plane. Brave is not watching the news anxiously for hours whenever there's been an attack, or a new plot has been uncovered.

"You call that brave?! Why, that's nothing!" Yes, it's barely anything. I'm presenting a minimum standard here. Something almost anyone should be able to do, small acts of bravery to *begin* with. Once you've managed this, go and seek larger challenges. Go on vacation to a city that has recently been bombed, for instance.

Some anti-terror warriors will say that I hate my own culture and secretly want the terrorists to win, (maybe even subconsciously - yay Freud!) Others will say that if everyone thinks like me the Islamists can just walk in and take over. Suicidal tolerance! But if the only major weapon the terrorists have is fear, then the best way to fight them is surely to confront that fear. Hack it away, piece by piece. Liberate yourself.

And then what can terrorists do to us? Tell me that. If we learn to be rational about our fear of terrorism, while also doing as much as an open and free society can do to fight it - which is plenty -*what more can they do to us*?

Discussion Starters

1. Stoerk begins with the premise that terrorism will always be with us (unless the terrorists decide to stop). Do you agree with him? Why?
2. What does Stoerk mean that "fear" is the terrorists most powerful weapon? How does he suggest that people deal with the fear? Do you agree with him?
3. What do you think is the proper balance between maintaining a free, democratic society and doing what may be necessary to thwart terrorism?

What Americans Should Know about Canada

By Durty Dan

Durty Dan is a Canadian writer with over 200 published articles. His website is www. durtydan.com. In this essay, he presents American readers with fifty things they should know – and probably don't – about Canada, with a good degree of wit.

We're you're closest neighbor. We're your largest trading partner and your closest ally. Still, there's a lot of stuff you don't know about Canada. Here are few things to educate yourself with. If you use only two or three of them, to a Canadian it will look as if you know a lot about our country. They will be impressed.

THE LIST

1. We DO NOT have snow all year round. We DO NOT live in igloos. We DO NOT ride around on dog sleds. We DO NOT have to check the back yard for polar bears before we let our kids go out to play.
2. Stop asking if we know somebody in Canada when you find out we're Canadian. We DON'T know everybody in Canada.
3. Canadians do not find, "*Say 'eh' for me*," to be particularly funny.
4. Our president is called a Prime Minister.
5. We have never had a Prime Minister assassinated. Although we've been tempted a few times.
6. We're a lot bigger than you, in land mass, but our population is considerably less. The populations of Los Angeles and New York City would be around 30 million people. The entire nation of Canada has around 32 million people. Due to the fact that most of our country is in the northern latitudes, we huddle close to the border, for warmth.
7. In the War of 1812, we kicked your butts. The reason why your White House is white is because we set fire to it and it was whitewashed to hide the damage (for propaganda purposes). The west wing was almost completely gutted. Some Americans will say that THEY won the war. However, to win, a party must reach their objective. Your objective was to take over British North America (what Canada was called then), our goal was to stop you. You don't have any more northern territory along the Canada/US border than you did before 1812. So who won? (Alaska doesn't count, you BOUGHT that state from Russia.)
8. A form of baseball was played just outside of Toronto, Ontario three weeks before Alexander Doubleday played the "first" game of baseball in your country.
9. We do not find the term "Canuck" derogatory, like Americans find "Yank" derogatory. It apparently originated during World War One. Your soldiers were call "doughboys," ours were called "Johnny Canucks". I think the British coined the term, but I'm not sure.
10. We did not have a "Wild West." The forerunner of the Royal Canadian Mounted Police (Mounties), the Northwest Mounted Police, kept the peace. Due to the fact that they were

a national police force, you could not escape their jurisdiction. They always got their man. Or woman. We have had our share of outlaws, though. Many famous pirates had their headquarters on the east coast of Canada.

11. Speaking of Mounties, they do not all ride horses. So don't try to outrun them if you see their lights in your rear view mirror.

12. We get the same TV shows and channels as you do. So don't ask "Do you get [name of show] up there in Canada?"

13. We are not "just like Americans;" we have our own national identity, we just haven't figured out what it is, yet. Someone once said that, "*Canadians are unarmed Americans with health care.*" That pretty much sums it up, I guess. We are internationally (but unofficially) known as the "World's Most Polite Nation."

14. Our national animal is the beaver. Sure it's just a rodent, but they're not even CLOSE to being extinct. You can still get money for beaver pelts. It is NOT our main unit of exchange, we have money, just like you.

15. We do not find the fact that Americans wear Canadian flag pins (so they can get better treatment in Europe) very amusing. So stop it.

16. Contrary to popular belief, the Klondike Gold Rush happened mostly in Canada, not Alaska. American prospectors were stopped at the border and had their liquor, gambling paraphernalia and firearms confiscated by the Mounties.

17. We have Thanksgiving in October, so we don't look like copycats (it *IS* an American originated holiday, after all). However, we celebrate Christmas, Easter, Halloween, Passover and other holidays at the same time you do.

18. We were formed, as a nation, in 1867. ·

19. We do not trade in beaver pelts, blankets and gunpowder. We have currency. Unlike you, however, we have a two dollar bill. (Although you had them during your bi-centennial celebration.) Actually, our two dollar bill is a *COIN*. Our bills have pictures of birds on them and are multi-colored. Our one dollar coin has a picture of a loon on it, so it's called a "Loonie." The two dollar coin has a picture of a polar bear on it, so it's called a "Toonie." (Don't ask, I'm as confused as you are on this one.) There are plans afoot to mint a five-dollar coin, but we have no idea what to call it.

20. November the 11th is called Remembrance Day, up here. It is a day when all Canadians honor our war dead and the veterans who are still amongst us. Its significance is that on the eleventh hour of the eleventh day of the eleventh month the Armistice was signed, ending World War One.

21. Not every Canadian speaks French. In fact, Canada is the only country where speaking French is not cool.

22. We spell words differently. Hon*ou*r, val*ou*r, defen*c*e, neighb*ou*r, col*ou*r, cent*re* and other words are from the British way of spelling. We also pronounce the last letter of the alphabet "zed", not "zee".

23. The Queen of England is not our national leader. She's just a figure head and somebody to put on our money with the birds. (Some Royalists in Canada will have something different to say about his, but they're a minority.)

24. In Canada the term "bilingual" does not mean the person can speak two languages, it specifically means "speaks both English and French." Canada has two official languages; they

are (coincidentally) English and French.

25. Members of our Senate are appointed by the national party in power. It is a life time position. Even though they are not elected by the people, they can still control government legislation.

26. Our states are called Provinces.

27. We have three Territories. A territory is created through federal law. In this case, Crown (government) lands in the territories are retained by the federal government in the *Crown in right of Canada*. This differs from the provinces, which own provincial lands in the *Crown in right of the province*. Secondly, in a territory, federal Parliament may enter into provincial-type affairs, such as school curriculum. Thirdly, territorial governments are not included in the *Constitutional amending formula* (this is the way Canada decides if we want to change something in the Canadian Constitution). Provinces get a vote when a change is proposed—territories don't.

28. Our Federal Governments are formed by the party who received the majority of votes (just like your system). Unlike your system, we do not vote for the person who we would want to be leader of our nation, we vote for the local representative in the territory they are responsible for (called a Riding). The party who had the most local representatives (seats) voted in—is the ruling party. The party who came in second is known as Her Majesty's Loyal Opposition. (This is done because we have more than two national parties.) The Opposition's job is to keep the ruling party honest and prevent them from getting into any skulduggery. (It doesn't always work.) We have elections every four years, but the ruling party can call an election earlier.

29. Our Prime Minister does not have a limit on how many terms in office they can serve. The most recent record is held by Liberal leader Pierre Eliot Trudeau who stayed leader of the country for around 16 years. It is known as the Trudeau Era. A WWII era Prime Minister, William Lyon MacKenzie King, served for longer than this, by the way.

30. We have had a woman Prime Minister. Her name was Kim Campbell. She was Deputy Prime Minister (that's what we call our Vice President) when the Prime Minister of that time, Brian Mulroney, quit. There was an election shortly after that (the Deputy PM is not allowed to finish the term, like the Vice President is).

31. You don't have to be born in Canada to be Prime Minister.

32. Many Canadians have never played hockey in their lives. There are many who do not like hockey.

33. Besides, our national sport is not hockey, it's lacrosse. It's one of the few sports that originated on the North American continent; it was played by the Indians.

34. We didn't invent hockey, we just made it better.

35. Canadian football is different. The Canadian Football League (CFL) has larger end-zones, the football is bigger, and they have one less "down." We don't support it much and a few teams have gone bankrupt. Despite the fact that many say it is better than American football, others (who don't particularly like Canadian football) use the expression *"run, pass, kick"* to describe the game. Apparently, they feel this best describes every offensive strategy in the CFL.

36. Even if an "American" team wins the Stanley Cup (the "World Series" of hockey) it doesn't matter to us, because all your best players are Canadian.

37. On the other hand, if a "Canadian" team wins the World Series we ignore the fact that all our baseball players are American.

38. New York City has more murders in a week than the entire nation of Canada does all year.

39. We have no right to keep and bear arms. So leave your guns home if you're visiting, otherwise they'll be confiscated at the border. We have very strict gun laws, and fully automatic weapons are pretty much illegal. It almost takes an Act of God to get a license to own a pistol. (This may be a contributing factor as to why we only have about 600 homicides a year, nation-wide.)

40. The border between Canada and the US holds the title of the "World's Longest Undefended Border."

41. Our side of Niagra falls is nicer looking than your side. In fact, even when Americans use images of the Falls in advertising and movies, they film the Canadian side. It's called Horse Shoe Falls.

42. That movie you thought was filmed in New York, or Seattle, or Chicago, or Los Angeles—may have just been filmed in Vancouver, Montreal or Toronto.

43. On average four hundred thousand Americans visit Canada each year.

44. Canada has rednecks, too.

45. We pay anywhere from forty to forty-five percent income tax. This does not include Provincial Sales Tax (from 0% to 11% of many purchases, dependent on the particular province) or the national sales tax, the Goods and Services Tax (7% of any purchase over $1.00). Visitors to our country can get the GST they paid reimbursed by filling out a simple form.

46. Our country got its name by mistake. When Jaques Cartier, a French explorer, came to the new world (around where present day Nova Scotia is) they met with local Natives who invited them to their 'kanata' or village. The Jesuit priest with Cartier's party (who was supposed to be providing translation services) misunderstood the native's meaning and told Cartier the name of the country was "Kanata" or Canada.

47. Canada is the only nation to have committed genocide (the complete eradication of a race of people). The Beothuk (*bee-ah-took*) Indians of Newfoundland were hunted like animals. The last one died in prison in the early 1800's. There are no more Beothuk Indians left in the world.

48. We call Eskimos "Inuit" because that's what they call themselves.

49. We own the North Pole, and therefore Santa Claus is Canadian. The internationally recognized mailing address for jolly old St. Nick is: Santa Claus, North Pole, Canada H0H 0H0. So you better not pout, you better not cry, you better not shout, I'm telling you why: Santa Claus is a Canuck.

50. Forget about Columbus and Plymouth Rock. Canada was the first place in North America to be settled by Europeans. There was a Viking colony, established by Leif Ericson, circa 1000 B.C. However, Indians attacked the settlements and the Vikings decided that it would be better for everybody if they just went home.

So there you have it. Now you just might know more about Canada than most Canadians do.

Discussion Starters

1. What did you learn about Canada that you didn't already know? What did you find most interesting? What did you find most amusing?

2. Comparing Canadian governance to the U.S., what similarities and differences did you find? What system do you find most preferable? Why?

3. Why do you think many Americans know little about Canada? What are your own impressions of Canada as a country and as a place to visit?

XII. Technology

Social Media's Positive Influence

By Josh Rose

Josh Rose is the digital creative director of the ad agency Deutsch LA and contributor to Mashable. com, which covers social media news. In this essay, Rose provides examples of the positive impact of social media technology on human interaction, including his personal experience.

Two events today, although worlds apart, seem inextricably tied together. And the bond between them is as human as it is electronic.

First, on my way to go sit down and read the newspaper at my coffee shop, I got a message from my 10-year-old son, just saying good morning and letting me know he was going to a birthday party today. I don't get to see him all the time. He's growing up in two houses, as I did. But recently, as I handed down my old iPhone 3G to him to use basically as an iPod touch, we both installed an app called Yak, so we could communicate with each other when we're apart.

The amount of calming satisfaction it gives me to be able to communicate with him through technology is undeniably palpable and human. It's the other side of the "I don't care what you ate for breakfast this morning" argument against the mundane broadcasting of social media. In this case, I absolutely care about this. I'd listen to him describe a piece of bacon, and hang on every word. Is it better than a conversation with "real words?" No. But is it better than waiting two more days, when the mundane moment that I long to hear about so much is gone? Yes. I guess one man's TMI is another man's treasure.

Moments later, I sat down and opened the paper. A headline immediately stood out: "In China, microblogs finding abducted kids" with the subhead, "A 6-year-old who was snatched when he was 3 is discovered with a family 800 miles away." Apparently, the occurrence of reclaimed children through the use of China's version of Twitter—and other online forums—has become triumphant news over there. I'm reading about the father's tears, the boy's own confusing set of emotions, the rapt attention of the town and country, and I'm again marveling at the human side of the Internet.

I recently asked the question to my Facebook friends: "Twitter, Facebook, Foursquare...is all this making you feel closer to people or farther away?" It sparked a lot of responses and seemed to touch one of our generation's exposed nerves. What is the effect of the Internet and social media on our humanity?

From the outside view, digital interactions appear to be cold and inhuman. There's no denying that. And without doubt, given the choice between hugging someone and "poking" someone, I think we can all agree which one feels better. The theme of the responses to my Facebook question seemed to be summed up by my friend Jason, who wrote: "Closer to people I'm far away from." Then, a minute later, wrote, "but maybe farther from the people I'm close enough to." And then added, "I just got confused."

It *is* confusing. We live in this paradox now, where two seemingly conflicting realities exist side-by-side. Social media simultaneously draws us nearer and distances us. But I think very often, we lament what we miss and forget to admire what we've become. And it's human nature to want to reject the machine at the moment we feel it becoming ubiquitous. We've seen it with the printing press, moving pictures, television, video games and just about any other advanced technology that captures our attention. What romantic rituals of relationship and social interaction will die in the process? Our hearts want to know.

In the *New Yorker* this week, Adam Gopnik's article "How the Internet Gets Inside Us," explores this cultural truism in depth. It's a fantastic read and should be mandatory for anyone in an online industry. He breaks down a whole slew of new books on the subject and categorizes it all into three viewpoints: "the Never-Betters, the Better-Nevers, and the Ever-Wasers." In short, those who see the current movement as good, bad or normal. I think we all know people from each camp. But ultimately, the last group is the one best equipped to handle it all.

Another observation from the coffee shop: In my immediate vicinity, four people are looking at screens and four people are reading something on paper. And I'm doing both. I see Facebook open on two screens, but I'm sure at some point, it's been open on all of them. The dynamic in this coffee shop is quite a bit more revealing than any article or book. Think about the varied juxtapositions of physical and digital going on. People aren't giving up long-form reading, considered thinking or social interactions. They are just filling all the space between. And even that's not entirely true as I watch the occasional stare out the window or long glance around the room.

The way people engage with the Internet and social media isn't like any kind of interaction we've ever seen before. It's like an intertwining sine wave that touches in and out continuously. And the Internet itself is more complex and interesting than we often give it credit for. Consider peer-to-peer networking as just one example, where the tasks are distributed among the group to form a whole. It's practically a metaphor for the human mind. Or a township. Or a government. Or a family.

The Internet doesn't steal our humanity, it reflects it. The Internet doesn't get inside us, it shows what's inside us. And social media isn't cold, it's just complex and hard to define. I've always thought that you really see something's value when you try to destroy it. As we have now laid witness to in recent news, the Internet has quickly become the atom of cultural media; intertwined with our familial and cultural bonds, and destroyed only at great risk. I think if we search our own souls and consider our own personal way of navigating, we know this is as true personally as it is globally. The machine does not control us. It is a tool. As advanced today as a sharpened stick was a couple million years ago. Looked at through this lens, perhaps we should re-frame our discussions about technology from how it is changing us to how we are using it.

Discussion Starters

1. What positives does Rose see in social media communication and the Internet? Do you agree with him?
2. What is the "paradox" that Rose refers to regarding social media communication? How can social media "simultaneously draw us nearer and distance us" at the same time? Do you agree with him?
3. What is your own experience with social media communication? How does it affect your shorter-distance and longer-distance relationships with people?

Built-In Obsolescence

By Anouch Seydtaghia

Anouch Seydtaghia is a journalist for Le Temps, a Swiss daily newspaper. In this essay, Seydtaghia provides evidence of tech companies creating built-in obsolescence in their products to get tech-hungry consumers to buy their latest models.

On the left, a wall of washing machines and stoves. On the right, a man is taking apart a vacuum cleaner, another a food processor. A little further away, an employee looking through a powerful magnifying glass pokes at a telephone with tweezers. In the background, a television set without its shell is broadcasting a reality show.

"La Bonne Combine" [The Good Deal] in Prilly, in the province of Vaud, is the appliance-repair Mecca of French-speaking Switzerland. "Look at this," says Felice Suglia, bringing over a circuit board. "This is the heart of a television set. The condensers are soldered right next to a heat sink connected to the transistors. The condensers are sensitive to heat. Why did Samsung put them here, even though there is room at the other end of the board?" the repairman asks.

This simple question is one of many about the reliability of appliances and electronic devices. More and more of them seem to be manufactured with planned obsolescence in mind—something that is often suspected, but rarely proven.

Electronics and appliance manufacturers are accused of deliberately shortening the lifespan of their products in order to force consumers to purchase new ones sooner. "It is impossible to be sure, but we often have strong suspicions," says Christopher Inaebnit, who runs La Bonne Combine. "Look at the latest washing machines. Big-name companies set the ball bearings into the drum. Because new drums are so costly, that makes it almost impossible to replace the bearings when they're worn out." It means that appliances have become less and less repairable. "A few years ago, we could repair eight appliances out of 10, both large and small. Nowadays, it's seven in 10. It's even less for electronics," says Inaebnit. Some appliances are designed in a very surprising way."

Further along, Inaebnit indicates a disemboweled iPad. "Apple uses double-sided tape that is stronger than we've ever seen before. To get to the electronic components, you have to unglue this tape with a hot-air gun. The smallest mistake and the tablet is destroyed," he says.

Planned obsolescence takes a wide variety of forms. Huma Kamis, of the Swiss-French Consumer Federation (FRC), says, "For the past eight years I have been doing comparative tests. It is indisputable that the obsolescence is programmed in. Metallic parts in cell phones have been replaced by plastic, so they are more fragile. Changing the connector for the charger is another kind of obsolescence. Often for no reason, the manufacturer will change them, just to force consumers to buy new ones. The iPhone 5's new Lightning connector is one example, but many other manufacturers also make accessories that are incompatible from one model to the next. It is really regrettable." The FRC hopes to make consumers more aware of the problem in 2013.

The most extreme form of planned obsolescence is for the manufacturer to program a precise life expectancy into its machines. "You will find a lot of testimonials on the internet that seem too real not to be true," says Toni Conde, a multimedia and communications expert who teaches at the EPFL Swiss Federal Institute of Technology in Lausanne. "Some manufacturers of memory cards for cameras or telephones limit the number of possible photos or videos. Past a certain quota, the card becomes unusable. This is true of printers too. Some are programmed to stop working after a certain number of print jobs."

In February 2011, The French-German television station Arte showed a documentary called "Ready-To-Toss," spotlighting an Epson printer that showed an artificial error message after 18,000 copies. When contacted, the Japanese manufacturer confirmed: "Our printers are equipped with pads that absorb the extra ink. They must be changed regularly in order to function properly. If not, there is a risk, in the worst case, of stains on furniture and rugs. Therefore, our printers are equipped with a counter to control their condition. When the pad needs to be changed, it is impossible to print anything more." Schahin Elahinija, marketing head for Epson Germany, adds that the service is free when the printer is still under warranty. Afterwards, it costs about $34.

At the beginning of the 1990s, the specialists at La Bonne Combine detected a similar technique in coffeemakers. "After 3,000 coffees, Jura coffee machines would stop working and would show a message saying it was time for service," says Inaebnit. "Later, Jura changed this so that the error message no longer blocked the machine. Certainly, the manufacturers of this kind of machine play on the naïvety of some consumers, displaying alerts that are not always relevant." When contacted, Jura denied that it "worked with planned obsolescence" and stated that a machine needs to be serviced every three to four years.

Some manufacturers make it very difficult to acquire parts. "Recently, we ordered a part from a television manufacturer. It cost about $300. By mistake, the shipper had left on the price tag for Slovakia, which was...60 euros ($78). Sometimes, they do everything to discourage repairs, especially in Switzerland," Inaebnit says.

Some computer manufacturers refuse to deliver any components, forcing La Bonne Combine to supply itself from businesses that make copies of the required parts. "Others will send us parts we didn't order, and afterwards refuse to take them back." When contacted, HP maintains that it provides spare parts for all its machines.

Another concern is quality. "Chinese suppliers have figured out that there are opportunities in the market for spare parts. But the quality varies widely. Finding good parts is a challenge," says Miro Djuric, one of the managers of iFixit.com, a website loaded with guides and instruction manuals. Its goal is to help consumers to repair their own machines. "Planned obsolescence is spreading," Djuric says. "On the first Android phones, it was possible to change the battery. Now, it is much harder to get to the battery, just as it is on the iPhone."

Distributors are often blamed for problems. "Several times, when we brought a camera or video recorder into a big store to be repaired, we noticed that the total price of the estimate and the repair was slightly less than the cost of a new one," says Régis Chatelain, director of Swissecology, a sustainable development engineering organization. "It is obviously a strategy to force consumers to buy new things."

When contacted, Interdiscount responded: "Because of the continual lowering of prices, it is sometimes cheaper to buy a new machine than to repair an old one."

Another example of programmed aging is software. "Take Windows: Microsoft stops supporting earlier versions after a few years. This forces users to buy the latest version and also a new computer, even though the earlier versions are still fine for the majority of users. There is also the vicious circle of the race to produce more powerful computers and faster chips," says Conde.

Are consumers themselves partly responsible? "The marketing for certain products works very well," says Kamis. "Every 12 to 18 months, the cell phone operators put another 'smartphone' in the hands of their customers. Which they could refuse to buy…"

Discussion Starters

1. What does "built-in obsolescence" mean and what is its purpose? What examples does the essay provide to show its existence? Are the examples convincing?
2. What can consumers do to combat built-in obsolescence? How would we have to change our consuming habits to make a difference?
3. What experience if any have you had with built-in obsolescence in your cell phones, computers, printers, play stations, etc.? Are you prone to want the latest version of whatever electronic gadget you use? How are consumers in part responsible for the success of built-in obsolescence as a marketing tool?

The Flight From Conversation

By Sherry Turkle

Sherry Turkle is a professor of the Social Studies of Science and Technology at the Massachusetts Institute of Technology. She has written several books focusing on the psychology of human relationships with technology. In this essay, Turkle contends that communication technology isolates humans and breaks down the face-to-face conversation that is at the heart of human connections.

We live in a technological universe in which we are always communicating. And yet we have sacrificed conversation for mere connection.

At home, families sit together, texting and reading e-mail. At work executives text during board meetings. We text (and shop and go on Facebook) during classes and when we're on dates. My students tell me about an important new skill: it involves maintaining eye contact with someone while you text someone else; it's hard, but it can be done.

Over the past 15 years, I've studied technologies of mobile connection and talked to hundreds of people of all ages and circumstances about their plugged-in lives. I've learned that the little devices most of us carry around are so powerful that they change not only what we do, but also who we are.

We've become accustomed to a new way of being "alone together." Technology-enabled, we are able to be with one another, and also elsewhere, connected to wherever we want to be. We want to customize our lives. We want to move in and out of where we are because the thing we value most is control over where we focus our attention. We have gotten used to the idea of being in a tribe of one, loyal to our own party.

Our colleagues want to go to that board meeting but pay attention only to what interests them. To some this seems like a good idea, but we can end up hiding from one another, even as we are constantly connected to one another.

A businessman laments that he no longer has colleagues at work. He doesn't stop by to talk; he doesn't call. He says that he doesn't want to interrupt them. He says they're "too busy on their e-mail." But then he pauses and corrects himself. "I'm not telling the truth. I'm the one who doesn't want to be interrupted. I think I should. But I'd rather just do things on my BlackBerry."

A 16-year-old boy who relies on texting for almost everything says almost wistfully, "Someday, someday, but certainly not now, I'd like to learn how to have a conversation."

In today's workplace, young people who have grown up fearing conversation show up on the job wearing earphones. Walking through a college library or the campus of a high-tech start-up, one sees the same thing: we are together, but each of us is in our own bubble, furiously connected to keyboards and tiny touch screens. A senior partner at a Boston law firm describes a scene in his office. Young associates lay out their suite of technologies: laptops, iPods and multiple phones. And then they put their earphones on. "Big ones. Like pilots. They turn their desks into cockpits." With the young lawyers in their cockpits, the office is quiet, a quiet that does not ask to be broken.

In the silence of connection, people are comforted by being in touch with a lot of people—carefully kept at bay. We can't get enough of one another if we can use technology to keep one another at distances we can control: not too close, not too far, just right. I think of it as a Goldilocks effect.

Texting and e-mail and posting let us present the self we want to be. This means we can edit. And if we wish to, we can delete. Or retouch: the voice, the flesh, the face, the body. Not too much, not too little—just right.

Human relationships are rich; they're messy and demanding. We have learned the habit of cleaning them up with technology. And the move from conversation to connection is part of this. But it's a process in which we shortchange ourselves. Worse, it seems that over time we stop caring, we forget that there is a difference.

We are tempted to think that our little "sips" of online connection add up to a big gulp of real conversation. But they don't. E-mail, Twitter, Facebook, all of these have their places—in politics, commerce, romance and friendship. But no matter how valuable, they do not substitute for conversation.

Connecting in sips may work for gathering discrete bits of information or for saying, "I am thinking about you." Or even for saying, "I love you." But connecting in sips doesn't work as well when it comes to understanding and knowing one another. In conversation we tend to one another. (The word itself is kinetic; it's derived from words that mean to move, together.) We can attend to tone and nuance. In conversation, we are called upon to see things from another's point of view.

Face-to-face conversation unfolds slowly. It teaches patience. When we communicate on our digital devices, we learn different habits. As we ramp up the volume and velocity of online connections, we start to expect faster answers. To get these, we ask one another simpler questions; we dumb down our communications, even on the most important matters. It is as though we have all put ourselves on cable news. Shakespeare might have said, "We are consum'd with that which we were nourish'd by."

And we use conversation with others to learn to converse with ourselves. So our flight from conversation can mean diminished chances to learn skills of self-reflection. These days, social media continually asks us what's "on our mind," but we have little motivation to say something truly self-reflective. Self-reflection in conversation requires trust. It's hard to do anything with 3,000 Facebook friends except connect.

As we get used to being shortchanged on conversation and to getting by with less, we seem almost willing to dispense with people altogether. Serious people muse about the future of computer programs as psychiatrists. A high school sophomore confides to me that he wishes he could talk to an artificial intelligence program instead of his dad about dating; he says the A.I. would have so much more in its database. Indeed, many people tell me they hope that as Siri, the digital assistant on Apple's iPhone, becomes more advanced, "she" will be more and more like a best friend—one who will listen when others won't.

During the years I have spent researching people and their relationships with technology, I have often heard the sentiment "No one is listening to me." I believe this feeling helps explain why it is so appealing to have a Facebook page or a Twitter feed—each provides so many automatic listeners. And it helps explain why—against all reason—so many of us are willing to talk to machines that seem to care about us. Researchers around the world are busy inventing sociable robots, designed to be companions to the elderly, to children, to all of us.

One of the most haunting experiences during my research came when I brought one of these robots, designed in the shape of a baby seal, to an elder-care facility, and an older woman began to talk to it about the loss of her child. The robot seemed to be looking into her eyes. It seemed to be following the conversation. The woman was comforted.

And so many people found this amazing. Like the sophomore who wants advice about dating from artificial intelligence and those who look forward to computer psychiatry, this enthusiasm speaks to how much we have confused conversation with connection and collectively seem to have embraced a new kind of delusion that accepts the simulation of compassion as sufficient unto the day. And why would we want to talk about love and loss with a machine that has no experience of the arc of human life? Have we so lost confidence that we will be there for one another?

We expect more from technology and less from one another and seem increasingly drawn to technologies that provide the illusion of companionship without the demands of relationship. Always-on/always-on-you devices provide three powerful fantasies: that we will always be heard; that we can put our attention wherever we want it to be; and that we never have to be alone. Indeed our new devices have turned being alone into a problem that can be solved.

When people are alone, even for a few moments, they fidget and reach for a device. Here connection works like a symptom, not a cure, and our constant, reflexive impulse to connect shapes a new way of being. Think of it as "I share, therefore I am." We use technology to define ourselves by sharing our thoughts and feelings as we're having them. We used to think, "I have a feeling; I want to make a call." Now our impulse is, "I want to have a feeling; I need to send a text."

So, in order to feel more, and to feel more like ourselves, we connect. But in our rush to connect, we flee from solitude, our ability to be separate and gather ourselves. Lacking the capacity for solitude, we turn to other people but don't experience them as they are. It is as though we use them, need them as spare parts to support our increasingly fragile selves.

We think constant connection will make us feel less lonely. The opposite is true. If we are unable to be alone, we are far more likely to be lonely. If we don't teach our children to be alone, they will know only how to be lonely.

I am a partisan for conversation. To make room for it, I see some first, deliberate steps. At home, we can create sacred spaces: the kitchen, the dining room. We can make our cars "device-free zones." We can demonstrate the value of conversation to our children. And we can do the same thing at work. There we are so busy communicating that we often don't have time to talk to one another about what really matters. Employees asked for casual Fridays; perhaps managers should introduce conversational Thursdays. Most of all, we need to remember—in between texts and e-mails and Facebook posts—to listen to one another, even to the boring bits, because it is often in unedited moments, moments in which we hesitate and stutter and go silent, that we reveal ourselves to one another.

I spend the summers at a cottage on Cape Cod, and for decades I walked the same dunes that Thoreau once walked. Not too long ago, people walked with their heads up, looking at the water, the sky, the sand and at one another, talking. Now they often walk with their heads down, typing. Even when they are with friends, partners, children, everyone is on their own devices.

So I say, look up, look at one another, and let's start the conversation.

Discussion Starters

1. Do you agree with Turkle that e-mail, texting, and Facebook have taken the place of conversation in negative ways? Why does she feel that conversation is much richer and more important than social media? Do you agree?

2. Turkle believes that being more "connected" to people via social media has in fact made us more alone. What does she mean? Do you agree with her?

3. What is your experience with social media? Does it often replace face-to-face conversation? How does it affect how you communicate with people?

Electric Cars: Is This Our Future?

By Joe Nocera

Joe Nocera is an op ed columnist for the New York Times. In this essay, Nocera evaluates his experience test-driving the Chevrolet Volt and offers his viewpoint on the future of electric vehicles.

The moment I realized that driving the new Chevrolet Volt was fundamentally a new experience was not when I first turned it on and went around the block. Yes, it was whisper-quiet, powered by its 16-kilowatt-hour, 400-pound battery, but it still felt like a "normal" automobile. And it wasn't when I drove the 100 or so miles from Manhattan to Southampton, N.Y., either. Although the battery's range is only about 40 miles, the car kept going even after the battery was drained; it just switched to its gasoline engine, in a transition so seamless I barely noticed it. It wasn't even when I arrived in Southampton that evening and plugged a special cord into an electrical outlet in the garage, to recharge the battery overnight.

No, what made the experience truly different—and what got me thinking about the Volt's potential to change the way we think about gas consumption—was what happened after that.

You know the story of the Volt, don't you? As the General Motors entry in the race to build a viable electric car—a race that includes the all-electric Nissan Leaf, a raft of Fords in various stages of development and an electric sedan that Tesla will soon begin selling—it may well be the most hyped American automobile since Lee Iacocca rolled out the Chrysler minivan. Begun four years ago, and championed by the legendary auto executive Bob Lutz, the Volt project managed to survive G.M.'s descent into bankruptcy, and emerge as the company's great, shining hope, a symbol of what American car manufacturers could accomplish. Or so it's been claimed.

Cars like the Leaf and the original Tesla—a Roadster that cost more than $100,000—are "pure" electric vehicles powered solely by their batteries. Classic hybrids like the Toyota Prius use a battery as a kind of add-on, to boost the gas mileage of a combustion engine. The Volt, however, is engineered differently. As long as the battery has juice, the car acts like an electric vehicle. When the battery dies, the combustion engine takes over, and it becomes an old-fashioned gas-consuming car. Once you recharge the battery, electricity takes over again.

The experience of driving it meshes with the way we think about using a car. There is no need to plan ahead, for instance, to make sure the car won't run out of battery life before we can recharge it. And the gas engine eliminates the dreaded "range anxiety" that prevents most people from embracing an electric vehicle. Indeed, G.M. likes to call the Volt an "extended range vehicle." Motor Trend, the car enthusiasts' bible, was so impressed that it named the Volt its 2011 car of the year.

The Volt went on sale last December. But because Chevrolet has been so cautious in rolling it out—dealers in only seven states have gotten cars so far, with fewer than 2,500 sold—it can sometimes seem like the world's most publicized invisible car. (A bigger rollout is planned for next year.) Which is why I asked G.M. if I could test-drive it over the Memorial Day holiday. I wanted to see for myself what all the fuss was about.

For four days, I drove it around town, used it to pick up the groceries, took it to visit friends. Sometimes, when I walked out of a store, someone would be standing next to "my" Volt, wanting to ask me questions about it. Though I am no automotive expert, I was pleasantly surprised by the car's power, pickup and handling. "People think it's going to be a dorkmobile," said Mr. Lutz, who retired last year. "But it's fun to drive."

Here's what really got me, though: on the dashboard, alongside the gauge that measures the battery life, the Volt has another gauge that calculates the vehicle's miles per gallon. During the two-hour drive to Southampton, I used two gallons of gas, a quarter of the tank. Thus, when I drove into the driveway, it read 50 miles per gallon.

The next day, after the overnight charge, I didn't use any gas. After driving around 30 miles in the morning, I recharged it for a few hours while I puttered around the house. (It takes 10 hours to fully recharge, unless you buy a special 240-volt recharging unit.) That gave the battery 10 miles, more than enough to get me where I needed to go that evening on battery power alone. Before I knew it, my miles per gallon for that tankful of gas had hit 80. By the next day it had topped 100. I soon found myself obsessed with increasing my miles per gallon—and avoiding having to buy more gas. Whenever I got home from an errand, I would recharge it, even for a few hours, just to grab a few more miles of range. I was actually in control of how much gas I consumed, and it was a powerful feeling. By the time I gave the car back to General Motors, I had driven 300 miles, without using another drop of gas beyond the original two gallons. I'm not what you'd call a Sierra Club kind of guy, but I have to tell you: I was kind of proud of myself.

When I began to describe for Mr. Lutz the psychological effect the Volt had had on me, he chuckled. "Yeah," he said, "it's like playing a video game that is constantly giving you back your score."

People who follow the car business like to say that this particular moment in automotive history is the closest we'll ever come to seeing what the industry was like a century ago. Back then, there were dozens of auto companies, all experimenting with different ways to power a car, a race ultimately won by the gasoline-powered combustion engine. For good reason: nothing else provided more power, more efficiently.

Now the race is on to come up with an affordable, mass-market electric car. Everybody in the game has a different theory about how to go about it. Elon Musk, the PayPal co-founder who is the driving force behind Tesla, built his original Roadster by strapping together nearly 7,000 lithium ion cells—essentially laptop batteries—that consume the bulk of the car's mass. (It's a two-seater in part because there is no room for anything else but batteries.) Although his Roadster will never be a mass-market car—in fact, it's being phased out in favor of Tesla's new Model S Sedan—Mr. Musk has claimed victory because, he says, the car, with a range of well over 100 miles, offers "proof of concept" that an electric vehicle can be built to go long distances between charges. Starting at $57,400, the Model S is about half the price of the original sports car.

Carlos Ghosn, the flamboyant chief executive of Nissan, has made a different kind of bet, placing his chips—billions of them—on the $32,780 Leaf, which has a 24-kilowatt-hour battery pack that can get 73 miles to the charge. Mr. Ghosn is said to believe that range anxiety is overblown, and that once people become accustomed to an electric car, 73 miles per charge won't be an issue. Well, maybe in Europe and Japan, but most analysts I spoke to think he's likely to get his head handed to him in America, and I tend to agree.

"We've had 120 years of gasoline dominance," said Lindsay Brooke, a senior editor of Automotive Engineering International Magazine. "The habits and expectations that have been engendered—How far will the car go? How quickly can you get it refueled?—aren't going to go away overnight." Americans like the idea that they can get in their cars and drive halfway across the country—even if they never actually do it.

Besides, nobody yet knows what kind of infrastructure will develop around the electric car. Is lithium ion ultimately the right battery chemistry? How quickly will the cost of the battery—which is the most expensive feature in an electric car—come down? When will the battery size shrink, and its power increase?

One of the reasons there is so much experimentation right now is that no one knows how this is all going to play out. Until some answers begin to emerge, it is highly unlikely that any electric car will gain mass acceptance. Early adopters may be willing to give an electric car a chance, but the rest of us won't. Most people want to drive proven technologies, not roll-of-the-dice bets.

Which is also why the Volt is such an appealing alternative—"the right answer for right now," said Michelle Krebs, a senior analyst with the automotive Web site edmunds.com. It gives people a taste of the electric car experience without sacrificing any of the things we expect in a gas-powered car. In fact, the Volt's engineering is a direct byproduct of G.M.'s dismal experience with its original electric car, the legendary EV1, which had more or less the same range as the Leaf. Between 1996 and 1999, G.M. leased 800 EV1's, but faced with mounting costs, they were all repossessed at the end of production.

Chris Paine directed a scathing documentary about G.M.'s decision to kill the EV1, called "Who Killed The Electric Car?," which blamed the failure on the automaker's perfidy, but G.M. has always been convinced that the real culprit was range anxiety. "People just weren't willing to make the compromises you had to make," said Andrew Farah, the Volt's chief engineer, "starting with the range."

Mr. Farah, who worked on the EV1, recalled that G.M. used to attach rolling generators to the outside of the car so that the engineers could keep using it even after the battery died; that became the kernel of the idea behind the Volt. For his part, Mr. Lutz was the one who kept insisting that the battery had to be able to achieve 40 miles per charge, a figure he based on the many studies that showed that the vast majority of Americans drove 40 miles or fewer per day. (The government officially puts the Volt's battery range at 35 miles, but in the right conditions—warm weather, flat terrain—the range can go as high as 50 miles. During the time I drove the Volt, the battery range was consistently in the low 40s.)

That insistence gave rise to some inevitable compromises. The battery can't be under the hood because a combustion engine is still there. So G.M. had to eliminate the middle seat in the back to make space for the big T-shaped battery the Volt required. Its small body, originally modeled on the Camaro, had to be made more aerodynamic because that was the only way to hit the 40 mile-per-charge mark.

And for a car intended for the mass market, it's awfully expensive. The Volt retails for around $41,000; from what I hear, that's pretty much what it costs to build. G.M.'s profits on this first iteration of the Volt, in other words, are essentially zero. Though there is currently a $7,500 tax credit on electric car purchases—the first tax incentive for hybrid gas-electric cars was introduced during the presidency of George W. Bush, in case you were wondering—it won't last forever. Consumer Reports has advised readers to avoid the Volt because it costs too much. G.M. badly needs battery technology to keep improving, both so that it can lower the cost of its electric cars, and begin making Volt-like vehicles in other sizes and shapes, including wagons and S.U.V.'s that will attract families. That's the only way it will finally reach the mass market.

Having said all that, driving it did convince me of two things. The first is that, Consumer Reports notwithstanding, the Volt has a better chance of success than anything else on the market. Yes, G.M.'s track record for making cars people want has not exactly been inspiring in recent years. But the company has been through hell and back, and a good number of the institutional impediments that prevented it from making good cars are now gone.

Though the Volt has its share of flaws, it is unquestionably a good car. More to the point, as I discovered when I drove it, the Volt makes sense for the economic and cultural moment we're in now. The psychological grip it held me in, the smugness I felt as I drove past gas stations, the way it implicitly encouraged me to stick with battery power as much as I could—others are going to feel that as well. Somewhat to my surprise, I actually felt a pang of enviro-guilt when I gave the car back and returned to my gas-guzzling ways. Mr. Farah told me that Volt owners often drove 1,000 miles or more before they needed to buy gasoline. I believe it. It has extremely high word-of-mouth potential.

The second thing it convinced me of is that the electric car is no longer some environmental pipe dream. Several years ago, I drove the Tesla, and though it was a wonderful experience, its high price and limited utility did not give me confidence that electric cars were ready for prime time. The Volt has made a believer out of me. At this moment of maximum uncertainty about how the future will play out, the Volt is comforting in its combination of new technology and old. Eventually, we'll have batteries that can get 300 miles per charge, and an infrastructure solution that will replace gas stations. Eventually.

In the meantime, we've got the Volt. It's a start.

Discussion Starters

1. Why does Nocera believe that the Volt is superior to and more marketable than other electric cars on the market? Do you agree?
2. What was the "psychological effect" of driving a Volt that Nocera experienced? Might driving a Volt have a similar effect on you?
3. What do you think the future is for electric cars? What would have to happen to popularize them? Would you consider buying one yourself at some time?

Japanese Robotics

By Yumi Tanaguchi

Umi Taniguchi is a freelance writer and Asian-culture expert. In this essay, Taniguchi reveals the advanced robotics in Japan compared to other countries, why the Japanese have embraced robots, and what the future may hold.

Japanese are more accepting of robots because the native Shinto religion often blurs boundaries between the animate and inanimate. To the Japanese psyche, the idea of a humanoid robot with feelings doesn't feel as creepy as it might in other cultures.

While robots are a long way from matching human emotional complexity, the country is perhaps the closest to a future—once the stuff of science fiction—where humans and intelligent robots routinely live side by side and interact socially.

Robots are already taken for granted in Japanese factories, so much so that they are sometimes welcomed on their first day at work with Shinto religious ceremonies. Robots make sushi. Robots plant rice and tend paddies. There are robots serving as receptionists, vacuuming office corridors, spoon-feeding the elderly. They serve tea, greet company guests and chatter away at public technology displays. Now startups are marching out robotic home helpers. They aren't all humanoid. The Paro is a furry robot seal fitted with sensors beneath its fur and whiskers, designed to comfort the lonely, opening and closing its eyes and moving its flippers.

For Japan, the robotics revolution is an imperative. With more than a fifth of the population 65 or older, the country is banking on robots to replenish the work force and care for the elderly. In the past several years, the government has funded a plethora of robotics-related efforts, including some $42 million for the first phase of a humanoid robotics project, and $10 million a year between 2006 and 2010 to develop key robot technologies. The government estimates the industry could surge from about $5.2 billion in 2006 to $26 billion in 2010 and nearly $70 billion by 2025.

Besides financial and technological power, the robot wave is favored by the Japanese mind-set as well. Robots have long been portrayed as friendly helpers in Japanese popular culture, a far cry from the often rebellious and violent machines that often inhabit Western science fiction. This is, after all, the country that invented Tamagotchi, the hand-held mechanical pets that captivated the children of the world.

Still, Japan faces a vast challenge in making the leap—commercially and culturally—from toys, gimmicks and the experimental robots churned out by labs like Takeno's to full-blown human replacements that ordinary people can afford and use safely. "People are still asking whether people really want robots running around their homes and folding their clothes," said Damian Thong, senior technology analyst at Macquarie Bank in Tokyo. "But then again, Japan's the only country in the world where everyone has an electric toilet," he said. "We could be looking at a robotics revolution."

That revolution has been going on quietly for some time. Japan is already an industrial robot powerhouse. Over 370,000 robots worked at factories across Japan in 2005, about 40 percent of the global total and 32 robots for every 1,000 Japanese manufacturing employees, according to a recent report by Macquarie, which had no numbers from subsequent years. And they won't be claiming overtime or drawing pensions when they're retired. "The cost of machinery is going down, while labor costs are rising," said Eimei Onaga, CEO of Innovation Matrix Inc., a company that distributes Japanese robotics technology in the U.S. "Soon, robots could even replace low-cost workers at small firms, greatly boosting productivity."

That's just what the Japanese government has been counting on. A 2007 national technology roadmap by the Trade Ministry called for 1 million industrial robots to be installed throughout the country by 2025. A single robot can replace about 10 employees, the roadmap assumes—meaning Japan's future million-robot army of workers could take the place of 10 million humans. That's about 15 percent of the current work force. "Robots are the cornerstone of Japan's international competitiveness," Shunichi Uchiyama, the Trade Ministry's chief of manufacturing industry policy, said at a recent seminar. "We expect robotics technology to enter even more sectors going forward."

Meanwhile, localities looking to boost regional industry clusters have seized on robotics technology as a way to spur advances in other fields. Robotic technology is used to build more complex cars, for instance, and surgical equipment. The logical next step is robots in everyday life.

At a hospital in Aizu Wakamatsu, 190 miles north of Tokyo, a child-sized white and blue robot wheels across the floor, guiding patients to and from the outpatients' surgery area. The robot, made by startup Tmsk, sports perky catlike ears, recites simple greetings, and uses sensors to detect and warn people in the way. It helpfully prints out maps of the hospital, and even checks the state of patients' arteries. The Aizu Chuo Hospital spent about some $557,000 installing three of the robots in its waiting rooms to test patients' reactions. The response has been overwhelmingly positive, said spokesman Naoya Narita. "We feel this is a good division of labor. Robots won't ever become doctors, but they can be guides and receptionists," Narita said.

Still, the wheeled machines hadn't won over all seniors crowding the hospital waiting room on a weekday morning. "It just told us to get out of the way!" huffed wheelchair-bound Hiroshi Asami, 81. "It's a robot. It's the one who should get out my way. I prefer dealing with real people," he said.

Another roadblock is money. For all its research, Japan has yet to come up with a commercially successful consumer robot. Mitsubishi Heavy Industries Ltd. failed to sell even one of its pricey toddler-sized Wakamaru robots, launched in 2003 as domestic helpers. Though initially popular, Sony Corp. pulled the plug on its robot dog, Aibo, in 2006, just seven years after its launch. With a price tag of a whopping $2,000, Aibo never managed to break into the mass market.

One of the only commercially successful consumer robots so far is made by an American company, iRobot Corp. The Roomba vacuum cleaner robot is self-propelled and can clean rooms without supervision. "We can pretty much make anything, but we have to ask, what are people actually going to buy?" said iRobot CEO Helen Greiner. The company has sold 2.5 million Roombas—which retail for as little as $120—since the line was launched in 2002. Still, with the correct approach, robots could provide a wealth of consumer goods, Greiner stressed at a recent convention.

Sure enough, Japanese makers are catching on, launching low-cost robots like Tomy's $300 i-Sobot, a toy-like hobby robot that comes with 17 motors, can recognize spoken words and can be remote-controlled. Sony is also trying to learn from past mistakes, launching a much cheaper

$350 rolling speaker robot last year that built on its robotics technology. "What we need now isn't the ultimate humanoid robot," said Kyoji Takenaka, the head of the industry-wide Robot Business Promotion Council. "Engineers need to remember that the key to developing robots isn't in the lab, but in everyday life."

Still, some of the most eye-catching developments in robotics are coming out of Japan's labs. Researchers at Osaka University, for instance, are developing a robot to better understand child development. The "Child-Robot with Biomimetic Body" is designed to mimic the motions of a toddler. It responds to sounds, and sensors in its eyes can see and react to people. It wiggles, changes facial expressions, and makes gurgling sounds. The team leader, Minoru Asada, is working on artificial intelligence software that would allow the child to "learn" as it progresses. "Right now, it only goes, 'Ah, ah.' But as we develop its learning function, we hope it can start saying more complex sentences and moving on its own will," Asada said. "Next-generation robots need to be able to learn and develop themselves."

For Hiroshi Ishiguro, also at Osaka University, the key is to make robots that look like human beings. His Geminoid robot looks uncannily like himself—down to the black, wiry hair and slight tan. "In the end, we don't want to interact with machines or computers. We want to interact with technology in a human way so it's natural and valid to try to make robots look like us," he said. "One day, they will live among us," Ishiguro said. "Then you'd have to ask me: 'Are you human? Or a robot?'" A robotic world once the sole domain of science fiction may soon become reality in Japan.

Discussion Starters

1. What reason does the essay give for Japan being far ahead of Western countries in developing and using robots? Do you agree?
2. The essay mentions the positive effects of using "industrial robots" in the workplace. What if any negative effects may there be?
3. What types of robots introduced in the essay did you find most interesting or surprising? What do you think the future role of robots might be in the U.S.? Do you believe Hiroshi Ishiguro's comment, "One day, they will live among us?"

Cyber Bullying

By Anton Hout

Anton Hout is the founder of OvercomingBullying.com. In this essay, Hout reveals the serious problem of cyberbullying, its devastating effects, and what the targets of cyberbullying can do to fight back.

Home sweet home is no longer a sanctuary into which victims of bullying can escape their tormentors. Bullies can now stalk their prey after school hours long after their targets have gone home.

Social isolation, public humiliation and malicious gossip have long been the stock in trade of bullies. With the advent of modern communications such as email, chat, text messaging and cell phones as well as the ability to publish online on websites, blogs and social networking sites such as Facebook and MySpace making their message instantly available to millions, the bully's reach and powers of social manipulation have been increased exponentially.

Parents are well advised to pay close attention to how this new threat can impact their children. We have already seen too many cases of children subjected to a cyber bullying attack who have been so traumatized that they have committed suicide as a direct result. "Bullycide" is the term that has been used to describe suicides caused by relentless bullying. "Cyberbullycide", to coin a phrase, would describe someone driven to suicide following a cyberbullying attack.

In the *book Bullycide In America: Moms Speak Out about the Bullying/Suicide Connection*, compiled by Brenda High, the story of Jeffery Johnston serves as a warning about cyber bullying. Jeffrey's mother Debbie Johnston writes,

> "A bully doesn't have to be eye to eye to bully someone. Sometimes he or she gets into cyberspace, and then there's no place to hide from their torment. With the keyboard as his weapon, the bully violated the sanctity of my home and murdered my child just as surely as if he had crawled through a broken window and choked the life from Jeff with his bare hands. It was not a death that was quick and merciful. It was carried out with lies, rumors and calculated cruelty portioned out day by day."

Cyber bullies, like any bully, want to feel power and control over their victim. They want to get under their victim's skin. Many kids live and breathe the internet. It is essential to how they see themselves and how they socialize with their peers. The computer is as essential a social tool today as the telephone was decades ago.

This is part of why a cyber bullying attack can be so devastating. Cyber bullies cut to the core of their victim's social life and self image. Targets are faced with threats and intimidation in emails and instant messages, but it is not only fear that the cyber bully can instill over the web. It is not good enough anymore for bullies to simply beat up their victims. With digital video becoming ubiquitous, beatings are now digitally recorded and uploaded so everyone can have a front row seat and the bloodlust can be enjoyed again and again.

How can cyber bullies be so heartless? Perhaps the internet lends itself to this indifference. Bullies don't have to see their victims or answer for their actions. Like the cowards they are, they hide behind their computers - behind a veil of anonymity.

Even though the effects of cyberbullying can be every bit as dangerous as offline bullying, if not more so, parents are even less likely to hear about it happening to their child.

To understand why, you have to understand how important access to the Internet is for many kids. They will remain silent about cyberbullying because they are afraid if their parents find out they will go off the deep end and cut off access to their computer, Internet and/or mobile phone. Years ago this would be the equivalent of a child who complained of bullying being grounded and losing their telephone privileges. Loss of Internet access would be deemed by many kids now to be the cruelest of punishments.

The first step in combatting cyber bullying is to stop responding to the cyber bully. Do not reply to emails, posts, IM's or text messages. This is what the bully wants. They want you to engage with them. They want to manipulate you into responding.

If you respond in any way that is emotional or lets them know that they are getting to you and are able to make you upset, it only encourages the cyber bully.

Remember, bullies often suffer from low self-esteem and they want to feel better about themselves. Instead of doing something positive or succeeding at something or making a new friend, a bully has learned to make themselves feel better by controlling, abusing and tearing down others. This gives them a sense of control and power they don't have in their lives. Most bullies are actually quite weak and the same is true of cyber bullies. If you respond in a way that lets the bully know that you are angry, upset or afraid, they will only be happy because they have managed to control your emotional state. Even if you do feel like that, don't give the cyber bully the satisfaction and encouragement by letting them know.

It is especially important not to respond emotionally because this could make you send a reply that you might regret later. Messages sent on the Internet are almost impossible to take back. If you lash back in anger you could find yourself the one who is being accused of being a cyber bully and the tables could be turned against you.

Bullies are hoping to get you upset so you slip up and make a mistake. Don't send flames and don't get into flame wars.

While you should not respond to the cyber bully online (or offline), you should also not delete their messages. That's right, do NOT delete their messages. Cyber bullies are especially cowardly and like to hide behind the anonymity that the Internet gives them. Or does it? Messages sent on the Internet are traceable. Make sure to keep all messages as the police will be able to use this information to track down the culprit. Do not delete any messages and save as much information you can about chats, IM's, text messages, blog posts, websites, etc.

This will also help show just how often the cyber bullying takes place, at what times and even from which location. Every computer, server and device connected over the (TCP/IP) network has a unique IP (Internet Protocol) address. Police along with the cyber bully's ISP (Internet Service Provider) can use this information to trace the bully right to his or her house.

You need to let appropriate authorities know about the cyber bullying or they cannot take corrective action. Cyberbullying is not something you want to ignore. It is your responsibility to report this behavior so the perpetrators can be dealt with. This helps not only to protect you (or your child, if you are a parent) but to intervene before the cyber bully harms even more kids. Bullies often behave in a serial fashion attacking multiple victims either at the same time or one after another. Once the high of abusing one victim is over they move to their next prey.

While bullies may have had a free ride up until now, they are more and more running into the long arm of the law. Cyber bullying needs to be brought to the attention of the police. Be sure to provide them with as much information as you can. They can then contact the cyber bully's ISP and track them down.

If you are a parent, inform your child's school if the cyber bully is a student. While the school administration may say they have no legal obligation as the bullying is taking place outside of school hours and off school property, many schools are adopting code of conduct-type contracts with their students and parents. This allows for schools to take action in such cases where the bullying still impacts on another student while he or she is at school. Targets of cyberbullying are traumatized and often lose focus on their schoolwork as a direct result of the harassment. Even if your child's school does not have such a policy, they still need to be made aware of the abuse so they can be alerted to potential further bullying that may be taking place while your child is at school.

If you are a parent or older sibling, pay close attention to your kids or younger siblings. Are they acting strangely? Are there unexplained pictures or odd messages on their computers or cell phones? Are they having trouble sleeping or falling behind at school? Do they seem depressed or more aggressive? Are they being evasive and don't want you to know who they are talking to, or do they close windows on their computer screen whenever you come near? Don't ignore what your instincts are telling you. If you think something is wrong, don't wait until it is too late.

Cyber bullying can be every bit as dangerous as face-to-face bullying, more so in some cases. Awareness is the key. And children need to know that cyber bullying is not their fault. It is not because of something wrong with them. The fault and the problem both lie with the cyber bully.

Discussion Starters

1. What is Hout's depiction of a cyber bully's make-up? Does it fit the make-up of bullies as you perceive or have encountered them?
2. What are Hout's recommendations for dealing with cyber bullying? Are there any that you question or any that you would add?
3. Have you had any personal experience with cyber bullying (as victim or assailant)? How did the experience affect you? How did you deal with it? How would you suggest that other victims deal with it?

XIII. Politics and Governance

America's Changing Demographics

By Billy Hallowell

Billy Hallowell is a journalist and commentator who has been published and featured in political and cultural books and is a contributor to The Blaze and Huffington Post. In this essay, Hallowell contends that America's changing demographics have dramatically altered the national political landscape in ways that both Republicans and Democrats must address to be politically relevant.

It's not just the economy, stupid. It's the demographics – the changing face of America. The 2012 elections drove home trends that have been embedded in the fine print of birth and death rates, immigration statistics and census charts for years.

America is rapidly getting more diverse, and, more gradually, so is its electorate. Nonwhites made up 28 percent of the electorate this year, compared with 20 percent in 2000. Much of that growth is coming from Hispanics.

The trend has worked to the advantage of President Barack Obama two elections in a row now and is not lost on Republicans poring over the details of the election results. Obama captured a commanding 80 percent of the growing ranks of nonwhite voters in 2012, just as he did in 2008. Republican Mitt Romney won 59 percent of non-Hispanic whites.

Romney couldn't win even though he dominated among white men and outperformed 2008 nominee John McCain with that group. It's an ever-shrinking slice of the electorate and of America writ large. White men made up 34 percent of the electorate this year, down from 46 percent in 1972.

"The new electorate is a lagging indicator of the next America," says Paul Taylor of the Pew Research Center. "We are mid-passage in a century-long journey from the middle of the last century, when we were nearly a 90 percent white nation, to the middle of this coming century, when we will be a majority-minority nation." Another trend that will be shaping the future electorate is the stronger influence of single women. They vote differently from men and from women who are married. Fifty-four percent of single women call themselves Democrats; 36 percent of married women do. With women marrying later and divorcing more, single women made up 23 percent of voters in the 2012 election, compared with 19 percent in 2000.

The changing electorate has huge implications for public policy and politics. Suddenly, immigration overhaul seems a lot more important, for one thing. Ask white voters about the proper role of government, for another, and 60 percent think it should do less. Ask Hispanics the same question, and 58 percent think the government should do more, as do 73 percent of blacks, exit polls show.

You can hear it in the voice of Alicia Perez, a 31-year-old immigration attorney who voted last week at a preschool in Ysleta, Texas. "I trust the government to take care of us," she said. "I don't trust the Republican Party to take care of people."

Sure, the election's biggest issue, the economy, affects everyone. But the voters deciding who should tackle it were quite different from the makeup of the 1992 "It's the economy, stupid" race that elected Democrat Bill Clinton as president. Look no further than the battleground states of Campaign 2012 for political ramifications flowing from the country's changing demographics.

New Western states have emerged as battlegrounds as the Hispanic population there grows. In Nevada, for example, white voters made up 80 percent of the electorate in 2000; now they're at 64 percent. The share of Hispanics in the state's electorate has grown to 19 percent; Obama won 70 percent of their votes.

Obama won most of the battlegrounds with a message that was more in sync than Romney's with minorities, women and younger voters, and by carefully targeting his grassroots mobilizing efforts to reach those groups.

In North Carolina, where Romney narrowly defeated Obama, 42 percent of black voters said they had been contacted on behalf of Obama, compared with just 26 percent of whites, exit polls showed. Obama got just 31 percent of the state's white vote, but managed to keep it competitive by claiming 96 percent of black voters and 68 percent of Hispanics.

Young voters in the state, two-thirds of whom backed Obama, also were more often the target of Obama's campaign than Romney's: 35 percent said they were contacted by Obama, 11 percent by Romney. Among senior citizens, two-thirds of whom voted Republican, 33 percent were contacted by Obama, 34 percent by Romney.

Howard University sociologist Roderick Harrison, former chief of racial statistics at the Census Bureau, said Obama's campaign strategists proved themselves to be "excellent demographers." "They have put together a coalition of populations that will eventually become the majority or are marching toward majority status in the population, and populations without whom it will be very difficult to win national elections and some statewide elections, particularly in states with large black and Hispanic populations," Harrison said.

One way to see the trend is to look at the diversity of young voters. Among voters under 30 years old this year, only 58 percent are white. Among senior voters, 87 percent are white. Brookings Institution demographer William H. Frey says policymakers and politicians need to prepare for a growing "cultural generation gap." "Both parties are getting the message that this is a new age and a new America," says Frey. "Finally, the politics is catching up with the demography." Just as Republicans need to do a better job of attracting Hispanics, says Frey, Democrats need to do more to reach out to whites.

The face of Congress is changing more slowly than the electorate or the population, but changing it is. House Democratic leader Nancy Pelosi of California was happy to highlight the news that for the first time in history, more than half the members of her caucus next year will be women, black, Hispanic or Asian. She said it "reflects the great diversity and strength of our nation." House Speaker John Boehner of Ohio, whose caucus is far more white and male, said Republicans need to learn to "speak to all Americans – you know, not just to people who look like us and act like us."

Former Secretary of State Condoleezza Rice, one of the GOP's most prominent black women, said the party needs to understand that "the changing demographics in the country really necessitate an even bigger tent for the Republican Party." "Clearly we are losing important segments of that electorate and what we have to do is to appeal to those people not as identity groups but understanding that if you can get the identity issue out of the way, then you can appeal on the broader issues that all Americans share a concern for," she said.

All sides know the demographic trends are sure to become more pronounced in the future. In the past year, minority babies outnumbered white newborns for the first time in U.S. history. By midcentury, Hispanics, blacks, Asians and multiracial people combined will become the majority of the U.S. Since 2000, the Hispanic and Asian populations have grown by more than 40 percent, fueled by increased immigration of younger people as well as more births.

Currently, Hispanics are the largest minority group and make up 17 percent of the U.S. population, compared with 12 percent for blacks and 5 percent for Asians. Together minorities now make up more than 36 percent of the population. Hispanics will make up roughly 30 percent of the U.S. by midcentury, while the African-American share is expected to remain unchanged at 12 percent. Asian-Americans will grow to roughly 8 percent of the U.S.

"The minorities will vote," said demographer Frey. "The question is will their vote be split more across the two parties than it was this time?" For both Republicans and Democrats, he said, the 2012 election is a wake-up call that will echo through the decades.

Discussion Starters

1. What is the voting coalition, according to the essay, that was responsible for electing President Barack Obama? Why do you think that coalition of voters votes primarily Democratic?
2. Given the changing demographics, what do you think the Republican Party must do to remain competitive in national elections?
3. How do you view the changing demographics in America? How will they affect the future of the country and its politics?

Tea Party Movement's Positive Impact on American Politics

By J. Wesley Fox

J. Wesley Fox is the Chairman of Restore America's Legacy, a conservative political action committee formed "to advance the interests of young Americans." In his essay, Fox contends that the Tea Party movement has had a positive effect on American politics and is much more than a passing political fancy.

In the last few decades there has been no political movement comparable to the Tea Parties. The Tea Party Movement is unique because it is entirely grassroots and desires to change American politics from the bottom-up.

The mainstream media and the Democratic leadership all misunderstand and grossly underestimate the movement. They have labeled it a movement of extreme right-wing nuts that are angry at having a black President, or don't want to pay taxes, or "cling to guns and religion." They are wrong. In fact, the Tea Party Movement is a mainstream "awakening" that has been long overdue and will not whither and die within a couple years as some predict.

The Tea Party groups are a loose and decentralized coalition of libertarians, conservatives, disenchanted independents and moderate Democrats. Tea Partiers are not a concentrated group of ideologues but a diverse collection of regular groups that are alarmed at the direction of the country. It began with the wasteful Stimulus Package and was further amplified by taxes built into cap'n'trade and healthcare reform. Tea Partiers are also upset at the corruption and utter lack of transparency in the Obama administration and the Democratic Congress.

The biggest issues for Tea Partiers are excessive government spending, the economy and the expansion of government power over the past two years. Some tea party groups may have additional issues of concern or have differing priorities but nearly all tea party groups share these concerns. Tea Partiers also share three core ideals: (1) limited government/individual freedom; (2) fiscal responsibility; and (3) free markets. They strongly support limiting the power of the federal government and are alarmed at the dramatic increase in federal power. Tea Partiers are also outraged at the massive budget deficits, the growth of the national debt, and the generational theft taking place. Finally, they are strong proponents of economic freedom and believe strongly that President Obama and the Democratic Congress are dismantling our free market economy in favor of a more centralized, socialist economy.

Another important element of the movement is their attitude toward partisan politics. Tea Partiers have consistently expressed their frustration and discontent with the Republicans as well as Democrats. In general, Tea Partiers are anti-establishment and want wholesale changes in their representatives. They are highly suspicious of career politicians and the influence of the national party leadership in local elections. As a result, they have rejected the traditional or establishment candidates in a number of primaries, preferring more independent or activist candidates.

The Tea Party Movement is not all-white, all-conservative, violent or racist. These accusations have been thrown out without any evidence to back them up. Polls have found that supporters of the Tea Party Movement are largely mainstream in terms of demographics. About 49% of Tea Party supporters are Republican while a surprising 43% are independents. They come from every socio-economic class, age group, and ethnic group. Only 79% of Tea Party supporters are white which is comparable to the percentage of whites in the general population. Despite the despicable accusations of Democrats and elitist media personalities, Tea Partiers are representative of the American people in almost every way.

Another baseless accusation is that Tea Partiers are violent gun-touting maniacs. The movement does not advocate the violent overthrow of the government. At nearly every demonstration and protest, Tea Partiers have countless signs reading "remember in November." Tea Partiers want change through elections not gunfire. Like any other movement, there are individuals that are unhinged and violent, but the media's focus on this extremely small sect demonstrates their lack of integrity and liberal bias. In reality, the Tea Party Movement is one of the most peaceful large scale political protests in recent memory.

The objective of the Tea Party Movement is to change the Republican Party from within. The Tea Parties have already flexed their muscle in a number of primary elections. In Illinois, the son of former Speaker Dennis Hastert was defeated by a lesser-known Tea Party candidate named Randy Hultgren. In the Nevada and Kentucky Senate primaries the Republican establishment strongly supported Sue Lowden and Tray Grayson. However, their close relations with the party leadership led to suspicion and their eventual defeat to lesser known candidates Sharron Angle and Rand Paul.

The Tea Party Movement has also contributed to the removal of incumbent Republicans including Sen. Arlen Specter, who was forced to switch parties. Other defeated incumbents include Rep. Bob Inglis of South Carolina and Sen. Bob Bennett of Utah. The primaries of the past few months clearly demonstrate the Tea Party Movement is very influential within the Republican Party and has already had a number of successes getting their own candidates on the ballot in November. In other words, they are successfully changing the party.

Restore America's Legacy and the Tea Party Movement have a lot in common in terms of ideology. The Tea Party strongly supports three of RAL's five principles (limited government, fiscal responsibility, free markets). The Tea Party has also made a very strong effort to become better informed and more active in the traditional political process. RAL wishes to do the same, providing information to supporters, raising funds to support campaigns, and evaluating candidates using a unique and selective criteria. Both also are highly critical of career politicians and want to support candidates with real world experience.

The Tea Party Movement is a positive development in American politics and RAL strongly supports their activities. If the Tea Party Movement is successful in the Midterm elections, it will prove that career politicians can be held accountable and that it is the people that hold the power. It would also prove that a strong anti-establishment and anti-government movement can manifest itself peacefully through a massive grassroots effort and legitimate political activity, not intimidation or violence. It will also strike a blow to cynics who believe that the people cannot change Washington.

Discussion Starters

1. What according to Fox do Tea Party followers believe in politically and economically? Do you agree with any or all of their beliefs? Why?
2. The Tea Party was very successful in helping to elect "their" candidates to Congress in 2010. Why do you think they were so successful?
3. Do you think the Tea Party is a positive or negative influence on the Republican Party? Why? What do you think the future of the Tea Party will be?

Overcoming Powerlessness

By Ralph Nader

Ralph Nader is a long-time political activist, writer, and lecturer, and a former candidate for President. In this essay, Nader sounds a clarion call for a grassroots political movement to change the power structure in America and close the ever-widening gap between the haves and have-nots in America.

In the Depression-wracked 1930s, the famous British economist John Maynard Keynes wrote an essay titled "Economic Possibilities for our Grandchildren." In that piece, he made a prophecy that we have shamelessly failed to fulfill. At the time of his writing, the world economy had reached a level of productivity that would enable society to eliminate the "economic problem"—that is, the persistence of abject poverty. "The economic problem may be solved, or be at least within sight of solution, within a hundred years," he wrote. "This means that the economic problem is not—if we look into the future—the permanent problem of the human race." Keynes argued that there was no economic excuse for not abolishing poverty and for providing everyone with the necessities of life, including retirement security.

I say "shamelessly failed to fulfill" because Keynes was right—that our economy is hugely more productive per worker but also unjustly distributed in its gains and misdirected in its investments. The growing disconnect between corporate profits and the conditions of the great majority of American workers and families represents the expanding failure of corporate capitalism—and the corporate state in Washington, D.C., that feeds and protects it—to deliver the goods.

American workers labor longer than any of their counterparts in the Western world, but they are also worse-off than any of those counterparts. They are not receiving their just desserts. Let's do something together about this abomination. The problem is, there is no civic or political infra-structure at the ready, no viable machine to bring about action, to help replace the bad with the good.

Our nation has millions of skilled bikers and joggers, birdwatchers and bowlers, stamp and coin collectors, dancers and musicians, gardeners, card and chess players—and more power to them. But we have no masses of skilled citizens who know how to practice the democratic arts, to use the power of numbers to bring about change.

We need more organized and connected Congress watchers, more democracy builders, more sentinels over the industries or government agencies that affect us so seriously. We need to close our gigantic democracy gap, a people-power vacuum so noticeable that it serves as an open invitation for commercial and bureaucratic rascals. The corporations know that the few valiant civic groups and active citizens are so short in staff, resources, and media platforms that no significant corporate abuse is at risk of being stopped by their small efforts. Indeed, most of the larger corporations and government agencies have no dedicated outside monitors at all.

Do you remember the advice from the American revolutionaries: "Eternal vigilance is the price of liberty?" We've forgotten how to pay that price. Civic engagement for the vast majority of

Americans is terra incognita. They've never been there, and they have their excuses: "I don't know what to do." "I don't have the time." "I don't want to risk the backlash." "Would it really make a difference anyhow? The big boys will get whatever they want."

There you have it: the rationales for the American society of apathy. But the real reason for apathy is usually a feeling of powerlessness. The first step to changing this is getting people in small groups to spend time in a civic space, just talking with one another. Every civic movement starts with one-on-one conversations, or with an experienced citizen activist offering guidance and support. That was the conclusion of former Tennessee Valley Authority chairman Arthur Morgan in his classic 1942 book, *The Small Community*. Such conversations always start with what the people think is wrong and should be changed in the community. Although they may begin in living rooms or around conference tables, they lead to action at state and federal levels.

The trouble is we live in a culture where individuation and instant gratification are kings—and civic work requires selflessness and patience. This is the key challenge in developing one's civic personality, in developing a thirst for righting a wrong or achieving justice to the point where your goals become the principled equivalent of self-improvement.

Candy Lightner, the founder of Mothers Against Drunk Driving, was so profoundly self-motivated by the loss of her own daughter that her passion for the cause led her to organize community campaigns, successfully, for tougher anti-drunk-driving measures all over the country. There are many stories of passive people, absorbed with their own daily lives, who are transformed after encountering a horrific tragedy and respond by confronting the situation head-on. Lois Gibbs, a mother, was living with her children near Niagara Falls when the news of serious contamination of the nearby Love Canal hit the headlines. After she saw symptoms of the toxic environment in her children and her neighbors' children, she wrote and protested extensively on the subject, and her successful struggles with the corporate polluters led her to start the nation's most extensive grassroots coalition of local anti-pollution activists.

In the fall of 2011, the Occupy Wall Street movement, standing for the "99 percent," spread into scores of communities to put the inequities of the big business–dominated political economy on the media front burner. With less than 250,000 people in all its marches and encampments, Occupy, still a work in progress, has been motivating people with demonstrations, workshops, collaborations, and democratic assemblies.

We need more grassroots efforts to train aspiring activists around the country. Any issue involving mass injustice, patterns of abuse, invasion of constitutional rights, or deprivation, can be addressed if private citizens transform themselves into public citizens and demand it together as a persistent force.

Most people who are powerless don't feel good about being powerless; they just accept it. Over time, though, feelings of powerlessness can gnaw away at one's sense of self-worth—even for those who are leading the so-called good life. So when they start meeting other powerless people like themselves who want to learn how to take part in shaping their own futures, something wonderful is created: a small community with a serious purpose.

Perhaps some enlightened wealthy people can help fund these initiatives. Justice, as its practitioners have known for centuries, needs money, not just small donations. Imagine what a thousand organizers could accomplish!

Discussion Starters

1. What forces in America does Nader urge citizens to organize against and what examples does he provide of their negative impact on working Americans? Do you agree with him?
2. Why does Nader believe that most Americans aren't engaged as civic activists? Do you agree with him? Could there also be other reasons?
3. Nader has been trying for years to help build a strong, effective activist movement that could change American politics and the economy. Do you feel the time is ripe for such activism? Would such participation interest you? Why?

The Constitution: Who Needs It?

By Alexander C. Kafka

Alexander C. Kafka is the Deputy Managing Editor of The Chronicle Review at the Chronicle of Higher Education and has written for a wide range of publications. In this essay, Kafka presents the viewpoint of Constitutional law professor Michael Seidman that the Constitution should not be viewed as an infallible document whose authority should never be questioned.

It's a Monday evening in October in a warm lecture hall a few blocks from the U.S. Capitol. In front of a couple dozen students in an introductory course on constitutional law, a low-key, shirt-sleeved Georgetown University professor, Louis Michael (Mike) Seidman, summarizes the ways the Constitution can be interpreted.

It can be read according to our best guesses as to the founders' original intent. Or by how the public first understood the document, in 1789. Or by the meaning people ascribe to it now. Or by the meaning that produces the best outcome. Even when we can reach consensus on what the Constitution's articles mean, "there is always the question in front of us," says the bearded 65-year-old scholar, "as to whether we should obey them."

What's that again? Did this former clerk for District of Columbia Circuit Judge J. Skelly Wright and Supreme Court Justice Thurgood Marshall just tell a group of law students that there are times when we should ignore the Constitution? Yup.

Seidman doesn't harp on the point. He moves on, as his listeners sip coffee and tap away on their laptops, to a detailed discussion of Youngstown Sheet & Tube Co. v. Sawyer, a 1952 Supreme Court ruling, concerning a steelworkers' strike during the Korean War, that limited presidential power. But he explores his constitutional skepticism in depth in his forthcoming book from Oxford University Press, *On Constitutional Disobedience*, part of the publisher's big-picture Inalienable Rights series of constitutional critiques.

Seidman's argument boils down to this: We the current American people are not the people who agreed in the 18th century to be governed by the Constitution (that's assuming that the colonists themselves agreed, a proposition about which he is also dubious). More practically, politicians, judges, and advocacy groups contort the Constitution's often vaguely worded precepts to match whatever they're pushing for. That makes citizens cynical and distracts us from considering what policies would be best for the country in regard to health-care finance, gun control, antiterrorism, and countless other matters.

Although Seidman is willing to bypass the Constitution, he still teaches it thoroughly, nuances and all. "There is this complicated body of constitutional doctrines," he says, "and I view my obligation as to make sure the students understand it and use it to write briefs and opinion letters—all the things that lawyers do in constitutional cases."

"At the same time, I do want the students to think, and think hard, about what I take to be really fundamental questions about the role the Constitution ought to play."

Without wanting to get specific, Seidman says his experiences clerking at the Supreme Court and a few years working in the D.C. Public Defender Service helped inform his constitutional wariness. "When you see how the law works up close, you just cannot miss the tremendous gap between the story law tells about itself and the way things actually function," he says. The Supreme Court "is more arbitrary, more at the mercy of eccentric views of individual justices,...less principle-driven" than one would suppose or hope.

Seidman doesn't ask us to forget that the Constitution exists. It could be, he writes, "a symbol of national unity if we focused on its commands at the most abstract level." For instance, "almost everyone supports liberty and equality in the abstract." He urges embracing "the Constitution...as a work of art, designed to evoke a mood or emotion, rather than as a legal document commanding specific outcomes."

Seidman knows that his viewpoint might be perceived as insane—"utopian at best and just plain crazy at worst." Among mainstream politicians, it will be considered heresy, perhaps traitorous. Even among scholars, who debate the nature of constitutionalism, "very few people think that we should give up on it altogether," he writes.

There is a long tradition of discussion about how constitutional ideals fare in the real world, says Seidman. That includes arguments, like Seidman's, regarding what hold an 18th-century document should have over modern Americans, and regarding how much guidance the Constitution can offer in creating effective public policies in an ever-changing society. During his 2005 confirmation hearings for the Supreme Court, John Roberts famously compared judges to umpires calling balls and strikes. Siegel says that any legal scholar offering that view would be laughed off the lectern.

But Seidman's approach, calling for a reassessment of whether the Constitution is fundamentally valid and should be obeyed, goes beyond that. And if Seidman's argument is not something that's ripe to be acted on in some short-term way, Siegel says, neither is it to be shrugged off as if from outer space.

Seidman's views may be extreme, but they didn't occur suddenly. He has taught law since America's bicentennial. And over the past 36 years, he's had ample time to anticipate critics' objections to disobeying the Constitution. Here are his top 10 rebuttals, very roughly summarized:

1. **Article VI makes the Constitution the supreme law of the land.** That just begs the question. It's the supreme law of the land only if you obey it, and that's what we're debating.

2. **But why would you frame a Constitution if you weren't planning to obey it?** Of course the framers wanted to be obeyed. Anyone asserting power wants to be obeyed. But we can't obey any and every authority who seeks to rule us.

3. **"We the People" consented to the Constitution by ratifying it, and so are bound to obey it.** Did we? Many of the framers were genuinely concerned about the country's future. But the convention was also driven in part by speculators who had bought up Revolutionary War debt and wanted a strong federal government that would enforce taxes to ensure that the debt was paid.

Other markedly unlofty considerations during constitutional negotiations included navigation rights on the Mississippi, whether states with ports would be able to collect fees from their neighbors, and whether Massachusetts Governor John Hancock would receive the founders' support for his re-election. Even if, despite the parochial concerns, we deemed the document's precepts worthy, remember that women, slaves, American Indians, and those without property were excluded from participating in ratification. Assent that flimsy should have no binding power over us 223 years after the Constitution took effect.

4. **We can always amend what we don't like.** Not really. Amendment is a bear, requiring two-thirds vote by both houses or a call to convention by the legislatures of two-thirds of the states. Then it needs ratification by three-quarters of the states—not the 13 original ones, but the 50 wildly disparate current ones. Out of some 11,000 proposed amendments, only 27 have been ratified. Ten of those, encompassing the Bill of Rights, were necessary to get the original states on board, and the 13th through 15th Amendments entailed a Civil War that almost destroyed the country and were essentially forced on the Southern states as the price of readmission to the Union. More fundamentally, the amendment argument is again circular, because at issue is whether we should obey the Constitution that sets out its provisions.

5. **The framers were wise and gave us a great document to build on.** They advanced political theory in key respects, no doubt. But the framers were products of their time, and many of their notions now look weird, if not actually repugnant. Many thought it was OK for people to own other people; to ignore women, nonwhites, and people without property; and for small or sparsely populated states to carry the same authority as large and/or populated ones. "On this view," Seidman writes, "constitutional obligation amounts to an intergenerational power grab that modern Americans should resist." To the extent that the framers were wise, there's nothing stopping us from keeping the provisions we like not because we have to but because we think it would be smart.

6. **If we don't obey the Constitution, anarchy will ensue.** Why? England and New Zealand function quite nicely without constitutions, don't they? Also, we've often, in practice, violated, or at least dramatically stretched, constitutional precepts—sometimes, indeed, in an effort to avoid anarchy. Think of President Franklin D. Roosevelt's clashes with the judiciary over New Deal programs during the Depression. People don't generally like anarchy and are usually good at taking sensible measures to avoid it.

7. **Through Americans' experience as a nation, we have come to believe that it is wise to obey the Constitution.** Really? How many Americans have actually thought about whether constitutional obedience leads to smart policies? And once more, the assertion is circular; it seeks to avoid the argument by claiming that it's not an argument worth having.

8. **The framers were wise enough to write the Constitution so vaguely that we don't need to disobey it.** That's lukewarm praise at best. Where the Constitution is vague and ostensibly

benevolent, as in the 14th Amendment's equal-protection language, it is harmless but also toothless (see No. 10). And on some matters, it's very specific and arguably silly—mandating, for instance, that someone who moved here as a baby can't be president, or that someone under 30 can't be a senator. Article I is "pretty clear" on the point that as presiding officer of the Senate, a vice president would have to "preside over his own impeachment," Seidman notes. Grist for a Marx Brothers routine, but hardly evidence of the fathers' wisdom.

9. **The framers took the long view, whereas we might change something impulsively, in a fit of passion or a moment of crisis.** See No. 3. You're overestimating the founders' wisdom, and quite possibly underestimating ours. More than that—if we don't make our best judgments about what America needs now and in the future, we're not living up to our responsibility as citizens.

10. **Well, OK, maybe the Constitution is flawed. But it's still vital because it protects our civil liberties.** Sadly, no. In times of crisis, it hasn't. It didn't protect slaves. "When slavery was eventually overthrown," Seidman writes, "it happened not because people felt bound to obey the Constitution, but because they were willing to fight a devastating war to change it." The Constitution didn't protect African-Americans during Jim Crow, either. It didn't protect dissenters during the early years of the Republic under the Alien and Sedition Acts, during World War I, or during the McCarthy era. Nor did it protect Japanese-American internees during World War II.

   Laws nominally protecting civil rights in 1954 didn't truly protect minorities until civil-rights activists, a decade later, persuaded Northern whites that Southern bigotry was intolerable, Seidman argues. In *The Federalist Papers*, James Madison presciently doubted the ability of mere "parchment barriers," laws on paper, to resist "the encroaching spirit of power."

But "without a constitution, how would we know that a measure passed by Congress is a law and not just meaningless ranting by a bunch of pompous and superannuated poseurs?" Ah—that is an existential jurisprudential quandary, Seidman admits, but not one that a constitution can resolve. For a constitution to legitimate laws, the document itself must be legitimate, and that brings us back to the arguments we started with.

Without constitutional grounding, on what basis would court rulings be made? Well, on what basis are they made now in cases involving limits on affirmative action, say, or the freedom to have gay sex? Those decisions, Seidman writes, are "at best tenuously tied to the constitutional text," and reflect, instead, a mix of policy judgment, interpretation of tradition, moral boundaries, and so on.

Without a constitution, for better and for worse, he writes, "the Supreme Court would no longer be able to hide behind the pretense" of mere constitutional interpretation. "Instead it would have to defend openly the proposition that an elite, deliberative, and reason-giving body should have a check on the political branches." In lieu of constitutional foundations, Seidman suggests that we sort through rationalist, existentialist, Rawlsian, and contestation theories, the last including the requisite that any foundation "must preserve the possibility of legitimate contestation" rather than prejudge outcomes.

Seidman hopes his reasoning will elicit a glimmer of recognition from a populace already wary of how the Constitution is manipulated in the course of everyday policy discussions. "The abstract Constitution is said to be a symbol of national unity, while the actual Constitution does no more than mirror our national divisions," he writes. "The situation is unstable and is ripe for exploitation by constitutional skeptics."

Seidman knows that a cultural shift away from the Constitution seems unimaginable—but so, until recently, did a black president or gay marriage. "I don't want to be grandiose about this book," he says. "I count myself lucky if my wife reads what I write, let alone starting a national conversation." But "I do think what we're talking about here is cultural change." America is "at a stage where there is a growing realization that a lot of constitutional law is empty posturing."

How does a new conversation about constitutional legitimacy begin? Well, maybe through books, Seidman says. But more immediately, "at the granular level, it is produced by ordinary individuals who challenge conventional wisdom." When someone claims that something's unconstitutional, he argues, "each of us should answer with a perfectly straightforward, but deeply subversive, two-word question: 'So what?'"

Discussion Starters

1. According to the essay, what are Seidman's main arguments for questioning the authority of the constitution? Which arguments do you find most compelling? Which do you find less convincing?
2. What counter arguments might you present against Seidman's anti-constitutional viewpoint?
3. Do you believe that a "new conversation about constitutional legitimacy" will occur? What is your opinion on the value of the constitution?

The Obama Era: A Post-racial Society?

By Lydia Lum

Lydia Lum is a freelance journalist and contributing editor to Diverse: Issues in Education. In this essay, Lum raises the question of whether the election of Barack Obama was an indication that America is moving towards a truly post-racial society.

With Barack Obama ensconced as the nation's first Black president, plenty of voices in the national conversation are trumpeting America as a post-racial society—that race matters much less than it used to, that the boundaries of race have been overcome, that racism is no longer a big problem. "It's smack down to think America is still all about racism," says Dr. John McWhorter, a Manhattan Institute senior fellow. "Racism is not Black people's main problem anymore. To say that is like saying the earth is flat."

But longtime scholars whose life's work intertwines with race disagree, even while applauding Obama's presidency as a milestone. Race, they say, still matters. A lot.

To these scholars, claims of post-racialism hold mirage rather than merit because far too many significant, statistical disparities remain between Whites and minorities in educational attainment, income and net worth, career advancement and health care outcomes. Post-racialism is a goal not yet reached. Therefore, casting aside the role race plays in these inequities as well as race-conscious remedies such as diversity programs, they warn, doesn't bode well for minorities still struggling.

While the term "post-race" has emerged in national discourse within the past few years, many scholars say the same subtext already lived in catch phrases like "color blind" more than a decade ago. Post-racialism parallels the same ideas that gained traction alongside other historical markers such as the first Martin Luther King Jr. national holiday in 1986.

"The idea of post-race is old wine in new bottles," says Dr. Troy Duster, a New York University professor of sociology. McWhorter, for one, gladly takes a drink. "Post-racialism is a good direction to move in because if there's some separation between Blacks and Whites, it's as if some unpleasantness is going on, like one has his foot on the other's neck. "Are there racists? Yes. But not enough to keep a Black family out of the White House."

Post-racialism has also birthed offshoots in a variety of hues. Richard Ford, Stanford University's George E. Osborne professor of law, prefers describing America's current divide as "racism without racists." In other words, many inequities are the legacy of long-ago marginalization. Race might not even be a factor in some injustices, Ford says, because the so-called offender is merely repeating actions originated by someone else.

In conversation, many academic skeptics of the post-race construct aren't initially fazed by the fact it's embraced and much discussed in workplaces, living rooms, the news media and the blogosphere. What's different now and going forward, other scholars concede, is that the most vocal and influential pushers of post-racialism have its most daunting poster pinup in Obama.

For the foreseeable future, post-racialism will likely attract more believers than it will lose them. Efforts to dismantle or ban affirmative action, for instance, will likely accelerate. McWhorter predicts doubts over postracialism will taper off if Obama's agenda and impact as a role model help reduce recidivism among Black men exiting prison and prod more Black fathers to help raise their children. He also predicts today's children might adopt post-racial mindsets more easily than adults. "They'll see the Obamas on TV every day. That's a powerful influence." But Dr. Sandra Graham, a University of California, Los Angeles professor of psychological studies in education, considers the latter prediction "myopic."

"There are so many competing TV images involving Blacks and violence that it will take much more than a figure in the White House for youth to become post-racial," says Graham, who studies peer relations among youth in Los Angeles schools. It is the persistence of these competing images and racial stereotypes—and their impact on people of color—that cause some scholars to scoff at the notion of a post-racial America.

"We still carry those in our heads," says Angela Harris, a University of California, Berkeley, law professor, referring to stereotypes. "Asian men are seen as smart with no social skills. Black men are seen as violent criminals. And people act and respond, based on those stereotypes."

The mindset tying Black men to crime and violence might explain some public reactions to a fatal shooting last month of an unarmed, 22-year-old Black man at an Oakland, Calif., train station. Transit agency police detained the young man and others while investigating complaints of a fight early New Year's Day. Passengers' recorded video showed the man lying face down on concrete in the course of submitting to police. A White officer shot the man in the back, and has since been arrested and charged with murder.

A week after the shooting, after passengers' video had been widely broadcast on TV and the Internet, a local news station interviewed Dr. Howard Pinderhughes. A University of California, San Francisco associate professor of social and behavioral sciences, Pinderhughes' research includes racial attitudes among youth. During the interview, Pinderhughes described what he saw on video "as an execution." He was roundly condemned by viewers accusing him of bias because he's Black and criticizing him "for saying 'execution' while the shooting was an incident under police investigation." "Two people can watch the same tape, and while I see an execution, someone else sees only an incident under investigation. This country is so far from being post-racial," Pinderhughes says.

Some disparities, such as K-12 academic achievement, can't be overcome without a racial lens and diversity-based solutions, scholars insist. Dr. Gloria Ladson-Billings, who holds the Kellner Family Chair in Urban Education at the University of Wisconsin- Madison, says Black students, including middle- income Blacks, lag too far behind Whites not to use special outreach and affirmative action. For instance, among 25 school districts around the country examined by Ladson-Billings, high school graduation rates among Whites were higher than those of Blacks by an average 12 percent for a three-year period ending with 2007-08 academic year. Blacks passed third-grade, district-level math tests in 2005-06 at rates lower than Whites by an average 23 percent.

The data come from the Minority Student Achievement Network, a coalition of the 25 districts, including suburban-urban schools in the Cambridge, Mass.; Shaker Heights, Ohio; and Phoenix areas. They boast more resources than their counterparts in neighboring cities and historically have had high academic achievement, Ladson-Billings says. "These are what's considered good school districts. Even if you focus on socioeconomics, you can't look at middle-income Blacks the same way you do Whites because Black wealth usually traces back only a generation, versus multiple generations for many middle- income Whites." "Race is still salient," she adds.

Furthermore, she and others worry about the apparent resegregation of schools everywhere. A growing number of Blacks have little or no contact with White students, according to UCLA's Civil Rights Project/ Proyecto Derechos Civiles (CRP). About 44 percent of today's students are non-White, according to the CRP at UCLA. In 2006-07, 39 percent of Blacks attended schools where minorities made up at least 90 percent of total enrollment and Whites were barely 1 percent. To address the resegregation, Graham of UCLA suggests creating more magnet schools that would recruit a diverse population. "K-12 is 20 years behind higher education in terms of promoting and encouraging diversity."

Based on Graham's studies of and surveys at 11 urban Los Angeles middle and high schools, fewer students reported themselves as victims of bullying at the schools with more diverse enrollments. "They felt less lonely than the kids in less diverse schools," she says. "They felt safe in bathrooms and other places where adults aren't around much. If a child has regular contact with different races, that's how he learns tolerance. That's how you improve his attitude." Racial disparities aren't limited to education. Take jobs, for example.

Last November—when Obama was re-elected—the Black unemployment rate of 11 percent was almost twice that of Whites, according to the Bureau of Labor Statistics. Disparities were ingrained before the current recession. In 2007, the Black unemployment rate of 8 percent was twice that of Whites. "As long as Blacks are disproportionately represented in joblessness, there's chronic economic subordination," says Dr. William Julius Wilson, the Lewis P. and Linda L. Geyser University Professor at Harvard's Kennedy School of Government who has written for more than 30 years about unemployment and poverty. "Race is still a significant aspect of society. It will be a long time before we're post-race."

Wilson predicts "post-race will fade like other silly fads. Post-race has made people like me explain to students, colleagues and others why it's silly. This could be positive, because the conversations I'm having, at least they encourage people to rethink post-race." Still, Wilson and his contemporaries eagerly watch for how race plays into Obama's social and economic agenda.

Ladson-Billings, for one, had publicly stated, long before Obama's election, that she doesn't believe true desegregation of schools as well as other changes in the racial divide are likely. But in an interview, she emphasized, "Just because something is near impossible to overcome doesn't mean it isn't worth doing or trying or hoping for."

"Two years ago, it was impossible to think of Obama as president," Ladson-Billings says. "Let's give him a nation to govern. Let's engage ourselves on all levels."

Discussion Starters

1. What arguments are presented supporting the contention that we live in a "post- racial" society? What arguments are presented against the contention? Which do you find more convincing? Why?
2. Why do some individuals quoted in the essay believe that general acceptance of our living in a post-racial society could actually hurt minorities? Do you agree?
3. Do you think we live in a post-racial society? What have you experienced or witnessed that informs you opinion?

Thomas Frank Interview: Political Ascendency of the Right

By Elizabeth DiNovella

Elizabeth DiNovella is Culture Editor for The Progressive magazine and writes about activism, politics, music, books, and film. In this essay, DiNovella interviews author and cultural critic Thomas Frank about the political ascendency of the Republican right, its causes and consequences.

Cultural critic Thomas Frank loves a paradox. Why has the worst economic crisis in generations led to a resurrection of free market orthodoxy? How can Budget chairman Paul Ryan, Republican from Wisconsin, rail against "corporate cronyism" and then enjoy $700 worth of wine with hedge fund manager Cliff Asness?

In his provocative new book, *Pity the Billionaire: The Hard-Times Swindle and the Unlikely Comeback of the Right*, Frank looks at the conservative arguments for austerity in an economic downturn. In the aftermath of the collapse of Wall Street, the Republican Party morphed anger at big business into anger at big government. The GOP's "anti-big-business message catches the bitter national mood," Frank writes. "What the Right actually does is deliver the same favors to the same people as always."

Frank may be best known for his 2004 book, *What's the Matter with Kansas? How Conservatives Won the Heart of America*. His other books include *The Wrecking Crew* and *One Market Under God*. A columnist for *Harper's* and a founding editor of *The Baffler*, he is also a former opinion columnist for *The Wall Street Journal*. I spoke to him by phone.

Q: What are your thoughts on Occupy Wall Street?

Thomas Frank: I wish them success. They've brought a lot of ideas into the national debate that were completely outside the debate before, and that's so important. Speaking from personal experience, I wrote a book twelve years ago where one of the main points began with the concentrations of wealth in this country. And that was regarded as an unacceptable, stigmatized topic back then. It was outside the consensus. Well, it's inside the consensus today. The President is talking about it; even the Republican candidates are talking about it. We have Occupy Wall Street to thank for that. That is a great thing.

Q: Do you think that there's a space for a populist alliance between the tea party and Occupy Wall Street?

Frank: No, I don't think there is. You're not going to get the tea party leaders to sign up for something that demands we re-regulate Wall Street. That's just not going to happen. These guys are laissez-faire ideologues at the end of the day. But you can fight for the support of the voters that were swayed by the movement. You can do that, and you should do that.

Q: You covered many tea party rallies and one of the big mantras you heard early on was, "Let the failures fail."

Frank: "Let the failures fail." It's attractive, isn't it? It sounded good to me when I heard it at the very first tea party rally in Washington, D.C., in February 2009. A protester had that on a sign he was carrying. At that moment, people were infuriated by the bank bailouts. The bailouts were just an outrage, straight up. An abomination. "Let the failures fail" was a good slogan for that anger. Let all the losers go down. Why prop them up? At a certain gut level, that sounded exactly right to me.

But if you look into it a little bit deeper, that's actually the philosophy that the United States did not accept in the Great Depression. That's the opposite of the road that we actually went. That's what Hoover's Treasury secretary wanted to do. Just let the Depression take its course. Let everyone get ruined. And then, people will recover and things will be fine on the other side. Hoover rejected that advice, and, of course, Roosevelt did the very opposite of that. But the leading protest movement was urging us to accept that advice.

Q: You write in *Pity the Billionaire* that the tea party's actual function was to ensure the economic collapse caused by Wall Street did not result in any unpleasant consequences for Wall Street. We see that happening now. No one's gone to jail and there's little new oversight over Wall Street.
Frank: Look at what Republicans are doing. They've all sworn to reverse the Dodd-Frank law that set up the new Consumer Financial Protection Bureau. If they can't overturn the law, they say, they won't fund the office, they won't appoint anybody to run it. They'll disable it somehow. They've all sworn to do this.

That's how conservatives actually run the government here in Washington: They run it by running it into the ground. They sabotage it. Sabotage is the word for their governmental philosophy.

Q: In 2008, the American right was supposedly finished, yet by 2010, the right was in ascendancy all over again. What happened?
Frank: That's the big question of our times. You have this financial catastrophe that was directly a result of ideology as anything I've ever seen in my lifetime, with the possible exception of the collapse of the Soviet Union. You have this largely deregulated financial sector and these fly-by-night mortgage lenders who are outside anybody's regulatory purview. You have this shadow banking establishment, and between them, they contrive to completely destroy the global economy.

When that happened, pundits here in Washington assumed this was the end of the road for conservatives, that they've had their thirty years and we did what they wanted and it ended in disaster. The pundits said that the Republican Party had to moderate itself or face irrelevance. The Republican Party didn't do that; they did the opposite. They swung hard to the right, and enjoyed one of the greatest victories of all time in the 2010 elections.

They declared that conservatives had really never gotten a chance. We had never gone all the way with conservative ideology. We'd never completely done away with government, or the liberal state, so conservatism was in no way responsible for what happened, they claimed. Therefore, the only alternative was to double-down on our commitment to the free market ideal. This became a utopian faith on the right. You especially saw this at tea party gatherings.

Q: But the right also depicted itself as an enemy of big business. Can you talk about that?

Frank: This is the secret to conservatism's success. The right was able to recast itself as a populist movement. Well, they've been doing that a lot in the past thirty years, but it was even worse this time around. They became a protest movement for hard times. Sometimes they pretend to be protesting the enemy—big corporations and big banks. If you read their literature, they say things like that all the time.

Congressman Paul Ryan wrote an article in *Forbes* magazine called "Down with Big Business." If you read it, it sounds like he's very critical of capitalism and the big corporations that run this country. But at the end of the day, he thinks the way to bring big business down is by going after big government. Very fascinating, this sort of twist that they always do. You can say all you want about how the banks screwed everybody over, but the culprit is the same as it ever was: government. That's who you're supposed to be rising up in anger against.

Q: Meanwhile, Ryan is raking in big money from these big corporations that he's supposedly denouncing.

Frank: They fund him extravagantly. It's not really a surprise to find out that these people who are doing all the denouncing are also the favorites of people like the Koch brothers, the oil billionaires in Wichita, Kansas.

One PAC that supported Newt Gingrich made a video attacking Mitt Romney for being a venture capitalist. It really went after him in a very strong, populist way, talking about how many workers' lives Romney and Bain Capital ruined over the years. It's very powerful, but what's funny is that they also claim that this is not real capitalism. What Mitt Romney does is not real capitalism. [Laughing] You know, if we could just get back to real capitalism, the authentic thing, then we wouldn't have Bain Capital out there buying up steel mills and firing everybody. Which is completely absurd.

Q: Ideology trumps reality.

Frank: That's right. And all of that stuff is taken from the literature of the 1930s. There are a lot of cultural patterns that are repeating themselves.

One of the stranger ones is this ideological blindness that people would inflict on themselves in the 1930s. I'm specifically talking about the left here, the far left. We're talking about the Communist Party. Either the Communist Party members or people who sympathized with it would go on trips to the Soviet Union, a famous set-piece of '30s literature. And they would somehow never manage to notice all the disasters that were going on around them. They were completely conned. They would blow off all the reporting that they had seen when they were back home here in America. They would not believe anything bad about their heroes in the Soviet Union, right up until the day that Stalin went out and signed a treaty with Adolf Hitler. It took them all by surprise.

That ideological blindness is repeating itself. But you see it now on the right, which similarly has a utopian idea, a utopian political solution that we're supposed to be working toward. Some of these guys deliberately mimic Communist language and Communist strategy from the old days, such as Dick Armey's group, FreedomWorks, which is funded by the Koch brothers.

Their utopia is a different one. It's a free market one. If we could just get to that point where government completely drops out of the picture and the business class is completely unshackled from the restraints of the liberal state, then we will finally reach economic utopia.

The idea of my book is that this should not be attractive to people in the middle of a recession that just won't go away because this is the very philosophy that got us into trouble in the first place. But in some ways, this is exactly what people reach for in hard times: A philosophy that removes doubt and that offers you some reassurance in what is frankly a very frightening time.

Q: So where were the Dems when all of this was happening? The tea party spent the summer of 2009 talking about death panels.

Frank: It's all well and good to sit around and make fun of the funny things that conservatives say and the hilarious gaffes that they make, but one of the only reasons that it works is that the Democrats let it happen. They never seem to be able to fight back, never seem to be able to figure it out. They really cannot talk about the philosophy that motivates their actions and their legislative deeds.

Look, I'm very liberal. I support a lot of the things that the Democrats have done. I want some kind of national health care. I don't think they went anywhere close to far enough on that. I liked the stimulus. I'm really glad that the Obama Administration had a big stimulus package.

However, the Democrats, from President Obama on down, have been almost completely unable to tell us why it is that government needs to get involved in these sectors of the economy. They just can't talk about it. And when they do talk about it, they always defer to the experts. "We need to do this because the economists say we need to do it." That's not going to convince anybody.

The politics of it, they think, will take care of themselves. People will naturally want a stimulus package. People will naturally be happy that they bailed out the banks and kept Great Depression II from happening. It never occurs to them that they have to go out there and fight for these things.

Discussion Starters

1. How according to Frank was the Republican Party able to cast itself as a populist movement during the recession? What economic and psychological factors caused many Americans to embrace that "movement?"
2. What according to Frank was both appealing and destructive about the Republican right's mantra, "Let the failures fail." What evidence did he provide that that would be the wrong course to take in a recession. Do you agree?
3. What role, if any, should government have in private sector oversight and regulation? Why is such oversight important to individual citizens?

Acknowledgements

Adichie, Chimamanda Ngozi. "Our 'Africa' Lenses." Reprinted by permission of the author.

Anders, Elyse. "What Pregnant Women Won't Tell You – Ever." Reprinted by permission of the author.

Andre, Claire, Myer, Michael, Shanks, Thomas, and Velasquez, Manuel. "Ethical Relativism." Reprinted by permission of the Markkula Center for Applied Ethics at the University of Santa Clara.

Andre, Claire and Velasquez, Manuel. "A Healthy Bottom Line: Profits or People?" Reprinted by permission of the Markkula Center for Applied Ethics at the University of Santa Clara.

Anonymous. "I'm an Illegal Alien at Harvard." Reprinted by permission of *The Daily Beast/Newsweek*.

Aratani, Yumiko, Chau, Michelle, and Wight, Vanessa. "Who are America's Poor Children?" Reprinted by permission of the National Center for Children in Poverty.

Balco, Radley. "Back to 18? Reconsidering the Minimum Drinking Age." Reprinted by permission of *The Huffington Post*.

Barrett, Paul. "Weather on Steroids." Reprinted by permission of *Bloomberg*.

Bartlett, Tom. "Dusting off GOD." Reprinted by permission of the *Chronicle of Higher Education*.

Begley, Sharon. "Why Money Doesn't Buy Happiness." Reprinted by permission of *The Daily Beast/Newsweek*.

Belanger, Jeff. "Dr. Hans Holzer - A Lifetime of Explaining the Unexplained." Reprinted by permission of the author.

Bishara, Marwan. "Egypt Paves the Way for Revolution of Consciousness." Reprinted by permission of the author.

Chua, Amy. "Why Chinese Mothers are Superior." Reprinted by permission of the author.

Conover, Ted. "The Way of All Flesh." Reprinted by permission of the author.

Dan, Durty. "What Americans Should Know about Canada. Reprinted by permission of the author.

DiNovella, Elizabeth. "Thomas Frank Interview: Political Ascendency of the Right." Reprinted by permission of *The Progressive*.

Eltahawy, Mona. "I Stayed to Fight—Being a Muslim Immigrant in Post 9/11 America." Reprinted by permission of *Diverse: Issues in Higher Education*.

Enayati, Amanda. *"For Kids, Better to Give than Receive."* Reprinted by permission of *CNN*.

Estrada, Ishmael. "Who Would Peter be Today?" Reprinted by permission of *CNN*.

Foust, Michael. "If Same-Sex Marriage is Legalized, Why Not Polygamy?" Reprinted by permission of the *Baptist Press*.

Fox, Wesley. "Tea Party Movement's Positive Impact on American Politics." Reprinted by permission of the author.

Gonzales, Luz, Vuong, Mui, and Walton, James. "First-Generation College Graduates: Their Stories." Reprinted by permission of California State University of Fresno.

Gorski, Terence. "Sentencing Children as Adults." Reprinted by permission of the author.

Green, Lorna. "Giving Students Room to Run." Reprinted by permission of *Teaching Tolerance* magazine.

Hallowell, Billy. "America's Changing Demographics." Reprinted by permission of the author.

Halperin. David. "Gay Men: Fusing the Erotic and Aesthetic." Excerpted from *How to be a Gay Man,* reprinted by permission of *Harvard University Press.*

Hanson, Victor. "A Nation of Promiscuous Prudes." Reprinted by permission of the author.

Hartwell-Walker, Marie. "Fathering in America: What's a Dad Supposed to Do?" Reprinted by permission of *PsychCentral.*

Hira, Ron. "U.S. Workers in a Global Job Market." Reprinted by permission of *Issues in Science and Technology.*

Hirschorn, Michael. "The Case for Reality TV." Reprinted by permission of *The Atlantic.*

Hout, Anton. "Cyber Bullying." Reprinted by permission of the author.

Hustmyre, Chuck, Dixit, Jay. "Marked for Mayhem. Reprinted by permission of the authors.

Jackson, Camille. "Weighing In – Healthy at Any Size?" Reprinted by permission of *Teaching Tolerance* magazine.

Jackson, Robert E., Salzman, James, "Geoengineering for Atmospheric Restoration." Reprinted by permission of *Issues in Science and Technology* journal.

Jayson, Sharon. "More College 'Hookups' but More Virgins Too." Reprinted by permission of *USA Today.*

Johnson, Jean and Rochkind, Jon. "With Their Whole Lives Ahead of Them." Reprinted by permission of the Public Agenda organization.

Kafka, Alexander. "The Constitution: Who Needs It?" Reprinted by permission of the *Chronicle of Higher Education.*

Karon, Jeff. "A Positive Solution for Plagiarism." Reprinted by permission of the *Chronicle of Higher Education.*

Kass, John. "The End of Football." Reprinted by permission of the *Chicago Tribune.*

Klein, Herbert S. "The Changing American Family." Reprinted by permission of the author.

Kristof, Nicholas. "Sewing Her Way Out of Poverty." Reprinted by permission of the *New York Times.*

Laats, Adam. "To Teach Evolution, You Have to Understand Creationists." Reprinted by permission of the *Chronicle of Higher Education.*

Libby, Ellen. "The Favorite Child." Reprinted by permission of the author.

Lum, Lydia. "The Obama Era: A Post-racial Society?" Reprinted by permission of *Diverse: Issues in Higher Education.*

Marshall, Jennifer. "Marriage Shows the Way Out of Poverty." Reprinted by permission of The Heritage Foundation.

Moody, Nekesa Mumbi. "Is Rap Music Dead?" Reprinted by permission of the Associated Press.

Nader, Ralph. "Overcoming Powerlessness." Reprinted by permission of *The Progressive.*

Navarro, Maria. "Decriminalizing Marijuana Usage." Reprinted by permission of the author.

Nocera, Joe. "Is This Our Future?" Reprinted by permission of the *New York Times.*

Onwuachi-Willig, Angela. "Good Silences, Bad Silences, Unforgiveable Silences." Reprinted by permission of the *Chronicle of Higher Education.*

Pitts, Leonard Jr. "How Black is Black Enough?" Reprinted by permission of the *Miami Herald.*

Platt, Shawna Platt. "Overcoming Abuse: My Story." Reprinted by permission of the author.

Rampell, Catherine. "Tough Job Outlook for College Grads." Reprinted by permission of the *New York Times.*

Rauch, Jonathan. "The End of Middle Class Growth." Reprinted by permission of *The Atlantic* magazine.

Rodriguez, Richard. "What a Wall Can't Stop." Reprinted by permission of the author.

Rose, Josh. "Social Media's Positive Influence." Reprinted by permission of *Mashable.com.*

Rosin, Hanna. "The End of Men." Reprinted by permission of *The Atlantic* magazine.

Rubin, Jeffrey. "The Roots of Brazil's Success." Reprinted by permission of the author.

Ruetschlin, Catherine. "Retails Hidden Potential." Reprinted by permission of *Demos.org.*

Sander, Libby. "Colleges Confront a Gender Gap in Student Engagement." Reprinted by permission of the *Chronicle of Higher Education.*

Seagal, Jeanne. "Domestic Violence and Abuse." Reprinted by permission of *HelpGuide.org.*

Seydtaghia, Anouche. "Built-in Obsolescence." Reprinted by permission of *Le Temps* newspaper.

Sharrock, Justine. "Executioner's New Song." Reprinted by permission of *The Progressive* magazine.

Shute, Nancy. "The Amazing Teen Brain." Reprinted by permission of *U.S. News.*

Smith, Fran. "Why Arts Education of Crucial." Reprinted by permission of the author.

Snyder, Kristie. "Gun Control Doesn't Work." Reprinted by permission of the author.

Snyder, Kurt. "My Personal Experience with Schizophrenia." Reprinted by permission of the author.

Staerk, Bjorn. "Living with Terrorism." Reprinted by permission of the author.

Stepp, Laura. "Black Teenagers Defy Pop Culture Portrayals." Reprinted by permission of *CNN*.

Stimson, Charles. "Legalizing Marijuana: Why Citizens Should Just Say No." Reprinted by permission of the author.

Storck, Thomas. "What is Wrong with Capitalism?" Reprinted by permission of the author.

Strickus, Paul. "STDS Still a Growing Problem Among Young Adults." Reprinted by permission of the author.

Taniguchi, Yumi. "Japanese Robotics." Reprinted by permission of the author.

Tisdale, Sallie. "Living with the Mystery of Headache." Reprinted by permission of *Harper's* magazine.

Turkle, Sherry. "The Flight from Conversation." Reprinted by permission of the *New York Times*.

Van Tassel, Kristin. "The Professor Lady Spits Rhymes." Reprinted by permission of the *Chronicle of Higher Education*.

Wilcox, Christie. "The Science of Heartbreak and How Music Heals." Reprinted by permission of the author.

Wilson, Eric. "Poetry Makes You Weird." Reprinted by permission of the *Chronicle of Higher Education*.

Womack, Larry. "Gun Control and Metal Detectors: The Failure of Congress." Reprinted by permission of the author.

Woodard, Colin. "The Intelligence of Beasts." Reprinted by permission of the *Chronicle of Higher Education*.

Yang, Wesley. "Paper Tigers." Reprinted by permission of *New York* magazine.